Masculinity, Law and the Family

Among the now considerable literature addressing masculinity there are few texts which take as the specific object of study the relationship between masculinity and the law. This book explores the diversity of the masculinities of law and bridges the critique of masculinity and the critical study of law through analysing the relation between masculinity, legal discourse and the family. It seeks to unpack representations in law of male sexuality, authority, paternity, fatherhood and male violence in the family. All of these are areas of law in which understandings of masculinity, law and power have assumed a central importance just as dominant ideas of male heterosexuality have become increasingly problematic.

Richard Collier begins his analysis by asking how we might understand the relation between law and masculinity. He proceeds to explore how the law has gendered the male body in the family. The author argues that men's subjectivities have been valorised in law through reference to a naturalised heterosexual subject position and that, though socio-economic shifts over the past century have reconstituted or 'modernised' heterosexual masculinity, the law continues to be concerned to protect a dominant ideal of masculinity. In particular, through exploring the relation between changes in legal conceptions of fatherhood and paternity and wider shifts in the historical construction of heterosexuality, Richard Collier argues that it is the idea of the *family man* which has come to signify a range of ideas about heterosexual masculinity in law. This book is about our understanding of masculinity, law and family life – about what it is to be a man in law and society.

Richard Collier lectures in law at the Newcastle Law School, University of Newcastle-Upon-Tyne.

Masculinity, Law and the Family

Richard Collier

London and New York

First published 1995
by Routledge
11 New Fetter Lane, London EC4P 4EE

Simultaneously published in the USA and Canada
by Routledge
29 West 35th Street, New York, NY 10001

© 1995 Richard Collier

Typeset in Baskerville by LaserScript, Mitcham, Surrey
Printed and bound in Great Britain by
Mackays of Chatham PLC, Chatham Kent

British Library Cataloguing in Publication Data
A catalogue record for this book is available from the British Library.

Library of Congress Cataloging in Publication Data
A catalog record for this book has been requested

ISBN 0–415–09194–2 (hbk)
ISBN 0–415–09195–0 (pbk)

I would like to dedicate this book to the memory of my father, Stanley George Collier, and to my mother, Nancy Collier. With love and thanks.

Contents

Preface and acknowledgements

This book is about how the law has constructed heterosexual masculinity. It assumes no prior knowledge of either law or of the debates which have emerged within feminist and men's anti-sexist critiques of masculinity. It is a book about what it means to be a man in legal discourse and, therefore, what it is to be a man in our society. Beginning by asking 'how might we understand the relation between law and masculinity?', it proceeds to analyse how law has gendered the male body in the family. It seeks to do this through exploring a variety of areas in which, I argue, dominant ideas of male heterosexuality have become increasingly problematic.

In one sense this book serves as a bridge between developments which have taken place in recent years within legal theory and within the range of critical studies of men and masculinity which have sought to explore the sociality of masculinities. In a number of recent feminist texts,[1] for example, we find critical accounts of the power of law in which the legal construction of masculinity, of male sexuality, fatherhood, paternity and male authority, has assumed a central significance. However such work tends to be concerned primarily with the ways in which law constructs *women* and women's experiences; 'it is for other men to make us see masculinities, and to bring these into question' (O'Donovan 1993: 88). This is what *Masculinity, Law and the Family* seeks to do.

By way of contrast to such feminist legal scholarship, the object of analysis in critical studies of masculinity[2] has been the social construction of men and masculinities. At times the effects of law and legal regulation have figured heavily in such accounts. (How has law gendered men? How might we challenge such representations?) What has not tended to be within the ambit of such work, however, is a critical engagement with the power of law from a perspective which has been informed by the recent developments in legal theory and those feminist jurisprudential texts which have also begun to question the power of masculinity.[3] In particular, the power of law frequently tends to be 'taken for granted' in such studies of masculinity (broadly involving a positivist conception of law which is, perhaps ironically, compatible with the dominant methodology of legal education and practice).

Masculinity, Law and the Family seeks to complement the existing work on critical studies of law, the family and masculinity through seeking to address the relationship between all three. I am concerned to present a systematic and coherent analysis of male heterosexuality in law and to introduce the reader to a number of debates currently raging about law and the family. The book does so, importantly, from a perspective informed by both critical legal theory *and* feminist and men's anti-sexist accounts of masculinity. As well as being a synthesis of existing work and contemporary issues in this area it also, I hope, raises important questions about how we understand the power of both masculinity and of law.

Chapters 1 and 2 integrate current developments in legal theory with a historical and sociological analysis of the family and seek to establish a theoretical base from which to begin to analyse the social construction of masculinity in law. These chapters, alongside Chapter 3, present an overview and analysis of approaches to theorising law, gender and the family, entailing a critique of traditional legal method and a fundamental questioning of how 'sex' and 'gender' are understood in legal discourse. Chapter 4 builds on the picture of male heterosexuality which has emerged at this stage whilst keeping in the frame a focus on the politics and practice of reproducing discourses of masculinity.

Moving from the more abstracted discussion of 'what is sex', Chapter 4 considers sexuality in the institution of marriage via an analysis of cases in which understandings of male sexuality have been considered central in establishing whether or not a marriage can be said to exist. In Chapters 5 and 6 I relate changes in legal conceptions of fatherhood and paternity to wider shifts in the historical construction of heterosexuality and to the emergence of a distinct discourse which I identify as familial masculinity. Through exploring the idea of paternal masculinity, these chapters challenge the dominant (law-centred) focus on men's (versus women's) rights and seek to explore how men's subjectivities have been valorised in law through reference to a naturalised heterosexual subject position. This is a discursive position which law continues to be concerned to protect though, from the late nineteenth century to the present day, the mechanisms by which it does so have changed.

It is an argument of this book that the dominant masculinity of legal discourse has served to privilege certain men. Socio-economic shifts over the past century have, I shall argue, reconstituted or modernised heterosexual masculinity in law. This, in turn, has important implications for how we understand the idea, common to much of the emerging literature, that we are now undergoing a form of contemporary *crisis* in masculinity. This misreading of the masculinity/law relation has diverted attention from 'dangerous' masculinities in the family, even though it was feminist challenges to these masculinities which had been influential in constructing the masculinity-problematic in the first place.

The fragmentation of masculinity which takes place in Chapters 5 and 6 feeds into a historical analysis (illustrated by the case studies of prostitution and child sexual abuse) of how familial masculinity continues to be rendered *safe* at the same time as it is reconstituted in law. The emergence of an idea of *respectable* familial masculinity in contrast to other undomesticated masculinities must be related to more general changes in discourses of masculinity in the late nineteenth and twentieth centuries. It is the idea of the *family man*, I argue, which has come to signify a range of ideas about heterosexual masculinity in law. What follows is, I am aware, one particular reading of the legal subject; other readings may focus on other aspects of heterosexual masculinity, on race, class, religion and ethnicity.

This book constitutes the beginnings of an unpacking of this notion of 'the family man' in both law and popular culture (understood here as a paradigm and not the apotheosis of masculinity). What follows is, I hope, a contribution to the wider debates taking place around the family, law and gender. It is not a traditional 'family law' textbook, in that it does not seek to expound a catalogue of rules relating to a specific area of the legal sub-discipline 'family law'; it is not the purpose to state, as Graycar and Morgan (1990: 13) put it, 'all there is' in a doctrinal sense on family law. It is, rather, an analysis of how legal catagories and doctrines are themselves constructed. This book exists more in opposition to the black-letter tradition of legal scholarship. As Freeman has pertinently warned, lawyers who remain technicians cannot contribute to the current debate raging about the family (Freeman 1985: 154). However the conclusions of this interdisciplinary study of masculinity and law raise important questions, and not just about the legal regulation of families, about gender and the place of law in the reproduction of relations of power between men, women and children. They also, importantly, relate to the politics and very concept of 'family law' itself.

In the writing of this book I have received encouragement, support and criticism from many friends and colleagues. I would like to thank them all. I would like, in particular, to acknowledge the encouragement and help given by Les Moran, Tony Jefferson, Fiona Cownie and Tony Bradney, Marie Fox, Katherine O'Donovan and Carol Smart. My greatest thanks are to Fiona Coleman, who has been a constant source of support during the writing of this book and has helped in countless ways with her unceasing kindness.

Chapter 1

Introduction
On law and masculinity

INTRODUCTION

Why another book on masculinity? It is becoming difficult to keep up with the books and articles exploring the social construction of masculinity. Each week, it seems, sees the publication of another. Yet amongst this now considerable literature addressing masculinity, it is curious that there are few texts which take as the specific object of study the relationship between masculinity *and law*. What follows draws on this existing literature on masculinity – variously termed 'the new sociology' or 'critical studies' of masculinity[1] – but its object is quite specific and novel. It is an attempt to theorise the relation between masculinity and legal discourse and to explore the construction of masculinity in areas of law pertaining to the family. Specifically, it seeks to unpack representations in law of male sexuality (Chapters 3 and 4) and paternity, fatherhood and men's violences (Chapters 5 and 6). It is a book which attempts to 'defetishise' the law – to engage in an analysis 'whereby the given is shown to be not a natural but a socially and historically constituted, and thus changeable reality' (Benhabib 1986: 47).

Though the focus of this book is law and the family, and the ways in which roles therein are differentiated according to gender, the conclusions have implications for legal studies generally as well as for gender studies and the sociology of masculinity. The book is, in short, not just concerned with the relationship between masculinity and law; it is about the very ideas and understandings we have of masculinity, law and family life – and of what it is to be a man in our society.

Given that the problematic, contested and political nature of masculinity and male sexuality has long been identified by feminist

legal scholars to be central to theorising the connections between
law and power, the absence of critical accounts of masculinity and
law might seem surprising. Indeed, in what has been termed the
'quest for a feminist jurisprudence' (Smart 1989a: 66) the problematic nature of masculinity and male sexuality has assumed a
central significance. One result of the marginalising of feminist
scholarship within legal studies generally has been to negate those
analyses of the gendering of law and legal method which have
sought to render the law/masculinity relation problematic. There
are now many texts which argue that addressing the masculinism
of law and legal practice must be central to feminist engagements
with the power of law; and, most importantly, debates have now
moved beyond the initial pointing out of the 'sexist' assumptions
which have underscored legislative provisions and judicial pronouncements (e.g. Sachs and Wilson 1978: Atkins and Hoggett
1984).[2]

Therefore, I wish to begin this chapter by asking how we might
seek to theorise the masculinity of law and legal method and how
we understand the contours of the law/masculinity relation itself.
With the exception of feminist interventions, legal studies have
remained largely oblivious to the insights of the critical studies of
masculinity which have emerged in recent years. This is notwithstanding the fact, I shall argue, that 'taking masculinity
seriously' can have much to contribute to the study of law. It is
interesting that law and legal regulation have already figured
prominently in a number of recent studies of masculinity. Sometimes this has been implicit; at other times it is central to the
argument. For example Jeff Hearn, in his book *The Gender of
Oppression* (1987), has questioned what the study of masculinity
might tell us about law and the legal institutions of government,
and about the

> structures of power, the enormities of which are so obvious and
> taken for granted within the social sciences. How can there be
> so many books, articles and treatises written on parliament,
> industry, the City, the professions, and so on, that do not even
> mention the power of men?

> (Hearn 1987: 22)

In his later work on masculinity Hearn proceeds to address the
power of law in a much more explicit way in his analysis of the
emergence of forms of masculinity at specific historical moments

(Hearn 1992: 111–26). Elsewhere, other work on masculinity has repeated such calls to take on the gendering of law and legal regulation in accounting for the construction of masculinity (e.g. Connell 1987).

Yet such critical engagements with masculinity have not tended to take place from within the context of legal theory (it is frequently presumed, for example, that we all know what law 'is'). This is, perhaps, understandable when we remember that, with the significant exception of feminist scholarship, legal studies have themselves singularly failed to address these connections between the power of men and the contingent and social nature of masculinity. Analyses of the relation between masculinity and the gendered dimensions of the institutions of law have tended to emerge from a specifically feminist standpoint (for example Smart 1989a; Thornton 1989a; Naffine 1990; O'Donovan 1993). So, the vast majority of law students – students of constitutional and administrative law, criminal law, family law, welfare law, company and commercial law and even of jurisprudence and legal theory – will find few mentions of masculinity and power in their studies (even though the subjects they are studying have been constructed from a masculinist vantage point.)

This absence of explicit discussions of masculinity does not mean that male legal scholars have not been concerned to write at length on gender and law, however. Rather, men's involvement with gender and law has tended to take the form of writing about *women*, writing on an abstracted 'Woman' – as an enigma, as the Other and as the object of male inquiry (and fantasy?). So the questions asked of law have traditionally been focused on women. How does the law treat women? Are women discriminated against? How might the law promote (or deny) 'equality' between women and men? How are women constructed in law? In part the emergence of studies of 'women and law' within the doctrinal mainstream can be seen as a sign of feminism's impact on the legal academy – how the law treats women has certainly become an issue to be addressed by legal studies. Yet, as we shall see, the objects of the study – both 'women' and 'law' – remain pre-theoretical; they are given.

When male legal scholars seek to develop such studies of women and law the methodological and epistemological problems are compounded. This is not just because when men have tended to speak of 'woman' or 'feminism', it has usually been 'in order to speak about "something else" – some "larger issue'" (for example, marxism or postmodernism) (Jardine 1987: 55) This is also a matter of how masculinity has *itself* been silenced. As Jardine asks about those male scholars who focus their attention on the 'woman problem':

> What are the mechanisms, linguistic and otherwise, whereby these men are able to evacuate questions of *their* sexuality, *their* subjectivity, *their* relationship to language from their sympathetic texts on 'feminism', on 'woman', on 'feminine identity'.
>
>   (Jardine 1987: 56) (emphasis in original)

Indeed, Jardine notes, 'Anglo-American academic male critics do seem to be very into feminism these days' (1987: 55). This issue is not specific to law (where a resistance to theory continues to mark out legal studies as the intellectual black sheep of the academy). It appears throughout the social sciences and humanities. Male academics have historically been obsessed with women, or rather obsessed with finding the answer to the often repeated conundrum 'What do women want?' As de Beauvoir (1972) argued, women have been and continue to be objectified from the male vantage point, the Object to Man's Subject. What this means, of course, is that Man as the Object of study and men as social and accountable beings fades from view within the hierarchic structure of a discourse which casts Man as Subject and masculinity as somehow the essence of the man. In this asymmetrical sexual economy Woman is marked as 'Other', as the embodiment of 'sex' and 'sexuality', whilst Man is absent. But, crucially, we do not see his absence.

It is at this point, prompted by the impact of feminism in the disciplines of history, politics, philosophy, sociology, economics and now law, that it has become increasingly obvious that masculinity is most marked by its absence, its invisibility. The rights and responsibilities that mainstream legal studies analyse are 'either explicitly those of men (for example the reasonable man) or implicitly those of men. . . . In law school courses, as in life, man is the central figure and woman is the other (Mossman 1985: 214; see also O'Donovan 1981). The trouble is that we do not see the absence of men (or the nature of the masculine presence); and of what we cannot see, we cannot know. It is time this absence was corrected. We cannot expect feminism to do this work, however.

Making us 'see' the masculinities of law is what this book seeks to do.

This book, in short, is about redressing an absence. It is about the silences, prohibitions and exclusions of the law – about what is not said as much as what is said – about being a man in law. Of course in a sense, and as feminists have pointed out, masculinity is everywhere – so how can it be absent? As Richard Dyer has commented, male sexuality is a bit like air – you breathe it in all the time, but you aren't aware of it much (Dyer 1985). The same might be said of masculinity. How can there be any arguments in favour of studying masculinity when post-Enlightenment intellectual traditions are already all about the study of men (Canaan and Griffin 1990; Moore 1991), when the focus of legal studies is already, in so many ways, the lives of men?

The answer to this depends on how we theorise masculinity. What has not been addressed, what is *repressed* in a sense, is the sociality of masculinity. To return to law, there is now a wealth of feminist scholarship which explores how women have been constructed in legal discourse (see Graycar and Morgan 1990). There are also, we know, many texts which are concerned to explore men and masculinity (too numerous to cite here; see Ford and Hearn 1988; August 1985). What we are now beginning to see, however, is work on the relation between masculinity and law which seeks to fuse this scholarship on the sociology of masculinity with an account of the construction of gender in law informed by recent developments in legal theory (Moran 1990; Collier 1992a; O'Donovan 1993: 65–73).

Through drawing on the implications of feminist legal scholarship for the study of masculinity and law, the following chapters seek to question not just the relation between law and the social construction of masculinity but also the relationship between feminism and men in legal studies. The situations of men and women are so different that it is difficult to construct an idea of 'masculinity' as a mirror to feminism's treatment of 'femininity' (or, indeed, for any study of masculinity to simply mirror the theoretical movements of feminism). More generally, therefore, this book seeks to address some of the methodological and epistemological implications of researching men, masculinity and law. But it also seeks to explore how gender differentiation has itself been socially constructed, how it 'violates the ideals which men

officially espouse'. One consequence of such critique is 'a redistribution of existing possibilities according to the explicit ideals
those arrangements violate' (Middleton 1992: 165). Yet we cannot
begin to address the masculinity/law relation until we are clear
what we mean by these concepts in the first place.

Where does all this fit into legal studies? In one sense this book,
like all other critical texts about law, is marginal to mainstream
legal scholarship as it currently exists in institutions of law in the
UK, though its concerns are central to the sociology of law and
gender. It is, in a frequently cited but useful distinction, a book
about law rather than a book *of* the law (Able 1973). On one level
some of the issues raised by feminist legal scholarship could be said
to have been accommodated in legal studies (notably in relation to
the politics of equal rights, discrimination and the idea of sexual
difference in law). Nonetheless it remains the case that, as Smart
(1989a: 25) comments, there are at present no UK law schools
which would introduce Women's Law as part of a compulsory
syllabus (see further Stang Dahl 1987). Written by a man in institutions which, I shall argue, have been suffused by an ideology of
masculinism, this book might perhaps be most accurately located
as both within and against the grain of legal scholarship in the UK.

The more general methodological and epistemological issues of
researching men and masculinity have been considered in depth
elsewhere (Middleton 1992: Chapter 5; Morgan 1992). I shall
address some of these issues in the following chapters as and when
they bear on the relation between masculinity, law and the family.
Nonetheless there are important questions which I believe must be
asked at the outset about law and masculinity, about the masculinism which informs the social sciences as a collection of disciplines
and about the relation between masculinity and the continued
exclusion of feminist and other non-patriarchal discourses in legal
studies. The remainder of this chapter acts as a guide, or map, to
introduce masculinity and law to those readers unfamiliar with the
terrain.

THE SOCIOLOGY OF MASCULINITY: A CONTEXT

Those people who speak of masculinity as an essence, as an
inborn characteristic, are confusing masculinity with masculinism, the masculine ideology. Masculinism is the ideology that
justifies and naturalises male domination. As such, it is the

ideology of patriarchy. Masculinism takes it for granted that there is a fundamental difference between men and women, it assumes that heterosexuality is normal, it accepts without question the sexual division of labour, and it sanctions the political and dominant role of men in the public and private spheres.

(Brittan 1989: 4)

One of the most difficult questions which has faced the study of masculinity in recent years has been actually defining the object of analysis. What is masculinity? 'Is it a discourse, a power structure, a psychic economy, a history, an ideology, an identity, a behaviour, a value system, an aesthetic even?' (Middleton 1992: 152). Or is it, as Middleton proceeds to ask, 'all these and also their mutual separation, the magnetic force of repulsion which keeps them apart? . . . a centrifugal dispersal of what are maintained as discrete fields of psychic and social structure' (ibid.: 152). To support the claim that the critical analysis of masculinity might have important implications for the study of law, gender and the family involves clarifying what is actually meant by 'masculinity' in the first place. The distinction Brittan (1989) makes between masculinity 'as an essence' and 'masculinism' as an ideology, is, I shall argue, of use in approaching the relationship between masculinity and law. First, however, it is necessary to place the study of masculinity in a historical context.

Throughout the 1970s and 1980s, and now into the 1990s, the subject of masculinity has generated a literature of considerable quantity (if not always quality) throughout the social sciences and across academic disciplines.[3] Much of this research has attempted to avoid, though with variable success, the pitfalls of a naturalist conception of masculinity which proclaims there to be an immutable essence of maleness. It sets out instead to analyse the involvement of men in social relations from a viewpoint which is informed by feminism and the 'second wave' of women's liberation. More recently this work has sought to accommodate into the analysis the plurality of masculinities and the differentiation as well as the communality of male experience. With the very terminology of the study of masculinity open to question, therefore,[4] the relationship of the critical study of masculinity to feminism has been, at best, problematic (Middleton 1992: 159).[5]

In the recognition that masculinity is a social construct, and thus liable to change, these analyses of the production of representations of masculinity have focused on diverse areas: literature,[6] religion,[7] the media,[8] sport,[9] race and ethnicity,[10] the experiential domain[11] and cultural representations of masculinity[12] are just some of the areas singled out for analysis.[13] More generally studies of masculinity have sought to explore such subjects as father absence, male sexuality (e.g. Abbott 1990) and the perceived emotional impoverishment of men's lives through reference to methods as diverse as object-relations psychoanalysis, humanistic psychologies and poststructuralist theories of language, the unconscious and discourse. Other studies, though not necessarily from an explicit anti-sexist position, have further sought to explore how masculinity varies through men's lives focusing, for example, on boyhood,[14] adolescence[15] and the experiences of the elderly.[16] Some of these writings are academic, many are more popular and journalistic in tone. What they tend to share, however, is an assumption that *something* is happening around masculinity (and, judging by the profusion of texts on the subject in recent years, that people want to read about it).

Carrigan *et al.* (1985) have identified a 'new sociology of masculinity' which has emerged in a steady stream since the early 1970s (specifically from the US and other advanced capitalist countries).[17] If it has a core assumption it is that men, as individuals, as social and economic categories and as a historically constituted sexgroup, have become increasingly problematic both for other men but, more especially, in their relations with women and children. As Astrachan puts it, these men seem to worry 'about three things, singly or in combination: relationships with other men, the male sex role, and the way women keep changing the rules of the game' (Astrachan 1986: 290). Masculinity has, put simply, been politicised by feminism.

Taking their cue from the women's movement and the responses of individual women to the socially destructive consequences of (generally, though not exclusively, heterosexual) masculinity, these men 'writing about masculinity and themselves' have drawn out the contours of intellectual and political project. For Connell (1987: xiii) it is this 'politics of masculinity' which should be the business of the heterosexual men who bear the brunt of the feminist critiques of masculinity and who 'are not excluded from the basic human capacity to share experiences, feelings and hopes' (ibid.: xiii; see also Jefferson 1989). For Hearn (1987: 21) men concerned to oppose sexism and who want to study gender should focus primarily on the critique of men and masculinity and not the study of women, and they should do so with an explicit anti-sexist commitment. Hearn has argued (1987, 1992) that through such an 'anti-patriarchal praxis' men should not try to 'solve' women's problems for them but recognise instead men's responsibility to each other to change relationships with both women and other men. (Compare this relation to feminism with, for example, that of Charver 1983; see further Middleton 1992: 159.)

This is the starting point: that masculinity is a social construct and that men have a potential to change, but that at present that potential is, in Connell's terms, blunted. Implicit is this dynamic of change and critique, a critique both of contemporary masculinity and of previous attempts to understand gender and power (Morgan 1992). It would be inaccurate to present the anti-sexist men's movement as an organised grouping, however.

> The men's movement . . . is a decentralised, heterogeneous network of magazines, small consciousness-raising groups, gay men's organisations, and alliances within psychotheraputic movements. There is no general theory, political structure or social background which unites these men.
>
> (Middleton 1992: 119)

It would be also inaccurate to present the literature of the 1970s and 1980s as constituting the first attempt to present a sociological analysis of masculinity. However 'intellectually disorganized, erratic and incoherent' (Carrigan *et al.* 1985) such research may have been, there existed an extensive discussion of masculinity before the main impact of the 'second wave' of feminism; that is, a 'prehistory' of research, indeed a distinct sociology, on men and masculinity before women's liberation and the profound questioning of masculinity by feminism (Carrigan *et al.* 1985: 553–78). The methodology of this 'old' sociology of masculinity was, however, problematic and suffered from a gender-blindness common to traditional sociological research methodologies (Morgan 1981; Roberts 1981; Bowles and Klein 1983; Stanley and Wise 1983).

The research tended to take the form of singling out a particular group of men or boys for analysis because, for some reason, their behaviour would be deemed by the academic researcher to constitute a social problem. For example, the discipline of criminology has traditionally concerned itself with men and crime (Allen

1988). Yet in so doing it has failed to recognise the social and contingent nature of the masculinity/crime relation itself and the fact that it was men, and not humankind, who constituted the object of study (Brown 1986a; Cain 1990; Gelsthorpe and Morris 1990; Smart 1990a). Criminology may not have necessarily *excluded* women from its discourse – women are present – but women and womens' subjectivities have been rendered systematically marginal to the discipline of criminology (Smart 1976). Criminology has failed, in other words, to address the gendering of its object of study (Scraton 1990) and the fact that most crimes remain unimaginable without the presence of men:

> Excluding soliciting . . . and shop-lifting . . . all other crimes, be they crimes of property or crimes of violence, crimes of the powerless or crimes of the powerful, crimes committed against the state or crimes committed by the state, are dominated by men. The question is: how does this knowledge, usually ignored because so taken-for-granted, help us to think about the problem of crime?
>
> (Jefferson 1992: 10)

The example of criminology illustrates the problem of 'taking masculinity seriously' (Stanko and Hobdell 1993). There exists an extensive literature addressing such subjects as 'juvenile delinquency' (Cohen 1955; Cloward and Ohlin 1960), street-corner gangs (Thrasher 1927; Whyte 1943; Miller 1958), 'techniques of neutralization' (Matza and Sykes 1961) and the causes of educational underachievement and emergence of youth subcultures amongst groups of males. That these texts constituted accounts of masculinity and that the masculinity being studied was itself a social construct was usually unstated. It was simply part of the subject of 'criminology'. Criminology thus failed to ask what it may be about men

> not as working-class, not as migrants, not as underprivileged individuals, but *as men* that induces them to commit crime? Here it is no longer women who are judged by the norms of masculinity and found to be 'the problem'. Now it is men and not humanity who are openly acknowledged as the objects and subjects of investigation.
>
> (Grosz 1987: 6, quoted in Allen 1988)

Similarly, what this earlier sociology of masculinity failed to account for is the fact that the object of research was historically and culturally specific forms of masculinities and not groups of 'youths' or 'adolescents' in general. In speaking of 'men' the research remained blind to the social production of men *as men*, to the communality and differentiation within male experiences. What theoretical coherence there was, the concept of the 'sex role' provided (Parsons and Bales 1956; cf. Pleck 1987b) and, by avoiding wider questions of social structure wherein gender is constructed, particular manifestations of masculinity became both pathologised and individualised. In a sense this resulted in the problem of masculinity fading away before it was even recognised to be a problem.

It is, crucially, the gender blindness of this sociological research which proponents of a theoretically coherent social analysis of masculinity have attempted to remedy. Through its failure to address the central question of power relations between men and women the literature seemed oblivious to one of the 'central facts about masculinity . . . that men in general are advantaged through the subordination of women' (Carrigan *et al.* 1985: 590). In contrast, more recent research has sought to utilise the notion of foregrounding masculinity so as to establish a position from which to analyse the sociality of masculinity. As Morgan (1981: 95) observes 'taking gender into account is "taking men into account" and not treating them by ignoring questions of gender as the normal subject of research.' (For a more detailed account of researching men and masculinity see Morgan's 1992 book *Discovering Men.*)

Thus, in contrast to the earlier sociology of masculinity, more recent texts[18] have explicitly attempted to explore the 'maleness' of men and to bring the 'he' hidden from (male) stream sociological inquiry into the light of day (Hearn 1987: 35–6) This research on masculinity addresses and draws upon the fundamental feminist insight that masculinity was, in a sense, forming an object of research before us all along – only when we presumed we were looking at humankind we were looking at historically and culturally specific *masculinities* (Brod 1987b: 40; Brittan 1989: 1). Far from rendering visible (that which was already over-visible) this rendering *otherwise* of masculinity can be said to constitute an organising perspective of the sociology of masculinity.

The form that this 'foregrounding' of masculinity should take has been, however, a matter of some debate and on the issue of

strategy and politics various differences of approach have emerged
which have rendered the study of masculinity, and more generally
the relationship of men to feminism, an epistemological and methodological minefield (Jardine and Smith 1987; Morgan 1992;
Middleton 1992: 113–65). For writers such as Brod (1987a), while
the practical political implications of men's engagement with
feminism remain problematic, it is seen as necessary and desirable
to develop the study of men and masculinity as a subject in its own
right. This, Brod argues, might best be achieved under the rubric
of 'men's studies'. What marks such studies out from the earlier
sociology of masculinity literature is, he argues, the recognition,
and epistemological presupposition, that relations between men
and women are relations of power and that these relations are
both individual and structural.

This recognition of power is undoubtedly a major step forward
in theorising masculinity. Here the study of masculinity is seen as
arising out of explicit support for feminism. However, it would be
a mistake to assume at the outset that 'men's studies' (whatever
this might be) are necessarily pro-feminist and the relationship
between men, feminism and researching masculinity has in recent
years prompted extensive and sometimes heated debate
(Showalter 1987; Canaan and Griffin 1990; Moore 1991; Griffiths
1992). The idea, for example, of seeking to develop a discipline of
'men and law', parallelling the 'women and law' approach to
gender (epitomised by Atkins and Hoggett's (1984) book *Women
and the Law*) is both methodologically and theoretically objec-
tionable. I shall explore these issues in more depth in Chapter 7 in
the light of the following analysis of masculinity, law and the
family.

At this point it is more constructive to turn the focus to law and
to explore some of the connections between these sociologies of
masculinity and law. I shall do this through seeking to relate three
of the principal themes of the studies of *masculinity* to the study of
law.[19] These are what I shall term (1) the crisis thesis, (2) the
development of the 'men against sexism' movement (or MAS; see
further Rutherford 1992: 2–11) and (3) the idea of 'men's liberation'. In each there are to be found implicit assumptions about
the nature of law and legal regulation. Each, I shall argue, fails to
adequately address the relation between masculinity and law and
leads ultimately to a misleading assessment of the power of each.

In Chapter 2 I shall put forward an alternative, and preferable, approach to theorising masculinity, law and the family.

The 'crisis' thesis: law as indicator of social change

The critique of masculinity has been, first and foremost, about the possibilities of *changing* men. However, the strategies by which this is to be achieved, and the theoretical presuppositions underlying political practice, vary considerably from, for example, 'new age' metaphysical texts (Bly 1991) to psychoanalytic and object-relations inspired neo-marxist and materialist accounts of masculinity and male sexuality (Tolson 1977; Metcalf and Humphries 1985; see, alternatively, Somerville 1989). More recently poststructuralist accounts have increasingly influenced the masculinity genre (Middleton 1992). Here masculinity is presented through reference to the structuring of language and the unconscious, a 'de-centred' male subject constructed through discourse and desire of the other. In short, there is no *one* politics or method to the critique of masculinity and no one theory of masculine subjectivity.

> The causes and the explanations of the problematisation of men and masculinity are many, and not mutually exclusive. In this process, men and masculinity become more liable to critique, more open to critique, and perhaps more able to respond to critique by changing.
>
> (Hearn 1987: 30)

On what has prompted this critique in the first place, however, there has been some agreement around the idea of a 'crisis of masculinity'. In particular, it has been argued that there is a *contemporary* 'crisis' of masculinity (Hearn 1987: 16–31; Connell 1987: 183–6; Brittan 1989: 25–36):

> there have been recent changes in the constitution of masculinity in advanced capitalist countries, of at least two kinds: a deepening of tensions around relationships with women, and the crisis of a form of heterosexual masculinity that is increasingly felt to be obsolete.
>
> (Carrigan *et al.* 1985: 598)

This crisis has had, commentators have noted, a specifically legal dimension and has been marked perhaps most clearly by perceived changes in men's lives in relation to both the family and work. One aspect of the crisis, for example, has been identified as the occurence of a breakdown of traditional masculine authority in relation to the family and around men's relationships with women and children. The scale of the transition in men's familial relations has been marked by the perceived diminution of specifically legal rights – notably over women, children and property. It is this issue which constitutes the focus of Chapters 5 and 6.

These ideas of 'change' and 'crisis' in masculinity have coalesced in the context of the politics of family law reform. It is in this area that an international fathers' rights movement and advocates of 'men's rights' (groups such as Families Need Fathers and Dads After Divorce in the UK) have sought to campaign, via a variety of strategies, to bring about law reform which might promote men's interests. In the early 1990s disputed readings of past legal reforms have been at the heart of these debates in England and Wales (in particular around legislative reforms of the 1960s and 1970s). More recently the emergence of the 'sex war' rhetoric of proponents of a more overt anti-feminism (for example Lyndon 1992; Thomas 1993) has in turn sought to utilise the idea of masculine crisis in order to argue, first, that family law now 'favours' women *vis-à-vis* men, and second that it is feminism which has brought about these tensions in men's lives. For some these events constitute no less than a 'backlash' against feminism (Faludi 1992).

It is interesting to see just who has been singled out as the subject of these 'deepening of tensions' within the crisis thesis, however. Generally the crisis thesis is taken as referring to the tensions within the masculinities of the younger professional intelligensia of western cities, a group which, as we shall see, overlaps not only with those men who are most likely to seek the services of a solicitor over divorce and custody, but also represents the constituency which has most visibly and audibly advocated arguments for extending men's formal legal rights in the family. The idea of change/crisis in masculinity is broad therefore; it can embrace both pro- and anti-feminist perspectives.

Law, and contested notions of the power of law, have been bound up within understandings of these changes in men and families. Alongside changes in men's familial relations a stronger version of the crisis thesis cites a more general crisis of masculine authority in society as a whole resulting from significant changes in mens' lives. The causes of such a crisis vary, though common

reference is made to significant social and economic shifts in the
'world order', for example military changes (Tolson 1977: 13;
Hearn 1987: 16–19) and the development of nuclear weapons
(Easlea 1983, 1981, 1987) The general point is well captured by
Carrigan *et al*.:

> Forms of masculinity well-adapted to face to face conflict and
> the managment of personal capital are not so well suited to the
> politics of organizations, to professionalism, to the managment
> of strategic compromises and consensus.
>
> (Carrigan *et al.* 1985: 599)

On one level these structural changes can be related to the emergence of the bureaucratic–administrative state (Kamenka and Tay
1975) and the growth of large bureaucratised corporations which
have accompanied the transition to technocratic modes of decision
making and control. Recent analyses of the organisational sexual
politics of a variety of institutions have, not suprisingly, located
these historical changes as having ramifactions for male and female
behaviour in institutional settings (Hearn and Parkin 1987). One
result, for example, has been the transformation of 'traditional'
forms of male power and prerogative in the face of a fracturing of
the social and economic infrastructure within which such male
power had been traditionally held (Chapman 1988: 249; Cockburn
1983, 1988). What such studies have shown is that a shift in the
structure of employment does not a priori produce significantly
different forms of masculinity, even though the reorganisation of
capital and the technological restructuring of the 1980s have undoubtedly transformed many men's and women's lives.

It is also possible to locate the growth in recent years of interest
in masculinity, in both the media and the academy, in the context
of an economic recession across western economies which has put
pressure on the hitherto (relatively) secure employment of
middle-class males. In November 1993 the charitable organisation
The Samaritans released figures showing an 80 per cent increase
in suicides by young men in England and Wales over the past ten
years, whilst the suicide rate for women was decreasing. Taking up
the idea of crisis, the Chief Executive of the Samaritans declared
'We have this concept of the "new man", but it seems he is a
confused young man and he is not quite sure how he is supposed
to behave, respond or relate in different relationships. . . . In a
sense it is almost an identity crisis' (*Guardian*, 3 November 1993).

The media, interestingly, made much of the masculine crisis idea, declaring the 'Rise in suicides linked to identity crisis of "new man"' (*The Independent* 3 November 1993) and that it was the '"New Man" behind rise in suicides' (*The Times* 3 November 1993). This idea of an identity crisis in the lives of primarily middle-class white men, and its possible destructive consequences, also informed readings of the internationally popular 1993 film *Falling Down*.

The 'crisis' would seem to appear on different levels therefore – mens' lives in relation to family, work, sexuality and the state are all encompassed by the idea of crisis. It is, however, easy to over-state this idea of a 'crisis' in masculinity. I shall argue in the following chapters, through a historical analysis of matrimonial law, that 'traditional' expressions of masculine authority have in many respects been untouched by feminism. The 'crisis thesis' should at the outset be used cautiously, therefore. As Banner (1989) notes, for all the arguments that masculinity has periodic-ally fallen into 'crisis' (and is thus 'vulnerable and mutable' (Brod 1987a: 57),

> almost any historical period can be defined as 'in crisis' if one is clever at historical analysis. In my mind, the bedrock of mascu-linity has remained essentially the same from Odysseus's slaying of the suitors in the ninth century B.C. in defense of home and family to the cowboy's and detective's and vigilante's slaying of villains in the twentieth century: heroic violence lies at the heart of the patriarchal masculine definition of self.
>
> (Banner 1989: 707)

It is not necessary to accept the reductionism implicit in Banner's depiction of the 'bedrock of masculinity' to take the point that masculinity (rather like capitalism or the criminal justice system) may be more accurately considered not so much on the brink of a 'collapse' but, more appropriately, at a critical juncture. The emer-gence of studies of masculinity might, alternatively, be seen as indicative of a more general cultural insecurity around sexuality and gender at the *fin de siècle* (Showalter 1992). They are also, perhaps, indicative and symptomatic of the insecurities which bedevil many a would-be radical male academic who has been, in so many ways, left on the side-lines by the feminist rejuvenation of critical scholarship and the collapse of previously comforting metanarratives.

It is with reference to the cultural climate in which gender configurations are produced that I wish to locate the analyses of masculinities in this book. For advocates of the crisis thesis, law has been seen as a barometer of historical changes in relation to shifts in ideas of masculinity and the power of men in society (law is, as we shall see, certainly part of a politics of masculinity). Thus, law X can be depicted as 'causing' change Y in men's position in the family. Yet the issues at stake here go beyond any specific textual analysis of representations of gender in an area of legal discourse. At issue here are more general questions about gender and culture at the end of the twentieth century. It is essential to place the discourses of masculinity which are the subject of this book in the wider historical, social and economic context whence they derive their meaning, therefore. It is also necessary to place a study such as this in a wider political context and to address the practices to which the differential theorising of men's power lead. The idea that changes in 'law' signify any 'crisis' of masculinity is, as we shall see, deeply problematic.

Two of the principle genres within recent writings on masculinity, what Carrigan *et al.* (1985) have termed the 'men against sexism' and 'men's liberation' approaches, produce very different conceptions of the power of law and the possibilities of engaging with law to bring about change. Both these perspectives will figure in the following chapters, underpinning arguments for and against specific legal changes. Each, for different reasons, is to be rejected at the beginning.

'Men against sexism': law as male power (men vs women)

The development of the 'men against sexism' and 'men's liberation' perspectives can only be understood in the context of the historical development of the men's anti-sexist movement generally (Rutherford 1992: Chapter 2). Both represent strains, or themes, within a heterogeneous grouping of texts and practices which have followed the impact of feminism on men. For readers unfamiliar with the history of the anti-sexist movement generally, some idea of what was said about men and masculinity might prove useful.

The first meetings of anti-patriarchal men's groups appear to have taken place in the United States around 1970 (the magazine *Brother* appeared in San Francisco in 1971). Certainly, by 1970 men's groups had been formed in the United States, drawn predominantly from university educated New Left activists (Carrigan *et al.* 1985: 574). Following the organisation of 'Men's Centres', parallelling the (higher profile) Women's Centres in the United States, by the mid-1970s talk of a 'masculine mystique' (Farrell 1974) had surfaced as proponents of such bodies as 'Men's Awareness Networks' advocated the formation of a national organisation along the lines of the National Organization of Women (NOW). Contemporary advocates of 'men's studies' in the United States (Brod 1987b; Kaufman 1987a) and male consciousness raising (Snodgrass 1977) continue this parallelling of feminism's development, which is further reflected both in political strategies and theoretical concepts (see further Bliss 1986). It is interesting, therefore, that it was clearly feminism, and not gay liberation, which was the model for the developing men's anti-sexist movement. From its very beginnings the literature has been premised on the responses of heterosexual men to feminism and, as Carrigan *et al.* note, the 'author's girlfriend' soon became a collective presence in the emerging genre. If male sexuality was to be located as problematic then it was a certain type of sexuality – heterosexual.

By 1972 the first such 'men's groups' had been formed in Britain (Rowen 1987: 19) and from this point on the men's anti-sexist literature has flourished. The term 'movement' itself does not, Carrigan *et al.* suggest, accurately describe the phenomenon:

> an intermittent, thinly spread collection of support groups, therapeutic activities, and ephemeral pressure-group campaigns might be nearer the real picture; and it is hard to think of any significant political effect it has had in any country over ten years.
>
> (Carrigan *et al.*, 1985: 575)

One notable example of literature from the anti-sexist movement in the UK is the magazine *Achilles Heel* which, though only one of many such magazines (Ford and Hearn 1988), has had, along with the *Men's Anti-Sexist Newsletter* (MAN), probably the highest profile of such works (see further the collections of *Achilles Heel* readings edited by Seidler 1991; 1992; also Rutherford 1992: 27). *Achilles Heel* described its target readership (Issue 6/7: 3) as 'many active trade unionists who have become interested in feminism . . . single parent fathers; men whose male identity is threatened by unemployment or divorce; men who read *Spare Rib*.' Common reference is made in much of the anti-sexist literature generally to texts often classified as 'radical feminist', with frequent citings of, for example, Dworkin (1981), Daly (1979, 1984), Brownmiller (1975) and Griffin (1981). Though the *Achilles Heel* of the 1990s is very different from earlier incarnations, the deference to feminism and women's experiences remains a dominant theme.

The fusing of the personal/theoretical dimension was central at the outset and two central themes rapidly emerged in the men against sexism tradition as a response to feminism. First, the perceived emotional impoverishment of contemporary masculinity, the idea that men are somehow 'out of touch' with our feelings; and second, what is frequently the existence of an acute sense of guilt and shame at the oppressions perpetrated by the sex-class men. Recognising the inherent oppressions of all men, and seeking to struggle towards some degree of emotional literacy, thus became the task in hand for men concerned to change. Jeff Hearn's recollections appear not atypical of this response to feminism:

> While holidaying in Tenby in South Wales I was surprised to find in a local bookshop a copy of the SCUM manifesto. This quiet Welsh coast had offered up nothing less that the document of the Society For Cutting Up Men. And yet hurtful as these words might appear, they slid off me because I knew them partly to be true.
>
> (Hearn 1987: 7)

Solanas's SCUM manifesto in fact reads as follows:

> Every man, deep down, knows he's a worthless piece of shit. Overwhelmed by a sense of animalism and deeply ashamed of it; wanting, not to express himself, but to hide from others his total physicality's total egocentricity, the hate and contempt he feels for other men, and to hide from himself the hate and contempt he suspects other men feel for him.
>
> (Solanas 1967)

Much of the anti-sexist literature repeats this association between masculinity and emotional impoverishment, if not always in the stark terms of the 'egocentricity . . . hate and contempt' of a 'worthless piece of shit'. Seidler (1985), for example, argues that while men might hear women's cries of anger and frustration, and while men might understand these intellectually, men continuously find it difficult to accept that things could really be so bad.

Elsewhere (1989: 186), Seidler writes of men 'who have been brought up to identify so directly with our minds' that it has become difficult to recognise the importance of 'feelings and emotions as sources of knowledge and understanding'. The argument echoes Dworkin's assertion that

> The poet, the mystic, the prophet, the so-called sensitive man of any stripe, will still hear the wind whisper and the trees cry. But to him, women will be mute. He will have learned to be deaf to the sounds, sighs, whispers, screams of women in order to ally himself with other men in the hope that they will not treat him as a child, that is, as one who belongs with the women.
>
> (Dworkin 1981: 49)

Perhaps understandably in response to such views, Seidler comments that 'it is as if all long-term heterosexual relationships in our time are doomed' (see also Rowen 1987: 7). In a similar vein, one of the clearest, and (in the UK) most influential conceptions of men's emotional poverty can be seen in the collection of essays *The Sexuality of Men* (Metcalf and Humphries 1985). Here the theorising of sex/gender is allied to (and, according to Somerville (1989), undermined by) a materialist account of psychoanalytic object-relations theory. Running through much of the men against sexism writings is a thin line between depicting masculinity as a social and historical construct and seeing it as somehow ontologically fixed (Morgan 1992: 41). At times the men against sexism writings veer towards the latter. It is thus men as a *sex-class* which is problematic within this strand of writing on masculinity and it is *heterosexuality* which is the principal (though not exclusive) object of discussion. In time the absorption of a number of feminist arguments, most notably around men's emotional inarticulacy and the impoverished/oppressive nature of male heterosexuality, resulted in a depiction of heterosexual masculinity as itself inherently oppressive. One consequence of this sometimes seemingly pervasive guilt on the part of men writing about masculinity was a political pessimism (given 'how men are', how could things be different?) and a replication of the underlying essentialism evident in particular strands of feminist thought (Segal 1987).

Yet it is far from clear what politics follows from the men's movement's trust in emotion (or, indeed, the idea that men are somehow emotionless; this depends on how we understand 'emotion'). As Middleton (1992: 131) has questioned, 'Can we be sure that "feeling is good for us"? Aren't some feelings demonstrably dangerous, misleading and oppressive? . . . Emotional expression is not always good, authentic and natural.' It is, I shall argue in this book, essential to theorise masculine subjectivity but in a way which can accommodate both practice and social structure (Jefferson 1994). The focusing on emotion, however, and the related politics of guilt, has had a number of consequences for understanding the place of law in the men against sexism analysis.

It has, in particular, led to a view of law and the state as being inherently male, oppressive and as embodying a masculine 'world view'. From this perspective law and legal method themselves become somehow essentially male. Indeed, classic tenets of liberal legalism – individual separation, physical autonomy – become quintessentially 'masculine' values (West 1988). Setting up a (false) dichotomy between 'doing' theory and 'doing' practice (Smart 1992b: cf. Bottomley and Conaghan 1993b), law does not simply equate with the power of men; it comes to constitute, in its purest form, that power. In an influential tradition of feminist scholarship on law this approach is perhaps exemplified by the work of the North American feminist Catherine Mackinnon, for whom 'the state is male in the feminist sense. The law sees and treats women the way men see and treat women' (Mackinnon 1983: 644). According to this view, the state, Mackinnon argues, appears most 'neutral', most male 'when it is most sex-blind, [and] it will be most blind to the sex of the standard being applied'. 'Once masculinity appears as a specific position, not just the way things are, its judgements will be revealed in process and procedure, as well as adjudication and legislation' (Mackinnon 1983: 658). Concerned not just with how women are constructed in legal discourse but also how that knowledge about women is derived, Mackinnon argues that male dominance

is perhaps the most pervasive and tenacious system of power in history . . . it is metaphysically nearly perfect. Its point of view is the standard for point-of-viewlessness, its particularity the means of universality.

(Mackinnon 1983: 638–9)

Such an approach, which conceives of all men as a homogeneous group and law as an embodiment of the power of all men, sits uneasily with accounts which seek to accommodate the differences between masculinities. Yet it remains a perspective which has been carried through in a number of pro-feminist accounts of law and masculinism. In accounting for the masculinism of criminological discourse, for example, Scraton (1990) simultaneously endorses Mackinnon's essentialist conception of law as male power (1990: 21) whilst also seeking to maintain a position sensitive to the variation in masculinities (for example, noting the 'false universalism' of the term 'all women' (1990: 15, 21)). What emerges from his analysis (which concludes, in effect, by submerging feminism within a reconstituted 'critical criminology' (1990: 23)) is a ringing endorsement of a number of key feminist texts (Rich 1977; Mackinnon 1983) yet in ways in which the discursive construction of masculinity clashes in many respects with the universalising which underlies Scraton's own use of 'masculine discourse'.

Alongside Mackinnon's powerful critique of the purported neutrality of liberal legalism, therefore, is an implicit essentialism and a political pessimism which follows the invoking of a model of unitary masculinity. Indeed, this approach to the power of law is infused with 'a paradoxical mix of debilitating pessimism and unfathomable optimism' (Jackson 1993: 211). Here the law 'reflects' the power of men. Law is infused with the qualities of masculinity. The power of men and the power of law become one and the same, inseparable, as the state itself is identified as somehow 'male' in the form and content of its laws.

Central to Mackinnon's analysis is a depiction of male sexuality as sustaining the power of masculinity and of law which is common to other writers in this strand of feminist discourse:

> male sexual aggression is the unifying thematic and behavioural reality of male sexuality; it does not distinguish homosexual men from heterosexual men. . . . An absense or repudiation of this aggression, which is exceptional and which does exist in an *eccentric and miniscule minority* composed of homosexual and heterosexual men, distinguishes some men from most men, or, to be more precise, the needle from the haystack.
>
> (Dworkin 1981: 57; my emphasis)

Such an analysis has led to a view of law as the embodiment of male power and it is this depiction of law which has resurfaced in the men against sexism perspective which, like Mackinnon, largely continues to construct men/women as pre-theoretical categories and the cultural construction of 'sex' itself as pre-discursive. It is not surprising that a problem for the anti-sexist men's movement has been establishing whether they are part of that 'eccentric and miniscule minority' or, rather, like the rest of men, are part of the patriarchal 'haystack' which is the problem. Thus, what is essentially an individualised issue of identity has prompted much self-reflection and, according to Somerville (1989), much 'hair-shirt penitance' and 'piety' (see also Canaan and Griffin 1990). In its more popular journalistic manifestation the (vacuous) distinction between 'new' and (presumably) 'old' men manages to side-step the construction of masculinities in a more general sense.

In much of the men against sexism writings what in fact has occurred is a shift in the male/female, subject/object relationship. As Eisenstein points out:

> In this perspective, culturally defined maleness [is] very far indeed from the normative role ascribed to it by Simone de Beauvoir. On the contrary, a women-centred analysis presented maleness and masculinity as a deformation of the human, and as a source of ultimate danger to the continuity of life.
>
> (Eisenstein 1984: 101)

What has occurred here is a discursive twist: man – and masculinity – becomes the object of political focus (possibly a good thing) *but* only at the cost of framing the questioning of masculinity in such a way as to assume that there is a normative woman-centred position (non-patriarchal) in opposition to the all-pervasive and oppressive masculinity. 'Masculinity' becomes interchangable with 'patriarchy' or, indeed, liberal legalism. This position itself derives from an essential, natural womanhood which is seen as uniting all women yet which in so doing negates the discursive construction of the feminist subject 'woman' and the differences in women's lives (Butler 1990: 1–16). The meaning of 'woman', other feminists have pointed out, differs as much as women's lives differ; indeed it is the very 'diverse positionality' of women's lives that malestream knowledges (such as law) have denied (Grbich 1991: 75).

Thus, the man/woman hierarchical dualism repeats itself – we know what we mean by man/woman as each are taken as pre-discursive categories. Put simply, women have the answers and men must turn to women to find out what they are. Essential, benign, positive and life-affirming womanhood (Daly 1979, 1985) is set up in opposition to an essential, destructive, negative and oppressive masculinity. In one variant it becomes women who embody authentic connection: 'women are actually or potentially materially connected to other human life. Men aren't' (West 1988) and 'crime and coercion are sustained by men. Solidarity and self-help are sustained by women. It is as stark as that' (Campbell 1993: 319). This is not to argue that legal method is not, in so many respects, an embodiment of 'masculine' values (Menkel-Meadow 1985; Spiegelman 1988) or that law has not identified an ethic of care and human connection most strongly with women. However, in much of the men against sexism literature we can see a powerful sense of guilt at simply being a man, notwithstanding the fact that this is a politics aimed at changing men. This essentialism has ironically tended to paralyse any political praxis. After all, given how men and women 'are', how could things be different?

This issue has been faced by feminists (Eisenstein 1984: 105–45) who have argued that 'the prescription that women should suppress heterosexual desire to further the cause of feminism is one I believe to be strategically and morally wrong' (Segal 1987: 46; see also Campbell 1980: 1). Mackinnon's use of 'authenticity' (see also West 1988) and depiction of consciousness-raising as *the* feminist methodology have similarly been criticised by feminists concerned about the positing of one feminist 'truth' over and above other perspectives (particularly when experiential data would appear to contradict the theory: Buffalo Symposium 1985; Colker 1988, 1991; Smart 1989a).

Nonetheless an essentialist view of masculinity, male sexuality and power has continued to inform men against sexism critiques which remain predicated on an essential man/woman dualism. Reynaud's (1983) polemical *Holy Virility*, for example, is in many respects a forceful and powerful critique of masculinity and male sexuality. Yet it is limited by a position which presents all men as the omnipotent and conscious oppressors of all women: 'what pleasure can he really feel with a weapon between his legs?' (Reynaud 1983: 42). At its most reductionist all heterosexual men are misogynists and the best that might be achieved, politically, is to recognise as much:

> when a man is suffocated by the paltriness of his existence, and he tries to put an end to power once and for all, he need not go far to find the enemy: his struggle is first and foremost within himself. Getting rid of the 'man' buried inside him is the first step for a man aiming to rid himself of his power.
>
> (Reynaud 1983: 114)

What is this 'man'? What is his essence? Is it beyond culture and society, a product of biology? Whether Reynaud's vague tautology is confronting patriachal power structures is questionable.

This is not to reject out of hand the diverse writings which might be placed under the 'men against sexism' rubric, not all of which share the essentialism depicted above. Nor is it to dismiss the politics of the anti-sexist tradition (which in Britain has tended to have a more clearly defined materialist focus than the North American counterparts. For example, from the UK see Tolson 1977; Metcalf and Humphries 1985). Yet in the end the attempted political effect of these engagements with masculinity seems to have been to make political – and more specifically socialist – movements aware of masculinity as an issue and to 'support' feminists in this way. However, as Stuart Weir (1993) recalls about his days editing the magazine *New Socialist*, 'putting the sex into socialism' has proved a notoriously difficult task.

More recently, in Britain we have seen, in a move perhaps related to a different form of political pessimism resulting from a fourth Tory term in office, the increasing influence of a range of 'new age' metaphysical and mytho-poetic texts many of which originate in North America (for example Bly 1991: Stewart 1991; Tatham 1992). These works indicate that the individualistic focus of 1970s self-actualisation is alive and well at a time when the distinction between men against sexism and men's liberation (see below) is becoming increasingly blurred. Such work on masculinity concentrates on 'Celebrating the Male Mysteries' of the 'King Warrier Magician Lover' (Moore and Gillette 1992), or on 'Reclaiming Our True Masculinity' (Lee 1991; Thompson 1992). At times it is not clear whether men are to 'get rid' of or 'reclaim' the man inside; but the idea that there is such a univocal and coherent 'man inside' remains.

To sum up, the men against sexism tradition contains many positive qualities – not least an admirable commitment, thoughtfulness and focus on social practice. This is not to dismiss the insights and effects of a diverse range of texts which have sought to redraw the terms in which masculinity is conceptualised. However, as a perspective to inform engagement with *law* it is limited by its theoretical presuppositions. It fails to engage with the fluid, dynamic nature of gender and with the ways in which gender is itself embedded and constituted through representation and in the symbolic realm. In particular, it fails to engage with how masculine subjectivities are constituted in the first place through ideas of subjectivity, language and, I shall argue, the activation of familial commitment. Crucially, this leads to a limited analysis of the power of law in this process. If this tradition replicates the essentialism of radical feminist politics, however, as well as remaining epistemo-logically predicated on the male/female dualism, then the failing of the 'men's liberation' tradition is that it is unable to transcend the limitations of liberal legalism while reproducing an incipient anti-feminism.

'Men's liberation': law as equal rights

It is a central contention in much of the literature on masculinity that men are oppressed within patriarchy in a manner which might be compared to women's oppression. It is this view which has resurfaced in the 1990s in the form of a particularly vituperative and bitter anti-feminism (Lyndon 1992; Thomas 1993). As a political movement, the idea of 'men's liberation' should not be overemphasised. Nonetheless, the idea of men's liberation has continued to inform and legitimise the attempts of politically powerful and influential individuals and organisations to 'improve' the legal rights of men.

An undoubted appeal of men's liberation is that it gets round the guilt and frustration inherent in some male responses to feminism. From this perspective men are seen as victims of their own advantages, their characters distorted by the pressure of 'being a man' in contemporary society (Stearns 1979). There is one issue which reappears in different forms: 'The torture of being a man' and whether men are 'really as bad as women make them out to be' (*The Independent* 16 September 1992). The 'costs' of masculinity the writings tend to focus on are male anxieties, neuroticism and low self-acceptance and, in particular, sexual difficulties (see Chapter 4). The disadvantages of being a man are thus listed at length, the maladaptive effects of male sex role socialisation lamented as the call is made for new, more humane ways of being a man. In some instances this stance has been allied to an explicit right-wing agenda (Gilder 1986). In another variant current sexual confusions (for example around date rape and sexual harassment) are related to a failure, prompted by feminism, to understand the 'realities' of male sexuality and masculinity (Amiel 1991).

In much of the men's liberationist writings by men it is the destructive effects of employment which are identified as central to the impoverished nature of a '*breadwinner masculinity*', which involves, as its does, considerable emotional costs for men, not least in excluding men from childcare (Gould 1974; Ochberg 1987). It is this idea of men's liberation which also underscores the campaigns of those groups which seek, in their own terms, to 'redress' a legal balance which has swung too far in favour of women. How these issues around work and the family have fed into legal change will be explored in detail in Chapters 5 and 6.

This concept of men's liberation is, at the outset, deeply problematic. While it recognises the complexities of oppression, it constitutes, like men against sexism, a limited approach to masculinity and law. One problem is the tendency to psychologise feminist critiques of masculinity (Interrante 1981). That is, the problems of masculinity become matters of individual psychology rather than structural relations of power. This is, in part, a problem of the methodology and the understanding of power within the men's liberationist stance. Within this framework, feminist arguments that it is the family and a compulsory heterosexuality which are fundamental to women's oppression are ignored or passed over. Feminism itself is frequently presented as a matter of women 'breaking out' of inappropriate/oppressive roles rather than fundamentally challenging men's power. Elsewhere a more blatant anti-feminism is evident, not just in the 'sex war' rhetoric, but in the advocacy of men's legal rights which might be used to best advance the collective interests of men (David and Brannon 1976). Thus the interests of men (as individuals and as a collectivity) are to be advanced through the utilisation of rights based claims. This has been particularly the case, both internationally and in the UK, with regard to the care of children after divorce and separation.

If men's liberation is theoretically problematic, however, it is also politically suspect. It constructs the power of law in terms of equal rights. Yet to argue that men too need liberating entails a redefinition of 'liberation', from meaning a struggle against the powerful to meaning a breaking free of conventions which are somehow seen as inimical to men's well-being (Carrigan *et al.* 1985: 568). Thus feminism is, in one strand of writing, reconstituted as 'good for men too' and is approved of as a worthy means of self-help. It is part of a politics of personal liberation for *men*, however, rather than as an attack on the power and privilege of those who are already powerful. It should not be surprising, therefore, that the explicit anti-feminism of the 'sex war' proponents is in effect the other side of the coin of the 'new age' and 'backlash' masculinists' attempts to reclaim the 'real man'. A latent misogyny has never been far below the surface of the men's liberationist stance (see Faludi 1992; Greer 1992, in contrast, suggests that the 'backlash' discourse is in fact little more than the same old male brutality by another name).

In a mirroring of feminism's political development, it has been seen as imperative for the pro-feminist liberationist to become involved in self-help groups, therapy, consciousness raising, role sharing and changing occupations; this is the practice to back up the theory. Yet the focus is on a lifestyle, a superficiality and surface which is endemic in media accounts of representations of masculinity (Collier 1992b; Moore 1988) and which is, on one level, indicative of the fragmentations and cultural valorisations of postmodernity. Yet the very idea of men's liberation is both naive and dishonest in the first place through failing to address the legal basis of men's power in society (Connell 1987: 234).

It is curious that feminism is transformed by the men's liberationist into little more than a humanistic growth movement. When this is allied to a critique of law, feminism becomes the cause of an ill-judged and immoral attack on men's liberties and family life. It is this modernising of masculinity which, I shall argue, has been reflected in and reproduced by changes in the law relating to the family. Men's liberation depoliticises gender. The oppression of women becomes a problem of role identity, not individual and collective power. Homosexuality is (significantly) ignored. Yet if sexuality and the family *are* important social-structural arrangements in the constitution of subjective commitments then it is essential that familial and (homo) sexual politics should not be ignored. As Connell argues:

> it is clear what its point is: not contesting inequality, but modernizing heterosexual masculinity. The discontent many men feel as holders of power under challenge is to be relieved by a change of personal style – a change of tactics in dealing with women, perhaps a changed self-concept – without any challenge to the institutional arrangements that produce their power.
>
> (Connell 1987: 236).

This book will explore how masculinity has been conceptualised in these debates. It is about how the law – in relation to sexuality, paternity, fatherhood and male violences – has sought to modernise masculinity. It focuses on the areas which Brittan (1989: 4) identifies as elements of the ideology of masculinism: ideas of 'natural' difference between men and women (Chapter 3), the 'normality' of heterosexuality (Chapter 4), the legal structuring of the sexual division of labour (Chapters 5 and 6) and the 'political and dominant role of men in the public and private spheres' (Chapter 2).

The 'modernising' of masculinity is an important part of the contemporary debates about family law reform which will be central to the arguments which follow. The idea that men too need 'liberating' must not be dismissed as a simple cultural manifestation of shifts in gender relations, however. It should be seen as constitutive of a significant change in the discursive construction of masculinity. Ideas of change and crisis – and law reform – have emerged as potentially positive or regressive from a feminist perspective. As embodied in debates around substantive legal reforms, the men's liberation discourse is an important part of the politics of the family and of law. These developments, as shall become clear, have historically fed into debates around legal reform. Adoption of both the 'men against sexism' or 'men's liberation' perspectives in theorising the relation between law and masculinity is not, however, the most useful way of beginning to understand such changes.

THEORISING LAW AND MASCULINITY

We have seen that defining masculinity is a complex and contested enterprise. In turning to theorise the relationship between masculinity and *law* one comes up against an immediate problem – the widely held belief in the legal academy that 'masculinity' and 'law' are somehow incompatible subjects. From my own experience of presenting staff seminars to (I suspect) frequently bemused legal scholars, it is not so much a hostility one faces (though at times it certainly is) as an unwillingness or inability to recognise that theorising a relation between masculinity and law may have any intellectual validity in the first place. This is, in part, a consequence of a general resistance to theory in the legal academy and of the stranglehold which doctrinal positivism continues to exert on many law schools. I suspect it also relates to the fact that tackling masculinity raises difficult questions about the 'public persona' of the academic (Thornton 1989a; Collier 1991). It also, crucially, relates to how law claims power through denying the legitimacy of those discourses which might challenge its scientific status.

An immediate counter may thus be made to my claim that the relation between masculinity and law can be an important and valid subject of study. From the traditional perspective of positivist legal method masculinity and law have little, if anything, to do with each other. The social construction of masculinity is not something with which any 'serious' legal academic should be concerned. In the terms of the doctrinal tradition its study certainly counts for little in terms of academic 'kudos' and might serve (depending on the contextual/interdisciplinary tradition of the law school) to further marginalise gender politics and other attempts to raise feminist arguments on doctrinal law courses. 'Masculinity', whatever we might take this to signify, may be perceived by the legal scholar to be an appropriate concern of the sociologist, psychologist or psychoanalyst (though, as we have seen above, sociology until recently has not been much concerned with the sociality of masculinity). For the lawyer, it is difficult to see what masculinity has to do with law and therefore difficult to see what it might have to do with legal method and education. And that, it seems, is the end of the story.

Working within the confines of doctrinal exegetical method, or traditional 'black-letter' law, there may be little to say of masculinity. This is not to claim that issues of sex and gender do not figure in many law courses, however. For example, from a liberal feminist perspective and in the name of 'equality' of opportunity, the law teacher might point out the 'sexist' assumptions of a judge in a particular case or highlight the iniquities of the legal process. The student of the Anglo-Welsh legal system will note the (relatively few) numbers of women judges and legal professionals compared to men. Certain judicial statements may be highlighted by the law lecturer perhaps so as to provoke outrage or humour (or both) amongst law students. However, masculinity here remains like economics, sociology, psychology and feminism, somehow 'out there'. It is what other people do and it has the most tenuous or complex of relations to one's own speech and behaviour. At the outset it is necessary to transcend the limitations of such positivist conceptions of law to begin to speak of the masculinism of the law itself.

Beyond traditional legal method

The problem of trying to put masculinity onto the agenda in legal studies is epistemological and relates to the intellectual straitjacket that is traditional legal method. Doctrinal positivist conceptions of the relation between gender, sex and law are of little assistance in trying to place masculinity within any kind of political economy which recognises the dimension of power or that gender relations themselves have an institutional dimension which transcends matters of personal 'choice' (see, for example, the broadly positivist texts on the relation between sex and law by Slovenko 1965; Honoré 1978). The doctrinal lawyer might discuss the rules relating to rape but to expound on their jurisprudential validity is not to engage in a critical analysis of the context and content of the rules themselves. Within the positivist paradigm law is conceived, in such works as Tony Honoré's *Sex Law* (1978), to be a catalogue of rules concerned with negation and denial of the sexual. Yet crucially, 'law', 'sexuality', 'natural/unnatural', 'male/female', all appear pre-theoretical and unproblematic. What *is* signified by the 'sexual', and how it relates to law, is given. Similarly, just as positivist conceptions of the sex/law relation are power-blind, positivist conceptions of law afford no grip on the gender regime of the institutions of the law nor on the gendered dynamics of legal method and legal practice.

To go beyond these limitations it is necessary to adopt an interdisciplinary approach to law which might transcend the restricted and inadequate positivist framework. Such an inter-disciplinary study is not

> that of juxtaposing legal knowledge with that of other, essenti-ally separate, knowledges (pluridisciplinary), nor would it be that of absorbing other disciplines or sciences into legal expertise (transdisciplinary) for the purposes of providing a further technical dimension of legitimation to legal discourse. The interdisciplinary study of law is aimed rather at breaking down the closure of legal discourse and at critically articulating the internal relationships it constructs with other discourses.
>
> (Goodrich 1987: 212)

It has been, I have argued above, the emergence of an interdisciplinary feminist legal studies which has placed the masculinism of
law onto the political agenda. Yet law remains, in many respects,
impervious to the feminist challenge (Mossman 1986). It is, Mossman
has argued, the very structure of law (the way it determines
'relevant' facts and defines legal issues) which has made it resistant
to feminist influence. This has, in turn, led to a dilemma for
feminist legal scholars, practitioners, teachers and students who
seek to become proficient at 'the law' whilst seeking to question its
very legitimacy (Dalton 1988; Olsen 1989). Feminist challenges to
normative notions of 'reasonableness', for example, might then
function as a justification for dismissing or disqualifying those who
are adjudged not to conform through rejecting the 'reason' of law
(Lahey 1991). 'Too often', Mossman notes, 'it seems almost impossible to be both a good lawyer and a good feminist scholar'
(Mossman 1986: 297; see also Lahey 1985; alternatively, see
Schneider 1991). Or, as Fineman puts it, feminism 'has not and
cannot transform the law. Rather, the law, when it becomes the battle-
ground, threatens to transform feminism' (Fineman 1991b: xii).

The argument that doctrinalism negates a questioning of the
social, historical and political nature of law, and that law is not a
self-contained, politically neutral institution, is well-established in
legal studies. There exists a voluminous literature addressing the
intellectual limitations of the 'black-letter' approach (Kennedy
1982; Thornton 1986). Even the most traditional of undergradu-
ate jurisprudence courses will (one hopes) contain some critique
of doctrinalism. There now exist many journals, books and articles
which take issue with doctrinal exegetical method. The interdisciplinary approach to law, whether under the ill-defined rubrics
of 'law in context' (for example O'Donovan 1985a; Lacey *et al.*
1990) or 'critical legal studies' (Kairys 1982; Unger 1983;
Fitzpatrick and Hunt 1987; Stanley 1988), is now an established
part of legal education in the UK (see further Grigg-Spall and
Ireland 1992). There even exist law schools whose purported defining aim is to teach the law 'in context' (Folsome and Roberts
1979). Few law schools today would deny wholesale the purchase
of a contextual approach to law, though they may restrict it to
certain subjects, such as criminology, which are considered 'appropriate' to such an interdisciplinary approach because of their
already culturally marginal status in the law school.

The notion of an interdisciplinary legal studies is well-established; indeed, recent attempts have been made to integrate the contingencies of gender and power whilst remaining in a broadly doctrinal text-book framework (for example Dewar's (1989a) book *Law and the Family*). Yet the point is that, despite the occasional 'grafting on' of theory in such a way, it remains the case that legal studies in the UK are grounded in a broadly positivist methodology which 'kills thought, stops it dead in its tracks: there is merely allegiance to tradition without understanding and, more importantly, without anything more than merely superficial questioning' (Stanley 1988: 84). This exclusion of questions of gender in the constitution of a normative and univocal epistemology within which, for male and female, the law is studied and taught continues to make it extremely difficult to get a grasp on how law and masculinity may be related. It is as if masculinity, and masculinism, is everywhere – any law lecturer or legal practitioner grappling with the politics, not just of rape or child custody, but also of company and commercial law, must be aware of this. Yet we cannot see it or theorise the power of masculinity – because we do not know what it is we are looking for and because, as 'lawyers', it is not our concern. (I believe masculinity is no less obvious on a company law course than in family law.)

It is at this point that the critical study of masculinity can have significant implications for legal scholarship. On one level there are signs that masculinity is emerging as a legitimate object of study within legal studies (Moran 1990; Collier 1992a). However, as we have seen earlier in this chapter, the opening out of the study of law to a politics of masculinity raises many questions about intent and object in developing any 'pro-feminist' legal studies on the part of men. If men are to 'take feminism seriously' (Bottomley *et al.* 1987) then it appears necessary to consider carefully the relationship betwen men and feminism in the law school (Collier 1991; see further Chapter 7, p. 267). This relates not just to questions of intellectual appropriation of feminism but also to a methodological self-reflection which, though it may be well-established in sociology, could not generally be said to be part of legal consciousness.

Locating masculinity as a valid object of legal study, therefore, at the outset means first challenging those practices which have functioned to de-legitimise the gender/law relation in the legal academy. This clearly means rejecting black-letter doctrinalism as a methodology to engage with the power of law. Yet if masculinity is not to be an abstraction, if it is not to remain 'out there', then it is necessary to address the masculinism of legal method itself and of those institutions – 'black-letter', 'critical', 'socio-legal' or whatever – which together propagate understandings of the power of law. This point requires clarification.

The masculinism of law

> The male jurisprudential tradition can . . . be seen as a professionally constituted and legitimated vision of the male as an authority, as one kind of authorship which underwrites the relations of power.
>
> (Grbich 1991: 75)

One of the central tenets of critical legal studies has been to question the ideological content of a legal curriculum which 'induces [a] pedagogical conservatism which masquerades as liberal consensus' (Stanley 1988: 43). Internationally, critiques of doctrinal orthodoxy are now well-established in terms of both the institutional politics of law schools and the jurisprudential curriculum. In focusing on the constitution of subjectivity within discourse and, ultimately, in privileging ontology over epistemology (Goodrich 1986), contemporary critical legal scholarship has, in particular, sought to subvert law's claims to validation as a science with its own method (doctrinal exegesis) and its own language and logic (Douzinas and Warrington 1987; Goodrich 1987; Young 1990 154–72). Breaking with doctrinal method remains an essential first step in putting analyses of gender and power on the agenda in legal studies; meanwhile recent studies of gender and power have opened out to analyse the social construction of sexuality, rendering both masculinity, masculinism and men's power accountable, political and liable to transformation (notable amongst this work is Connell's (1987) influential book *Gender and Power*).

This literature has significant implications for the teaching and study of law which I shall, in following chapters, seek to address. In what might tentatively be termed postmodern jurisprudence the aim has been to analyse legal discourse utilising a methodology of deconstruction which fundamentally questions the 'need to debate, if not yet to teach, the rhetorical status of law' (Goodrich 1986: 211). However, the point I wish to stress here is that linking the discursive field of law to masculinity has proved to be the contribution of a feminist scholarship 'intended to draw upon an understanding of how the constitution of law and the constitution of masculinity may overlap and share mutual resonances' (Smart 1989a: 86). It is *feminism*, and not critical legal studies, which has put masculinity on the agenda, notwithstanding the resistance of legal studies to addressing the sociality of gender in a more general way (and the fact that 'even' 'critical' texts might, in some respects, reproduce masculinist assumptions). From this feminist perspective it is the masculinism of law and law teaching which must be central to the deconstruction of the power of law. It is 'men and the law' which has masqueraded as 'people and the law' (Boyle 1985a) and the 'he' of malestream discourse which excludes women: 'Law has developed over time in the context of theories and institutions which are controlled by men and reflect their concerns' (Fineman 1991a: xiii).

Feminist legal scholarship is no longer an 'uncatalogued item, a yet-to-be-recognized enterprise' in legal studies (Lahey 1985; see Graycar and Morgan 1990). It has challenged purportedly neutral and objective doctrines by engaging with the realities of women's lives (Lahey 1985; Stang Dahl 1987) and, in focusing on the *gendering* of these processes, has sought to question the masculinism not just of legal discourse but also of the practices and institutions of law and legal education (O'Donovan 1989). Feminisms have thus challenged the masculinism of legal studies and have redrawn the relationship between masculinity, men and the power of law in the institutions of legal education. For example, just because a 'progressive' critical text might espouse a critique of doctrine (be it from a marxist or poststructuralist position) this does not mean that it does not bear the imprint of an appeal to science, hierarchy and truth *or* that it does not propound a specifically masculinist world view (see Green's (1992) criticisms of Goodrich (1990) on equating 'human' with 'male'; Boyle 1985a: 430). Feminist critiques of legal doctrine challenge what Graycar and Morgan (1990: 21) have termed the 'hard-edged' or 'serious' parts of law, disturbing traditional legal categories (Bender 1988; Coombs 1988; Becker 1989; Finley 1989a), exposing the hidden gender of the textbooks and casebooks used in teaching law (Frug 1985; Boyle 1985a) and the sexism of legal language (Scutt 1985; Busby 1989; Griffith 1989; Williams 1989).

Proponents of an interdisciplinary approach to law argue that legal studies have much to gain from the convergences within the histories and sociologies of social practice, and in particular from feminism and theories of discourse. We know that, for all the challenges of the recent past, the dominant methodology of the legal academy remains doctrinal legal method. Yet any intellectual break with doctrine or recourse to a modified neo-marxist or deconstructionist orthodoxy does not necessarily imply any progressive attitude to gender either in the resulting legal scholarship or the institutional practices of the law school. As Fineman (1991b: xi) notes, the difference between feminist and 'more traditional' approaches to theory is a belief in the 'desirability of the concrete'. Far from the 'grand theorising' discussed above, this points to 'middle-range' theories, both 'inside' and 'outside' law, which might seek to mediate between the material circumstances of women's lives and theoretical engagements with the power of law (Fineman and Thomadsen 1991; Bottomley and Conaghan 1993a).

There are different strands to feminist critiques of the masculinism of law, therefore, encompassing (at least) a woman-focused methodology (as opposed to the masculinist malestream), a critical evaluation of the concepts of legal discourse, a challenge to the existing social order and an evolutionary concern with contributing to ongoing debates, rather than substituting a male 'truth' with a feminist 'truth' (Fineman 1991a). In short, feminist legal scholarship has challenged both the *institutions* of the law and the masculinism of legal *method* itself. Masculinity has been rendered problematic not just in relation to *what* is taught as 'the law' but also to *how* the law is taught. We have seen that traditional legal method, or 'black-letter' law, has been identified by feminist legal scholars as a pervasively masculine methodology (Mossman 1986; Thornton 1986; Mackinnon 1989; Smart 1989a), a method with a 'hidden gender' (Graycar and Morgan 1990) whose supposedly neutral norms and universal principles belie a masculine vantage point (Fineman 1986; Dalton 1987–8; Torrey *et al.* 1990). The power of law as a dominant discourse is self-contained (though incomplete and imperfect), self-congratulatory (though not introspective or self-reflective) and self-fulfilling (though not inevitable nor infallible).

(Fineman 1991b: xii)

Far from pre-fixing 'woman' to the study of law (Mossman 1985; Lahey and Salter 1985), this scholarship has sought to move towards a more co-operative and less authoritarian and hierarchical style of law teaching (Menkel-Meadow 1988; Hantzis 1988; Cain 1988) and to listen to women's many voices (Grbich 1991; Bottomley and Conaghan 1993a). Alternatively, attempts have been made to seek a woman-centred law (Stang Dahl 1987) or to develop a value-system based on an 'ethic of care' (Larrabee 1993).

If a 'critical' approach to law, family and gender is to be any different from the prevailing orthodoxy then it is necessary to recognise that the determination of what is to count as 'knowledge' of the law must itself be related to the structure of gender relations in which the institutions of legal studies, the promulgators of doctrinal method, law students and future lawyers are at present bound up (Polan 1982; Rhode 1986). This means addressing all these dimensions to the masculinism of law.

From masculine law to masculinities

It is possible to read the masculinism of law on different levels. In relation to the legal academy, for example, Margaret Thornton (1989a) speaks of a 'personal dimension' which privileges all men. This, it is argued, is premised on a liberal conception of the self as 'public persona', a persona maintained by an elaborate silencing of questions in men's lives and resulting from the 'psycho-sexual power flowing from the maintenance of women in subordinate roles as wives, mistresses, secretaries and research assistants' (1989a: 118). Thornton describes aspects of this masculine 'persona' as inimical to women's success within the academy and in so doing describes the forms and effects (though not the construction) of a particular (hegemonic) form of masculinity. This hegemonic masculinity, she argues, has important implications for the viability of strategies of equal opportunity both within the academy and elsewhere (this analysis of 'public persona' is not confined to the institutions of law). More generally masculinist assumptions have been identified as similarly inimical to women's advancement in a legal profession which has historically embodied and entrenched discriminatory attititudes towards women (Kennedy 1992).

Carol Smart (1989a), involved in a rather different engagement pitched at the level of theorising the masculinism of both legal method and the institutions of law, argues that law is constituted as a masculine profession on empirical grounds (there are comparatively few women lawyers or judges) and that 'doing law' (whatever that is) and being identified as masculine are congruous. However, Smart does not argue that men are most suited to law because of any biological imperative. Rather, the analysis points to (though does not explicitly address) the nature of the *connections* between the power of masculinity and of law:

> both law and masculinity are constituted in discourse and there are significant overlaps in these . . . . So law is not rational because men are rational, but law is constituted as rational as are men, and men as the subjects of a discourse of masculinity come to experience themselves as rational – hence suited to a career in law. In attempting to transform law, feminists are not simply challenging legal discourse but also naturalistic assumptions about masculinity.
>
> (Smart 1989a: 86–7)

What is significant in this passage is the notion of 'men as the subjects of a discourse of masculinity'. This opens up the plurality, and the contingency, of those discourses which speak of masculinity in the legal context. Indeed, it is this idea of discourses, of the plurality, of masculinities – as opposed to a single unitary masculinity – which could be seen as very much the 'state of play' within the sociology of masculinity (for example, see Segal 1990; Hearn 1992; Morgan 1992). This means, as Brittan (1989) and others have argued, that there is no one, essential masculinity. Thus, as we have seen above, if we are to unproblematically take 'all men' as an object of study perhaps the only thing they have in common is their penises (Connell 1987). Increasingly reference has been made, therefore, not to masculinity but to this plurality of masculinities (Segal 1990; Middleton 1992). Brittan (1989) explicitly adopts the notion of the pluralities of masculinities in his wide-ranging analysis of *Masculinity and Power*, while Brod, very much a proponent of 'men's studies', similarly states:

The most general definition of Men's Studies is that it is the study of masculinities and male experiences as specific and varying social–historical or cultural formations. Such studies situate masculinities as objects of study on a par with femininities, instead of elevating them to universal norms.

(Brod 1987a: 40)

Adopting the plurality of masculinities enables the integration of the contingencies of ethnicity, physical ability and sexual orientation in the discursive construction of male subjectivities. However, though we have lost the 'false universalism' of other approaches to masculinity, this is not in itself an unproblematic enterprise. This does not mean there is no 'essence' to masculinity (or can we not speak of it without falling into a crude reductionism?). Morgan (1992) has addressed this question, claiming that 'there is not simply a diversity of masculinities, rather like a well-stocked supermarket, but that these masculinities are linked to each other, hierarchically, in terms of power' (1992: 45). However, to talk of a plurality of masculinities 'seems to imply an array of different statuses each one of which possesses something we might call a 'masculinity' (ibid.: 45). Might not such a plurality, therefore:

blunt the critical cutting edge of feminism. . . . In the ever proliferating multiplication of masculinities is there a danger of losing a sense of dominance, of patriarchy and of control? Might not this pluralization seem . . . to be yet another male strategy?

(Morgan 1992: 46)

The solution may be, Morgan suggests, to recognise that, first, 'masculinity' remains a term used in our society and that it is necessary to explore its usages; but also that (b) the use of the term 'masculinities' 'is a theoretical and political strategy designed to deconstruct conventional stereotypes . . . [but] what may be an aid to understanding now may serve as a blinker in the future' (1992: 46). As an essential correction to the ethnocentrism of so much research on masculinity, therefore, this approach also facilitates identification of the race specific aspects of male experiences and opens out the analysis of masculinity.[20] In rejecting the idea that all men, in the same way, are the benefactors of a patriarchal law/ state and social order, this goes against the notion of masculinity which underscores both the 'men against sexism' and 'men's liberation' approaches discussed above. This involves rejecting the conception of a seemingly universal, omnipotent, pervasive and inherently oppressive masculinity.

This does not mean that men, as a sex-class, do not benefit under patriarchy by virtue of being men. It does, however, open up those 'resonances' between the discursive constitution of both law and masculinities of which Smart speaks. Both, for example, are constructed as rational through the invoking of naturalistic and essentialist presuppositions. Rejecting such naturalistic conceptions of masculinity and disturbing the masculine/rational association, strands in both poststructuralist theories of masculinity (see Middleton 1992: 131–45) and feminist poststructuralist texts (for example Weedon 1987) have proceeded to stress the importance of decentring liberal-humanistic notions of coherent unified subjectivity. Such a de-centring is, it is argued, of the essence in a deconstruction of masculinity (Moi 1985).

The masculinism of law can thus be identified at both the institutional and methodological levels. To return to law and legal education and the institutions through which legal method is propagated, the case for linking the masculine/rational dualism with a legal method which has historically negated questions of gender and power is perhaps all the more acute. As we have seen, in theorising the sex/law relation, doctrinal exegetical method has been underscored by a positivist conception of law as a unified, coherent entity which renders unproblematic the categories of male and female. The legal subject may be a 'rational' actor but traditional legal method renders illegitimate any questioning of gender and power in relation to the differential constitution of male and female and as gendered rational subjects in the first place (Naffine 1990). Thus, it should not surprise us that we find the criminal law or family law lecturer who cannot, at least within the narrow parameters of doctrinal law teaching, analyse the constructions of masculinity and femininity which unite these two seemingly disparate areas of law. Doctrinal positivism does not provide the analytic tools to begin to do so – it can neither explain nor deconstruct the gender of law. This is not to say that an analysis of power relations cannot take place within doctrinal law teaching (on some courses, if not generally, it does so). However, it remains an enormous *struggle* to do so in relation to doctrinal based courses because of the closures engendered by the law as science model.

What this means for legal studies is that we cannot even begin to unpack the masculinism of legal method and the institutions of law unless we transcend the doctrinal model. There is a convergence between the construction of both masculinity and law in that both are enmeshed within notions of hierarchy, authority, rationality and abstraction; each involve a distancing of the personal, the emotional and the sexual in the constitution of a univocal authoratitive voice. The 'man of law', as we shall see in the following chapters, is a man who has inherited and enacted a 'public' reason and the 'public face' of market forces (O'Donovan 1985a: Naffine 1990). However there are subdivisions (or rather masculinities) within this general category, each with very different personae. There is, in short, no one 'man of law'.

If one accepts the phallogocentrism of legal discourse – the fusing of the masculine, heterosexual imperative and the fixing of sign/signifier within a partiarchal structure of power/knowledge relation (Smart 1989a: 86) – then law as a phallogocentric discourse can be seen to be inseparable from the ideology of masculinism (Brittan 1989: 4). Phallocentric culture can here be taken as referring to 'the needs of the masculine imperative which receive a cultural response' (O'Donovan 1993: 5). Law is part of such a cultural response. Yet the concept also involves the unconscious, the psyche and subjectivity; that is, it is also at the level of subjectivity that, crucially, patriarchal relations are reproduced (legal agents are, after all, humans and not degendered 'oppressors'). The question then becomes – how are these gendered identities constructed? (Jefferson 1993). And how are subjectivites constituted through the masculine imperative reproduced in law?

The deconstruction of law and masculinity can be related through how each stakes a claim to power; the power of law to disqualify that which is not part of its method (subjectivity, alternative accounts of 'reality', the transgression of the heterosexual imperative) is bound up with the power of men and hegemonic masculinity to exclude that which might challenge masculinism itself as a pervasive ideological support of male power. That is, the naturalisation of sexual difference, the sanctioning of the political and dominant role of men and the institutional enforcement of hegemonic heterosexuality which can be seen as constitutents of masculinism (Brittan 1989: 4). Law is, in other words, an important part of how subjectivities are constructed within a phallogocentric culture.

It is the challenge of feminist, gay and lesbian studies, and other

alternative knowledges that they deny the legitimacy and naturalism of male authority, that they challenge the neutral competence
and purportedly objective reason of masculinity and that they subvert the pervasive masculinism and hegemonic heterosexism of
the institutions of law. They render masculinity accountable, as
liable to change and contingent; they place masculinity firmly
within the terrain of the sexual politics of law. Thus, it is possible
to speak of a sexual politics of law through recognising the power
of resistant discourses, such as feminism and critiques of masculinism, and embracing the contingencies of gender and the
possibility, and inevitability, of change.

It is at this point that it becomes possible to bring together these
issues and address just what is meant by masculinity in this study. It
is not my intention in the chapters which follow to reduce masculinity or male power to the status of functional product of essentialist/
biologic disposition. Nor is it, as we shall see in Chapters 3 and 4,
to claim that heterosexuality is necessarily problematic *per se*. It is,
rather, to subvert essentialism and embrace the pluralities and
contingent nature of masculinities, both heterosexual and homosexual. It is to locate masculinity not as a fixed entity, but as
something continually 'in process', as a heterogeneity and
(crucially) as liable to change and to be challenged. I have here in
mind a sense of a '*sujet-en-proces*' (the subject in process) (Kristeva
1981: 165). It is to embrace the 'performative possibilities' of
gender (Butler 1990) and to place masculinity within an active
process within which meaning is manufactured.

Masculinities must be constantly produced and reproduced,
and the gender regime at any historical moment is always in a
dynamic (Connell 1987). That is, social strucures are constantly in
the process of constitution; 'structures identified by analysis . . .
exist only in solution, they are not absolutely prior to the subject
but themselves always in process of formation. Social and personal
life are practices' (Middleton 1992: 153). Masculinity is never
finally closed, fixed or resolved therefore. This is as true of a
specific institutional setting, for example, a law school, barristers'
chambers or a firm of solicitors, as in society generally. It involves
locating the politics of masculinity not simply at the level of the
personal (be it as a matter of choice, conditioning, human nature
and so forth) but also as embedded in the gender regime of
specific institutions (Segal 1990), as part of politics and organisational sexuality of institutions and society generally.

Masculinity . . . is best understood as transcending the personal, as a heterogeneous set of ideas, constructed around assumptions of social *power* which are lived out and reinforced, or perhaps denied and challenged, in multiple and diverse ways within a whole social system in which relations of authority, work and domestic life are organised, in the main, along hierarchical gender lines.

(Segal 1990: 288)

The idea that discourses of masculinity have an institutional dimension is important in understanding the power of law. Although masculinities are produced both in and by a heterogeneity of discourses of representation, statements about masculinity must be located within a specific system of dispersal. In order to assign any particular significance to representations of masculinity, therefore, it becomes also necessary to analyse the social relations within which they are reproduced. Outside of such an institutional context such representations have no self-evident meaning. Thus

To speak legitimately of a discourse of masculinity it would be necessary to show that a particular set of usages was located structurally within a clearly defined institution with its own methods, objects and practices. Otherwise the reference to discourses of masculinity is simply a reference to repeated patterns of linguistic usage, which may be significant, but cannot be theorized in the way some legal and medical discourses can. Masculinity is produced within some discourses in the stricter theoretical sense, but most examples of 'masculine' utterance are not discourses.

(Middleton 1992: 142)

Law provides not just a set of usages for discourses of masculinity which are located structurally but also a clearly defined institution with its own methods (doctrinal exegetical method), objects and practices. Discourses of masculinity, in other words, have had an established and entrenched link with the histories of power and knowledge of law.

TOWARDS A STUDY OF LAW AND MASCULINITY: CONCLUDING REMARKS

I have argued that gender relations are not fixed but are constantly produced and reproduced. The politics of masculinity are not simply a matter of personal choice (though traditionally masculinity has been and continues to be discussed as if it were a personal political issue and not in the domain of 'real' politics (Weir 1993)). The gender order is also institutional and structural and relates to networks of power which transcend specific institutions (Segal 1990: 288). Valorisation of authority, hierarchy and violence, as components of the ideology of masculinism, is not specific to legal (or any other) institutions but is bound up within those discourses which construct masculinities. In relation to workplace practices generally

> To explain rather than merely describe the sexual hierarchies of the workplace, we need to understand the interaction between the logic of capitalist accumulation and men's needs and desires to maintain their dominance in the workplace.
>
> (Segal 1990: 299)

This involves linking the wider, structural context and the personal dimension and transcending the public/private dichotomy which underscores both the 'public persona' to which Thornton (1989a) refers and also the idea of 'state intervention' which has underscored liberal legalism (Olsen 1985; Rose 1987). It is this connection that I shall seek to explore in the following chapter. The exclusion of women, discussed above, has been central to the ideology of masculinism and it brings together the ideas of violence, hierarchy and homosociality which have surfaced in accounts of legal education and the legal profession. The competence, authority and prerogative of the male 'fine mind' as a public persona within this hierarchical institutional setting is a social construct which depends in part on the exclusion and ideological subordination of women. Perhaps, with this in mind, we may be now closer to understanding how men have, and continue to, resist women's entry into and progress within the legal sphere and how this relates to the ideology of masculinism.

Women's presence within the legal world, albeit partial and the result of hard struggle, has met with and continues to meet systematic resistance from men. Feminism meets similiar resistance within law schools today (Graycar 1986; Thornton 1986; Bottomley 1987; Smart 1989a). Yet it is surely curious that a common technique of exclusion is a statement of familiarity with feminist projects, an expressed belief that we live in 'post-feminist' times (or at least the enlightened liberal men of the academy – or the 'needles in the haystack'? – do). A clearer picture of the relation between masculinism and law now begins to emerge. The masculinity/ rationality conjunction has itself been employed in the dynamic of exclusion of alternative discourses, such as feminism, which threaten the power of masculinity and law. Removed from the realm of the rational, questions of gender and power are denied validity within traditional legal method: 'They're at it again, leave them alone'; 'It's not law, you would be happier doing sociology.' To be 'passionate' here connotes the irrational, the feminine and the antithesis of the 'reasoned' and 'logical', of the academic 'fine legal mind'. Law excludes gender as it excludes those who do not play its game. Legal discourse disarms alternatives at the moment of their articulation just as masculinist institutions deny the validity of discourses which would question their naturalistic status and seek to marginalise that which deviates from the hegemonic norm.

This has important consequences for understanding the gender of law and the process of professional socialisation *into* the dominant legal method. The public/private, work/home dichotomies central to liberal legalism (Chapter 2) pervade assessments of what is, and is not, of concern to the lawyer. The private, personal and subjective is thus irrelevant to the dominant epistemology of legal method, doctrinal exegesis, which proclaims the law a science unto itself, self-referential and seeking no justification other than its own claim to 'Truth' and scientific status. The challenge to doctrine is thus a challenge to the exclusions engendered by this model of understanding the law. When feminists challenge law's exclusions – for example in the areas of rape, child sexual abuse or domestic violence (the areas to be covered in Chapter 6) – feminism is also challenging men to deny the 'truth' of the experiential, of desire, and of their own sexuality and power. Change, therefore, means bringing the experiential, the subjective, the personal back onto the agenda.

To this end it is not suprising that recent accounts of masculinity should have sought to fuse theory with an autobiographical focus (Jackson 1990). What is personal is what is banished from the masculine. It is for this reason, in part, that the following study of masculinity and law is concerned with the family, sexuality and affective relationships and with what our culture, and our laws, understand by the 'family life' of men. However, it is insufficient to focus just on this. That women and men are constructed differentially by law in their familial relationships is now beyond doubt (see O'Donovan 1985a, 1993); it is the contours of these differences which feminist legal scholarship has begun to detail.

The following chapters argue that potent ideas of masculinity, in particular representations of male sexuality, authority, fatherhood and paternity, continue to be constructed in law and that these ideas are crucial to the constitution of subjective commitments to family life for both women and men. What follows is, in part, an attempt to

> examine the new ways of thinking and acting which these languages of the family have introduced into our reality . . . they actually constituted new sectors of reality, new problems and possibilities for personal investment as well as for public regulation.
>
> (Rose 1987: 68)

In this introductory chapter I have presented an overview and analysis of some of the issues and themes which have emerged within the sociology of masculinity. These are issues which will be explored further in the following chapters. I have attempted to place this literature in a wider context, both with regard to theorising masculinity in sociology generally and in relation to feminism and feminist analyses of male power. I have discussed both the strengths and dangers of studying masculinity and law, introduced some of the difficulties and issues which arise in defining masculinity and have presented the beginnings of a theoretically coherent approach to studying law and masculinity.

The following three chapters seek to transcend the theorisation of masculinity in terms of a bifurcation between heterosexual and homosexual identity and, with regard to law, to locate the place of legal discourse in the constitution of normative and deviant forms of male sexual behaviour. In Chapter 2 I shall look in more detail at the construction of the public/private division in law and the concepts of power and oppression. In addressing the construction of masculinity in law – to hopefully open up the possibilities of 'new ways of thinking and acting' – what follows is a contribution to debates about the politics of the family and gender, as well as a rethinking of the personal investment of both women and men to marriage and the family.

Chapter 2

Theorising masculinity and the family

We have seen in Chapter 1 that the doctrinal ideal of 'black-letter' law continues to dominate the intellectual and cultural climate of law, notwithstanding the periodic crises occasioned by legal realism, socio-legal studies, the sociology of law and, more recently, critical legal studies. With regard to the law relating to the family, the legal subdiscipline 'family law' has been maintained and constructed through a range of legal textbooks (for example Bromley and Lowe 1987; Dewar 1989a; Cretney 1990, 1992). These proclaim what the author considers to be the relevant laws which apply to the family. Usually this has involved consideration of laws on marriage and divorce and the 'private' obligations of husband and wife, with a heavy bias towards legal regulation of the care and control of children and the allocation of property entitlements following the termination of relationships. In the 1990s many university family law courses in the UK continue to construct the subject in terms of the rights and responsibilities of husband (H) and wife (W) and through reference to the 'sacramental associations' of the sacred texts and myths of family law (O'Donovan 1993: 9). Yet for all its increased respectability the subject family law continues to be perceived within the legal academy and profession as in many ways inferior to the 'proper' doctrinal subjects such as contract, tort and criminal law.

What this conception of the subject of 'family law' singularly fails to do is to question the inherent theoretical presuppositions of the object of analysis and its method of inquiry. What exactly is 'the family' in law? What do we mean by 'state intervention' in the family? Where does 'family law' come from in the first place (not simply in the sense of deriving from common law, legislation, custom and history; see O'Donovan 1993: Ch 2)? Perhaps most

complex of all, how does legal regulation of emotional relationships relate to the reproduction of the gender order and the
constitution of individual subjectivities? In other words, how does
it relate to the activation of commitments of men and women to
their lives in 'the family' and, in this process, how does it construct
heterosexuality itself? What is the power of law in this area and how
does it relate to gender?

Recent scholarship has sought to critically theorise this relationship between law and the family and in so doing has fundamentally
questioned a number of presuppositions about law and power
which underlie the idea of a liberal 'state' which 'intervenes',
through law, in the 'family' (Freeman 1985; Olsen 1985).
Interdisciplinary analyses of the family *in* law have, prompted in
part by the feminist critiques of legal method, opened out the legal
structuring of gender within this familial domain to examination
through seeking to explore connections between legal and other
discourses which construct the familial. Within this reconstructed
remit of 'family law matters' (O'Donovan 1993) such an interdisciplinary study of law has aimed at 'breaking down the closure
of legal discourse and at critically articulating the internal relationships it constructs with other discourses' (Goodrich 1987: 212).
Not surprisingly recent developments in social theory, notably
around postmodernism, have filtered through in debates about
law and the family as the discursive status of both the 'family' *and*
'law' has been thrown into question.

One result has been to draw into the arena of legal studies a
range of discourses which have sought to privilege the political and
social nature of masculinity. It is the growing acceptance of this
'interdiscursive status of the legal text' (Goodrich 1987: 212)
which, I shall argue in this chapter, has facilitated a critical dialogue
between law, feminism and those knowledges which might seek to
put the problematic of masculinity onto the sexual political
agenda. Masculinity may not be an issue in the traditional family
law textbook but, in the end, perhaps we should not be too concerned about this. After all, what the concept of law as 'social
discourse' facilitates is 'the re-reading of the law and the rewriting
of the legal textbook' (Goodrich 1987: 208).

'CRITICAL' FAMILY LAW

Reconstructing the legal textbook in this way is a far from simple task. Such a 'reconstruction' of the legal subject has been attempted in a number of areas, notably from an overt 'contextual' perspective (for example, on criminal law: Lacey *et al.* 1990). At times critiques of doctrinalism have self-consciously distanced themselves from the textbook tradition, proclaiming themselves to be a 'critical commentary [which] is considered marginal' to the mainstream (O'Donovan 1993: 18). Generally, however, there has been little methodological orthodoxy to recent critical writings on the family and law. Indeed the very concept of 'critical family law' is open to question (Freeman 1985; cf. Eekelaar 1989). It is perhaps not surprising that the different intellectual traditions of critical legal studies – feminist, liberal, marxist, neo-marxist, postmodern, etc. – should each be replicated in critical accounts of law and the family. However, the existence of any larger movement of 'critical family law', and in particular one that would reproduce the metanar-ratives of existing paradigms, remains deeply problematic.

Nonetheless, if there is a recurring theme in recent critical writings on law and the family then it appears to be the perceived need to address and transcend the limitations of doctrinal legal method and to seek to make sense of developments in matri-monial policy and politics (that is, to address the law in practice as well as the law in books). To this end, and in keeping with the need to simultaneously take the power of legal doctrine seriously, critical texts on law and the family have sought to integrate questions of policy and socio-economic context within a broadly interdisciplinary and contextual understanding of the substantive law. Family law is, in short, inescapably political. Thus the critical approach to law and the family has not so much involved rejecting out of hand the cases and statutes of the traditional 'family law' textbook as integrating into the analysis the recognition

> that law needs to be socially located . . . family law cannot be understood as if it is assumed to operate neutrally, ahistorically or cocooned from indices of power. Just as existing theory is designed to shore up the status quo, so critical theory has . . . a particular goal as well. Critical family law is an integral part of a struggle to create a more socially just society.
>
> (Freeman 1985: 154–5)

It is necessary to go beyond the the conventional boundaries of family law (Olsen 1985). Indeed, policies towards the family can-not be confined within the traditional conceptual field of liberal legal theory (Freeman 1985: 158). The 'integral part' of political struggle envisaged by Freeman in his article *Towards a Critical Theory of Family Law* (1985) is in fact an amalgam of a range of developments in relation to feminism and discourse theory, critical legal studies and poststructuralism. It also covers paradigms, disciplines and perspectives which may not be necessarily compatible in their theoretical presuppositions (see also O'Donovan's *Family Law Matters* (1993: 18)). Notwithstanding this proviso however, it has been the crucial insight of studies such as this that it is necessary to start the analysis of law, gender and the family with *families* themselves – as social, psychological, economic and political units – and not with *law*. The meaning which one gives to the 'family' in law can have far-reaching implications and it is important to question at the outset what the word 'family' in legal discourse signifies. As sociological, historical and anthropological studies have shown, there is no one essential transhistorical and transcultural 'family' which the law can then be said to be regulating (Bernardes 1988a). Before we can theorise the relationship between masculinity and the family, therefore, we need to state what we understand by family in the first place.

DEFINING THE 'FAMILY'

The concept of 'the family' covers many issues relating to kinship, household organisation and sexuality which sociologists of the family, in a now voluminous literature, have sought to explore. The subject of 'the family' may be taken for granted but it is not legally defined. Methodologically, many different research techniques have been used; analysis of demographic patterns (developments in mortality rates, fertility, population trends), large scale empirical surveys (Wilmott and Young 1962) and smaller qualitative, ethnographic and interactionist studies (Turnstall 1962; Komarovsky 1964) have all been utilised in researching the family. Critical deconstructions of gender in law have frequently taken the form of textual analyses (of cases, statutes), whilst empirical socio-legal research has provided important information about what happens 'in practice' (e.g. Eekelaar *et al.* 1977). All have involved complex moral and ethical questions and one thing is clear from these studies – that household structures have varied historically and that the 'family' can mean different things in different contexts (historical change in familial masculinity is explored further in Chapter 5).

Utilising as ideal-types the models of 'extended' and the 'nuclear' families, historical sociologies of the family (Shorter 1975; Fletcher 1977; Stone 1977) have sought to explain historical shifts in household structures. Together this scholarship constitutes a body of work which has shed considerable light on the changing roles of men and women in the family – and it has also, implicitly, provided much information about historical shifts in the forms of masculinity within the family domain (Anderson 1971, 1980; Aries 1973; Laslett 1977; Davidoff and Hall 1987). The focal point of such historical studies of the family has been the marriage-bond, the affective, sexual ties between husband and wife (a bond which is, we shall see, central to legal definitions of the familial). The sexual relationship of husband and wife is at the centre, for example, of Fletcher's definition of the family as

> a small, relatively permanent group of people, related to each other in the most intimate way, bound together by the most personal aspects of life, who experience amongst themselves the whole range of human emotions . . . who experience continual responsibilities and obligations towards each other; who experience the sense of 'belonging' to each other in the most intimately felt sense of that word.
>
> (Fletcher 1977: 26–7)

These 'most intimate' and 'most personal' dynamics of family life are the unstated core of Fletcher's idea of the 'family'. Yet his is just one of the defining 'essences' of the family which sociology has offered (cf. Leach 1955; Gough 1959; Mair 1971; Harris 1979; see further, and more generally, Hoggett and Pearl 1987: 1; Bernardes 1988b). Marriage, it appears, can be all things to all people and, as cross-cultural and anthropological studies have shown (Mead 1935, 1943, 1950), there is no one transhistorical family form. Rather, 'despite idealisation of the heterosexual family, there is no consistent model of what a family is' (O'Donovan 1993: 34; see also Elshtain 1982; Thorne and Yalom 1982).

The most cursory look at contemporary households shows that there is no 'one' single, British family form but rather a plurality of 'families'. There has occurred in the past twenty years a number of (much reported) major changes in the number of families which fit the 'stereotyped' view of the nuclear family (breadwinner/male, childrearer/female with two children), not least the increase in the number of single person households and in levels of cohabitation and the percentage of births outside marriage (Deech 1980; Weitzman 1981; Freeman and Lyon 1983). Any analysis of the family, law and masculinity must take account of the historical specificity of the contemporary context in which we must locate debates about matrimonial law therefore, as well as the variations of ethnicity and culture which inform our understandings of 'family life' and the fact that all households are not, and never have been, constituted in the same way.

'The family' in law

There is no one universally applied idea of what constitutes a family to be found in legal discourse (though this does not mean that the law has not sought to privilege a particular version of 'the familial' over and above others). Instead, legal determinations have focused on the meanings of specific legislative provisions. For the lawyer this can be of considerable significance, for the meaning which one gives to 'family' in a particular legal context can have far-reaching implications (Dickey 1982; Olsen 1984; Minow 1985a). For example, assessment of the effects of a piece of legislation such as the Divorce Reform Act 1969 turn on the definition of family taken. If 'family' is held to constitute a lifelong union between a man and a woman then the 1969 Act and the subsequent Matrimonial Causes Act 1973 may be argued to have weakened the family, diminishing respect for 'family life' and bringing about a rising divorce rate. However if 'family' is understood to be a temporary arrangement (heterosexual serial monogamy) then it is arguable that the family is as respected as ever, with chances of marrying higher today than they were in the late nineteenth century. Indeed, in 1988 the UK had the highest rate of marriage in the European Community (Central Statistical Office 1991: 2.11).

Lawyers have traditionally tended to adopt simplistic approaches to the word 'family', implying that the concept means the same thing in all situations. Yet there is no essential family form in law (Dickey 1982; Dewar 1989a). This is usefully illustrated by analysis of legislation where the word 'family' is used. For example the wording of the Increase of Rent and Mortage Interest (Restriction) Act 1920 states that a person who was 'a member of the original tenant's family', and who was residing with the tenant at the time of the original tenant's death, may then become a tenant of the deceased tenant's property if they continue in residence of that property. This Act clearly envisages some meaning for the 'family' of which the tenant might then be held in law to be a member (Berkovitz 1981). Similarly, in an example used by Bradney (1979) and O'Donovan (1993: 34), Schedule 1, paragraph 3 of the Rent Act 1977 permits a statutory tenancy, in the absence of a surviving spouse, to devolve to any person who was 'a member of the original tenant's family' and who was residing with the deceased at the time of, and for six months preceding, his death. The question has explicitly fallen in law to be answered therefore – what does a 'member of the tenant's family' actually mean?

The answer is far from obvious (see further Ghandi and MacNamee 1991). As Bradney (1979) shows in his analysis of the Rent Acts, the word 'family' should be given its 'proper meaning' (Brock v Wollams [1949] 1 All ER 715: also Sefton Holdings v Cairns [1988] 2 Fam Law Rep 108). However, in determining this meaning it is clear that it is the *sexual* relationship between the parties which is to be subject to judical scrutiny. In Gammans v Ekins [1950] 2 All ER 140 Asquith L.J. considered that

> if their relations were platonic, I can see no principle on which it could be said that these two were members of the same family, which would not require the court to predict the same of two old cronies of the same sex innocently sharing a flat. If, on the other hand, the relationship involves sexual relations, it seems to me anomalous that a person can aquire a 'status of irremovability' by living or having lived in sin. . . . To say of two people masquerading, as these two were, as husband and wife . . . that they were members of the same family, seems to be an abuse of the English language.[1]

Sex, the 'special intimacy' to which Fletcher (1977) referred, would appear central to defining a legally constituted relationship in this case. In the later case of Dyson Holdings v Fox [1976] QB 503 the Court of Appeal were clear that a relationship between an unmarried man and an unmarried woman living together over a very long period might constitute a family relationship necessary to satisfy the relevant section. Bridge L.J. considered that 'the ordinary man in 1975 would, in my opinion, certainly say that the parties to such a union, provided it had appropriate degree of apparent permanence and stability, were members of a single family whether they had children or not.' In this case the sexual relationship was present. The conclusion may be different in this case but family status continues to be determined by an assessment of whether or not there is seen to be, by the court, a sufficiently stable and appropriate sexual union.

In the subsequent case of Helby v Rafferty [1979] 3 All ER 1016, however, a relationship was considered to be insufficient to constitute a family. Here 'there was no charade. . . . Nor was there any attempt made, as I understand it, to throw dust in the eyes of friends as to the true nature of the relationship . . . the parties . . . were less intimate than was in fact the case.' The test would appear to be 'whether the "ordinary man"' would recognise the relationship as establishing 'a broadly recognisable familial nexus' (Carega Properties v Sharratt [1979] 2 All ER 1084; O'Donovan 1993: 35). Given the centrality of the heterosexual bond in defining the family in this context, it follows that the family in law must also not be based on a homosexual relationship (see Chapter 3). Thus, in Harrogate Borough Council v Simpson [1985] 17 HLR 205; [1986] 2 FLR 91 the court declared that it would 'be surprising in the extreme to learn that public opinion is such today that it would recognise a homosexual union as being akin to a state of living as husband and wife.' (See also R v Immigration Appeal Tribunal, ex parte Windestedt [1984] *The Times* 12 December 1984.)

These cases illustrate two important points about masculinity and law which will be elaborated on in following chapters. First, we can see here the centrality of *sexual* relations and a particular normative sexuality in assessing whether or not a legal relationship can be said to exist. It is heterosexual intercourse which gives rise to familial rights; non-heterosexual relations do not. Second, these cases reveal an important aspect of the *power of law*. In defining whether or not a particular institution/household grouping is to be regarded as a 'family' it is the intervention of law, the calling upon of the judicial gaze, which is necessary in order to bring a 'family' in law into being. In particular, this works through reference to the idea of the 'ordinary man' (in effect, a judicial determination of what is considered to be popular morality).

Defining a family in the above cases involves making not just certain assumptions about heterosexuality but also about masculinity and femininity (assumptions the narrow doctrinal approach to law disempowers us from beginning to analyse). It is crucial to the power of legal method that the question of *what* is to be taken to constitute a 'fact' about the family and the question of *whose* reality it is that the law is involved in privileging is rendered an accountable, social and political issue. These are contingencies that any truly 'critical' family law must seek to deconstruct.

Alternative constructions of the family in law are possible.[2] Barrett and McIntosh (1982: 7) have argued that the family might more usefully be understood in two senses. First, as a social and economic institution in which, by and large, households are assumed to be organised on a sexual division of labour between primary breadwinner/male and childrearer/female. On this analysis certain structures of masculinity and femininity may be said to be particularly compatible (if not functional) to the familial institution. Barrett and McIntosh argue that although these are assumptions about gender roles which are not based on the empirical reality of family life for the majority of people, they must nonetheless be considered part of the familial sphere since they form elements of the conditions under which men and women are employed and live their lives. They contain assumptions which are both reflected in levels of wages, taxes and benefits and which are also reproduced in the domain of leisure, advertising and so forth. In O'Donovan's (1993) terms these have become part of the powerful 'myths' through which we experience family life.

The second sense in which the family may be understood is through the concept of familial ideology, or the family as an ideology. While social institutions and ideology are reciprocally related, the ideology of the family, Barrett and McIntosh suggest (1982: 8) is stronger than is commonly allowed

> It should be remembered that the currently dominant model of the family is not timeless and culture free. . . . This hegemonic form is a powerful ideological force that mirrors in an idealised way the characteristics of contemporary family life. It has only a tenuous relation to co-residence and the organisation of households as economic units.
>
> (Barrett and McIntosh 1982: 33–4)

Understanding the family as a collection of ideological and cultural factors which are imbued within certain power relations, Barrett and McIntosh argue that a particular definition of the 'family' is constantly idealised within contemporary society as the goal to which all should aspire. In the following chapters I shall explore the power and place of law in the construction of experiential commitments to this family life for both women and men. There is no *one* family, just as there is no one familial masculinity, or femininity. But this does not mean that a specific ideology of the family may not itself be powerful. Starting with families, and not law, one faces the immediate problem in that it remains difficult to say what the family actually is.

There have been many approaches, many theories and methods, applied to the study of the family (Bernardes 1988a). In the remainder of this chapter I shall focus on three: functionalism; the 'public/private dichotomy'; and the 'familialisation' approaches to the study of law and the family. Each, I shall argue, involve different conceptions of masculinity and law. There are other approaches,[3] or other ways of 'telling stories about law' (O'Donovan 1993: 18, following the approach of Dewar 1989a). My concern here is with how theorising the law/masculinity relation (Chapter 1) has been implicated in each. It has been, in particular, the public/private dichotomy which advocates of critical family law have sought to 'transcend' in seeking to open out the family and law to an analysis of gender and power.

FUNCTIONALISM

Functionalism has arguably being the most historically influential of these three theoretical perspectives, dominating the sociology of the family in the 1940s and 1950s (notably through the work of the American sociologist Talcott Parsons; Parsons and Bales 1956; Parsons 1964). Functionalist sociology developed analyses of social systems and their inter-relationships in such a way as to construct gender relations in the family as being fundamental to linking the individual with the wider social group. Within the functionalist paradigm the family is presented as playing a central role in the processes of socialisation whereby an individual learns her or his 'role ' in society. The 'function' is thus what the family does or is assumed to do. In particular, it is the family which socialises the child into the values required for adult life which provides an orderly means of reproduction and which provides a means of controlling, though marriage, the potentially destructive forces of sexuality.

There is clearly a model of masculinity and male sexuality implicit in this functionalist idea of a normative, functional, male gender 'role'. A more recent exponent of this idea of a male 'sex role' has been Joseph Pleck. In his book *The Myth of Masculinity* (1981) Pleck argues that masculinity may be understood as a role which undergoes significant change during the lifetime of an individual. Pleck is concerned to reject essentialism in the study of masculinity and he locates psychological identity as central to his concept of masculinity. Rejecting the crude dualisms of androgyny (Bem 1976, 1974; Eichler 1980: 67–92; see further Connell 1987: 171–5) it is Pleck's argument that masculine conformity can often be socially dysfuntional. However, though his analysis is quite sophisticated (and is clearly allied to an anti-patriarchal political stance) Pleck's depiction of masculinity continues to rest on the implicit assumptions of functionalist role theory such as sanction, norms and conformity.

Law, as a mechanism of enforcing such norms, is implicated in such an analysis of masculinity if one accepts that law, as an embodiment of the values and norms of society, sanctions or renders illegitimate certain behaviour. Yet just what this 'male role' involves is far from clear. Masculinity becomes a meaningless abstraction if it is to signify no more than 'male gender' or 'how men are', thus somehow floating free of the power relations within which it is itself constituted (Connell 1987: 47–54). It is this abstraction and depoliticising of masculinity, therefore, which remains one of the major problems of the sex role paradigm (Brannon 1976; Pleck 1981; cf. Carrigan *et al.* 1985; though note the change in Pleck's later work; Pleck 1987b). Nonetheless this has not stopped the language of the sex role from becoming the principal means through which judges have addressed gender in law. The rhetoric of sex roles, though theoretically flawed, has continued (as we shall see in the following chapters) to pervade judicial pronouncements on gender.

The problem is with the concept of a sex 'role' itself. The idea of a culturally/legally imposed role presumes the existence of a 'true' inner self which is considered to be separate from the proscribed behaviour which may be taken as the expression of 'masculinity'. If change is something which happens to the 'sex role' (from society or from an unalienated 'real' self), irrespective of human agency, then it is difficult to see where change originates in the first place. Sex role theory thus remains oblivious both to the dialectics inherent in gender relations between social structure/ human agency and to the fluid and double-edged nature of law and legal change. We shall see in this book that law does not unproblematically reinforce any one 'male role' in the family but is involved in an altogether more complex mobilisation of subjectivity, interests and desires towards particular (though unspecified, indeterminate) ends. Indeed, as we shall see below, there is no one abstracted male 'role' in legal discourse which can be identified as fully capturing all the complexities and contradictions of male experiences.

Masculinity is more complex and contradictory than functionalist role theory allows. The family is similarly more heterogeneous than the functionalist paradigm would present it. For example, physical protection and economic and emotional support for adults and children (purported 'functions' of the family) are not always provided through the family unit. There is no guarantee that economic rewards will be distributed and consumed equally. Indeed, there is a wealth of evidence to show that the law has not historically protected women and children from men's violences and the socially destructive aspect of modern (and past) masculinities. The central functionalist ideas of 'function', 'need' and 'stability' are deeply problematic, therefore. They rest on conservative, consensual presuppositions which fail to account for historical change in family structures. Implicitly, the gender regime of family life is conceived as a social good, the key to the 'fit' between social system and structure through the depiction of different functional roles for male and female (see, for example Wilmott and Young 1973; Berger and Berger 1983). The politics of the family, law and gender are thus evaded.

It is interesting that, despite functionalism's ethnocentrism, underlying tautology and frequent overemphasis on urban communities (Morgan 1975: 57), it is a perspective which continues to be adopted in studies of law and the family and a range of quasi-legal agents of the 'psy' professions (and not just judges) continue to promulgate ideas of functional/dysfunctional families. There is certainly an appeal for the 'family lawyer' in approaching a subject which might appear at first to be defined by the functions the family is assumed to perform. Functionalism presents one framework for exposition of a subject whose academic and legal origins are dubious (Bromley and Lowe 1987: 2–3). Focusing on assumed 'goals' facilitates the positivist socio-legal researcher through providing identifiable parameters for 'success' or 'failure' (and thus, in turn, justifying research proposals and funding). Ultimately, however, functionalism is a flawed perspective from which to begin to approach the family. It is blind to the structures of gender and power (and thus to power in the family), falling apart perhaps most of all because there is no one type of family or no one masculine or feminine 'sex role' which can perform these 'functions'. Just what the 'goals' of the family are remains far from clear and, instead of somehow intervening when things go 'wrong', law can itself be the source of the problems of the family in the first place.

THE PUBLIC/PRIVATE DICHOTOMY

The range of problems in family law which which may be formulated in terms of the boundary between public powers and private freedoms is considerable. Questions such as how, and to what extent, the state should intervene in family life (Goldstein, Freud and Solnit 1973), what personal morality is the concern of the law (Wolfenden 1957; Devlin 1959; Hart 1963) and the extent to which welfare professionals should intervene in the family (Dingwall, Eekelaar and Murray 1983, 1984) have all been couched in terms of the dichotomy between the 'public' and the 'private' spheres. The issues addressed in the language of 'public/ private' and 'state intervention' range through divorce (McGregor 1957), child care and child abuse (Butler-Sloss 1988; Campbell 1988; Woodcraft 1988), marriage (Weitzman 1981; Smart 1984a), sexuality (Weeks 1981), the provision of maintenance (Eekelaar and Maclean 1986), responses to domestic violence (Dobash and Dobash 1980; McCann 1985) and moves to conciliation in the decision making process (Parkinson 1983, 1987; Bottomley 1984). Central to each is the question of the extent to which the 'public' state/law can or should intervene in the 'private' family.

The public/private dichotomy has a long history (Freeman 1985: 166; O'Donovan 1985a: Ch. 2; Thornton 1991: 448–51) and the fact that the division is gendered is now well established in feminist theory (Okin 1979; Elshtain 1982; Benn and Gaus 1983; Olsen 1983; Nicholson and Linda 1986; Pateman 1983, 1988). Indeed, the public/private dichotomy has been central to the development of a recognisable body of feminist thought within legal scholarship (Graycar and Morgan 1990: 30–40). The dichotomy can be found in the natural rights theories of Locke (Locke 1967), and the philosophical foundations of contemporary liberal legal theory are evident in the political philosophy of Mill (1910, 1929), for whom the realm of morally legitimate state regulation was to be contrasted with a realm of privacy, personal choice and freedom from state intrusion (O'Donovan 1993: 23–4). This classic liberal foundation has more recently underscored considerations of the law on homosexuality and prostitution (Wolfenden 1957) and pornography (Williams 1979). The parameters of the private sphere perhaps most recently resurfaced in the criminal law context in debates around the legal legitimacy of sado-masochistic sexual practices (the 'Spanner' case: R v Brown [1993] 2 WLR 556: *The Guardian* 2 December 1992: 3; *The Independent* 10 December 1992).

There is a certain paradox to the public/private division in all of this; or, as Lacey (1993: 93) puts it, 'the more we criticize the public/private dichotomy, the more we get trapped within its conceptual framework'. It has been presented as central to theorising the law/family relation (Glendon 1978; Elshtain 1982; Gamarinkow *et al.* 1983; Freeman 1985; Olsen 1985; O'Donovan 1985a, 1993; Weintraub 1990). Yet it is also argued that it is a division which confines and limits understanding of reform strategies around law through failing to account for the power of law and liberal legal discourse and through negating the gendered and discriminatory nature of the division in the first place (Rose 1987; Thornton 1991). The public/private dichotomy, it might seem, is to be accepted, rejected and 'transcended' all at the same time.

In effect the 'public/private' division has been held to have a conceptual utility precisely because it is a dichotomy which does *not* hold up to analysis beyond the terms of liberal legal discourse. Freeman (1985) argues that the private sphere does not exist outside of the state. He suggests that the public and the private each contain the other at the level of social practices and strategies of power. The division has nonetheless been utilised in analyses of law as an example of (one of) a range of binary oppositions which pervade liberal legal discourse (Katz 1978; Gardiner 1983). These divisions have, in turn, been considered to be fundamental to the shaping of consciousness in a capitalist/patriarchal social order in such a way as to foster acceptance of existing social arrangements (Kennedy 1982; Horowitz 1982). O'Donovan (1985a) welds this argument to a sexual political agenda, arguing that the private is as constructed a space as the public but is presented through patriarchal law as the sphere to 'which the King's writ does not seek to run, and to which his officers do not seek to be admitted' (Balfour v Balfour [1919] 2 KB 571, 579: also Semayne's Case [1604] 77 ER 194). The division legitimates a reading of the family as a place of refuge and source of social security, somehow beyond the law and society. Yet 'law is not only central to the concepts of private and public, and to the division between the two, but also plays an important part in the construction of that division' (O'Donovan 1985a: 3).

Set up in this way questions of morality, subjectivity, sexuality and gender all become 'not the concern of law'. They are part of the familial and the world of (legally entrenched) male power and authority. From this perspective it is law which supports and reproduces power differentials between men and women, masking the injustice of existing sexual relations through presenting the sexual division of labour (premised on the public/private division) as 'natural' and 'inevitable' in the first place (Rosaldo 1974; Taub and Schneider 1982; Eisenstein 1984; in relation to social contract theory Pateman 1988).

Feminist critiques of the dichotomy have thus explored how the division is itself infused within the ideology of masculinism; with gendered notions of the worlds of work, the market and individualism, of politics, competition and the state. It is these which are associated with men and masculinity whilst the private sphere is depicted as 'the world of women'. What this means is that the domestic, familial and the personal, traditionally the sphere of sexuality, desire and emotion (and that which is, we have seen, central to the definiton of the familial), is then fixed to the feminine, not masculine, polarity (Weeks 1981: 81–96; Polan 1982; Olsen 1983). Thus, the 'absence' of legal regulation of the 'unregulated private' (O'Donovan 1985a: 11) has served to facilitate the exercise of the power of men over women and to mask the fact that this ostensibly 'private' world of the family is actually formed by and through structures which are external to it – for example by welfare policies and the legal structuring of employment practices, marital relations and so forth. Yet it is difficult to see how the 'private' can simultaneously be that which is both unregulated and indirectly regulated by law (see Graycar 1987–8). On this view it is the state, through law, which defines what is to be private whilst at the same time maintaining that 'the private' has itself been preconstituted naturally. From a feminist perspective this is then seen as serving to legitimate the refusal of the state to intervene in the family whilst negating the fact that the liberal conception of 'privacy' has in fact historically meant little more than the right of men to dominate women and children. Any 'failure' on the part of courts to enforce contracts between husband and wife, for example, does not so much arise from a reluctance to intrude into a private relationship; that 'private' relationship was already regulated by the marriage contract (Pateman 1988; Okin 1989).

The argument that the public/private dichotomy has served to mask the power of men has considerable force. However, the underlying conception of a 'male' state which then 'intervenes' in the private family assumes a particular model of the public/private which has recently come under attack. It is far from clear, for example, whether particular laws may be classified as 'intervention' or 'non-intervention' (Olsen 1983; Freeman and Mensch 1987; Fudge 1987). Theoretically, understood in terms of the public/private dichotomy, legal reforms on this view become a matter of 'increasing' or 'decreasing' legal intervention and family privacy. Understanding law to be an expression of state policy, such a conception of state intervention mobilises a conception of power which is implicitly juridical – of power as expressed through the legal form and as a reflection of state policies (Pateman 1983, 1988; Minow 1985b; Olsen 1985; Freeman 1985: 168). Power is thus understood in terms of a zero-sum equation; an increase in the power of the state means a decrease in the power of the family, and vice versa. The state is here understood to be the sole point of reference for judicial, administrative and political functions which had historically hitherto been distributed among other elements of the polity (Kamenka and Tay 1975; O'Donovan 1985a: 4–5). Law, the extent of legal regulation, then serves as the measurement, it becomes the barometer, of the freedoms of the familial sphere whilst – and crucially – the family is itself set up as reflection of the state. And it is, we must remember here, the affective private sphere against which the public domain (the world of men and masculinity) has been defined in the first place.

There are, therefore, two concepts which are central to the understanding of law and the family in terms of the public/private dichotomy. First, an implicit unity is here given to the concept of the state and 'state intervention'. It is the 'state' which 'intervenes' in the family. Second, this theorising involves a specific (juridical) conception of power conceived in zero-sum terms. This construction of state and power requires clarification for it has directly fed into conceptions both of the state/law as reflection of male power (which we have seen in Chapter 1 is politically questionable) and of the idea of masculinity as fixed, immutable and transhistorical (and thus a negation of the idea of masculinity in process and readings of the historical specificity of the emergence of discourses of masculinity). Most importantly, it is this understanding of the state and power which is rendered problematic, and transcended, by the familialist approach. Rethinking the public/private dichotomy thus entails questioning the concept of the state as the 'locus of all political power and of the interests which the law – as expression of state policy – is deemed to serve' (Rose 1987: 66).

Beyond the state

Traditionally the state's regulation of sexuality has been theorised with an implicit acceptance of the public/private dichotomy. For example, and from a historical perspective which does (initially at least) seek to integrate poststructuralist theoretical developments around sexuality and power, the work of Jeffrey Weeks (1981) has presented a wide-ranging overview of many legislative changes in the regulation of sexuality. It is forcefully argued by Weeks that the state has both overtly and covertly controlled sexuality, for example by criminalising homosexuality, legislating on the age of consent and attempting to regulate the circumstances in which prostitution takes place. Connell, in his wide-ranging book *Gender and Power* (1987), has similarly argued that the state intervenes in constructing a sexual division of labour premised on the public/ private division through utilising a range of regulatory mechanisms which have involved law. In the UK, for example, this has been done through developing equal opportunity policies (Equal Pay Act 1970; Employment Protection Act 1975) and passing legislation on sex discrimination (the Sex Discrimination Act 1975). When the law has been concerned to test equality, equal opportunity or difference, concepts which share law's constituent theoretical dualisms have been utilised. The assumption has been that individuals will be tested against the male norm – a normative, but unspoken masculinity. If found equal, the individual will be allowed 'equality'. Such a view of state intervention is also common to both marxist-feminist and neo-marxist accounts of the legal structuring of domestic labour (for example Wilson 1977; McIntosh 1978a: 255; Barrett 1980: 239). It has, to the present day, underscored debates about the politics of the family from positions as diverse as socialist-feminist (Barrett and McIntosh 1982), conservative 'new right' (Mount 1983; Scruton 1986; Morgan 1986), classical and neo-marxist materialist (Engels 1972) and radical psychological perspectives (Laing and Esterson 1964; Cooper 1971; Poster 1978).

Such scholarship considers the state to be central to the sexual political agenda. Yet, notwithstanding the fundamental insights of much of this work into the gendering of familial relations, these accounts have frequently reproduced a positivistic conception of law which has conceived of legal regulation as the source of either 'more' or 'less' freedoms, as defender or attacker of a private sphere in which one might or might not realise one's 'true' gender identity. As with doctrinal black-letter conceptions of law, it is not that gender issues and the politics of masculinity are not being addressed therefore; but implicitly the state is depicted as a coherent entity and the locus of power and decision-making which somehow exists apart from the familial domain.

Drawing on this tradition it is unsurprising that the 'masculinity of law' can then easily be seen as an indicator of the extent of patriarchal relations at any historical moment. The recognition of the state as an institutionalisation of gender has certainly not been a common view within social theory which has, like the humanities generally, ignored the gender-blindness of its originating paradigm. Yet accepting the gendered dimension to the variety of institutions and practices which together constitute 'the state' in liberal legal theory does not itself necessarily involve transcending, or going beyond, the terms of liberal legal discourse and the conception of public/private as distinct spheres. For example, in what has been termed the 'women and law' approach (Brown 1986a), a liberal feminist case for female emancipation has been built up which has been premised on the claim of equal rights (Eisenstein 1984: 15–27). It has been in the liberal terms of equality of opportunity that the long history of feminist reform campaigns around the family have been couched (Brophy and Smart 1981). However, this approach continues to view the state as a neutral arbiter of the claims of interest groups, a state which might, or might not, grant 'equality' through legal reforms. The dawning recognition that there is no *necessary* correlation between formal legal equality and the realities of women's and men's lives has served to render problematic such a liberal feminist perspective in which law is conceived as responsive to social demands and in which it has been the pursuit of formal legal equality which constitutes the goal of reform strategies (Smart 1989a: Ch. 4).

This search for equality through law remains something of a Holy Grail for a liberal legalism which has failed to recognise that there is no direct relation between quantifiable legislation and the perpetuation of relations of power. It is thus one of the problems of remaining within this liberal framework that politics here becomes a matter of seeking institutional forms of change (looking *to* law) rather than a questioning of the epistemological status of the law itself (which may involve re-locating law within a multiplicity of discourses in which gender is constructed). Feminism has, of course, now faced up to this problem that legislation based on 'equality' or 'rights' has also been used by men to claim new or to extend existing rights and privileges (Smart 1989a: 82) and that

> to rely on that paradigm [of individual entitlements] as a framework for true sexual equality is to misread the legacy of liberal legal ideology. Equal rights are, at this historical moment, too restricted in legal content and too divisive in political connotations to serve as an adequate feminist agenda.
>
> (Rhode 1986: 150)

We must remember that men resorting to their 'rights', on behalf of a beleaguered and misunderstood masculinity, has been central to the men's liberation position. Within such a paradigm the state is conceptually separate from 'the family', the domestic and the 'personal' concerns of a private sphere premised on the existence of a 'real' 'true' or (in marxist terms) 'unalienated' self (Collins 1982: 116–18). Of course this notion of a true unalienated self also appears in feminist thought, notably in Catherine Mackinnon's (1982, 1983) depiction of 'consciousness-raising' as a feminist methodology which presumes a true feminine state (from which a male state/law has alienated women; see further Jackson 1993). Both reductionist marxist and some radical feminist accounts of the state/law as embodiment of class/male power thus fail to break free of the terms of the categorical dualisms of liberal discourse which had ostensibly (and ironically) been the object of critique all along.

It is this andocentrism of positivist law, the underlying idea of the legal subject as a 'seamlessly unified self' (Moi 1985: 8), which recent feminist postmodernist work has sought to relate directly to masculinism and the power of men. Moi (1985: 8), for example, has argued that traditional humanism must be seen as part of patriarchal ideology, premised on the abstraction of a 'Man' devoid of all conflict, contradiction and ambiguity. Elsewhere it is argued that the modernist centring of 'man', as knowing actor and author of his own thoughts and actions, heralded a deep-seated positivism which has now become 'associated with some of the most deep-seated intellectual problems of the end of the twentieth-century' through reducing 'cultural and sexual differences to one dominant set of values and knowledge' (Smart 1990a: 75). As Weedon comments, making the connection between masculinity and modernism explicit:

> The decentring of liberal humanism, with its claim to full subjectivity and knowing rationality, in which man is the author of his thoughts and speech, is perhaps even more important in the deconstruction of masculinity than it is for women, who have never been fully included in this discourse.
>
> (Weedon 1987: 173)[4]

To summarise the argument thus far; in liberal legal discourse premised on the public/private dichotomy it has been the state which, through law, determines what is private and what is public. It is the state which is theorised as establishing a legal framework within which policy decisions are implemented. This conception has not been confined to traditional positivist constitutional concepts of juridical state power, but is also replicated in feminist, marxist and other ostensibly radical analyses of the public/private. The problem is epistemological ('it is not a simple problem of party membership' (Smart 1990a: 72)). On this view law is a 'player' in relations between men and women, to be contested for and 'won' by particular groups (such as men/women). It is law which does, or does not, support the interests of a particular group, law which is the neutral arbiter of competing interest claims. Law is thus understood to be a *source* of rights and responsibilities, of either moves to equality or of moves towards further discrimination; it is law which both produces and reproduces patriarchal relations.

It is this conception of law which critical theory of the family has begun to question:

The current controversy about the respective realms of the public and private, and about the limits of state intervention into the family . . . distort and perpetuate a mystifying discourse which sees 'the family' as separate from, and in opposition to, the state.

(Freeman 1985: 170)

The public/private dichotomy is part of the 'mystifying discourse' of liberal legalism. In purporting to both explain and to be itself explained by the productive power of law to constitute the social realms, such a conception of state intervention ascribes an enormous power to the law. Law is said to constitute the dichotomy in the first place, yet the dichotomy is then used to justify, or to critique, where the respective boundaries of legitimate state intervention have been drawn. However, it is not simply a matter of shifting the boundaries – a little more privacy here, a little less there – but more a question of rejecting the boundaries *per se*. The dichotomy has no determinate content in law but functions as an image/metaphor which has then been able to structure judicial arguments to existing values and beliefs (Rose 1987). It is not surprising, therefore, that judges should espouse the language of sex roles for this is in keeping with the liberal legal conception of gender and the dominant episteme of the social structure whence they derive their power.

Understood in this way the concept of the public/private constitutes not so much an analytic tool in deciding the amount of legal intervention but rather, as Rose (1987) argues, a form of political rhetoric central to the making of value choices and constructing subjective commitments within liberal legal discourse. The public/private dichotomy blinds us to the relation between law and power in the constitution of gendered identities and therefore wipes out any notion of masculinity as a social and performative practice (as well as the dialectic of social structure and psyche) before it even appears as such.

FAMILIALISM: RETHINKING LAW, POWER AND THE FAMILY

It is now necessary to outline the theoretical approach to the emergence of discourses of familial masculinity in law which I will develop in the following chapters. Rejecting the public/private dichotomy has major implications for how we understand the law/family relation in terms of analytic concepts (in contrast to the heuristic purposes of the 'family law' textbook writer, for whom these closures may appear self-evident). This is not a matter of replacing one atheoretical conception of family law with a new, ideological, perspective; rather,

> If we are to understand the politics of familialisation, and the transformation of political concerns into personal and familial objectives which it entailed, we need to fragment, disturb and disrupt some of the central explanatory categories of critique.
>
> (Rose 1987: 66)

We need, in particular, to transcend the public/private dichotomy. The law exercises power not just by its material effects but also in its ability to disqualify knowledges and experiences. It is, therefore, necessary to question the relation between law and other strategies of regulation and techniques of power which constitute the family domain. Analyses of the relationship between law and the subjectivities of men and women involves utilisation of a conceptual apparatus which is not part of the theoretical baggage of doctrinal exegesis or 'black letter' law and which also manages to reject positivist 'grand theories' of law and oppression (Smart 1989a: 68) and the metanarratives of modernity (Lyotard 1984; Kellner 1988).

The focus which emerges within what have been termed 'familialist' writings on law and the family is concerned more with the *effects* of rather than the intentions behind law (Dewar 1989a: 6). Such a 'consequentionalist approach' (O'Donovan 1993: 22) locates multiple sites of oppression within the family. It breaks from holistic theoretical explanations of power relations in terms of an overarching theory of oppression, be it of sex-group or social class. If the experiential dimension – the activation of subjective commitments, hopes, aspirations and beliefs – is to be integrated into an analysis of law and the family, then it is necessary to recognise that a range of regulatory apparatuses and discourses make claims to knowledge both about law and familial relations and also that law can exclude certain discourses from its practice.

The familialisation approach has been perhaps most evident in feminist thinking about the family and law (though this is not to argue that the writings one might term 'familialist' are necessarily pro-feminist; note in particular Barrett and McIntosh's critique of Donzelot, 1982: 95–105: cf. Bennett *et al.* 1981). This is not to fall back on ideas of a mythical past or essentialist notions of the family in constructing the modern family as somehow pathological (a position which is, in Donzelot's text, at times allied to an incipient anti-feminism; see also Lasch 1977).

I am here using familialism as a critical term – a method – in theorising law and the family which entails a move away from the language of the public/private and towards the discursive construction of the familial. As such, it must be seen in the context of wider developments within social theory and, in particular, of attempts to make social theories more politically intelligible (Weedon 1987; Featherstone 1988a, 1988b; Kellner 1988). In the rejection of grand theorising, and through rethinking the juridical concept of power, legal theory has turned instead to a focus on superstructure and the *socially* constructed nature of the present, subjectivity and of discourse (Harland 1987; Weedon 1987). Here it is history, rather than the search for any abstracted grand theory or absolute truth, which has been used to deconstruct the present.

In the analytical approach developed by such writers as Foucault (1980, 1981) and Donzelot (1980) the concept of 'genealogy' has been utilised not so much in terms of a methodology but more as a distancing process from a range of conceptual tools (for example the public/private division, state intervention) which are taken to have hitherto constrained study of the family and law (see further Minson 1985). This includes the categoricalism which underlies the identification of opposed, undifferentiated interests which has underscored accounts of law and power as diverse as feminist (Mackinnon 1982, 1983), marxist (Collins 1982: 17–35) and functionalist (on categoricalism in gender theory see further Connell 1987: 54)

In the language of familialisation the historical shift in discourses addressing the family – legal, medical, psychological, psychoanalytic and welfarist – has accompanied a shift from a model of law as a discourse of right (the juridical model) to a model in which law is but part of a process of regulation through a complex of mechanisms of surveillance and normalisation concerned with the constitution of the familial. It is not that law is irrelevant to this new form of regulation; rather, law is now located as part of a complex network of surveillance. Rethinking law in this way challenges not just the epistemological status of doctrinal exegesis. It also involves reassessing the institutions and practices of the law within the wider cultural configuration in which discourses of masculinity are produced. It involves recognising the diversity rather than the homogeneity of regulatory practices (and thus brings in the regulatory aspects of extra- and quasi-legal mechanisms of the 'psy' professsions such as medicine, education and social work). Law, in other words, is too important to be neglected, but is also not important enough to constitute the sole object of analysis. 'Law', understood in its broadest form, becomes a manifestation of power. It is in this sense that feminist legal theory has stretched the 'boundaries of law' (Fineman and Thomadsen 1991).

> Law can and should be the *object* of feminist inquiry, but to position law and law reform as the *objective* of such theorizing is to risk having incompletely developed feminist innovation distorted and appropriated by the historically institutionalized and inextractable dictates of the 'Law'.
>
> (Fineman 1991b: xv)

This 'de-centring' of law has several implications for understanding the relationship between masculinity and law. Law is here just one regulatory system within a network of powers which regulate the family. In some areas law can be seen to be withdrawing, in others a creeping legalisation is taking place (Smart 1989a: 15–20; O'Donovan 1993: 23). The emerging forms of rationalisation concerned with the transformation of the subjectivities of both men and women implicates both domestic, reproductive and conjugal politics (the traditional areas of 'family law') as well as the world of work and 'public' politics. It concerns the emergence and institutionalisation of discourses of both public and private masculinities (Hearn 1992) which are indivisible and must be understood one in terms of the other. Disrupting the unitary nature of the concepts of state and power, 'law' no longer can be said to operate on 'the family'.

A considerable range of laws are of relevance to the family. A selection from a traditional legal textbook account of family law (for example Bromley and Lowe 1987) might list laws relating to marriage, divorce, inheritance, the protection of children, domestic violence and custody. However, all of these have objects and powers which cannot simply be translated into each other because they all constitute 'law' and one 'legal subject' in each and every instance. Family law has been traditionally concerned with ascribing status. In different areas of law, however, 'husband' and 'wife', 'mother' and 'father' might have different meanings in different contexts. Just as there is no one 'family' in law, therefore, we should also expect to find no one 'father' or 'husband' which has the same meaning in every legal context. Similarly we cannot expect to find one masculinity in/of legal discourse. What we *will* find is a valorised, or idealised, masculinity through reference to which other masculinities are ascribed a status.

Within this approach the family constitutes the object of a range of regulatory programmes which go far beyond mere formal legal regulation. It is the very *diversity* of legal regulation which becomes the key to understanding the power of law:

> They [regulatory practices] do not operate according to a single division of 'public' and 'private' – spaces, activities and relations which are within the scope of regulation for one purpose are outside it for another. Unities and coherences must be analysed in terms of outcomes rather than origins or intentions. Rather than conferring a false unity upon the diversity of legal regu-lation, critical analysis should treat this diversity as both a clue to the intelligibility of the law and, perhaps, as the key to a political strategy in relation to law.
>
> (Rose 1987: 67)

It is recognising and integrating within an analysis of familial relations this wide range of factors which marks the familialisation approach evident in Donzelot's (1980) *The Policing of Families*. The influence of this perspective is echoed in Smart's claim that law should not be understood

> as a homogeneous entity but as a collection of practices and discourses which do not all operate together with one purpose. . . . I do not perceive the law as a superstructural reflection of the economic base but recognise that it contains within itself its own constraints and motivation as well as being influenced by poli-tical and ideological factors which are independent of economic development.
>
> (Smart 1984a: 22)

This recognises that institutions have their own internal dynamics, structures of power, gender and labour (including, of course, those institutions of law in which, I have argued in Chapter 1 we must locate the (re)production of discourses of masculinity). These dynamics are themselves bound up in complex and contradictory ways with voluntary initiatives and private actions which may not derive from a formally legal source. The powers which derive from statute (for example those of social workers) are not necessarily given effect and experienced in consistent and monolithic ways. Thus, it is difficult to speak of there being 'one' state policy which is implemented across all these concerns and which is invariant in the form of its regulation. To do so would also de-gender those legal agents delegated with putting laws into effect. The state here becomes part of a dispersed apparatus which works through dominant discourses (like law) and the constitution of consensus as much as it does through force.

In the following chapters I wish to take 'the family', not as the object of a unitary state policy, but as an *interdiscursive nexus* of legal, medical, religious and other discourses, the very diversity and the contingencies of which testify to the existence of hybrid ways in which the familial is constructed. The challenge of this approach to understandings of law and the family in terms of the public/private division does not stop here, however. This de-centring of law involves also rethinking the juridical conception of power and facilitates an integration of the idea of law as a social and accountable discourse.

Rethinking law and power

There exists a rich vein of literature in which power is held not simply to be negative, in the sense of repressive and inhibitory but also positive, concerned with exhortation, incitement and production (Donzelot 1980; Foucault 1981; Garland and Young 1983). Freeman (1985) has integrated this notion that power may be positive in his argument that law does not simply serve to reproduce social order but that

> it actually in part constitutes and defines that order. Family law (and not only family law, for labour law, tax law, social welfare law, immigration law and other laws and regulations are similarly creative of such an ideology) produces and reproduces patriarchal relations. The legal form is one of the main modalities of social practice through which actual relationships embodying gender stratification have been expressed.
>
> (Freeman 1985: 158)

In the influential analysis of power developed by Foucault (1981), power is not simply a negative, repressive entity:

> Underlying both the general theme that power represses sex and the idea that law constitutes desire, one encounters the same putative mechanisms of power . . . it is a power that only has the force of negatives on its side, a power to say no. . . . It is a power whose model is essentially juridical centred on nothing more than the statement of the law and the operation of taboos. All the modes of domination, submission and subjugation are ultimately reduced to an effect of obedience.
>
> (Foucault 1981: 95)

Foucault conceives of power as creating resistances and struggles against its operation which themselves bring about new knowledges and transformations within a power-field (Smart 1989a: 14–20). It is a concept which covers both physical 'force' in domestic relations as well as the dynamics of emotional relations (that which Connell (1987) terms the 'structure of cathexis'). Within this conception power is as much about an ability to mobilise subjectivities and constitute aspirations and beliefs as with prohibitions and negation of human behaviour and the sanctions of formal positivist law (though this is not to underestimate the repressive censure of the law). Power cannot be calibrated in zero-sum terms and the effects of power relations cannot be confined to the effects of law. Power is no longer a single object or a repetitive form. Rather the 'sources of power are multiple – from control over economic, political, cultural, or military resources to charisma, erotic attraction and desire' (Rose 1987: 68–9).

Discourses of masculinity are the result of such a construction of power. It is not that the Foucauldian analysis is denying juridical power, but rather that the success of the new forms of power has been proportional to their ability to hide their own mechanisms. The secrecy of power is thus indispensible to its success (Foucault 1981: 86) just as a blindness to the social construction of masculinity can itself be seen to be part of the power of the masculine norm.

The activation of normative mechanisms in the constitution of masculinity in law is, I shall argue, part of the more general powers of normalisation in a disciplinary society. From this perspective the non-economic concept of power is more in keeping with the mechanisms of regulation in the late twentieth century and with the diversity of regulatory practices which constitute the modern governmental order. This is not to deny that once power and judicial rights were linked; however, a historical transformation has taken place, away from this question of who 'has' power to the mechanisms of power and disciplinary coercion. Thus, it is misleading to claim that men simply 'have' power (a tendency, I have argued in Chapter 1, in much of the 'men against sexism' writings). Similarly, to assume that all men consciously intend to oppress women (and could thus end that oppression if they wished) misreads the use of the term 'oppression' as a 'causal explanation for social phenomena rather than a description of their governing conditions' (Middleton 1992: 147). Through the conflation of men as singular and collective subjects, and assuming that one man represents and is represented by all men, this relates to the theoretical difficulties which follow 'conceptualizing both intrapsychic and interactive relations . . . in terms of emotion, phallogocentrism and discourse' (ibid.).

> Groups are not united, singular subjects. Oppression and power are perfectly valid concepts within a restricted sphere of analysis. They explain the potential of groups to act in certain ways in relation to one another. They give answers to questions about experience by specifying not causes, but limiting conditions.
>
> (ibid.: 152)

These concepts of power, however, 'cannot be used to axiomatize relations between the sexes'. Rather, subjectivities are caught up within the results of oppression and power; the constitution of emotion and affective relations, the activation of commitment to the patriarchal marriage, must begin therefore from the displacement of the modernist fallacy that there is any authentic or fixed self in the first place from which emotion, power or oppression originates.

Addressing the sociality of ideas of men's emotion and familial power is an important part of reconstructing men as the subjects of legal discourse. More generally, the picture of a disciplinary society which emerges in Foucault's work can be seen as part of the processes of familialisation addressed above in which there has occurred no less than a reconstitution of the commitments of women and men to the familial. Law does not fade into the background, institutions of justice do not disappear. Rather, the

> judicial institution is increasingly incorporated into a continuum of apparatuses (medical, administrative and so on) whose

functions are for the most part regulatory. A normalizing society is the historical outcome of a technology of power centred on life.

(Foucault 1981: 144)

This governmentalisation of the state (Foucault 1979) involved a transformation of what could be governed, by whom and in what ways. Far from understanding reform strategies, legislative changes and social transformations as originating from 'the state', therefore, it becomes possible to locate heterogeneous sources of reform which are bound up within different networks of power. This makes it necessary to question the formation of all goverment objectives with regard to the family (Minson 1985: 182). Sexuality, masculinity, femininity and desire – all are implicated in this play of power relations. Unification of techniques and objectives into concepts of 'social control', however, negates the political engagement with desire, aspiration, sexuality and gender (an engagement with the emotional which has been crucial to the politics of masculinity but which has not figured in mainstream accounts of the political). Such a negation of praxis, of the politics of personal life and the sociality of ethical commitments, sexuality and desire must be resisted if analysis of law and the family is to take seriously the politics of masculinity.

To summarise, one effect of characterising law, state and power in this way is that law is no longer considered to be a homogeneous coherent unit which can be reduced to the expression of class – or male – interests. There can never be one overarching theory of the relationship between families and law. Nor can it be stated that the law always, in each and every instance, reproduces a particular family form or represents the interests of men (however much it might seem so given the frequent blatant sexism of law). This has important implications for understanding the construction of men and masculinity in legal discourse. Law and the state can no longer be understood to be unproblematically serving the interests of all men in the same way. The 'uneven development' (Smart 1986) of law is much more open-ended. A distinction can be made between 'legal regulation' and 'male control', between 'structures of power and mechanisms of regulation without attributing these to biological agents who then become the personifications of power and control' (Smart 1984a: 17). The integration of poststructuralist theory into accounts of law and gender brings into the equation how both law and masculinity are constituted in discourse and what connections, if any, might exist between each (Rose 1987: 72; Smart 1989a: 19). As Brown (1986b: 434) has argued:

> It is this model [of the law as male] which is (or should be) on the rubbish pile today, this model which is at issue in the attacks on the idea of a homogeneous content of women at law and in the rejection of the 'equal rights' analysis of legal effects and legal reform.
>
> (Brown 1986b: 434)

This is not to argue that laws do *not* serve men's interests. It is, however, to reject the model of law in which legal regulation is presented as, *a priori*, embodying a simplistic struggle of 'men versus women'. Perhaps ironically such a rejection of the conception of law as an embodiment of male interests serves ultimately to empower both women and men in taking control of their lives, inasmuch as it avoids the characterisation of all men as omnipotent, conscious oppressors of women or all women as ontologically 'superior' somehow to men. This approach, far from writing women out of history, involves a recognition that sexuality, aspirations, motivations and desire are all enmeshed within power relations and social objectives. Amongst the modes of operation of power 'the shaping of wills, desires, aspirations and interests, the formation of subjectivities and collectivities is more typical than the brute domination of one will by another' (Rose 1987: 69).

In Chapters 5 and 6 I shall explore the emergence of 'modern' familial masculinity in law. What is important about familialisation is that it signifies a *historically* specific range of programmes aimed at diverse aspects of familial life, but programmes which nonetheless share in common a concern to reconstruct the citizen, her/his ambitions, desires and subjectivities. It historicises, in short, the construction of the familial and is thus a useful perspective from which to undertake a non-reductionist analysis of law and masculinity. The familialisation of society has involved, I shall argue in the following chapters, no less than the constitution of historical discourses of masculinity which have been reproduced through law.

It is necessary at this point to shift the analysis from the theoretical level to a consideration of the substance and history of these developments. What does this process and theory mean for understanding the history of the family? What does it mean for the changes in relations betwen men and women therein? In particular, how does this compare with accounts couched in terms of the public and the private to explain the power of men – as husbands, lovers, fathers and sons – in familial relations?

Constructing the familial

The idea that the family is a social construct and that law may be one of the main modalities of its constitution has been a central theme of familialist writings on the family. In *The Policing of Families* (1980) Donzelot presents an analysis of the family which attempts to relate the 'Birth of the Family' to the emergence of a newly delineated domain of 'the political'. Contrasting the modern family with the types of social organisation of an earlier epoch, Donzelot's thesis illustrates certain aspects of the familialist approach. Donzelot rejects the 'meticulous restitution of the familial past' of traditional historical sociologies of the family because of 'the excessive leeway it gives pre-existing theoretical machineries' (for example, the dichotomies of liberal legalism). Instead, clarifying the Foucauldian-influenced genealogical approach (see further Minson 1985: 180–224), Donzelot declares

> The method we have employed tries to avoid this danger by positing the family, not as a point of departure, as a manifest reality, but as a moving resultant, an uncertain form whose unintelligibility can only come from studying the system of relations it maintains with the socio-political level. This requires us to detect all the political mediations that exist between the two registers, to identify the lines of transformation that are situated in that space of intersections.
>
> (Donzelot 1980: xxv)

Donzelot is concerned, in part, with addressing the problems of the liberal state via an analysis of the residue of pre-modern and early modern regulation of everyday life. In questioning the social welfare objectives which had previously been operated by moral policing, without ever over-extending the domain of 'state law' to the private domain, Donzelot constructs the problems facing the liberal state in such a way that they cannot be seen to be derived from the development of capitalism alone. Crucially, it is Donzelot's contention that society has become increasingly influenced by an *idea of the family*. It is the construction of this ideal in the processes of power which has been termed the 'familialisation' of society.

Without denying economic imperatives the focus shifts to the ways in which the problems of the family are constructed in discourse (Donzelot 1980: 199) and how, by the mid-twentieth century, from being 'the plexus of a complex web of relations of dependence and allegiance, the family became the nexus of nerve-endings of machinery that was exterior to it' (Donzelot 1980: 91).

Traditionally the liberal demands on the state have been expressed through the discourse of rights. The problem faced by the liberal state, Donzelot argues, has principally been one of administering a national population and providing welfare. The liberal conception of the state and law discussed above involved a plurality of overlapping and contradictory notions of the public and private domains (we have seen that there is no consistency as to when a 'private' area of family life will be rendered 'public'). It is not so much that the family has been the cause of the problems faced by the liberal state, however. Rather it is the modern family which has become 'a positive form of solution to the problems posed by a liberal definition of the state' (Donzelot 1980: 53).

The status of the family as a 'private' area is reconstituted in this analysis as a hybrid of attempts to differentiate between the private and public spheres within liberal legal discourse. It is the family which has become the 'positive solution' to the problems of regulating sexuality, morality and health in the process of reconstituting the subjectivities (and sexualities) of the modern order. For example, just what the problems of 'welfare' were to be arose from what was, and was not, defined as the limits of legally legitimate state action. How far could the liberal state go? Having defined an area outside the concern of the law as 'private' it is then the family which, on Donzelot's analysis, becomes the object of projects of social intervention concerned with surveillance, regulation and constitution; that is, the family as the legal institution through reference to which the performative possibilities of gender configurations are then constructed.

To recap; this account rejects the dichotomies of liberal legal discourse (for example the political/governmental, social/economic and the related public/private dichotomy). Crucially, it implicates in the construction of the family the establishment of a normative masculinity (as one privileged masculinity amongst a range of masculinities), a norm of sexual discipline and affectionate ties. The historical constitution of subjectivity has ultimately involved no less than the social construction of a binary division between masculinity and femininity. The family is not here under-stood to be a unitary, private institution but rather as the 'moving resultant' of a range of discretionary private spaces which have been constructed differentially for the different members of the family – for men, women and children – through reference to historically specific ideas of (among other things) masculinity.

It is the formation of subjective commitments to family life which Donzelot's thesis writes into the analysis and which renders it particularly relevant for a study of masculinity, law and the family. As we have seen, relocating law within the promotion of a range of bio-political objectives which may or may not be fulfilled involves other regulatory strategies than simply formal law. The constructed 'social' itself becomes suffused with regulation and power (Foucault 1981). Yet it is not necessary for formal law to be extended to every area of life

> For 'the social' is not society understood as a set of material and moral conditions that characterise a form of consolidation. It would appear to be rather the set of means which allow social life to escape material pressures and politico-moral uncertain-ties; the entire range of methods which make the members of a society relatively safe from the effects of economic fluctuations by providing a certain security – which give their existence possibilities of relations that are flexible enough, and internal stakes that are convincing enough, to avert the dislocation that divergencies of interests and beliefs would entail.
>
> (Donzelot 1980: xxvi)

To remain within the liberal legal conception of state and law leads to a position whereby power is seen to flow from the state *to* the family. In contrast Donzelot argues that just as families are influ-enced by economic and social forces society is also affected by families. It is this, in part, which explains why the definition of the family is itself flexible. The picture which emerges is one in which the 'family domain' is not so much the site of a universally stable core of family members (such as mother and child, father and son, premised on such legally ascribed 'roles' as breadwinner and homemaker – the classic functionalist position). Rather the family is a *working hypothesis* – a subject constructed in process (just like gender and social structure). Thus it might, at different historical moments, accommodate different subject positions in its embrace.

Donzelot's thesis is not without problems.[5] His argument that there has occurred with the emergence of the 'patriarchy of the state' a rebalancing of men's and women's interests will be examined further and rejected in Chapter 6. It is not here argued that familialist texts are not without difficulties or that a genealogical approach to the study of law and gender is the only viable methodology. Nonetheless, the debates generated by Donzelot's study are far reaching and have important implications for approaching the study of masculinity, law and the family. We have now one part of our starting point: that the familial is a social construct. It is now necessary to look to the concept of law as a social discourse in order to facilitate an analysis of how the historical changes outlined above might be related to changes in the law and the legal regulation of masculinities – and how we might read these changes through an analysis of legal texts.

Law as a social discourse

How does all this relate to the legal text therefore? To cases and statutes, the 'very stuff' of law and legal education? I have referred above to a feminist poststructuralist perspective (for example, see the synthesis and critique of Weedon 1987) which, far from constructing 'grand theories' of the nature of women's oppression, has instead focused on the notion of 'truth' and the hierarchies of discourse in which truth-claims are formulated. This emerging paradigm within legal studies (on methodology see Young 1990: 154–73) has profound implications for theorising the family, law and masculinity in facilitating a breaking out of the confines of a positivist conception of law in which 'feminists can only challenge [law] and maintain credibility within law by positing an equally positivist alternative' (Smart 1989a: 71).

It is here that the idea of law as a *social discourse* is of significance. Within the poststructuralist and postmodernist influenced strand of legal studies it has been the very possibility of making any claims to knowledge about the law which has been rendered problematic (Goodrich 1986; Douzinas and Warrington 1987; Douzinas *et. al.* 1990):

> the study of law as social discourse conceives law to be pre-eminently a practical category, a mode of social being and belonging which largely lacks justification. To view law as primarily an ontological, practical, category, is to refer philosophy of law

to the study of law in terms of social ontology, that is to its existence as social practice – to the influence it actually exerts, to the functions it performs and to the meaning and effects it realises . . . the need [is] to read law dialectically, in terms of the functions it performs within a complex political and social totality.

(Goodrich 1987: 211–12)

As a 'practical category', 'a mode of social being', this relates well to the focus on practice and the performative aspects of gender I have highlighted above – the practices whereby gender is reproduced through interactive and intrapsychic processes. Within contemporary legal theory the concept of law as a social discourse has been derived from a methodology of deconstruction (see further Derrida 1975, 1976, 1978; Norris 1982; Goodrich 1987) and the development of legal semiotics (Jackson 1985). This has highlighted the rhetorical status of law (Goodrich 1986, 1984), the political character of legal discourse and the relation of nihilism (or the refusal to believe in absolute values) to the exegetical exposition of law as a system of rules (Goodrich 1986: 211). More generally, this rejection of absolute truth relates to the collapse of the originating paradigm for disciplines such as criminology (and more generally sociology) which have sought to propound a unifying 'cause' of a range of human behaviour.

In the context of law, what proponents of deconstruction have argued is that the correct meaning of a legal text has no existence prior to its formulation in legal discourse; that is, that the formation of 'correct legal meaning' is a process involving choice and that this is a process which can be deconstructed and analysed. The purportedly 'coherent' legal text may thus, in one variant, be 'trashed' (Kelman 1984) in order to reveal the contingencies of its meaning and construction.

This is not to argue that previous cases are unimportant, however (such textual analyses involve, after all, taking doctrine seriously). It is instead to argue that the essence of the doctrinal legal reasoning seen in Chapter 1 is a *socially constructed argument*; an argument which is, within the terms of legal method, supported by appeals to authority, hierarchy, precedent and the social system from whence this legal/institutional order derives. The essence of textual deconstruction therefore is that there is no essence to the text. The concept of truth is, in effect, displaced by that of discursive *effect* (Debray 1984) as questions of ontology are privileged over epistemology.

This has a twofold implication for the analysis of family, law and masculinity. First, it opens out the textual construction of the legal case to analysis. Such an analysis of cases and statutes constitutes the primary object of this book. Second, it brings the legal decision into the realm of the political through exposing the contingency of what is purported to be judicial neutrality/genderlessness. It thus becomes possible to see how meanings of masculinity have been organised historically into sets of permissible or impermissible readings (Murphy and Rawlings 1982; Mossman 1986); it becomes possible to question how law 'exercises power not simply in its material effects (judgements) but also in its ability to disqualify other knowledges and experiences' (Smart 1989a: 11). In particular, it becomes possible to see how a form of (hetero)-masculinity has disqualified other masculinities.

It is this idea of law as a social discourse which provides a way of exploring the relations of affinity, or intertextuality, between legal discourse and other forms of discourse – political, moral, scientific and sexual. It provides a way round the separateness and autonomy of law and the seemingly pervasive power of positivism, a way of beginning to unpack the relation between law, power and masculinity. It is for this reason that the following chapters are concerned with unpacking the meanings of masculinity in legal texts and with exploring how these social constructions of masculinity relate to power and the construction of the familial.

> Ultimately, then, whether we explore the techniques of persuasion employed in these texts, analyse the conditions of existence and consequences of textual production, or examine the structure of the discourses contained in the text, we are led to questions of power and of how power circulates within a society.
>
> (Murphy and Rawlings 1982: 61)

Masculinity is, I have stressed, about power. This approach, however, opens up the legal text to alternative resistant readings which might themselves constitute claims to power of oppositional discourses such as feminism and any anti-patriarchal praxis on the part of men. Law is not an object waiting to be studied; rather, certain 'beliefs and questions about authority create our understanding of "law"' (Grbich 1991: 61). Deconstructing the subject within legal discourse opens to question the 'positionality of knowers about law, the negotiation of meaning about authority and the professional academic practices which exclude women's experiences from the development of legal theory' (Grbich 1991: 61). It also opens out the contingency and plurality of masculinities discussed in Chapter 1, historicising the law and recognising

> the peculiar and distinctive character of law as a specific, sociolinguistically defined, speech community and usage . . . [to] treat legal discourse or the legal genre as an accessible and answerable discourse, as a discourse that is inevitably responsible for its place and role within the ethical, political and sexual commitments of its times.
>
> (Goodrich 1987: 2)

This is not to negate the importance of the practices of the law. It is to question those legal texts which address the ethical and sexual basis of the social/legal order and to begin to unpack the gendered dimension of those subjectivities which have been constructed in and through the languages of law.

CONCLUSIONS: ON METHOD, MASCULINITY AND LAW

The presentation of the relationship between the family, law and masculinity in this chapter has opened out to analysis the place of law in seeking an answer to Foucault's now familiar question: 'why has sexuality been so widely discussed and what has been said about it?' (Foucault 1981: 11). In valorising human subjectivity and in privileging ontology over epistemology legal studies have began to reject the 'grand theorising' of metanarratives and absolute truths and to reject the androcentric and abstracted conceptions of law which have bedevilled analysis of gender and power.

Instead, recent studies of law and the family have sought to celebrate the diversity of legal regulation, to de-centre law within a wider network of power and to focus instead on local instances of power and resistance. This has involved the utilisation of a range of approaches and disciplines which have sought to transcend the limitations of black-letter law (for example, the 'synergistic reading' of Alison Young in her book *Femininity in Dissent* (1990)). This has, through the methodology of deconstruction, rendered the relation between the legal text, language and power problematic (Goodrich 1986, 1987; Weedon 1987; Douzinas *et al.* 1990).

The familial domain has, in short, been opened out to critical analysis. Rejecting the liberal conception of state intervention and the zero-sum calibration of power which underlies the public/ private dichotomy, it becomes possible to unpack the liberal-legal ideology which has fixed the sexual, familial and affective relation to a private unregulated/feminine sphere and the asexual, public and regulated/masculine world of work to the public domain. It is the *invisibility* of masculinity, the masculinism of the divide, which is itself here revealed as a social construct, a result of the play of power and resistance. Subjectivity and the sociality of the man/ woman division is itself put on the agenda:

> Domestic, conjugal and parental conduct is increasingly regu-
> lated not by obedience compelled by threat of sanction but
> through the activation of individual guilt, personal anxiety and
> private disappointment. Husbands and wives, mothers and
> fathers themselves regulate their feelings, desires, wishes and
> emotions and think themselves through the potent images of
> parenthood, sexual pleasure and quality of life.
>
> (Rose 1987: 73)

It is with representations of masculinity in law that I shall be concerned in the remainder of this book – the legal construction and socially contingent nature of those representations of masculinity in law which may realise, or deny, the capacities of the body (Weedon 1987: 74–107). The representations of masculinity to be found in law have an effect not merely at the level of pure ideas but also in promulgating languages of gender which are both historically and culturally specific and which are addressed to the social body, to life, health and to the question of how 'power spoke of sexuality and to sexuality: [sexuality] was not a mark or a symbol, it was an object and a target' (Foucault 1981: 147). These are, in particular, readings which challenge the material, social, personal and generational privileges of the institution of marriage.

Representations of masculinity in law, far from being preconstituted, unmediated artefacts, constitute a nexus of the physical and cognitive realms, of knowledge and experience of self and society and of ideas in which individual subjectivity has been articulated and constituted. Sexualities are thus not pre-given but are constituted through a sexual binary system in which:

> each individual has to pass in order to have access to his [sic]

own intelligibility (seeing that it is both the hidden aspect and the generative principle of meaning), to the whole of the body (since it is a real and threatened part of it, while symbolically constituting the whole), to his identity (since it joins the force of a drive to the singularity of a history).

(Foucault 1981: 155–6)

The family itself becomes a site for the exercise of power. It is not that power relations operate on the family so much as that power suffuses the family. The family cannot be separated from the environment in which it exists, which is within a network of relations of power. As such:

feminist critiques and proposals will be of limited value unless they can provide a positive analysis of the new types of power and authority which have come into existence over the last century and the ways in which they operate.

(Rose 1987: 74)

In the opening out of the complex of social powers to analysis it becomes possible to ask a quite specific question of the law: *What does it mean to be a man in legal discourse?* To understand this we need to question the assumptions which underlie legal constructions of men in familial relations.

In the following chapters I shall proceed to examine the claims to knowledge which legal discourse makes about masculinity and the family. These are claims about family life, child care and sexual pleasure, about health, happiness and fatherhood. The sexed male body is, we shall see, both an object and target of legal discourse, of a regime of examination and surveillance through which normal/perverse, natural/deviant sexualities and gender have been constructed.

In Chapters 3 and 4 I shall deconstruct male heterosexuality in law and tackle these constructions as they relate to the 'family man' in law. The discursive effect of the idea of the 'family man' will be considered further in Chapters 5 and 6. I shall build on the analysis of Chapters 1 and 2 to focus on the meanings, values, and forms of pleasure which have been central to the construction of masculinity in law. Men, constituted in discourse as masculine subjects, have had their interests represented by discourses such as law in which a particular construction of masculinity exists as part of a masculine vantage point or world view. Masculinity and femininity are themselves resultants of the play of power relations, of a cultural aquisition of subjective commitments to the existing order which is itself a social and accountable process (Burniston *et al.* 1978).

It is in this way that moving away from law, de-centring law, can be empowering through taking us to a position where we are no longer simply concerned with questions of whether the law does or does not embody a formal equality (whatever that may be) between men and women. It now becomes a question of the relation between law and how we actually *experience* ourselves as men and women, male and female. Valorisation of the social nexus within which the forms of regulation attain validity fractures law's unity. Law is, like all human relations, just part of structures of power informed by divisions and relations of gender, race and class. Relocating law within this network of regulatory mechanisms, however, one faces a paradox in that in many respects analysis of law may be the wrong place to start to understand regulatory strategies within the network of familial powers. Recounting the 'rules of law' in a given area of the sub-discipline family law, I have argued, does not simply mislead as to the practice and politics of law; it also obfuscates the place of law within this complex of regulatory practices.

To understand law's power involves looking elsewhere. I have argued in this chapter that it is in producing readings of legal texts, in the processes of interpretation, that the legal community has historically been engaged in temporarily fixing meanings and privileging particular social interests. It is now time to deconstruct what those meanings and interests are and what, in the end, they have to say about the masculinity of law.

Chapter 3

Law, sex and masculinity

INTRODUCTION

> Many years, it seems, must pass before the general public and its
> lawgivers will base their actions on the fact that men are animals
> and that sexual misdemeanours may be caused by the excessive
> production of a hormone or by a deficient education. . . . We do
> not apply our biological knowledge to the treatment of nympho-
> mania in girls, nor to the homosexual or homicidal tendencies
> which sometimes occur in men. In this field of humanism we have
> advanced only a very small way from the time when a woman with
> a beard . . . was regarded and treated as a witch; or a patient with a
> disease of the brain was put in chains and punished.
>
> (Burrows 1949: 169, quoted in Bartholomew 1960: 83)

These comments on 'the fact that men are animals' conclude
Bartholomew's (1960) discussion of *Hermaphrodites and the Law*.
The problem with law and lawyers, he has argued, is the failure of
each to 'take some account of the facts known to every medical
student' (Bartholomew 1960: 112). Yet ascertaining just what these
biological 'facts' are has proved far from clear with regard to
homosexuality and transsexualism. I shall argue in this chapter
that the interrelation between legal and medical discourses, and
the positivist claims of each to scientific status in establishing these
facts in the first place, has proved to be an important moment in
the construction of a naturalist heterosexual masculinity in law.
This chapter is concerned with transsexualism and homosexuality
because each involves sexualities which deviate from the dominant
paradigm of the feminine and the masculine.

The facts about heterosexuality have been taken for granted;
heterosexuality itself has been largely untheorised. In Chapters 4,

5 and 6 I shall proceed to explore the construction of male hetero-sexuality in law via an investigation of ideas of sexuality, paternity and fatherhood in legal discourse. First, however, it is necessary to explore the heterosexual nature of both marriage and masculinity for, as Barrett and McIntosh have argued 'the present ideology of the family is so steeped in heterosexism that any realistic engage-ment with familialism must locate the discussion within that frame-work' (Barrett and McIntosh 1982: 9).

The law's treatment of homosexuality is a useful starting point with which to begin to analyse historical shifts and variations in the ways in which legal discourse has constructed masculinity. In part this is because there is a massive literature on homosexuality as compared with the sociality of heterosexuality. The 'unexamined heterocentricity' (Rich 1980) of the humanities has tended to construct lesbianism and male homosexuality 'as "alternative life-styles" at best, "pathological perversions" at worst' (Wilkinson and Kitzinger 1993: 1). Yet these histories of homosexuality in law have also involved constructions of male heterosexuality. Changes in notions of male homosexuality have a significance therefore not just at the level of understandings of what is frequently taken to be 'deviant' or 'stigmatised' (O'Donovan 1993: 79) identities amongst a particular grouping of men; they have also involved significant changes in ideas of masculinity and sexuality *per se.* Within the structuring of legal discourse around the series of binary oppositions discussed in Chapter 2, the homosexual/ heterosexual dichotomy has been constructed in law through reference to other oppositions such as vice/virtue, cleanliness/ disease, natural/unnatural and public/private. These binaries have pervaded the theorising of desire and sexuality and have been fundamental to the institutionalisation of a heterosexual matrix,

> that grid of cultural intelligibility through which bodies, genders, and desires are naturalized . . . a hegemonic discursive/epistemic model of gender intelligibility that assumes that for bodies to cohere and make sense there must be a stable sex expressed through a stable gender (masculine expresses male, feminine expresses female) that is opposi-tionally and hierarchically defined through the compulsory practice of heterosexuality.
>
> (Butler 1990: 151)[1]

It is through the mode of legal regulation that processes of natural-isation, as motivated collective practices, have been institu-tionalised so as to override biological facts. The frequency of judicial appeals to 'nature' in legal cases – either to deny the social legitimacy of homosexuality or else to privilege a form of hetero-sexual relations – has occurred by way of assertion rather than explanation (heterosexuality is, after all, not in need of explana-tion). These techniques of naturalisation have served to exclude that which does not fit within the implicit narrative of familial ideology and the heterosexual matrix. Thus, we shall see in this chapter how homosexuality and transsexualism transgress this heterosexual familial norm and how each reveal aspects of the ways in which the discursive techniques of the heterosexual imperative have constructed male sexuality in marriage through essentialist terms.

It is for this reason that I shall look at the legal regulation of homosexuality and transsexualism in this chapter. The ways in which the law has established a definition of 'sex' has been central to the regulation of each. If the law is part of the assigning of a social definition with regard to homosexuality then the question needs to be reversed: what do these laws also tell us about male heterosexuality in law? Or, as the editors of the feminism and psychology reader *Heterosexuality* asked their potential contributors

> What is heterosexuality? and why is it so common? Why is it so hard for heterosexuals to change their "sexual orientation"? What is the nature of heterosexual sex? How does heterosexual activity affect the whole of a woman's life, her sense of herself, her relationships with other women, and her political engagements?
>
> (Wilkinson and Kitzinger 1993: 1)

The questions asked about women apply also to men; how does heterosexual activity affect the whole of a man's life? Indeed, in a sense masculinity and heterosexuality appear to have a similar discursive status: each is now that which is 'unexamined', 'given', 'invisible', 'pervasive' or 'largely untheorized'. The points that gay and lesbian writers have made about the pervasive heterocentricity of the humanities curiously echo feminist critiques of masculinity – both heterosexuality and masculinity have become that which is seemingly universal and taken for granted and that which is most in need of challenging (Hunter 1993: 157).[2]

THE LEGAL CONSTRUCTION OF HOMOSEXUALITY

It would be a major weakness of any work which set out to address the relation between law and masculinity if it were to fail to include an analysis of (what are usually taken to be) minority forms of sexuality. There are, of course, other forms of sexuality than simply heterosexuality and homosexuality. There exist a range of non-heterosexual and non-reproductive forms of sexual behaviour which any social analysis of masculinity and law must take account of. It is not simply that for centuries sex outside of marriage has been subject to moral and legal regulation (be that regulation canonical or secular) and that such an omission would 'miss out' an important part of the legal regulation of sexuality. It is at the level of the theorising of masculinity *per se* that this heterosexual/homosexual relationship must be rendered problematic.

The study of homosexuality can be seen as essential both in its own right and because of the light it sheds on the regulation of sexuality – on 'the development of sexual categorisation, and the range of possible sexual identities' (Weeks 1981: 96). The first thing which one notes about the legal history of homosexuality, however, is the remarkable hostility the law has shown to the 'pretended family relationships' of the homosexual (Weeks 1991. s. 28 of the Local Government Act 1988 is but one of the most recent examples of this attitude; see further Jeffrey-Poulter 1991). This hostility, and what it says about the heterosexuality of legal discourse, must be accounted for.

What is 'homosexuality' or a 'homosexual masculinity'? If 'masculinity' signifies a priori only heterosexuality then the homosexual man could not be considered a 'man' or 'masculine' at all. Sexual *identities* and *behaviour*, be they heterosexual or homosexual, are not necessarily congruent. For example, a man might feel himself to be heterosexual in identity yet he might then engage in activities which others might consider to be homosexual in orientation and vice versa. Perhaps an obvious example here would be the gender order of public schools for boys (as attended by considerable numbers of the judiciary), where apparently widespread early homosexual experiences appear compatible with 'stable' heterosexual identities in later life.

One thing is clear; homosexual behaviour is both trans-historical and transcultural. It has existed in different cultures and throughout history (Aries 1985). What has varied considerably, however, has been the legal and social responses to homosexuality (Davenport-Hines 1990; Jeffrey-Poulter 1991). Given this historical variation in the subjective meanings of homosexuality it can no longer be possible (if it ever was) to theorise homosexuality in *universal* terms (Weeks 1977). Analyses of law and homosexuality must take place against this historical context and be sensitive to the variation within legal responses and to the different constructions of homosexuality (and heterosexuality) in different social, cultural, religious and economic contexts.

Recent writings on gender and power, notwithstanding the occasional 'conclusive proofs' of neurobiologists, geneticists and cognitive psychologists for a particular cause of homosexuality,[3] have argued forcefully that homosexuality should not be understood as a form of deviance inhering biologically in the individual (McIntosh 1968). It is, rather, a discursive construction, a term in process, a becoming or a 'repeated stylization of the body, a set of repeated acts within a highly regulatory frame that congeal over time to produce the appearance of substance' (Butler 1990: 123). What is taken to be 'normal' or 'abnormal' is, in short, a social construct.

Contemporary sexual debates have increasingly focused not on gender as a product of irresistible biological force but instead on the processes through which certain genders are ascribed deviant status as socially and historically constituted products of a combination of factors which have together channelled sexual possibilities into one particular sexual orientation or identity (Connell 1987). Heterosexuality and homosexuality are seen as social constructions and not as pre-given, atheoretical categories and sexual identity is itself related to social definition and the wider cultural nexus within which gender norms are established. Fragmenting the idea of a singular, knowable self (see p. 66) reveals notions of 'identity' as a convergence of multiple sexual discourses, part of an 'appropriation and redeployment of the categories of identity themselves' (Butler 1990: 128). Rather than seeing heterosexuality and homosexual identities as fixed and immutable categories of gender, therefore, this approach recognises the significance of *social* responses to sexual behaviour in the formation of gendered identities – and these social responses implicate, at the outset, the law.

On one level the law can be understood to serve as a barometer of social reactions to homosexuality. 'Repressive' or 'liberal' laws may be taken to be indicators of the degree to which homosexuality is tolerated in a certain society at a particular time.

However, as I have argued in Chapter 2, the law has a significance other than simply as the indicator or fewer or greater sexual freedoms which are somehow granted by the liberal state. Law has been important in its capacity as a significant social source of stigmatisation of non-heterosexual behaviour.

What status has the law accorded homosexuality? The criminal law is concerned with homosexual relations in a number of different ways. The object of legal intervention has not tended to be homosexual desire as such so much as the carrying out of a specific range of homosexual acts. However, if the law has not been concerned to prosecute those men who are simply attracted to their own sex, then this is not to say that the law can be seen to approve of homosexuality or to condone homosexual activity. The law is not concerned, at least formally, with individuals who believe themselves to be homosexual. It is concerned with the denial of the legitimacy of homosexual relations as viable alternatives to the heterosexual norm (Weeks 1991).

A variety of political, social, economic, legal and religious considerations have historically informed the negation of the legitimacy of homosexuality. We know that social and historical variations in the regulation of homosexuality are well established in histories of homosexuality, frequent reference being made to ancient Greece and Rome where pedagogic homosexual relations were accepted as part of societal sexual mores (Dover 1978; Veyne 1985). Yet the avowedly Christian-Judaic taboos against homosexuality which have influenced the moral regulation of homosexuality in the UK have not been reflected in any consistent level of legal sanction (on conflicts in religious approaches see Schwarz and Sharratt 1990; Beaumont 1990). Rather; the western tradition has witnessed, and continues to witness, considerable variation in the criminal law's treatment of homosexuality (Weeks 1977; Boswell 1980). More generally, different countries continue to vary considerably in setting an age of consent for homosexual acts. Notwithstanding the recent parliamentary vote to reduce the age of consent for homosexuals from 21 to 18, Britain continues to embody substantive inequality in its laws. Even though other European countries have now seen fit to equalise the age of consent at which heterosexual and homsexual sex can take place, in Britain the distinction remains (see further Michael 1988).

Until the Criminal Law Amendment Act 1885 the law concerning homosexual behaviour had been constructed in terms of the offence of sodomy, a definition of which may be found in Chief Justice Coke's 'Institutions of the Laws of England' as

> A detestable and abominable sin, amongst Christians not to be named, committed by carnal knowledge against the ordinance of the creator, and order of nature, by mankind with mankind, or with brute beast or by womankind with brute beast.
>
> (Quoted in Caplan 1981: 149)

Significantly, this definition omits references to carnal knowledge of 'womankind with women' and does not actually name the sin to which it is referring. One effect of such a silence has been to cultivate an official and popular ignorance as to just what the sinful sexual acts are in the first place. According to Caplan (1981: 149) one result of this was that 'sodomy' became a generic term, a 'catch-all' for a catalogue of nameless vices. This sodomitical tradition continues today in the form of 'the love that dares not speak its name' and, along with all the definitional vagaries with which it is beset, this remains the basis of the law on homosexuality. The definition was taken up in secular statute during the Reformation in 1533 in the Act of Henry VIII which, codifying the law, brought buggery within the ambit of statute law. Homosexuality was, at this time, considered to be more a potential expression of human lust than any signifier of the 'essence' of the man, however. That is, homosexuality was a form of non-procreative sex which fell among a range of other sexual practices which the law rendered criminal. The idea of sodomy as just one of a range of non-reproductive sexual practices is clarified by a comparison with the more specific offence of 'buggery' in law.

Sodomy in law involves intercourse when a man's penis enters the anus of another man or woman. It is not sex specific in this sense. Buggery, in contrast, seems to be a wider offence covering both sodomy and intercourse with an animal (R v Cozins [1834] 6 C & P 351). Until 1861 buggery (sodomy or bestiality) remained punishable by execution (though it is not clear to what extent the laws were enforced; Weeks 1981: 100). Various attempts had been made to repeal the death penalty (for example, in 1826 and 1841) and, though it was not applied in practice after the 1830s, it was not to be until the Offences Against the Person Act 1861 that the death penalty was eventually replaced with sentences of between ten years and life imprisonment.

Before the statutory codification, therefore, the law was directed 'against a series of sexual acts, not a particular type of person, although in practice most people prosecuted under the buggery laws were probably prosecuted for homosexual behaviour (sodomy)' (Weeks 1981: 99). Part of the significance of the 1885 Criminal Law Amendment Act, very much the product of the social, economic and political climate of the mid- to late nineteenth century, lies in how it shifted the definition of the homosexual offence in law. The Labouchère Amendment to the Act brought all forms of homosexual activity within the criminal law and, at a stroke, the Act widened the range of offences covered by statute by bringing into the gaze of the law the new (though uncertain) category of 'gross indecency'. The law thus, in effect, made male masturbation as an intersubjective act a matter for the criminal law. Subsequent legislation, notably the Sexual Offences Act 1967, did not abolish the offences of the 1885 Act as such; they merely excluded consenting adult males in private from the operation of this law. The 1967 Act put the onus on the Crown of proving that an act was either not done in private, was without consent or that either party was under 21 years of age. It would be misleading to state that it 'legalised' homosexuality, however.

In law, any act which involves contact with the genitals of another man (unless justified by some good reason, for example, a medical examination) constitutes an act of 'gross indecency'. What this means is that masturbation in the presence of another man, even without contact taking place, might count as gross indecency (R. v Hunt [1950] 2 All ER 291). A succession of cases have subsequently sought to define gross indecency (with little success; Power 1993). Yet these discussions remain bound up within the parameters of a moralistic condemnation of homosexuality. Section one of the Sexual Offences Act 1967 states that homosexual acts between men are not to be criminal if they take place between consenting adults over 21 years of age and in private. This does not signify that homosexuality is legally legitimate. Whilst in 1967 (the year of the Sexual Offences Act) the age of majority was 21, section one of the Family Law Reform Act 1969 subsequently reduced the age of majority to 18. Although the law is now to be changed so as to reduce the homosexual age of consent to 18, a differential age of consent is to continue. Equality before the law, it would seem, is as elusive as ever. In a sense, therefore, homosexuality is similar to prostitution – not a crime, but clearly undesirable and contrary to public morality (Knuller v DPP [1973] AC 435: Shaw v DPP [1962] AC 220).

What is the law saying about the male body here? It is explicitly concerned with sex, desire and male genital interaction. The parameters of this concern are marked by a discourse premised on the naturalness of heterosexuality; the very moralistic language of the law is archaic and, in a sense, pre-sexual. It will be 'gross' and 'indecent' for two men to kiss in public or to act with clear sexual overtones (R v Preece [1977] 1 QB 770; R v Hornby & People [1946] 2 All ER 487; R v Hunt 2 All ER 291; R v Hall [1964] 1 QB 273). This is clearly not the case for heterosexuality where 'public' displays of sexuality (though within certain limits) are accepted if not encouraged (Helen (charles) 1993). Even a 'preliminary homosexual act' has constituted an offence in law, though what this might be is not clear (a glance, a stare, a touch or kiss?). Procuring homosexual acts (R v Miskell [1954] 1 All ER 137) and soliciting or importuning in a public place for 'immoral purposes' are each subject to legal sanction (s. 32 of the Sexual Offences Act 1956; see further Cohen 1982; Power 1993; R v Gray [1981] 74 CAR 324; R v Kirkup [1981] *The Guardian* 10 November: R v Plimmer [1975] 61 CAR 264; R v Ford, Redgrave [1981] 74 CAR 10). It appears to be the *visibility* of homosexuality which is the object of legal intervention (a concern which informed the background to s. 28 Local Government Act 1988; see Durham 1991: 123).

Police officers have sought to entrap gay men with a variety of techniques and '"soliciting" and 'importuning' . . . can be used by prosecutors to describe anything commonly understood as chatting up or making a pass – literally any physical gesture or words, depending on context' (Crane 1982: 115, quoted by Power 1993: 47). Ultimately these public displays of homosexual attraction involve a threat to no less than public order itself. In 1989, with an estimated 5,000 gay men convicted for consenting homosexual relations, laws as diverse as the 1986 Public Order Act and the Justices of the Peace Act 1361 had all been used to push the number of convictions of consenting male adults in England and Wales to the highest level since the mid-1950s.

We need to try to make sense of these laws, to understand how they have been and continue to be justified and what they say, not simply about homosexuality, but also about heterosexuality and the family in law. The criminal laws referred to above cannot be the sole focus for such an analysis, however. 'Homosexuality', if taken as a discrete object of legal analysis in much the same way as one might undertake study of the 'law' and the 'family', is a subject which traverses many areas of traditional legal scholarship. More often than not criminal law textbooks have covered homosexuality under the sexual offences rubric (I will not repeat the well-rehearsed arguments against heuristic doctrinalism on this point). However, family law and the civil law generally (for example in relation to redress for sexual discrimination, protection of 'fundamental rights' such as those guaranteed by Articles 8 and 12 of the European Convention[4]) also involve a politics of homosexuality (Michael 1988). Even within the confines of a doctrinal exegetical study of law, homosexuality is a relevant (if much neglected) area of study. For example, a book such as Tony Honoré's *Sex Law* (1978) is shot through with assumptions about the nature of homosexuality which involve (unstated) conceptions of the 'normality' of heterosexuality. In a book which seeks to discuss homosexuality an author can also say much about the nature of the norm – heterosexuality.

The example of Honoré's *Sex Law*

Tony Honoré's book *Sex Law* (1978) is one of the few doctrinal texts which seek to address the range of laws concerned with 'sex'. As such it is illuminating to look at some of Honoré's arguments in more detail for here is a book (by a respected legal academic) which *has* sought to explore the specific relationship between law and sex (and not just consider it as part of a larger study of some other issue). *Sex Law* also typifies aspects of the doctrinal construction of the heterosexual/homosexual dualism. Homosexuality, Honoré tells us, is unnatural:

> homosexual acts, and any form of sex other than normal intercourse between a man and a woman, are unnatural. They are unnatural in that there is no advantage from the point of view of the survival of the human species in these forms of sex, whereas in normal sex between men and women there is. It would be begging many questions to speak of a design set by God or nature, but clearly the normal act tends to the survival of human kind and the others do not.
>
> (Honoré 1978: 105)

The normal and natural are here reduced to the conjunction of penis and vagina and the attendant possibilities of conception (presuming lack of reliable contraception). Honoré's focus is a particular conjunction of bodies rather than any question of sexual identity: 'the genital organs are so made that in normal intercourse the man's (for the most part) fits the woman's fairly easily. This is not true of intercourse between men' (Honoré 1978: 105). We are, it seems, reduced to a question of 'fit' of genital organs. That which does not fit, or is associated with excreting, is unnatural. More than that 'the passive role in buggery is like the role of a woman in normal intercourse so it is thought womanly' (ibid.).

By this tautology, 'women's role' in heterosexual intercourse is established: it is passive. The argument, though ostensibly addressing male homosexuality, clearly contains implicit assumptions about male heterosexuality. Yet what is the essence of the legal objection to homosexuality (and the implicit naturalness of heterosexuality) as exemplified in Honoré's positivist account of *Sex Law*? There are two aspects to this, both of which resurface in later chapters of this book concerned with fatherhood – first, that homosexuality is unnatural and, second, that homosexuality represents a significant threat to the heterosexual institution of marriage.

Homosexuality as 'unnatural'

One of the most frequently espoused objections to homosexuality is that it is the antithesis of 'natural' heterosexual sex within the institution of marriage. This argument within the Judaeo-Christian tradition (for example, see May 1930; Comfort 1968: 138) derives from a range of biblical sources which stress the 'unnatural' nature of non-reproductive sexual behaviour (Exodus 22.19; Leviticus 18.22, 20.23; Romans 1.27). Religious objections continue to inform debates on law reform in relation to homosexuality, for example over issues around the acceptance of gay clergy and the desirability of gay and lesbian fostering and adoption of children.[5] However, biblical condemnation based on the 'unnaturalness' of homosexuality should be placed in the context of the wider condemnation of sexual practices within the Bible which includes homosexuality among a range of non-reproductive activities such as bestiality, coitus interruptus and masturbation (indeed, any form of sex, other than intercourse between a man and a woman, which might not lead to conception). The 'natural' argument has subsequently been used in a more explicitly political context (Honoré 1978: 103) and, as Moran (1991) has shown, homosexuality has also been seen as symptomatic of treason and political deviancy. Such attributes of homosexuality continue to stem from its inherent 'unnaturalness' and threat to public order.

Homosexuality as threat to marriage

Second, homosexuality is a threat to the heterosexual institution of marriage. Section 11 (c) of the Matrimonial Causes Act 1973 states that a man may not marry a man and a woman may not marry a woman. That is to say, women only marry men. Heterosexuality in marriage is thus legally compulsory in that the institution of marriage is preserved and reserved for women and men. However, an immediate distinction may be made between homosexual *acts* and legally recognised *relationships*. The law that homosexuals may not marry does not exclude homosexuals from marrying, provided that individuals with a homosexual orientation marry someone of the opposite sex. Many gays and lesbians do marry and have children (Bozett 1987; Matteson 1987). Section 11 (c) is not so much concerned with homosexuality in marriage, therefore (which may be dealt with by the law on consummation/nullity, or under the divorce grounds of the Matrimonial Causes Act 1973 depending on the circumstances), as with the exclusion of certain types of relationship at the point of entry to marriage. Marriage is a privileged institution for adult heterosexuality, an institution in which there is at least the potential for heterosexual intercourse (on gay and lesbian marriages see Nelson 1987; Brown 1990).

Cases have arisen where the parties to the marriage have not been 'respectively male and female'. Here there has been no question of sex reassignment surgery and some deceit has allowed the marriage to take place (for example, Talbolt (Otherwise Poyntz) v Talbolt [1967] 111 SJ 213; cf. the Canadian case of Re North *et al.* and Matheson [1975] 52 DLRP 280) This exclusion of homosexuality from marriage is predicated on biological imperatives which exclude same sex relations from entry to the institution. Advocates of legal reforms which would enable homosexuals to 'marry' have thus argued that the criteria for establishing a test for validity of a marriage should be based on commitment to a relationship and not matters of biological sex. Other jurisdictions have moved towards this position (notably Denmark: Act No. 372; see Nielson 1990).[6] Whether individual homosexuals would wish to marry is a different question. Nonetheless this continued exclusion of homosexuals from marrying establishes marriage as an institution for heterosexual sexual activity – a point which is central to understanding the constitution of hetero-sexuality in law.

This negation of legal recognition of same-sex relationships has been justified in different ways and reveals a complex set of fears and anxieties (Crane 1982). Honoré (1978), in one of the less convincing of arguments, argues that homosexuality should be condemned because it 'tends in general to frustrate population increase' and because acceptance of homosexuality would mean that men would no longer economically support women in marriage (Honoré 1978: 104). Although conceding that 'a minority' of homosexuals are 'no threat' to the rest of society, Honoré argues that homosexuals generally cannot expect to be 'as highly regarded' as other men who take on the financial burden of raising families and supporting women (Honoré 1978: 105). Homosexuality, it seems, is also economically disruptive.

There are two strands to the argument: first, that heterosexual men raise families and homosexual men do not. This is reduced to a crude functionalist presupposition of population policy. Second, it is assumed that heterosexual men in marriage support women, an argument based on the assumption that men in general support women economically. Implicitly the differentiation of male/female activities along the male/breadwinner, female/childrearer dualism is accepted; the legal denial of legitimacy to homosexual relationships is thus justified because homosexual men are less likely to marry and support wives. Homosexually orientated men should marry if only to 'support' women whatever the consequences for the sexual relationship in marriage (quite where this leaves the marital ideal is not clear). It is thus the marriage and not the quality of the relationship within it which would appear to count. Yet, as Michael Ross (1983) has shown in his study of *The Married Homosexual Man*:

> one of the major factors underlying the marriages of homo-sexuals has been demonstrated to be a highly anti-homosexual expected peer and societal reaction . . . the consequence of homosexuals marrying in terms of psychological adjustment are not at all obvious: while a low degree of maladjustment or situationally produced problems are apparent in some respon-dents, it seems clear that there is a high degree of compartmen-talisation in the lives of married homosexuals, thus minimising

such problems. If marriage had any effect on their homosexuality, it was to increase its importance.

(Ross 1983: 146; see also Bozett 1987)[7]

Interestingly it is male, and not female, homosexuality which is seen to have this economic consequence (lesbianism does not undermine the economic position of men). Implicitly, therefore, the naturalness of a form of male 'breadwinner' masculinity is accepted. Male sexuality is also set up in naturalist terms; both heterosexuality and homosexuality rest upon an 'essential' sexual urge but an urge which is quantitatively and qualitatively different depending on whether the man 'is' heterosexual or not. For example, it is stated that homosexual men are more promiscuous than homosexual women or heterosexual men 'perhaps because men are in general more inclined to seek variety in sex than all but a small percentage of women' (Honoré 1978: 85). The conclusion which follows is that though some homosexuals might form long-term attachments and even think of themselves as 'married', relations between men and men cannot be as stable as those between men and women (Honoré 1978: 85). Homosexuals might pretend to marriage but they cannot achieve the stability of the heterosexual union *because of their sexuality* which will, in the end, reveal them for what they truly are.

This is the crucial point. Sex cannot be denied. It is male sexual desire which this naturalist argument divides into two (the hetero-sexual and homosexual). This bifurcation is fundamental to the negation of homosexuality in the formation of heterosexual 'normality'. What heterosexual and homosexual men share is an essential sexual urge. This urge might take one or other direction depending on the influence of 'over-possessive mothers', or 'absent or weak fathers' (Honoré 1978: 88), but the central proposition remains that it is homosexuality, as a deviant manifestation of an otherwise natural male sexuality, which constitutes the threat to public order and to the marriage institution. As to why the moral rules relating to sex should be stronger than those relating to property or violence it becomes necessary for Honoré to make his underlying view of the male sexual urge explicit: 'This is [because] sexual urges are particularly strong, and are not likely to be held in check by anything short of clear, unconditional rules and attitudes' (Honoré 1978: 104–5). We are reduced to an essentialist model of male sexuality. The paradox is that the 'unnatural' male urge is also a natural phenomenon in that it too is biologically given. The argument is contradictory; it accepts the normality of homosexuality at the same time as that normality is denied.

Honoré's account of legal hostility to homosexuality is simply not good enough. Containing no more than biological positivistic assertion, such accounts of law and sexuality (and Honoré's *Sex Law* is but one example of this genre in legal studies) fail to account for the social nature of law and masculinity (both heterosexual and homosexual). It is just such a social analysis which, I have argued above, must be central to theorising law, gender and power.

The sociality of the heterosexual/homosexual dualism

It is a universal fact of human existence that what we know best, that which forms part of our everyday mental landscape, is also that which we most take for granted, and question the least. And so some of the strongest jolts to our awareness, the deepest reorientations in out thought, often come from being confronted with the obvious.

(Miedzian 1991, quoted in Hunter 1993: 150)

Heterosexuality and homosexuality are far from unproblematic opposites which maintain that you either 'are' homosexual or heterosexual according to whatever criteria the rigid dualism has taken to define as such. This is not to ignore the experiential 'fixed' nature of gender identity nor the importance of this experience in developing identity politics (on heterosexual feminist identity see Thomas, A. 1993; Yural-Davis 1993; Reinharz 1993). As Young (1993) notes, questioning the binary of hetero/homosexual is not to deny the powerful experiences of a fixed sexual identity. The dualism of heterosexuality/homosexuality fails to account for the psycho-sexual dynamics between the two and how sex itself is constructed through reference to a hierarchical binary. In a sense, therefore, the social nature of the dichotomy itself is evaded.

It is a mistake to take homosexuality as a unitary phenomenon. Female and male homosexuality are in many respects different in both their social expression and in the sanctions they receive, so that any notion that 'homosexuality' is itself a unitary concept must be treated cautiously (O'Donovan 1993: 84–6). The legal regulation of lesbianism has been and continues to be very different from the law's treatment of male homosexuality (Kitzinger 1987). As to why this should be the case, it is certainly necessary to improve on Honoré's falling back on claims that men 'are far more adventurous. There are more male than female homosexuals. The ways of women arouse less feelings than those of men. The objections to homosexuality apply more strongly to men than to women' (Honoré 1978: 110; on the ways in which lesbian love-making is constructed as sexual activity see Card 1991)

What is perhaps more probable is that legislators have failed to consider that women might have and express a sexual desire which exists independently of men and would highlight the importance of maintaining the boundaries which construct heterosexual masculinity. For example, according to the British government, a reason for the absence of legislation on lesbianism has been that 'the question of homosexual acts by females has never – so far as the Government of the United Kingdom are aware – been generally considered to raise social problems of the kind raised by masculine homosexuality' (quoted by Weeks 1981: 118; see further Carabine 1992). As a potential disturbance to a heterosexual phallocentric order lesbianism may escape criminal sanction relative to male homosexuality. Yet when female sexuality is seen as threatening the idea of essential womanhood in law (mother-hood) then the law's treatment of lesbian mothers shows that it would be inaccurate to say that the law treats lesbianism with legal impunity (Rights of Women 1984; Kitzinger 1987; Allen and Harne 1988).

We have, it seems, two central dichotomies, two axes of power relations to consider when addressing the law and homosexuality. First, that between male and female homosexuality and second, between heterosexuality and homosexuality itself. In contrast with the sexological tradition[8] which focuses on the differences between heterosexuality and homosexuality, it is alternatively possible to argue that there are considerable similarities between the two forms of sexual expression. The categories of homo-sexuality and heterosexuality are not pre-theoretical but are, like law itself, social constructs (West 1977; Tannahill 1980; Davenport-Hines 1990). Heterosexuality is thus relational, '. . . constituted in a matrix formed by the intersection of negotiated situations, desires, fears and attitudes' (Young 1993: 38) – a matrix to which we all, men and women, lesbians and homosexuals, contribute in our everyday interactions.

It is not simply that 'heterosexual' identified men have admitted to 'homosexual' sexual experiences (Kinsey *et al.* 1948: 65–6, 623) or that heterosexual behaviour (whatever we understand this to be) is necessarily confined to men who identify themselves as 'straight' (Ross 1983). Whatever research one looks to within the positivist paradigm to conclusively 'prove' either the causes or extent of homosexuality, it is clear that social expressions of heterosexuality and homosexuality can converge. As a 'variation' of sexual behaviour homosexuality corresponds to the cultural norm of heterosexuality in several respects (Hanscombe and Humphries 1987; Wilkinson and Kitzinger 1993). Both, for example, can be conceived in terms of repression of the other; the subjective experience of gender identity as 'fixed' is common to both heterosexual and homosexual identified individuals and relationships (Person 1980; Crawford 1993). If one wished to account for why men might resist homosexual identity formation then it might plausibly be understood to be a matter of rational self-interest in recognising the far-reaching social and legal consequences of 'coming out' as a homosexual male in a homophobic society (as evident in recent debates around the 'outing' of gay celebrities). Both masculinities arguably involve a prominent role for genital sexuality in the maintenance of masculine identity, be that masculinity heterosexual or homosexual. As well as the undoubted differences in social expression, therefore, it is important not to lose sight of the fact that there are considerable similarities and overlap between homosexual and heterosexual sexualities.

What does all this mean for the construction of heterosexual masculinity? Pleck (1980) has argued that the dichotomy between heterosexual and homosexual men serves as a central symbol for a hierarchical structuring of masculinity *per se*. The hierarchy, Pleck argues, is maintained across a number of dimensions (for example, wealth, age, strength), but that it is the heterosexual/homosexual identification which in particular is an important signifier of masculinity. Within Pleck's analysis the heterosexual/homosexual ranking serves to locate all men in a relative position of power to other men, it denotes a hierarchy based on sexuality but one that is adaptable to the contingencies of economic success, looks, charisma, physical ability, etc.

This insight is interesting for it renders problematic the male/male axis and the supposed 'otherness' of homosexuality. Pleck suggests that it is in relations *between* men that a central power dynamic between men and women is to be located. That is, that the dynamic between male heterosexuality and homosexuality has implications for understanding male/female power relations. This point is brought out clearly in a consideration of the use of homosexual derogation by heterosexual men and in the extent of male homosociality as valorised in popular culture (Lipman-Blumen 1976; see also on the re-claiming of effeminacy as a heterosexual 'sissy' Hunter 1993). The functional use of homosexual derogation is taken up by Hoch (1979) who notes that:

> A whole male culture . . . has grown up, providing an ambiguous collective reinforcement against the tabooed feminine and homosexual orientation . . . the more one retreats to an all-male environment, presumably the greater the homosexual temptation, and hence the continued need to 'up the ante' in the way of violence to prove one's manhood.
> (Hoch 1979: 85; also Easthope 1987: 105–8)

This points to the sense in which masculinity can be defined as that which is 'not feminine'. The dichotomy thus sets up a 'real' authentic masculinity (heterosexual) as opposed to a 'false', denied masculinity (homosexual) while at the same time denying the homosexual dimension to much 'heterosexual' male behaviour. Such a negation of homosexuality has also been evident in several sociological accounts of male heterosexuality. There are elements of this in the work of Willis (1977) on adolescent boys, which notes the frequency of anti-homosexual derogation in what he terms 'working class oppositional culture'. Hartley (1974) similarly argues that masculinity would not appear attractive were it not for the stereotypes of femininity which are counterposed to it, whilst Hoch's (1979) presentation of 'masculinity as the avoidance of homosexuality' argues a similar point (though from an explicitly psychoanalytic perspective). For Hoch (1979: 78–94) heterosexual masculinity functions in specific ways; as a defence against both impotence and homosexuality. It is possible therefore to identify patriarchy as a dual system in which men oppress women but in which there also exists a systematic structure of power relations between men based on sexuality and gender identity (Pleck 1980).

The derogation of the homosexual feeds into a defence of the homosocial. Indeed, the idea of male homosociality as reflected in a range of culturally proscribed male behaviour has constituted an important way of understanding men's playing out the dynamics of male heterosexuality and homophobia whilst, crucially, maintaining both the exclusion of women and male dominance in institutional and cultural settings. Thus, when a judge declares, as in the case of R v Aitken [1992] WLR 1006, that male 'robust games' and 'horseplay . . . in the light of the Royal Air Force ethos' might include consenting to being set fire to (and seriously injured), he is also saying something about what he considers to be 'normal' 'boisterous activities . . . jokes and undisciplined pranks' which men might legitimately engage in together. The popularity and social acceptance of homosocial bonding would seem to testify to the call of a homosocial world which goes on long after the majority of men have become engaged in 'secure' heterosexual relationships. Homosociality pervades the media, in films, television and literature. The simultaneous negation of homosexuality and celebration of heterosexual homosocial bonding can thus been seen as an integral part of the ideology of the essential natural sexual difference between male and female and the maintenance of the heterosexual public persona of authoratitive masculinity. The frequency with which the homosocial is valorised in popular culture, importantly, testifies to a fragmentation in heterocentricity (in the case of the transsexual, below, this heterocentricity is not fragmented; it is shattered).

We have seen in Chapter 2 that sexuality/emotion and affective relationships have been central to defining the familial. Here we can see that it is sexuality – sex, desire and the politics of the body – which is central to the dichotomy that one sex (women) exists as potential sexual object for the other sex (men), while the other sex (men) is negated as sexual object. It is to the role of law in the processes of negation of 'deviant' sexualities that it is now necessary to turn. Gay sexuality disturbs the polarity of 'men' and 'women' as complementary parts of the natural (conjugal) whole (Warner 1990). 'Harsh' punitive laws in relation to homosexuality might not construct the dichotomy (to argue as much would be to give too much power to law), but they do buttress a sexual division which is fundamental to the establishment of a form of heterosexual masculinity in law. Just as the public/private dualism discussed in Chapter 2 can be seen as central to liberal legal discourse, therefore, so the distinction between heterosexuality and homosexuality must be seen as central to the power of hegemonic masculinity and heteropatriarchy.

THE HOMOSEXUAL PERSONAGE AND THE EMERGENCE OF (HETERO) MASCULINITY IN LAW

The heterogeneous dimensions of the categories of masculinity and heterosexuality are each negated by a naturalist ideology which constructs masculinity and heterosexuality on the basis of essentialist presuppositions. The purported 'natural' and unchanging quality of heterosexuality is, in short, problematic. The emergence of the homosexual personage as 'a past, a case history and a childhood . . . a life form and a morphology' (Foucault 1981: 43) has itself been a historically specific phenomenon:

> There is no question that the appearance in nineteenth-century psychiatry, jurisprudence, and literature of a whole series of discourses on the species and subspecies of homosexuality, inversion, pederasty, and 'psychic hermaphrodism' made possible a strong advance of social controls into this area of 'perversity'.
>
> (Foucault 1981: 101)

Homosexuality, in Foucault's now familiar argument, was put together as a 'psychological, psychiatric, medical category' around the 1870s. However, the shifting sexual economy of the late nineteenth century involved not simply changing definitions of homosexuality but also changing definitions of childhood and the family (Pinchbeck and Hewitt 1969; Aries 1973), of sanity and illness (Foucault 1967) and, crucially, of the category of 'sexuality' itself (Tannahill 1980; Weeks 1981, 1985; Foucault 1981; Aries and Begin 1985; Gallagher and Laqueur 1987). The nineteenth and twentieth centuries have witnessed no less than a transformation in the constitution of both heterosexualities and homosexualities, the contours of which are only beginning to be mapped.

The process of the law's criminalisation of male homosexuality outlined above constituted one important moment in the establishing of a historic redefinition of masculinity in law. The 1885 Criminal Law Amendment Act represents an important moment in the transformation of men's relation not just to their own bodies but also to the bodies of women. This transformation was produced in part through the activation of criminal sanction and through a legal redefinition of the arena of legitimate and appropriate male sexual expression. This shift in the legal/juridical forms of regulation had an effect at the level of producing structural shifts in the constitution of discourses of acceptable male sexualities. However, such legal change must not be seen in isolation. Law has not worked alone, as it were, but must be seen as part of a nexus of cultural prescriptions of deviance, normality and illness which have together involved the production of 'the homosexual personage'. This argument requires some clarification.

By the end of the nineteenth century, notwithstanding the variation in patterns of secularisation and codification of law between different European states (and in particular the contingencies of the influence of the Catholic and Protestant churches), male homosexual behaviour had become subject to legal sanction in a form very different from the pre-modern order (which had been marked by the sodomitical tradition). A fusion of medical, scientific, religious and legal discourses concerned with detailing the deviance of homosexuality underscored the production of the idea of the 'homosexual' as a type of person at a specific historical moment.

> Homosexuality appeared as one of the forms of sexuality when it was transposed from the practice of sodomy onto a kind of interior androgyny, a hermaphrodism of the soul. The sodomite had been a temporary aberration; the homosexual was now a species.
>
> (Foucault 1981: 43)

This process was marked by a change in the focus of the law's concern, a move from specific acts (a conjunction of bodies) to an ontological concern with identity, self and citizenship. In *The History of Sexuality Vol. 1* (1981) Foucault addressed this making of the homosexual individual, identifying techniques of examination and surveillance and the construction of the polarities of normal and perverse which were to be utilised as part of a 'perverse implantation' (1981: 43–4). The homosexual thus 'became a personage, in addition to being a type of life, a life form, and a morphology, with a discrete anatomy and possibly a mysterious physiology' (ibid.: 43). Foucault terms this an 'incorporation of perversions and a new specification of individuals'. Central to the thesis is the idea that the homosexual's sexuality was all; it was 'everywhere present in him: at the root of all his actions because it was their insidious and indefinitely active principle' (Foucault 1981: 43). Sexual identity thus struck to the core of the homosexual's being. Foucault shows how shifting forms of homosexuality and heterosexuality took place within a historical context spanning the transition in household structures prompted by feudal and early capitalist economies through to the emerging industrial capitalist economy of the nineteenth and twentieth centuries. It locates sexuality itself as an interdiscursive, socio-economically specific construction bound up within wider social shifts in the heterosexual matrix.

It is to be remembered that Foucault's argument is historically specific. In the context of the bourgeois class struggle at the end of the eighteenth century the bourgeoisie set its own body and sexuality 'against the valorous blood of the nobles' (ibid.: 127–8) in a process in which the bourgeois subject 'sought to redefine the specific character of its sexuality' against the working class (ibid.: 128). 'Respectable' working-class sexualities, transformed from pre-industrial licentiousness, thus negotiated with a new familial order built round the divisions of homosexual/heterosexual, normal/deviant, public/private and so forth (the nature of these 'dangerous masculinities' in the present will be explored in Chapter 6). The cast was set; in the context of an intellectually pervasive biological positivism, the homosexual/heterosexual dualism constructed the other at the same time as it policed the self. It was a dualism which was, crucially, to be enshrined in law.

Foucault's now influential thesis – in short, that homosexuality is a historically specific social construct – has a precursor in McIntosh's (1968) argument that it is possible to historically locate the emergence of a particular male role (around the late seventeenth century) by reference to which the rest of the population in turn defined themselves oppositionally – as pure, 'normal' and not in need of treatment: that is, as heterosexual. The 'homosexual role', McIntosh argues, functioned both to segregate the deviant from the normal (thus limiting their behaviour or inscribing it within a limited social subculture) and also by setting up a dichotomy between that behaviour which society deems to be acceptable and that which is unacceptable. Central to this argument is a view of the law as instrumental in the denial of the legitimacy of homosexuality as an alternative sexuality.

Law has been significant in bringing 'the species' of the homosexual into being and in creating the categories and concepts of 'homosexuality' and 'heterosexuality'. The juridical gaze thus brings both the homosexual as well as the family into being in particular contexts. The process has involved the classification of subjectivities (into heterosexual/homosexual) which simul- taneously involves a justification and endorsement of the law's own powers to judge. The discursive construction of the homosexual 'person' as a deviant 'man of law' (Naffine 1990) (or perhaps as not a man at all) took place in and across legal, medical and psychological discourses in the construction of a new subject to be observed, policed and examined.

The significance of this for theorising heterosexual masculinity can now be unpacked. We know that in the nineteenth century the law in relation to homosexuality changed significantly, becoming harsher and more punitive. We know this construction of the homosexual personage involved a shift in naturalised conceptions of male sexual desire. Male desire continued to be premised on a reductionist and universalist model of potential lust but the sexual mapping of the male body at this historical moment became much more sophisticated than simply focusing on a matter of a con-junction of bodies engaged in a certain activity. Instead, the re-mapping of the male body which occurred in the latter part of the nineteenth century involved not just the construction of an ontological heterosexual/homosexual polarity but also a shift in the meaning of masculinity itself (the contours of nineteenth century fatherhood, for example, will be explored in Chapter 5). Homosexuality itself only became a matter for social concern when sexuality itself, as a general category, became a matter of major public importance. In the context of debates on 'natural' sexuality in the nineteenth century legal and cultural valorisation of the sanctity of the marital bond 'by a necessary rebound' demanded the more refined control of extra-marital sexuality (Weeks 1981: 107). One form that control took involved a shift in the legal regulation of homosexuality. However, the regulation of the extra-marital did not stop there. This 'more refined control' of extra-marital sexuality involved also the systematic valorising of a model of the marital, the privileging of a conjugal sexuality and the denial of the legitimacy of other forms of sexuality outside the heterosexual matrix. It involved no less than the construction of a form of marital male heterosexuality in law; it involved con-structing an idea of 'the family man' which remains in law (though substantially modified) to this day. (It is this 'family man' which is the focus of the following chapters of this book.)

The negation of homosexuality is central to theorising mascu-linity and law, therefore. This is not to argue that the homosexual population was from this point on socially 'controlled'. Homo-sexuality, through the valorising of the ontological, took on the status of a 'reverse discourse' which 'began to speak on its own behalf' (Foucault 1981: 101), to celebrate the labelled 'deviant' identity. The law should not be read as a straightforward attempt to reduce sexuality to the reproductive, heterosexual, marital, adult form. To argue as much would be to fail to 'take into account the manifold objectives aimed for, the manifold means employed in the different sexual politics concerned with the two sexes, the different age-groups and social classes' (Foucault 1981: 103). It would also be to ascribe too much power to the law.

It would be more accurate to see law as part of a complex unity involving the opening up of the body to speech and to practice. The law has a significance beyond simply constructing homosexuality and heterosexuality as bi-polar categories. Law speaks of the body, of self and subjectivity, of desire and power, in a much more complex way than in simply signifying a sexual status in terms of either/or. Law is not just concerned with the heterosexual/homosexual dimension of male sexuality. It is concerned with the *form* that heterosexual behaviour takes. Only certain bodies, certain sexualities, may be permitted to enter the married state. The trouble is, of course, that this heterosexual masculinity has been invisible because it has been so taken for granted.

SCIENTIFIC 'FACT' AND THE LEGAL PROBLEM OF TRANSSEXUALISM

We began this chapter with some comments made about the problem of establishing scientific 'facts' which could be 'known' to every medical (or indeed law) student. Raymond (1979: 165) has argued that the issues highlighted by transsexualism cannot be confined to the transsexual context. Rather, they 'should be confronted in the "normal" society that spawned the problem of transsexualism in the first place'. We have seen above that the setting up of the perversity of homosexuality involved a claim to scientific 'fact' to justify the turning to the law to control 'unnatural' sexual stimuli. This reasoning constitutes a hierarchic discourse which negates, rather than valorises, human agency; it involves a biological (positivist) ontological presupposition in which it is the body which determines what you are and what you will be. The deviance of homosexuality is thus quantifiable, it can be measured and assessed. In the case of the transsexual, however, this breaks down. The interrelation of legal and medical discourses has sought to establish what sex and gender mean in the marriage context. Yet both have spectacularly failed to address the issues raised by transsexualism in the 'normal' society that spawned the problem.

In the construction of the sex/gender division the law's treatment of transsexualism has a significance far beyond the (statistically) few men and women who seek to change the sexual status they were born with. In a succession of cases concerned with transsexualism the law has sought to determine what sex, gender and (ultimately) what a man and a woman actually mean for the purposes of forming a legal marriage. The insights to be gained from these cases are thus invaluable for a study of masculinity and law for they question what 'sex' and 'gender', 'man' and 'woman' in law involve in the first place.

Transvestism, transsexualism and gender dysphoria

Legal regulation of cross-dressing has a long history (Bowman and Engle 1957: 584), with the first apparent scientific discussion of the impulse to dress in the clothing of the opposite sex made by Krafft-Ebing (see also Hirshfeld 1952). The earliest section of the Judaic code of sex morality prohibited the wearing of the attire of the opposite sex in unequivocal terms: 'A woman shall not wear that which pertaineth to a man, neither shall a man put on a woman's garment; for all that do so are an abomination unto the Lord their God' (Deut. 22.5). Though 'very few reports describe the surgical transformation that is demanded by certain male transvestites' (Bowman and Engle 1957: 583; 1960), it is clear that transvestism and transsexualism are not the same thing, therefore. The transvestite might obtain gratification from dressing in the clothes of the opposite sex and may be of heterosexual or homosexual orientation – but this is not transsexualism:

> The term transsexualism has been applied to the person who hates his own sex organs and craves sexual metamorphosis. Transvestism in the broad sense may cover a wide range of cross dressing and sexual behaviour and feelings. At one extreme the individual may occasionally like to dress up in clothes of the opposite sex, but without overt deviant sexual behaviour. At the other extreme, he dresses and lives his whole life in so far as possible as a member of the opposite sex. At this extreme, too,

impulses vary. One person may consider life useless without sexual transformation while another contents himself with fantasised changes.

(Bowman and Engle 1957: 583)

In a sense a degree of transvestism is culturally sanctioned. Cross-dressing (notably within a politics of effeminacy; see Hunter 1993) has figured in both men's anti-sexist writings and work on masculinity and popular culture (Mort 1988). Bowman and Engle conceded in 1957 that the wearing of jeans, overalls, slacks, shirts and other 'male' attire may be a matter of convenience and custom to women at various times and places: 'similarly, men's styles in certain eras copy the silks, rufffles, elaborate hair dress and jewelry used by women in other eras' (1957: 583). Hoch (1979) similarly traces the place of cross-dressing and effeminacy in a historical overview of masculine styles, from the 'Renaissance Playboy' to the 'Playboy Gallant'.

Just as these expressions of cross-dressing can be seen to be historically variable, transsexualism is also a phenomenon which must be viewed in the social and historical context in which a range of signifiers of gender have been accorded meaning.

The imaginery status of desire . . . is not restricted to the transsexual identity; the phantasmatic nature of desire reveals the body not as its ground or cause, but as its occasion and its object. The strategy of desire is in part the transfiguration of the desiring body itself. . . . Always already a cultural sign, the body sets limits to the imaginary meanings that it occasions, but is never free of an imaginary construction.

(Butler 1990: 71)

Transsexualism has at least two dimensions to it: the medical/scientific and the social/psychological. Transsexualism has usually been regarded by the medical profession as being of psychological rather than organic origin (Smith 1971: 693–5). Doctors and lawyers have produced a voluminous literature addressing the medical and legal anomalies of 'gender-role disorientation' or 'gender dysphoria' (on legal issues see Pannick 1983; Dewar 1985; O'Donovan 1985c; Bradney 1987). What has become clear is that the realisation for the transsexual of those varying impulses towards sexual transformation depends on the sophistication and availability of the surgery which might bring 'sex change' about.

Sex reassignment was not in fact termed transsexualism until 1953 (Benjamin 1953: 13), though the phenomenon had been reported in various anthropological studies. As medical techniques have progressed, so sex-change operations have become increasingly complex; and as attitudes to transsexualism have shifted so the legal problems to which transsexualism gives rise have emerged within legal studies (Strauss 1967; Smith 1971; David 1975; Pace 1983; Taitz 1988). The development of drug treatment, (oestrogen, testosterone and androgen), and surgery (vagino-plasty, penis-graft and mastectomy) must be placed within the wider context of provision of health care services, therefore. Times have changed since Bowman and Engle's (1957: 588) declaration that 'male parthenogenesis does not yet seem to be within the realm of possibility' and it is because of these medical developments that the law has found itself faced with cases on the legal and sexual status of the transsexual which strike at the heart of the distinction between men and women in law. The high level of publicity which has attended the transsexual cases of the 1980s and 1990s, perhaps in particular that of Caroline Cossey, served to put the issues of transsexualism firmly in the public eye (Cossey 1992). This public profile has, possibly, been further heightened by the appearance of cross-dressing help-lines in tabloid newspapers in Britain and the treatment of transvestism in the successful 1992 film *The Crying Game*.

Psychologically, the argument that transsexualism might involve a gender 'dysfunction' is premised on a male/female polarity and the establishment of a rigidity in sex roles at birth. For the transsexual there is a subjective confusion when faced with a rigid dichotomous structure of man/woman whereby an individual must belong to either the male or female sex. The transsexual may be anatomically of one sex but believes that s/he belongs to the other. Transsexualism is neither a simple matter of sexual preference or necessarily 'about' modes of sexual conduct but should rather be located in the terrain of experiential psychology, subjectivity and identity: 'Transsexuals often claim a radical discontinuity between sexual pleasures and bodily parts. Very often what is wanted in terms of pleasure requires an imaginary participation in body parts, either appendages or orifices, that one might not actually possess' (Butler 1990: 70). The transgression of transsexualism is the subjective confusion it involves and not the sexual behaviour which it (possibly) involves. We have seen in relation to homosexuality that the law is concerned with excluding particular relationships from the institution of marriage. When it comes to transsexualism the problem is that an individual may 'seem' to be one thing and yet in fact be another.

It is perhaps for this reason that the law has found trans-sexualism such a difficult subject to deal with. The psychological and cultural dynamics within gender construction valorise questions of identity, subjectivity and desire and the (super)structural determinants by which they are constructed. The structuring of emotional relations is thus central to the case of the transsexual. Emotion, cathexis and the forces of desire and the body, at least for the transsexual, somehow override other considerations such as biological sex and the legal 'fact' registered on the birth certificate. For the transsexual any notion of a coherent, unified and stable subjectivity/gender identity structured around a dichotomous sex/gender system is fractured, 'blown apart' by the lived tensions of sex, gendered expectation and desires.

A paradox underlies the plight of the transsexual, therefore. For the transsexual social gender expectations (cultural norms of masculinity and femininity) are both misplaced and denied. They are to be rejected. Yet at the same time a form of hegemonic masculinity and an emphasised femininity (Connell 1987) is simultaneously confirmed and enforced in a startlingly crude way. (It is this 'invasion' of orthodox femininity by the transsexual that Raymond (1979) and others have taken exception to.) We are not so much here dealing with 'subordinate' or 'alienated' masculinities therefore as with *the concept of masculinity itself*. The male to female transsexual is denying *all* the cultural forms and structures of masculinity on offer *per se* – to the extent of wishing to physically change that most marked indicator of gender itself, the human body.

Raymond (1979) has argued that transsexualism is a consequence and symptom of such a rigid gender dichotomy (in particular a result of patriarchal stereotyping of women and femininity). O'Donovan (1985a, 1985c) has similarly used transsexualism as a way to contest the law's 'primary dichotomy' of man/woman through polarising the sexes into 'male' or 'female'. The dichotomy, she argues, is based on physical difference (the possession, or absence, of a penis). What both Raymond and O'Donovan share in their discussions of transsexualism (though their conclusions differ) is a crucial awareness that transsexualism is not an esoteric subject for legal study but is something which must be placed firmly on the sexual political agenda. It implicates the body, the power of law and the social and legal meanings of masculinity and femininity in the 'normal' society which spawned the problem in the first place.

The legal importance of sex signification

The assigning of sexual status in law, of establishing whether one is legally a man or a woman, has a wider significance than simply determining who can marry. Criminal law (R v Tan [1983] 2 All ER 12), employment law (E.A. White v British Sugar Corporation [1977] 1 IRLR 121) and social security, sex discrimination and taxation law all have addressed the question of whether or not an individual is a man or a woman (O'Donovan 1985a: 71–2, 206–10). However, it has been in the context of the formation of *marriage* that the 'fixed' nature of a transsexual's birth certificate, and the (lack of) legal rights of transsexuals to form a family, that the transsexual has caused perhaps the most problems for a legal system which has been predicated on the essential dualism of 'man' and 'woman'. In the light of the arguments of Chapter 2, the importance of this is obvious; sex is at the heart of marriage and marriage, we know, is at the heart of 'family' life.

Though the number of transsexuals may be small relative to the general population, there has occurred a 'persistent trickle' (Bradney 1987: 350) of cases since the first (apparent) reported British case of Re X. [1957] Scots Law Times 61 (see also Bartholomew 1960: 83). The sort of problems which transsexualism can raise in the area of matrimonial law are evident in the case of Dolling v Dolling [1958] (*The Times* 23 May 1958). Here a sex-change after marriage was held to not constitute cruelty for the purposes of establishing grounds for divorce. Similiarly in the earlier case of Re Swan (1949 unreported; Bartholomew 1960: 84) property was left to a woman who had during the course of her life changed sex and had died as a man. The court held that the estate could be dealt with on the footing that they were the same person, commenting 'There is nothing very terrible about this, it is a peculiar case, but not unknown.' From these two cases it might appear that there is nothing so very disturbing and unnatural about transsexualism (or at least when the main issue is divorce grounds or inheritance provision). But when the question is the formation of the marriage of a post-operative transsexual the position of the law is very different.

We have seen in relation to homosexuality that under Anglo-Welsh law section 11 (c) of the Matrimonial Causes Act 1973 provides that a marriage is to be void if 'the parties are not respectively male and female' (see De Reneville (Otherwise Sheridan) v De Reneville [1948] 1 All ER 56). The complex procedural regulations governing the formation of marriage to be found in the Marriage Act 1949 establish legal requirements relating to the preliminaries of marriage, the place and method of solemnisation and, by virtue of section 2 of the Births and Deaths Registration Act 1953, the birth of a child must be registered within forty-two days. The birth certificate will then record the sex of the child. In the majority of cases the record is correct and there is no problem. That, however, is not always the case.

The birth certificate: what determines 'sex'?

Where a mistake of assignation is made it is possible for a certificate to be amended in cases of medically certified error. In establishing the sex classification of the child the customary answer to the straightforward question of whether the child is a male or female has been to simply look at the baby's external genitalia. However, a number of possible errors may occur. For example, a straightforward error of entry may be made. The registrar may enter male when the child is in fact female (or vice versa). Second, and more understandably, the sex of the infant may be indeterminate: that is to say, it may seem to be one sex on the basis of the examination of external genitalia, but on further examination the biological sex of the child may be indeterminate. Sex classification errors may occur, for example, because of the presence of gonads of both sexes, too few or too many sex chromosones, a confusion over the assigned sex or perhaps due to missing internal sex organs. This has arisen in the case of the hermaphrodite when it is not simply that the sex assignment is incorrect but that the co-existence of biological signifiers of more than one sex renders objective assignation difficult. It is far more difficult to determine the sexual status of the hermaphrodite than the transsexual.

In the case of the transsexual the individual is dissatisfied with her/his assigned sex category at birth, believing, despite the biological evidence to the contrary, that they are psychologically not a member of the sex indicated on the birth certificate. The 'fixed' content of the certificate is therefore of great importance for it is the law which, by holding that the birth certificate cannot be changed, constitutes a cause of distress to those transsexuals who wish to live their lives according to their post-operative sex, perhaps wishing to marry but being unable to do so by virtue of s. 11 (c). For these transsexuals the status of the birth certificate is central to their legal status: 'The fact that I have proved that I have been a woman for the past 20 years and that I have been a very happy person for that time shows that they should catch up with events.' (April Ashley, *The Times*, 7 June 1980; see also Cossey 1992).

As the cases of the hermaphrodite and the transsexual show, therefore, there is no one way of assigning sexual status which can work in all instances and the medical determination of sex has been, not surprisingly, a complex and contentious subject. Katherine O'Donovan (1985c) argues that the English law's approach to sex and gender has proceeded on untested assumptions about biological determinism in such a way that 'from the entry on the birth certificate to the drawing up of the death certificate persons are assigned to category female or category male' (O'Donovan 1985c: 9). In fact there are a range of possible ways of testing sex and alternative explanations vie for acceptance. O'Donovan's conclusion is that no clear universally objective test for sexual classification could ever be found. Instead a number of practices vary according to the branch of the law in which the question has arisen (O'Donovan 1985a: 64–70). Smith (1971: 965), for example, points out that different variables can affect sex determination: chromosonal sex, gonadal sex, hormonal sex, the possession of internal accessory organs (the uterus in the female, prostate in the male), external genitals, assigned sex and the gender role. Within all of these it is possible for there to exist considerable variation (for example, in the quantity of the hormones testosterone and oestrogen present in the body, which vary both from person to person and within individuals according to psychological state and hormonal cycles). There is, Smith concludes, not necessarily any predominance of any of these variables. All vary according to contingent factors and each of these are constructed differently in different areas of law (Cole 1978).

Medicine may be far from clear in its answers but, then again, opinions also differ as to whether the final determination of sex assignation is itself a medical or legal question: does the medical finding determine the legal outcome or vice versa? According to Bartholomew (1960: 88) the question of 'what is sex' is best left to those who know of such things (the medical profession); it is considered impractical for the law to abandon the two-sex assumption and debate the highways and byways of sex determination. Smith (1971) concurs, stating that

> Ultimately it is not for the law to decide the sex of an individual. The law must accept medical decisions in this area and give them the legal effect that is in the best interests of the individual and society. What those best interests are is difficult to determine, especially since the issues are clouded by conventional morality and religion.

> (Smith 1971: 972)

Yet the problem remains that these medical discourses are not necessarily consensual and the relationship between law and medicine is far from clear. It is frequently argued that the law must largely depend on and follow the lead and guidance of medicine (this is implicit in legal cases on transsexualism). Yet it would appear that medical classifications must also be consonant with legal principles and, in particular, that the law must somehow recognise the practical relationships of everyday life. Medical and legal discourse thus appear to vie for legitimacy in the commentaries on transsexualism. One result has been that the cases concerned with the issue read as a rag-bag of medical and legal considerations. They do not only fail to clarify 'what is sex' in the first place but also singularly fail to address the 'practical relationships of everyday life' of the transsexual her/himself. This has been most clear in the case of the post-operative transsexual who then decides s/he wishes to marry.

SEX, GENDER AND MARRIAGE

We have seen that, whilst both marriage and family are open to many definitions, the law has looked to sexual relationships as primary in forming the marriage bond (Chapter 2, p. 52). The transsexual who wishes to marry faces an immediate problem in that s. 11 (c) of the Matrimonial Causes Act 1973 is unequivocal: a marriage must be between a 'male' and a 'female'. Though 'marriage' is not defined in legislation, one commonly cited judicial definition has been that it is 'the voluntary union for life of one man and one woman to the exclusion of all others' (Hyde v Hyde and Woodmansee [1866] LR 1 P & D 130, 35 LJP; see further Poulter 1979). If this is interpreted as meaning that a marriage must be between a man and a woman then it would appear that the marriage of a post-operative transsexual must be void. Or does it?

The answer depends on whether or not one is taking the sex at birth or the post-operative sex as the signifier of legal status. If the transsexual is to be unable to change their birth certificate, passports and other documents of legal significance to accord with their new identity then it would seem it is a case of 'once a man, always a man'. The post-operative transsexual who marries might have believed their relationship to be heterosexual, valid and thus 'normal' only to find that it is in fact homosexual, unnatural and thus void by s. 11(c). This was the background to Corbett v Corbett (Orse Ashley) [1971] P 83, [1970] 2 All ER 33, perhaps the most legally influential of the cases on transsexualism (despite its status as precedent). In this case Ormrod J. laid down what is often taken to be the fundamental definition of sex and gender in English law. The reasoning is worth considering in detail for it is the way in which this decision was reached which tells us much about the law's conception of sex, gender and the nature of masculinity.

George Jamieson had been registered at birth and raised as a male. After employment as a merchant seaman and female impersonator, and after a suicide attempt, in 1960 and at the age of 25 he underwent sex-reassignment surgery and adopted the name April Ashley. April Ashley worked as a female model and was recognised for National Insurance purposes as a woman. Arthur Corbett, a transvestite who had sexual relations with 'numerous men', then married Ashley. Though Ashley was classified as male at birth, both married with full knowledge of the operation. The respondent, Ashley, had possessed male external genitalia but had then been treated with female hormones and undergone surgery involving the removal of male genitalia and the construction of an 'artificial female vagina' (p. 90) (though a chromosome test after the operation showed the cells were male). The 'marriage' proved a failure and action was brought to have it declared null and void either on the grounds that both of the parties were male or that there had been incapacity or wilful refusal to consummate the marriage. After the presentation of expert medical testimony regarding sex-determination the court decided that the marriage was null and void. Ormrod J. held that at the time of the marriage ceremony both respondent and petitioner were male and therefore there could be no marriage in English law.

Corbett v Corbett makes clear not just that marriage is not permitted in such cases but also, at least in respect of matrimonial law, that surgery and hormone treatment do not constitute a change in the sex assigned to a person at birth. Regarding the relation between legal and medical discourse Ormrod J. was clear that the law could not decide the matter alone. The science of medicine was to be relied on and the law had to 'look outside itself in order to seek the criteria to judge sex' (Bradney 1987: 351). The 'truth' of medical discourse was thus turned to in order to establish what does, and does not, constitute the sex of a person. Yet, in the last instance, the decision remained legal; the medical finding could only be 'merely of assistance' (p. 100). Of the nine doctors called to give evidence all agreed that there were at least four separate criteria which might be used in judging sex: the chromosomal, genital, psychological and gonadal factors. (Some would have added hormonal factors.) Finding the psychological and the biological tests not to be congruent (indicating, respectivley, that Ashley was male and transsexual), Ormrod decided that his decision was all about *the nature of sex in the relationship of marriage.* Having presented this context within which he would be establishing the sex of an individual (the purpose of marriage) it became possible for him to conclude that:

> Having regard to the essentially heterosexual character of the relationship which is called marriage, the criteria must, in my judgement, be biological, for even the most extreme degree of transsexualism in a male or the most severe hormonal imbalance which can exist in a person with male chromosones, male gonads and male genitalia cannot reproduce a person who is naturally capable of performing the essential role of a woman in marriage.
>
> (p. 106)

What this meant in practice was that the law should adopt the chromosonal, gonadal and genital tests in determining sex for the purpose of marriage. The test is thus 'biological', it is sex, and not psychological gender, which is to be significant in determining sexual status. It was therefore possible to ignore the later operative intervention. The reasoning could not be clearer. The 'greater weight would probably be given to the genital criteria than to the other two.' 'My conclusion, therefore, is that the respondent is not a woman for the purposes of marriage but is a biological male and has been since birth' (p. 106).

Ormrod neatly sidesteps the necessity of giving a judgement as to Ashley's sex *per se* through making the marriage context his 'catch-all' concept (whereby subsequent definitions of sex are twisted and turned to suit purposes and argument). It is the 'nature of marriage' which glosses over the contradictions and inconsistency in the reasoning, a rhetorical 'glue' which holds together this particular coupling of sex, law and gender. A medical doctor himself (see the letter from James Comyn Q.C., attorney for April Ashley, to the *Cornell Law Review*, 5 January 1971; Smith 1971: 1005), Ormrod's reasoning in Corbett thus tells us much about the biological basis of masculinity – for what the case is actually about is heterosexuality in marriage. What the case decided was that it is biological sex, and not gender, which is to determine legal status in this context. So what does this mean for masculinity therefore? And what does it tell us about marriage?

The test is biological

First, sexual status is to be determined according to biological criteria and in cases of any confusion 'greater weight' is to be given to the genital test. In reply to the contention that, as society recognised the transsexual as a woman for the purposes of National Insurance, it would be illogical not to do so for marriage, the court stated that such a submission confused 'sex with gender. Marriage is a relationship which depends on sex and not on gender' (p. 107). It could not be more clear. Biological sex, and all that follows from this, is at the core of the marriage relationship. Subjectivity, social appearence, gender identity and psychology are irrelevant in determining whether a person is a male or a female. Even transformative surgery cannot change sex. The die is cast at birth:

> It is at least common ground between all the medical witnesses that the biological sexual constitution of an individual is fixed at birth (at the latest) and cannot be changed, either by the

natural development of organs of the opposite sex, or by medical or surgical means. The respondent's operation, therefore, cannot affect her true sex.

(p. 104)

Such a view, as O'Donovan (1985a: 66) and others have argued, is essentialist and draws on a biological reductionist conception of masculinity (which also underscores social biologistic accounts of gender). The psychological traits are determined by a biological imperative and, whether or not an individual is a man or a woman, sex is to be determined at or before their birth. Thus an individual born with male genitalia and a male chromosomal structure will be, as far as the purposes of marriage are concerned, a male. Whatever the gender identity, and notwithstanding the post-operative existence of female genitals or social appearance, this individual will be classsified as a biological male. If an individual has the genitals, gonads and chromosomes of one sex then even if their life is otherwise lived as a member of the other sex, for legal purposes, sex classification cannot be changed. At the root of masculinity in law is a biological mandate of once a male always a male.

It is questionable whether the decision in Corbett is now correct even within narrow doctrinal terms. English law now provides, in s. 11 (c) Matrimonial Causes Act 1973, that it should be gender and not sex which determines whether parties may marry. The contracting parties have to be 'male' and 'female', and not a man and a woman. If this means that marriage is then to be couched within terms of gender and not sex then Corbett can only be of persuasive authority (Bradney 1987) (that an appellate court may be loathe to admit the point is another question). But the basis of the decision is, more importantly, intellectually dubious. 'Sex' as signifier of a biological category (man/woman) and human activity (intercourse) is distinguished from gender. This dualism enables Ormrod to disregard that which is most troubling about Ashley's life – that she regarded *herself*, on her own testimony, to be a woman even though the birth certificate stated otherwise. If public law might consider sex to be mutable then the matrimonial phallocentrism of this case fixes sex at birth for the discursive polarities which regulate entry to marriage (man/woman, sex/gender) to remain in place. What it actually is that marks this difference between the public law determination of sex (for example, for National Insurance purposes) and the place of sex in the marriage context is, as we shall see, the privileged status and specific nature of sexual intercourse in legal discourse.

Other objections may be raised to the decision. It is not clear that sex is fixed 'at birth'. Ormrod gives no reason for adopting this as the test beyond mere assertion. Take away the fundamental premise – that marriage is heterosexual – then, assuming the 'primary significance' of the genitals (a genito-centric view), it is arguable that the law should take into account the removal of the most important organ (the penis) and the substitution of another (female) genitalia. If the genitals are of primary importance what happens when the genitals are removed? If the penis becomes an (artificial) vagina then why not look to the vagina?

Ultimately, as a legal signifier and not physical organ, a penis cannot be removed for the purposes of sex signification. Born a man, Ashley remains a man despite subsequent surgery. The definitional process is thus characterised by a 'lack' of a penis, for it is the absence/removal of the penis which renders intercourse (im)possible. Ormrod is saying the genitals are the primary test: they are the most important criteria. Yet he is also denying the significance of the wholesale removal of the male genitals and the construction of an (artificial) vagina which might then signify female sexual status. The reasoning is curious. Men may seek to enlarge, perfect and project the penis in multifarious ways, might undergo surgery to 'cure' impotence (Tiefer 1987) and 'work on' the penis to improve its sexual efficacy (Zilbergeld 1980). To 'improve upon' a penis may enhance marriage and heterosexual (and homosexual) lovemaking. But to 'lose' the sexual use of the penis, metaphorically in the case of impotence (Chapter 4) and literally in the case of the male to female transsexual, is, in this context, legally impossible. Once a man always a man even if the 'man' in question is incapable of the sex act on which the institution of marriage is built.

There is a certain paradox to the decision therefore. Ormrod is claiming to concentrate on biological factors as the conclusive proof of legal sex. Yet he is also denying the legal relevance of the operation on the genitalia which has taken place. Thus, even if the biological test is to be accepted, the test must be of an uncertain status when it denies a complete change in the most important factor of the test itself; that is, the genitals. It may be argued that the post-operative transsexual would continue to lack the secondary/internal female organs which a sex-change operation might not provide. Yet could it not then be countered that many women themselves lack such organs? Such a 'lack' does not mean they cease to be women or that they cannot marry.

Ormrod's denial of legal sex reassignment is not based upon any coherent theory of sex and gender. Nor is it based on the practical ramifications of allowing such a legal change to be made. Rather, it rests upon an objection to legal sex reassignment *per se*. What he is saying is that a man is a man and a woman is a woman. The disruption entailed by a fundamental questioning of the meanings of man and woman, of masculinity and femininity, would upset the dichotomy of the sex/gender system on which the institution of marriage is premised.

Ostensibly Ormrod is concerned with the private relationship of marriage and with what goes on in Corbett and Ashley's (or, later, Mark Rees', Caroline Cossey's or Miss B's)[9] marital bed. Yet the policy questions have wider import. As obvious as it may seem, it is important to recognise that marriage is not a private matter to be somehow 'negotiated' between individuals. It is a public institution for heterosexual intercourse. It is the institution with reference to which other relationships/structures of cathexis are defined and, ultimately, denied, an institution to which the terms of admittance cannot be negotiated (O'Donovan 1993: Ch. 4). It is also an institution through reference to which, we are beginning to see, a particular legal conception of masculinity is beginning to emerge.

'The essential role of woman (and man?) in marriage'

The reason for holding that George Jamieson is and always has been a man is that he would be incapable of 'performing the essential role of a woman in marriage'. The argument hinges on this *essential role* which the transsexual cannot meet. It is to be presumed that Ormrod did not mean by the 'essential role of woman in marriage' the ability to look and to act 'like a woman' (criteria a transsexual, if the surgery were sophisticated enough, might meet):

> Socially, by which I mean the manner in which the respondent is living in the community, she is living as, and passing as a woman, more or less successfully. Her outward appearance at first sight was convincingly feminine but on closer and longer examination in the witness box it was much less so. The voice,

manner, gestures and attitudes became increasingly reminis-
cent of the accomplished female impersonator. The [body] . . .
looks more like a female than a male as a result of very skilful
surgery. . . . 'The pastiche of femininity was convincing'. That,
in my judgement, is an accurate description of the respondent.

(p. 104)

Ashley is really not 'good enough' at being a woman. It is possible
to socially 'pass as a woman' but Ashley is only able to achieve a
'pastiche of femininity'. Might even more 'skilful surgery' improve
on this? As Smith (1971: 1007) notes 'the "essential role of a
woman in marriage" under this view is simply being a woman from
conception or birth'. Ormrod's criteria are phallocentric. They
rest on a denial of female characteristics and a celebration of the
possession of a penis as the essential validating factor in and of the
institution of marriage. As Pannick (1983) notes, there is no
reason why sex assignment in difficult cases should depend upon
the criteria stated by Ormrod J. rather than upon the absence, at
the date of marriage, of external male genitalia 'and the existence
at that time of secondary female sex characteristics, female sex
hormones and a social and psychological female role' (Pannick
1983: 294). The essential role of the woman (and, by implication,
of the man) relates to sex; it is sex which

> is clearly an essential determinant of the relationship called
> marriage because it is and always has been recognised as the
> union of man and woman. It is the institution on which the
> family is built, and in which the capacity for natural hetero-
> sexual intercourse is an essential element. It has, of course,
> many other characteristics, of which companionship and
> mutual support is an important one, but the characteristics
> which distinguish it from all other relationships can only be met
> by two persons of the opposite sex.

(p. 105)

Marriage may be many things but it is above all an institution in
which there must be, as an 'essential element', the 'capacity for
natural heterosexual intercourse'. It is thus intercourse which
makes marriage different from other relationships. Intercourse, it
is to be presumed, April Ashley, Mark Rees and Caroline Cossey
cannot experience (The Rees Case [1987] 2 FLR 111; The Cossey
Case [1991] 2 FLR 492). Is the 'essential role' a capacity to have

intercourse or an ability to procreate? If the latter were the case those countless marriages which do not beget children would be void. Many women and men, for various reasons, cannot beget children. So if procreation is not the purpose of marriage, what is? To this we find no answer:

> Since marriage is essentially a relationship between man and woman, the validity of the marriage in this case depends . . . upon whether the respondent is or is not a woman. . . . The question then becomes, what is meant by the word 'woman' in the context of a marriage.
>
> (p. 105)

We are trapped within a tautologous logic as we return again to the familiar conundrum 'what is a woman?' Is it significant that we are not here concerned to ask what is a *man* in marriage, what is masculinity and what might be *his* essential role? As usual questions of masculinity fade from view just as they emerge. It is possible that Ormrod's casting of the problem in such terms was because Ashley, after all, held out to be a woman; but one might reasonably doubt whether, had the case concerned a female to male transsexual, we would then find ourselves engaged in a debate as to what the 'essential role of a man in marriage' might be. (To provide for his wife? This, after all, would seem to be Honoré's (1978) definition.) We would be more likely, as with the case of homosexuality, to be defining masculinity in terms of what it is *not*.

The 'essential determinant' of marriage: intercourse

The 'natural heterosexual sex' to which Ormrod refers is the essence of marriage. It is sexual intercourse, penetration of the vagina by a penis, which makes the determination of sex and gender in Corbett different from other 'public' areas of law. Though Ormrod recognises that in some contractual relationships sex can be significant (for example in relation to life assurance and pensions schemes, conditions of employment or national insurance contributions, employment tax and so forth), in these areas of law sexual status is not such an 'essential determinant'. There is nothing in these cases to prevent the parties to a contract of insurance or a pensions scheme from agreeing that the person concerned should be treated as a man or as a woman as the case may be. Law grants this discretion (p. 105).

There is no such discretion in the marriage context which genital connection signifies. Sexual intercourse establishes marriage as a relationship of a different order from, for example, the sex-blind contract relationship. Given this it is hardly surprising that a marriage between two men could not be possible. It is the essence of the marriage relationship that there occurs, or at least may potentially occur, heterosexual intercourse. This raises a number of questions. Intercourse and marriage are said to be inseparable but this is not backed with any evidence that marriages actually are contracted with the intention of having 'legal' sexual intercourse. Such 'evidence' may be impossible to establish but this remains the assumption underlying Ormrod's stance. The legal institution of marriage is a historically specific, and relatively recent, phenomenon (Poulter 1979; Stone 1990). People do have, and always have had, sex 'outside' marriage. In some marriages sexual intercourse might itself not take place. So how justifiable is this legal definition of marriage? The parameters of human sexuality transcend the genital connections of the traditional marital sexual dichotomy.

Though Corbett v Corbett is now over twenty years old, its legal significance lives on. More recent interpretations surrounding Articles 12 and 8 of the European Convention for the Protection of Human Rights have modified but substantially followed the reasoning in Corbett (The Rees Case [1987] 2 FLR 111; The Cossey Case [1991] 2 FLR 492). Other jurisdictions are markedly more understanding of the transsexual's position and fourteen states which are party, in 1993, to the European Convention now make provision for the legal recognition of the new sexual identity of the post-operative transsexual (O'Donovan 1993: 51).[10] It has been clear for a while that when transsexualism comes to court in the future it is likely that the decisions will be made in the European Court; and the most recent case in this forum (B v France [1992] 2 FLR 249) in some respects indicates a shift in position. In B v France, the European Court of Human Rights held, by fifteen votes to six, that the frequent necessity of disclosing to third parties information concerning a post-operative transsexual's private life had resulted in a degree of inconvenience sufficient to violate Article 8 of the Convention. Accordingly, a sum for non-pecuniary damage was awarded. However, and importantly, Rees v UK [1987] 2 FLR 111 and Cossey v UK [1991] 2 FLR 497 were distinguished and not overruled. The court noted both the changes in social attitudes to transsexualism which had taken place and the uncertain legal status of surgical transformation; but it was concluded that no sufficiently broad consensus existed between the member states of the Council of Europe to persuade the court to overrule the Rees and Cossey judgements.

On the basis of decisions so far, therefore, it remains doubtful whether the transsexual in the immediate future will fare any better than they did before Ormrod J. The influence of the dissenting opinion in future cases of Judge Martens (B v France [1992] 2 FLR 249), which was based on humanistic grounds and is far removed from the essentialist reasoning of Ormrod, remains to be seen. It could be argued that transsexualism is, after all, statistically insignificant (Ormrod 1972: 87). However, as B v France shows, cases continue to arise which are as legally difficult as those of Ashley, Rees and Cossey. Ormrod had stated:

> Apart from marriage, I cannot see how this matter arises. . . . The only branch of law . . . in which problems of sex-determination may arise in practice is family law and in this branch it will only arise where the validity of a marriage is in issue. . . . The relative unimportance of sex determination in the law is demonstrated by the fact that there has only been one case in the history of the English Law in which the question had to be decided. That case was Corbett v Corbett.
>
> (Ormrod 1972: 85)

Yet Ormrod was wrong on two counts. First, far from its 'relative unimportance', the decision in Corbett has had major implications within family law, in the areas of financial provision on divorce (ss 23–5 Matrimonial Causes Act 1973), inheritance and with regard to the matrimonial home (see Dewar 1985). Second, to state that the only branch of the law in which problems of sex-determination arise is family law is, quite simply, incorrect. Cases following Corbett have concerened areas of law apart from 'family' matters. In R v Tan and Others [1983] 2 All ER 12, the Court of Appeal was called upon to determine the legal status of a person with a view as to whether they were liable to conviction for a crime where the sex of the parties was an essential determinant of the offence (s. 30 of the Sexual Offences Act 1956, which makes it an offence for a man to live on the earnings of prostitution). In this case Parker J. expressly approved of the judgement in Corbett, notwithstanding Ormrod's own assertion that he had not been concerned with determining the legal sex of the respondent at large. In stressing what he saw as 'both common sense and the desirability of certainty and consistency' Parker rejected the argument that if a person was 'socially female' then they should not be held to be a man. Yet this purported 'certainty' and 'consistency' is questionable. Pace (1983) makes a telling point:

> Had the Court of Appeal in Tan been faced with an hermaphrodite appellant, and with no readily accessible civil law decision as a refuge, it would have had to get to grips with the issues involved in a much more convincing way than it did when confronted with the relatively easy problem of transsexualism.
>
> (ibid.: 321)

The implications of decisions such as Corbett and Tan are far reaching. It would follow that a male to female transsexual prostitute could nonetheless be convicted of male homosexual soliciting and thus attract harsher penalties (s. 1 Sexual Offences Act 1959, s. 2 Sexual Offences Act 1956). It would seem also that a female to male transsexual could not be found guilty of an offence of unlawful sexual intercourse with a girl under 16 (s. 6 Sexual Offences Act 1956). On this reasoning the post-operative male to 'female' transsexual would also be incapable of being raped (and the transsexual would thus be denied a basic legal protection). Noting that the degree of penetration of the vagina by a penis necessary for marriage consummation is greater than that required for rape (R v Lines [1844] 1 Car & Kir 393), Pace points out the inconsistency which arises where a wife refuses to consummate and is forced by her husband to have sexual intercourse with him: 'Assuming marital rape to be possible on the facts, a slight degree of penetration would support a rape conviction yet the marriage would remain unconsummated' (Pace 1983: 320). This conception of sex and gender is not just intellectually and theoretically questionable therefore. Even within the narrow legalistic terms of doctrinal pragmatics it can lead to confusions and uncertainties across areas of legal discourse which transcend the initial 'family law' context.

CONCLUSIONS: THE SEXUAL BASIS OF HEGEMONIC MASCULINITY AND MARRIAGE

Bradney (1987: 353) has argued that insisting on sex at birth rather than post-operative sex as the signifier of sexual status is to take up a 'weak position'. As transsexualism becomes more and more acceptable, both officially and socially, the Corbett position may become more difficult to sustain (the reasoning in B v France illustrates that such a shift is taking place). Nonetheless it has been sustained in cases such as Rees, Tan and Cossey and this tells us several things about the sexual basis of both masculinity and marriage in law. We have seen in this chapter that it is the presence of the penis which pervades the legal construction of sex in relation to both homosexuality and transsexualism. It is the penis which constitutes the signifier of sexual difference which then makes possible the division of the sexes into 'man' and 'woman' and, ultimately (for it is 'essential' to it), grounds the institution of marriage in legal discourse. The reasoning in Corbett v Corbett assumes a unique link between sex and marriage which it is difficult to support in either law or social practice. Unless one resorts to a pre-modern theological position (in which case all non-marital sexual activity itself constitutes 'sin') it would be incorrect to say that marriage is the only context for sexual intercourse. Nor would it be true to say that the sexual element is necessarily going to be the most important component of any particular marriage for the individuals concerned.

Two issues are at stake here. First, by assuming that all sexual intercourse takes place within marriage, the law is valorising and giving primacy to an institution which has itself been defined by reference to the possibility of engaging in sexual intercourse. The transsexual cases, basing marriage on a biological dichotomy, ignore the 'social' aspects of the marriage relationship and focus instead on the sexual. If marriage 'depends on sex and not on gender' then legal discourse is valorising one particular medical interpretation of the relationship of sex and gender. Compassion, consideration, empathy and the ability to love and understand are all subordinated within an economy of masculinity which privileges intercourse above all else in the constitution of the marriage relationship. Other forms of human contact and pleasure are deigned legal validity within a position which takes it for granted that there is a fundamantal difference between men and women, and that heterosexuality is normal (that is, the key elements of the ideology of masculinism as identified by Brittan 1989: 4).

In this process gender is denied purchase and the subjective reality and personal happiness of the transsexual is negated (though the basis on which society has this right to prevent the transsexual from achieving such happiness is questionable; Smith 1971: 972; Judge Martens in B v France [1991] FLR 249). It is perhaps ironic that in other respects the law is concerned with consent and conscious understanding in the formation of a marriage. But the objection to the decisions is not simply that the reasoning involved is essentialist and that the law privileges inter-course over other signifiers of a committed relationship. O'Donovan (1985c: 20) points to a second, wider and more funda-mental issue transsexualism raises, a question which is at the heart of the politics of masculinity – 'the organisation of society on a gender basis [which] exacerbates gender dysphoria as exhibited by the transsexual.'

This point is crucial. Corbett presupposes the fixed and immut-able categories of male and female and the organisation of society on a gender basis. It assumes two closed categories of femininity and masculinity, each possessing certain biological characteristics. Yet, far from being fixed in this manner, 'gender is fluid, unstable, constantly reconstructed and embedded in the symbolic realm . . . subjectivity is, in part, an effect of . . . processes which always require the interaction of a self, language and their others' (Middleton 1992: 145). In challenging the foundationalist reason-ing of law it becomes possible to open up 'other configurations, not only of genders and bodies, but of politics itself' (Butler 1990: 142). It is clear that a minority of individuals cannot be so classified biologically (See Re C and D (falsely calling herself C) [1979] 28 ALR 524, 35 FLR 340; Bailey 1979). The decision leaves open the determination of the sex in marginal cases such as testicular femin-isation and testicular failure. In such cases the biological tests of the decision would lead to conflicting results. Ormrod has claimed the decision would lead to certainty as to sex in all instances. The problem is that it does not lead to certainty at all. Corbett is also at the very least 'difficult to reconcile' (Pannick 1983: 293) with the earlier judgement in SY v SY [1963] P 37, where Willmer L.J. in the Court of Appeal found that a woman who had abnormal sexual organs which prevented intercourse would nonetheless be capable of intercourse after 'the creation out of nothing of an artificial vagina, sufficient in size to enable full penetration to be achieved.'

To argue that a distinction may be drawn between an anato-mically 'normal' woman (as in SY v SY) and the transsexual, both of whom have had surgical treatment to the vagina, might make some sense if those biological components which are taken to constitute the difference between the two (perhaps hormone levels, ovaries) were themselves 'of the essence' to the act of intercourse taking place. However, this is not the case, for the act of 'consummation' entails penetration of the vagina by the penis (see further Chapter 4). Any subsequent consequences of the act (such as conception) which involve the 'secondary' sexual organs or biological features other than a vagina/penis are not fundamental to the legal definition of intercourse. Ormrod's distinction is illogical and in contradiction to other parts of his argument.

In the end there can be no answer to the question of whether an individual is 'really' a man or a woman, though different discourses continue to seek such an authorititive determination and proclaim their own findings as scientific 'fact'. All that can really be said with certainty is that certain sex organs are differentiated in different ways and by different discourses and that this biology, thus signified, bears some, though not specific, relation to social gender. To return to the sociality of the hetero/homosexual dichotomy,

> The implicit construction of the primary heterosexual construction of desire is shown to persist even as it appears in the mode of primary bisexuality. Strategies of exclusion and hierarchy are also shown to persist in the formulation of the sex/gender distinction and its recourse to 'sex' as the prediscursive as well as the priority of sexuality to culture and, in particular, the cultural construction of sexuality as prediscursive.
>
> (Butler 1990: 148)

This implicit construction of heterosexuality reappears also, we have seen, in the case of the transsexual. Strategies of exclusion and hierarchy pervade the reasoning in Corbett and the prediscursive, essentialist, construction of sex within doctrinal law (for example Honoré's approach in *Sex Law* (1978)). It is

> precisely the property of human sociality that it transcends biological determination. To transcend is not to ignore: the bodily dimension remains a presence within the social practice. Not as a 'base', but as an object of practice. *Masculinity invests the body.* . . . Social relations continuously take account of the body and biological process and interact with them. 'Interact' should be given its full weight. For our knowledge of the biological dimension of sexual difference is itself predicated on the social categories.
>
> (Carrigan *et al.* 1985: 595)

The formal equalities promoted by the Sex Discrimination Act 1975 and the Equal Pay Act 1970, both laws against discrimination on the grounds of sex, are concerned with 'sex equality'. Sex specific legislation has a long history (for example the Married Women's Property Act 1882; Infanticide Act 1938). Yet 'sex equality' is meaningless unless we have some conception of what 'sex' actually signifies in law. It is ironic that on the one hand we have laws concerned to abrogate reliance on stereotyped notions of sexual roles (the Sex Discrimination Act 1975) yet when it comes to determining sex assignment the law continues to embody and perpetuate a dichotomy whereby all individuals regardless of their psychological identity are either a man or a woman (see E.A. White v British Sugar Corporation [1977] IRLR 121). Such a failure to engage with the constitution of gender results in a perpetuation of masculine ideals: 'the best conse- quences of such a critique would be a redistribution of existing possibilities according to the explicit ideals those arrangements violate' (Middleton 1992: 165).

The law in relation to homosexuality, transsexualism and marriage replicates the essentialism and categoricalism I have argued against in Chapters 1 and 2. The dichotomous biological and social classification into male and female is reflected by a further division between biology (as material base) and sub-sequent social and legal classification. Part of the explanation may simply be that legal reasoning has failed to keep up with developments in medical research. This is not a sufficient explanation. The inability of the law to treat sex and gender with any coherence says much about the patriarchal and phallocentric nature of legal discourse and about the nature of legal reasoning itself.

Alternative perspectives do exist. A 'sex as continuum' thesis does not conceive biological sex in terms of the polar opposites of male and female but rather sees sex as a continuum, or cluster concept, where individuals may be placed at some point along a scale (O'Donovan 1993: 50). The consequences which follow from biological sex typing (for example, that you are a male at birth and will therefore legally be a 'man' for the rest of your life) can thus be separated from what might be termed 'contingent' conse-quences of social gender classification (though it remains unclear what the connection between the two is). In other jurisdictions a psychological test together with surgical reassignment has been held to be a more appropriate legal standard. Certainly, the

psychological gender-related test has a number of advantages.
Smith (1971) puts the point well:

> [T]he chromosomal sex is merely of abstract, scientific and
> theoretical interest in the case of transsexuals. . . . To insist that
> a person must live and be legally classified in accordance with
> his or her chromosomal sex violates common sense as well as
> humanity. It reduces science to a mere technicality and an
> absurd one at that. With the same justification, one may insist
> that Rembrandt's works are not paintings but pieces of canvas
> covered with paint.
>
> (ibid.: 966)

Overruling Corbett would give rise to its own problems (Dewar
1985), but these would follow only insofar as they result from a
conception of marriage as an a priori heterosexual institution. If
there is to be no reason why two people of the same sex, male or
female, should not be able to form the legally committed relationship of marriage – whether or not they are pre- or post-operative
transsexuals – then it is difficult to see what some of these difficulties are. Ultimately it is the heterosexual nature of marriage and
the phallocentrism of law and masculinity which transsexualism
and homosexuality render problematic.

We have seen in Chapters 1 and 2 that the plurality 'masculinities' integrates the differentiation as well as the communality of
male experiences. Connell (1987) has utilised the concept of
hegemonic masculinity in his analysis of gender and power in
order to question the processes whereby one particular form of
masculinity has assumed a hegemonic social and cultural ascend-
ancy. The hegemony of this exalted form of masculinity is specific
to a historical situation. As a culturally (and I shall argue legally)
exalted form of masculinity, hegemonic masculinity may or may
not actually correspond to individual men's lives, but whether or
not it does is not really the point. The concept of hegemonic
masculinity leads us to a questioning of the social, legal and cultural context, the circumstances in which power is won and held.
It gives us a way in to begin to understand the kind of masculinity
which we can now see is emerging in legal discourse.

> The construction of hegemony is not a matter of pushing and
> pulling between ready-formed groupings, but is partly a matter
> of the formation of those groupings. To understand the

different kinds of masculinity demands, above all, an examination of the practices in which hegemony is constituted and contested – in short, the political techniques of the patriarchal social order.

(Carrigan *et al.* 1985: 594)

Bringing together the themes and issues raised in this chapter it becomes possible to integrate the dynamics of male/male and male/female relations within an analysis of gender and power. Perhaps now we can begin to see how homosexuality and transsexualism are related to the production of just such a form of masculinity in law:

> The subordination of women and the marginalization of homosexual and effeminate men are sustained neither by chance nor by the mechanical reproduction of a social system but by the commitments implicit in conventional and hegemonic masculinity and in the strategies pursued in the attempt to realise them. . . . The collective project of oppression is materialized not only in individual actions but in the building up, sustaining and defence of an institutional order that generates inequalities impersonally.

(Connell 1987: 215)

Connell crucially identifies the relation between hegemonic masculinity, the oppression of women and the marginalisation of homosexual and effeminate men. In keeping within the language and politics of the constitution of subjective commitments to family life developed in Chapter 2, it is this 'building up, sustaining and defence of an institutional order' (an idea suffused with masculinism) which is fundamental to understanding law, gender and power. The production of hegemonic masculinity implicates the social, economic and legal relations within which one particular discourse of masculinity has assumed a social hegemony.

Masculinity, I have argued in Chapters 1 and 2, is not settled by biology; it is produced historically and socially. As such, reproduction of forms of masculinity becomes the outcome of a range of political strategies which have involved the law and legal discourse. In the field of constituting subjectivity and setting the socially sanctioned parameters of sexual interaction, sexuality and desire have been constituted in legal discourse through reference to both pain and pleasure by social injunction, prohibition and exhortation. I have argued in this chapter that masculinity is not a fixed, transhistorical entity; it is not an object that we can reach out and touch, quantify or qualify. It is more a resultant of a social process. It is something which is constantly constructed and (re)negotiated within a historically evolving social structure.

Homosexuality and transsexualism bear witness to and celebrate the diversity of masculinities, the possibilities of resisting the heterosexual familial (hegemonic) norm. They transgress the sexual basis of both marriage and masculinity in law. That they are excluded from marriage should not surprise us when to allow their entry would subvert the very basis of marriage as a privileged heterosexual institution. Ultimately what homosexuality and transsexualism lead us to is a questioning of the abstract determination of 'male' and 'female' and the sexual binary system underlying family law into which all individuals must be fitted at birth. Sexual response is not natural, given or inevitable in its form or content:

> For male sexual response to be aroused by any member of a large category of women does not require free-floating affect, ie, a quantum of lust roaming around looking for an object, so much as a capacity for ready physical response coupled with a massive blocking out of men as emotional objects.
>
> (Connell 1983: 29–30)

The dynamics which are involved in this (re)negotiation on a daily basis of male gender identity, within the parameters of a culturally dominant and socially proscribed form of hegemonic masculinity, are not stable. Hegemonic masculinity is not fixed and social expressions of sexual desire are not pre-given. Instead there exist a range of performative possibilities in the process of negotiation of male gender identity. Masculinity might more usefully be understood as something which is in a continuous process of discursive construction. The embedding of masculinity is social, historical and permanently in flux and, as Connell has argued (1983: 30–1), what is perhaps most striking about the construction of hegemonic masculinity is the length and the complexity of the process (see further the accounts of heterosexuality in Wilkinson and Kitzinger 1993).

In these processes law has been instrumental in ascribing normative sexualities. The legal structuring of heterosexual familial relations presented in this chapter is fundamental to the institutionalisation of a phallocentric gender order and in this process the normative bifurcation between heterosexuality and homosexuality has been crucial in the formation of hegemonic masculinity.

> The category 'men' needs to be exposed as a modern invention which nonetheless draws its legitimacy from appeals to a historical continuity supposedly guaranteeing its universality. The aim is to recognise that we are, sometimes, men, in all the ways which that recognition can be understood.
>
> (Middleton 1992: 160)

The construction of this 'modern invention' of men will be explored further in Chapters 5 and 6. The following chapter is concerned with the legal constitution of something which has emerged as central to this discussion of sex and marriage – sexual intercourse. We shall see how the mapping of the male body in legal discourse 'fine tunes' male sexuality in specific ways in familial relations whilst this dichotomy between heterosexuality and homosexuality remains primary. The fact that the re-construction of the history of homosexuality in recent years has taken place within the context of feminism and the emergence of new sexual movements should not be so very surprising: for within the history of homosexuality oppressive definitions and defensive identities have 'marched together' (Weeks 1981: 117). The last word is perhaps best left to Mark Rees, one transsexual whose application to the European court failed:

> For me the idea of marrying a man is ludicrous. . . . It would have been so even before reassignment therapy. I would very much like to marry and be able to adopt a child within a legal relationship. All transsexuals have to accept that reassignment surgery means they will not be able to procreate. In itself that is no bar to marriage under our law. Marriage is not denied to men or women who through acccident or injury are sterile. Other aspects such as caring companionship are important too.
>
> (Mark Rees)[11]

In the following chapter I shall consider further this relation between procreation, sexual pleasure and the meaning of sexual intercourse in law in an investigation of the sexed male as object in law. The law does not simply state that sex in marriage is to be heterosexual. It also stipulates the precise *form* that sexual intercourse is to take.

Chapter 4

'Love without fear'
Representations of male heterosexuality in law

INTRODUCTION

> Heterosexuality has to feature in our politics as more than a
> guilty secret . . . it must be restored as a legitimate part of
> feminism's concern. It is, after all, the primary practice of most
> women.
>
> (Campbell 1980: 10)

> The late Calvin Coolidge once remarked 'If I want 'em, I want
> 'em; If I don't, I don't'. True, he was speaking of apples. But he
> might have said precisely the same of women. And so might all
> men.
>
> (Chesser 1941: 35)

In both feminist and men against sexism writings there is one issue
which has, perhaps above all other, been singled out for debate
and analysis: the politics of male sexuality or, more specifically, the
oppressive, destructive and anti-social consequences of male
heterosexuality. In feminist writings on the relation between law
and male sexuality, in discussions of rape, child sexual abuse,
domestic violence, sexual harassment and pornography, it is the
destructive nature of male sexuality which is so often presented as
the social problem which needs to be addressed by our society.
Frequently texts conclude with a statement of the need to 'take
male sexuality seriously' or to 'tackle the problem' of men and
their dangerous sexuality. For Catherine Mackinnon, we have seen
in Chapter 1, the relation is unequivocal: 'the more feminist view
to me . . . sees sexuality as a social sphere of male power of which
forced sex is paradigmatic.' (Mackinnon 1983: 646). A similar
concern with male sexuality is echoed in the men against sexism

tradition and has been particularly clear in a strand of feminist writings which are, perhaps, exemplified by Mackinnon's comments (see also Dworkin 1987). In a sense male sexuality has assumed a standing in feminist discourse similar to masculinity itself; it is that which is somehow 'everywhere but nowhere', seemingly omnipresent yet invisible – so taken for granted that its sociality is negated in the mists of the myths and metaphors which surround our understandings of male sexuality.

This chapter seeks to make sense of these confusions. It is also about change and continuity in the construction of sexuality in law. It seeks to explore representations of masculinity and male sexuality in legal discourse and, through contrasting legal constructions of masculinity in the moral, sexual and economic context of the late nineteenth century with those of the contemporary *fin de siècle*, examine how certain ideas of male sexuality – ideas which continue to be constructed through myth and metaphor – have been granted a legitimacy through their grounding in law.

At a time when the laws of sexual identity and behaviour might seem to be breaking down, curiously echoing the existential anxieties of the 1880s and 1890s, the 'sexual anarchy' of the contemporary has been marked by a backlash to the perceived sexual liberalism of earlier decades (Showalter 1992). In part this has taken the form of an anti-feminism which has propagated the 'naturalness' of a phallocentric model of heterosexuality. Yet essentialist constructions of male sexuality have, we shall see, a long history in law. The specific object of this chapter is to investigate how the law has constructed 'natural' sexual intercourse in its institutionalised setting: that is, in marriage. The representations of male sexuality to be found in legal discourse hold out beliefs about self, subjectivity and society which link up with cultural constructions of sexuality. Marriage, we have already seen in Chapter 3, is based on a form of sexual consummation; heterosexual relationships are, we know, privileged in the legal consequences they attract. What we need to do now is explore the type of heterosexual sex that law has sought to privilege as constitutive of marriage and discover what this, in turn, tells us about masculinity, marriage and the family.

Chesser's comments above, writing in *Love Without Fear: A Plain Guide to Sex Technique For Every Married Adult* (1941), appeared in the context of a discussion of the respective sexual roles of men and women in marriage. The 'House of marriage', he declared, 'has to be built, stage by stage. Its orderly, happy construction demands a plan' (1941: 25). Those individuals who, before they enter the married state, take the steps urged by Chesser 'will have laid strong foundations upon which to build a structure both firm and enduring.' There exists in law an idea of male sexuality which is premised on essentialist presuppositions similar to those conjured up by Chesser in his 'happy construction' of marital sexuality. It is a male sexuality which is, above all, genito-centric and naturalistic; and it is the displacement of this male sexuality which has been central to feminist critiques of the heterosexual imperative, as well as those critical studies which have addressed the power of the ideology of masculinism. It is also, crucially, a form of male sexuality which is central to the construction of the institution of marriage as a 'restrictive practice' (Honoré 1978: 9).

Central to the ideology of masculinism is, I shall argue, an implicit dichotomy between the idea of potent/virile and impotent/non-virile masculinity, a division which is a core element of the form of hegemonic masculinity we have seen emerge in Chapter 3. Though in this chapter I shall ostensibly address representations of sexual intercourse in one specific area of law (the law relating to the formation and annulment of marriage), the politics of male sexuality have a more general relevance to social, economic and political life in the late twentieth century. Analysis of the *historical* specificity of masculinity and male sexuality in legal discourse, in keeping with the theoretical position detailed in Chapter 2, is an important part of a political engagement with the power of law. It is the purpose of this chapter, therefore, to subvert those readings of gender which negate the contingent and social nature of the myths and metaphors of the cultural sexual economy.

The following is in three parts. First, I shall explore some contemporary ideas of male sexuality and address the social context in which heterosexuality has been rendered problematic and political. Second, I shall relate to this contemporary context a historical overview of the ways in which, from the late nineteenth century to the present, the law has constructed male sexuality in the process of determining whether or not sexual intercourse can be deemed to have taken place so as to bring about a consummated marriage. Third, and drawing on the consistencies and contradictions between the present and the past, I shall explore at a more general level how the law has sought to construct male heterosexuality in the family and what this might mean for the study of law, gender and power.

In short, this chapter is concerned with dismantling the archaeologies of the constitution of male heterosexuality in law. In seeking to understand how the law has constituted familial affective relations it is essential to recognise the diversity, coherences and contradictions within and between discourses which speak of sexuality, the self and the body. This question has become, in the light of feminist, gay and lesbian questionings of heterosexuality, a matter of considerable importance. In the context of the spread of HIV and Aids the need for such analysis of the social and legal parameters within which heterosexual intercourse takes place is further heightened.

A CONTEXT: SEXUALITY AND SOCIETY

The twentieth century has seen the publication of many books concerned with the achievement of sexual fulfilment (Van der Velde 1928; Lindsey and Evans 1928; Havil 1939; MacAndrew 1946). More recently there has occurred in Britain a proliferation of hitherto 'explicit' videos and texts concerned with promoting sexual technique in a 'safe sex' context. This 'immense verbosity' (Brunt 1982) testifies to the purchase of Foucault's thesis that 'we . . . are in a society of "sex", or rather, a society "with a sexuality"' (Foucault 1981: 147). That sexual attitudes have changed is beyond doubt. For example, in January 1992 the Court of Appeal decided in R v Boyea [1992] Crim. LR 574 that the 'level of vigour' in sexual congress should be considered to be higher in 1992 than in 1934 for the purposes of determining what might constitute an indecent assault (R v Donovan [1934] 2 KB 498). What 'transient and trifling' bodily contact actually involves, therefore, is historically variable (*The Times*, 6 February 1992). However, if it is the case that attitudes to sex have changed since the 1930s, they have also, in some respects, stayed the same. Writing in her book *The Sex Factor in Marriage* in 1937, just three years after the Donovan decision, Helena Wright addressed her audience of those 'who are or are about to be married' as follows:

> Some of you . . . may shrink from reading such plain talk about the details of bodily intercourse, and the way in which to use the sex organs . . . and the cause of all this is not want of love. It is

want of knowledge . . . *we need to learn and practice the art of living the married life.* And that art is like all other arts in one thing: it has to be based on knowledge. There is a technique of married life, and husbands and wives need to know that technique just as surely as a painter needs to know the technique of his art.

(Wright 1937: 11–12; my emphasis; see also Griffith 1942: 170)

The idea that dissemination of knowledge of 'techniques' of sexual activity might contribute to 'healthier' or 'safer' sex life has been a recurring theme in discussions of sexuality throughout the twentieth century (Reuben 1970, 1972; Comfort 1977; Leigh 1979). Eustace Chesser, a contemporary of Wright's, similarly declared that:

the woman has to be taught, gradually, how to enjoy love on its physical side. For the husband to attempt too much . . . is a mistake . . . it is important that the bride who does not know, in advance, *what we have discussed* should be lovingly told by her husband what the position is.

(Chesser 1941: 76; my emphasis)

Importantly, these discussions have had an explicit teleology to them in the idea that obtaining such appropriate knowledge of the 'techniques of married life' will then lead to an improvement in the quality of sex and, implicitly, the quality of life itself (Altman 1984; Neustatter 1992). In recent years, however, prompted in part by Aids and HIV, the parameters within which these discussions of sexuality have taken place has changed. A 'knowledge' of sexuality and the body, and an associated rethinking of the place of penetrative intercourse within the (hetero)sexual reportoire, has become a matter of concern not simply in assessing the quality of an individual's sexual life. It has also, through the advocacy of 'safe', protected sex and a stressing of the dangers of unprotected sexual intercourse, become a matter of the protection of life itself.

The social practices of heterosexuality therefore, albeit belatedly, have now assumed a central significance in the development of Aids awareness programmes and, notwithstanding pervasive homophobia, the fact that Aids transcends sexual orientation has began to permeate public consciousness. It is, for the majority (one hopes), no longer simply a 'gay plague'. This has occurred, however, at the same time as a profound rethinking of the place of sexuality *per se* in the constitution of the self has taken

place, a reappraisal of identity, sexual practices and moral values
in the late twentieth century (Davenport-Hines 1990: 1). Central
to this project has been a reassessment of the purportedly 'natural'
quality of a phallocentric model of sexual intercourse and, at a
time when traditional sexual identities are increasingly breaking
down, we are witnessing the proliferation of cultural configurations of sex which transgress the familial ideal (Butler 1990;
Showalter 1992). The changing status of the transsexual and
homosexual seen in Chapter 3 exemplifies this process. In the
celebration of sexual diversity (Weeks 1985, 1986) the heterosexual cultural matrix has as a result become the object of sustained critique from those who have been excluded from the
discourses of the familial order. Perhaps ironically, the increased
commodification of male sexuality has itself been perceived as
leading to a disjuncture between cultural images of men's sexual
prowess and the realities of men's lived experiences (Hoch 1979;
Ehrenreich 1983; Metcalf and Humphries 1985).

It is difficult to say what Helena Wright, in 1937, would have made
of such developments. The challenge to the phallocentric order goes
to the very heart of the twentieth century gamut of sexual advice,
guidance and assistance which has been constructed with quite
distinct sexual scripts for men and women in mind. The 'knowledges'
of sex to which Wright refers – indeed, arguably our whole cultural
understandings of sex – have epitomised in their central theme the
consummation of the heterosexual trinity: that is, erection, penetration and orgasm as the 'perfect', 'complete' sex act. Wright see this
essence of intercourse as metaphysical sacrament:

> As the Act proceeds, the intensity of pleasure rises, thought is
> abandoned, a curious freeing of the spirit, very difficult to
> describe, takes place. It is as if there were, hidden among the
> sensations of the body, a spiritual counterpart, a pleasure of the
> soul, only attained for a few seconds, bringing with it a dazzling
> glimpse of the Unity which underlies all nature.
>
> (Wright 1937: 4)

Couched in such transcendent terms it is not surprising that consummation in law then becomes 'the final performative act of
consecration of the marriage. The primal act of heterosexual
intercourse . . . to be repeated as a generative act ad infinitum'
(O'Donovan 1993: 46). Yet this reductive construction of heterosexuality, of male orgasm as narrative closure, involves reducing

the potentialities of the body to one act, sexual intercourse. The very language of the law is revealing: 'to consume a body with mouth and teeth is cannibalism. Consummation with a sexual organ gives a different form of pleasure' (O'Donovan 1993: 46).

The word 'consummation' in fact originated around the fifteenth century from the Latin 'consumare', meaning to complete, and from 'summus', the highest, utmost. Sexual intercourse thus brings to completion or perfection, legally and spiritually, a solemnised marriage through the act of intercourse. As a legal concept consummation 'brings into being' a marriage and this, as Wright and Chesser make clear, is an act in which men and women have, both historically, culturally and legally, been accorded certain roles (Campbell 1980; Heath 1983; Hall 1991). '[T]he male is the seeker, it is he who makes the first advances. . . . The male has to arouse the female, and only if he does this properly does she experience active sex feeling' (Griffith 1942: 197). It is this form of 'sexual connection', 'constructed through men taking the initiative and women responding through choice or preference' (Coward 1982: 15), which has been central to the social construction of male sexuality as predatory and dangerous. It is the man afflicted with an 'unsatisfied sex hunger' who, 'unless restrained by very strong motives, . . . is apt to seek from some other woman what he now despairs of obtaining from his wife' (Wright 1937: 11). Certainly, at a time of sexual anxiety the appeal of the certainties and security of 'safe' sex in the monogomous marital context may be understandable. However, the apparent re-embrace of old certainties co-exists with the dislocation of the polarities of gender involved in the development of feminist post-structuralist thought which has sought to disturb the foundational dualisms of the institution of marriage (Weedon 1987; Butler 1990). Cultural naturalisations of gender and attempts to fix the dualisms of male/female, heterosexual/homosexual in place do not 'float free' of the law therefore. They are beliefs which have a history, a context and a legally based legitimacy.

THE LEGAL CONSTRUCTION OF SEXUAL INTERCOURSE

The legal and social construction of male virility has an obvious relevance for political engagement with the sexual politics of both masculinity and law. A number of immediate questions may be raised about the legal construction of sexual intercourse. Is it true that a 'masculine' sexual imperative is embedded in law? If it is then what does this involve? How does it relate to the 'truth' of sexuality – not in the sense of legal doctrine's determination of what constitutes sexual intercourse in a particular context, but in terms of the lived experiences of women and men? It is here that Smart's (1989) depiction of the phallogocentric is a helpful starting point through signifying

> the combination of phallocentric, which is the masculine heterosexual imperative, and logocentric, which is the term appropriated by feminists to identify the fact that knowledge is not neutral but produced under conditions of patriarchy. The elision of these two concepts in phallogocentric allows for a recognition that these two fields of sexuality and knowledge are interwoven.
>
> (Smart 1989a: 86; see also Smart 1990a; O'Donovan 1993: 5)

In seeking to investigate the convergence between the constitution of law and masculinity, the construction of sexual intercourse in law embodies the heterosexual imperative and the binding of power/knowledge in a particularly obvious form. Indeed, the heterogeneous dimensions of the categories of masculinity and heterosexuality are each negated by a naturalist ideology which constructs masculinity and heterosexuality on the basis of essentialist presuppositions. It is not suprising that the 'truth' of heterosexuality should then be so taken for granted, for heterosexuality stands in marked contrast to the plethora of texts which have sought to explore the historically specific construction of homosexuality and the shifts within meanings ascribed to 'the homosexual personage' (Weeks 1977; Foucault 1981; above p. 107). Unlike the 'deviance' of homosexuality, in the interweaving of sexuality and knowledge under the conditions of patriarchy heterosexuality remains monolithic and immutable. It is, above all, natural and the very naturalness of heterosexuality becomes the abiding truth of sexuality *per se.*

We have seen in the preceding chapter how homosexuality was put together as a psychological, psychiatric, medical category around the 1870s (Foucault 1981: 43, 101). However, the shifting sexual economy of the late nineteenth century, a time of scandal and crises of sex, race and class, involved not just changing ideas of homosexuality, but also changing constructions of childhood as a social problem (Dingwall *et al.* 1984), of sanity and illness and 'sexuality' itself (Caplan 1987, see p.106). Thus, if it is the case that homosexuality has been constructed as the antithesis of the norm, then it becomes necessary to question the nature of the norm itself; that is, how has male heterosexual *virility*, as opposed to the deviance of homosexuality or impotency, been understood in law? How does disturbing the polarities of heterosexuality/ homosexuality, male/female and potent/impotent serve to fracture the sexual economy of an institution (marriage) which has been, and which remains for the majority of men and women, a primary social institution? As part of a more general denaturalisation of gender, such a questioning of the hierarchical binary nature of sex involves us in no less than 're-establishing as political the very terms through which gender is articulated.' (Butler 1990: 148). How have the pleasures of sex been articulated, therefore? What is sexual intercourse in law?

There is nothing 'modern' about the cases which follow, at least in the sense that judicial investigation and assessment of marital coitus has a long history. Indeed, theological examinations of the mechanics of the sexual practices of husband and wife have been striking in the extent of their obsessive surveillance of the sexed body. Canon law had accorded much significance to sex and sexual morality and the Church Fathers expounded at great length on what constituted 'natural' and 'unnatural' sex (Flandrin 1985; Darmon 1985). Particularly influential (and much cited in legal judgements) have been the writings of Sanchez (*Disputationes de sancto matrimonii sacramento,* 1654, Book 7, Vol. 11), discussed in detail by Darmon (1985). Contemporary medical and popular journalistic texts continue this fascination with the causes and cures of sexual 'dysfunction' and the propagation of the (hetero)sexual aesthetic (Fallon *et al.* 1984; Apse *et al.* 1984; Perelman 1984).

What has marked the modern secular period out as different from that which preceded it, however, has been the establishment of regulatory and administrative mechanisms whereby heterosexuality might be, in Foucault's terms, 'put into discourse'. Thus, whilst the unconsummated marriage – its form and content – had been formulated by the Church, its manifestation in the new epistemic order, and the establishment of an apparatus for the minute investigation of marital coitus, has been legal in form. It has been through sexuality that

the juxtaposition of the techniques of discipline and technologies of the self produced a desire for the production of a
knowledge of things and for its intensification and perfection: a
desire that was fundamental to the new art of government.

(Moran 1990: 168)

In terms of heuristic classification it is possible to approach the
non-consummation of marriage through tracing the history of the
concepts of void and voidable marriages in law, the importance of
ecclesiastical law (Matrimonial Causes Act 1857 s. 2; Darmon 1985)
or the doctrinal development and multivarious technicalities of
the law relating to the formation and annulment of marriage (see
further Bromey and Lowe 1987: 69–103). The annulment of
marriage is an established subject within the substantive jurisprudence of family law and the related historical and procedural
issues have formed a subject for considerable analysis and debate.
However, such a doctrinal focus fails to place the unconsummated
voidable marriage, under s. 12 Matrimonial Causes Act 1973, in
the wider social and historical context (Collier 1992a: 485–6).

The cases which follow are not only commonly referred to as
constituting the substantive law in contemporary 'family law'
textbooks (for example, Bromley and Lowe 1987: 82–7). Certainly,
these cases are in an area of law which may be considered to be, for
practical purposes, increasingly obsolete. The cases which follow
emerged at particular historical moments. The majority arose as
ways of trying to get round the restrictive divorce legislation of the
time, whilst more recent cases on incapacity have arguably been
more concerned with restricted rights to marry. However, notwithstanding the contingencies of the legal context, it is possible to
isolate the following components of sexual intercourse in this area
of Anglo-Welsh law. Each involves, I shall argue, a particular
understanding of male sexuality which continues, in the 1990s, to
retain a cultural purchase.

Heterosexual sex is natural

First, heterosexual sex is natural and sexuality expressed in marriage
is a natural phenomenon. Naturalism denies any alternative organisation of the body, for what is natural is inevitable and cannot be
questioned. We have already seen how these essentialist presuppositions have been relied on to legitimise the 'natural' quality of the

institution of marriage and legally legitimate sexual intercourse (Chapter 3, p. 121; Corbett v Corbett [1970] 2 All ER 33).

It is important, however, to recognise that it is *male* sexuality which has been constructed as driven by this essential natural 'force'. In directing this natural sexual instinct into the institution of marriage the law has been constructed as minimising the social disorder which might ensue through sexual activity taking place outside the marriage relationship (D-e v A-g (falsely calling herself D-e) [1845] 1 Rob Ecc 280: 298). If law is ever out of step with the sexual dictates of nature then the ensuing disorder threatens not only the institution of marriage but ultimately social order *per se.* Thus, homosexuality, adultery and all non-marital sexuality become bound up within the web of potential social disintegration and political deviance (Devlin 1959; Moran 1991).

This essentialist construction of male sexuality continues to pervade areas of legal regulation (it is particularly evident in accounts of prostitution and child sexual abuse). In the succession of cases concerned with marriage and the legal status of the post-operative transsexual, we have seen above how a naturalised male sexuality has underscored the definition of sex and gender which grounds sexual intercourse firmly within the institution of marriage. Epistemologically, the claim to scientific 'fact' which this reasoning involves – an appeal to law to control 'natural' sexual stimuli – constitutes the setting up of a hierarchic discourse which negates, rather than valorises, human agency. The naturalist ideology continues to pervade the discourses of the 'psy' professions concerned with the techniques of normalisation, control and (dis)order which mark governmental regulation within the new epistemic order (Foucault 1970; Donzelot 1980; Chapter 2).

What is natural is heterosexual: the primacy of genital sex

Sexual pleasure in marriage is to be achieved through contact with the body of another but the other is not to be of the same sex (s. 11 (c) of the Matrimonial Causes Act 1973). Heterosexuality in marriage is thus legally compulsory in that the institution of marriage is preserved and reserved for women and men (Nelson 1987; Dewar 1989a). As a result heterosexist ideologies continue to be given a legally sanctioned purchase through the denial of legal legitimacy to homosexual relationships. However, the sexual economy of legal marriage is ordered in a more complex way than around a simple homosexual/heterosexual orientation dualism. The law is not just concerned to ensure that marriage is a heterosexual institution; it is also concerned with the *form* that sexual behaviour takes and, specifically, the nature of the genital interaction therein.

The hierarchical dualism of man/woman (man/active, female/passive) succeeds in reducing the polymorphous possibilities of the body to a genital conjunction which is ordered in a particular way. Specifically, this is a connection of penis and vagina in which male and female can be ascribed very different roles, pleasures and desires and whereby legitimacy is denied to other connections outside this genital economy, for example genital/oral, genital/anal, anal/oral (Moran 1986). Thus, it should not be suprising that both homosexual sexual relationships and the marriage of the post-operative transsexual should be denied entry to the married state if it is a genital test which is taken as determining sexual status in law. For there to constitute a legal marriage there must be the capacity for 'true' heterosexual intercourse (Corbett v Corbett [1970] 2 All ER 33). We have already seen in Chapter 3 how, rather than valorise questions of identity, subjectivity and desire (all of which might constitute alternative signifiers of sexual status), the current law denies the significance of the superstructural processes through which subjectivity is constructed. It seeks to embody instead an essentialist conjunction of genitals which then functions as the determinant of whether or not a marriage is to be possible between two individuals.

'True' sexual intercourse and (im)potent male sexuality

Is it any coincidence that, from Sparta to Nuremberg, the most disastrous ideologies have been founded largely upon a coherent mythology of virility? The analogy is neither forced nor gratuitous; to condemn an individual in the name of sexual normalisation is to issue an untenable dictate. . . . Must we continue to condemn to silence those who, by virtue of an ill-matched marriage, are exposed to sexual misery? If so, the trap is laid, and the fatal mechanism activated.

(Darmon 1985: 229)

Let us now turn to how the law has constructed male sexual virility. Darmon (1985: 1) has argued, in his analysis of those groups of individuals who suffered at the hands of the *ancien régime* in France (the poor, the insane, sodomites, alchemists and blasphemers), that the impotent have been a largely forgotten category in the scholarship of legal academics and historians. Yet it is arguably this very antithesis of male virility – impotence – which speaks of many of the tensions which seem to surround contemporary male heterosexuality. It would certainly seem to tap a raw nerve in many men, at least judging from the number of texts in which rethinking ideas of sexual potency has been central in attempts to overcome the emotional impoverishment of the forms of masculinity now considered redundant (Zilbergeld 1980; Carlton 1980; Bancroft 1982; Krane *et al.* 1983; Elliot 1985; Tiefer 1987). It also, most importantly for my present concerns, provides us with a much clearer picture of what the judiciary have taken to be the nature of the male pleasure which is to be derived from sexual intercourse.

If it is true that, culturally, 'sex' is often equated with 'intercourse' then impotence negates this sexual ideal. We are dealing here with the 'mistakes and sufferings which have darkened married life for thousands of couples' (Wright 1937: 9). In relation to the sexual economy outlined above, male sexual 'dysfunction' takes place in the context of a cultural construction of male sexuality in which genital sexuality has been identified as a 'mainstay' of male gender identity *per se* (Person 1980). This fusing of male gender identity with genital sexual performance has been a theme which runs throughout both feminist and men's 'anti-sexist' accounts of masculinity. In the case of law it has been possible to construct men as being 'overaggressive' 'over/ undersexed', 'sexually inadequate' and so forth precisely because male sexuality itself has never been conceptualised as a problem in the first place. Thus, if we are to view the impotent man as an object within a discursive field concerned with normalisation, it is unsurprising that he should be constructed as a 'dangerous individual' (Moran 1990: 169). Like the homosexual, he represents a threat to marriage and the social body. He is, like the homosexual, not really a man at all (Broker 1976). As victim of the 'mythology of virility' he is one whose sexuality speaks of the truth of his being and for whom entry to the married state is to be denied by reason of the Truth; he is incapable of sexual intercourse.

What is it that he is not? What is the nature of his transgression? We can begin to answer this by looking at how the law has constructed the masculinity of the potent, 'honourable' and decent man. The idea of the 'family man' constitutes a model of masculinity which surfaces regularly in legal discourse; he is the embodiment of a virile, responsible masculinity. In Chapters 5 and 6 we shall see that he has been established in law primarily through reference to his employment status and marriage; that is, he is in work and he is married. These contingencies, alongside sexual orientation and physical ability, constitute key elements of hegemonic masculinity in law. Such a form of masculinity is both class, sex and race specific; the 'man of law' is white and middle class, a man whose 'masculinity assumes a middle-class form . . . [he] is the man of reason. . . . His is a high-brow, cultivated form of masculinity, which depends upon an ability to think and act intelligently, not with brute force' (Naffine 1990: 116).

Many examples, traversing different areas of law, illustrate both the power and fragility of this form of masculinity. Its contours are complex and the relevance of different aspects of the signifiers of 'maleness' vary from area to area. However, what remains central to hegemonic masculinity is the significance of male sexual potency; that is, as several critical studies of masculinity have argued, in the maintenance of hegemonic heterosexual masculinity, a model of male sexuality as driven by a naturalistic force has been fundamental. It is also, we have seen, central to the determination of what is to constitute 'true' sexual intercourse in law.

The discursive status of the phallus is extraordinary. For a start it is transhistorical. We know from Corbett v Corbett that a penis might be physically removed but that it cannot be legally removed for the purposes of assigning sex. Within the mapping of this genital taxonomy as heterosexual and natural, it is the absense of the penis which signifies femininity and the absence of intercourse which signifies impotence and the unconsummated marriage. But what is natural about a penis? What are the 'natural' qualities of a penis which render it so legally significant? The difficult question of what 'natural' 'true' intercourse involves has been central in a succession of cases which have been concerned with the formation and termination of marriage.

Canon law had accorded much significance to sex in marriage and the Church Fathers expounded at length on 'natural' and 'unnatural' sex. Genital examinations were institutionalised in canon law in the thirteenth century (Darmon 1985: 142) as the bodies of men and women became points of entry for the values and norms of sacramental sex. The subsequent dissemination of printed books, confessors' manuals and theological treatises and factums made cases of sexual impotence common knowledge and this ecclesiastical obsession was to be carried into secular law following the passing of the Matrimonial Causes Act of 1857 (the Act which established civil jurisdiction in matrimonial matters, created civil courts and provided for absolute divorce). With embarrassment, a sense of duty and an at times obsessive relish, the courts have proceeded to show scant reluctance in scrutinising the marriage bed, the bodies of husband and wife and, in particular, the transgressive nature of sexual dysfunction. The question is, in so doing, what have they found?

The case of D-e v A-g (falsely calling herself D-e) [1845] 1 Rob Ecc 280 (p. 1039) is the cornerstone of the cases on the place of sexual intercourse in marriage. Indeed it was later to be described (Per Willmer L.J. in SY v SY (Orse W.) [1963] P 55) as 'a statement of commanding authority'. In the leading judgement, Dr Lushington declared that the court were 'all agreed that, in order to constitute the marriage bond between young persons, there must be the power, present or to come, of sexual intercourse' (p. 1045). He then proceeded, in a passage which is worth quoting at length, to define the legal meaning of sexual intercourse:

> Sexual intercourse, in the proper meaning of the term, is ordinary and complete intercourse; it does not mean partial and imperfect intercourse; yet, I cannot go to the length of saying that every degree of imperfection would deprive it of its essential character. There must be degrees difficult to deal with; but if so imperfect as scarcely to be natural, I should not hesitate to say that, legally speaking, it is no intercourse at all. I can never think that the true interest of society would be advanced by retaining within the marriage bonds parties driven to such disgusting practices. Certainly it would not tend to the prevention of adulterous intercourse, one of the greatest evils to be avoided.
>
> (p. 1045)

This is at the crux of Lushington's reasoning in D-e v A-g. First, intercourse (giving pleasure) is not in itself sufficient. It is admitted that intercourse has taken place in this case but it was not 'real' (ordinary/proper/natural) intercourse. 'Ordinary' and 'natural' must therefore have some meaning. Second, the 'disgusting practices' which might follow from 'unreal' intercourse are one of the 'greatest evils' against the 'true interest of society'.

These are the consequences of a legal recognition of 'imperfect' sexual intercourse in marriage. What sexual intercourse involves is a specific interaction of the male and female body (genital connection, penis/vagina) and what non-marital intercourse (adultery) might lead to is social disorder:

> Without that power [to consummate] neither of the two principle ends of matrimony can be attained, namely, a lawful indulgence of the passions to prevent licentiousness, and the procreation of children, according to the evident design of Divine Providence.

> (p. 1045)

There is in law a 'true' sexual intercourse which is capable of consummating a marriage. Other 'unnatural' connections and non-penetration, be it due to structural impediment or psychological inability, are not sufficient to consummate a marriage.[1] What such a construction does, of course, is to marginalise sexual practices outside the frames of the heterosexual matrix. It is, simply, penetration which defines sexual intercourse in law (see also O'Donovan 1993: 46). What constitutes the 'natural' quality of the genitals, however, is far from clear and would appear to vary from case to case (S v S (otherwise C) [1954] P 736; B v B [1955] P 42; cf. SY v SY (Orse W.) [1963] P 37; M v M (Orse B.) [1957] P 139).

The 'natural' quality of the genitals

Though canon law had been slow to recognise the possibility of female impotence (Darmon 1985: 35), a succession of twentieth-century cases concerned with female incapacity to consumate have raised the difficult question of at what point does surgical intervention transform the genitals into something so qualitatively different as to be 'unnatural'?

In S v S (Otherwise C) [1954] P 736 the husband petitioned for a degree of nullity on the grounds of the wife's incapacity and wilful refusal to consummate the marriage. After both parties had made, the court accepted, genuine but unsuccessful attempts at consummation, the husband began an adulterous association with a woman who then bore a child by him. In this case, the wife had been 'abnormal' only in the sense of having a thick hymen, which could be corrected by minor surgery with no danger to life or health. The conclusion was, therefore, that the husband had failed to satisfy the court that the marriage was not consummated owing to the incapacity of the wife (p. 743). One question was left open: what would be the conclusion if the surgery required had been more in line with a wholesale transformation of the genitals (which was, of course, to arise in the Corbett case)?

In B v B [1955] P 42, in contrast, the surgery required to enable consummation to take place did involve a radical transformation of the genitals. The wife had been born with certain male organs. These were removed in youth and, after an operation, an 'artificial passage of between four and six inches was created'. The husband petitioned for nullity on the grounds of the wife's incapacity, alleging that there cannot be consummation 'where the husband's erection penetrates into an artificial passage which in effect has no relation to the organ which should be there in the wife' (p. 46). Interestingly, in an argument which was to inform the court's final decision, counsel for the husband turned the question round:

> if the court were to hold that a connection in those circum-
> stances was consummation of a marriage it should hold that
> there was consummation in a case where a man who had no
> sexual organs was provided with a sexual organ with which he
> could penetrate the wife.
>
> (p. 46)

What, in such circumstances, would constitute a 'real' penis? If the court were to hold the 'artificial' vagina to be capable of being penetrated it would follow that a marriage could also be con-summated by the use of a similarly 'artificial' penis. The court did not explore the matter of what providing a man with such an artificial organ would entail. If a man's inability could be overcome with such an organ it is possible that the 'essential' role of the penis in intercourse would then be displaced (which would have also involved the court in judicial assessment of what constitutes an artificial penis).

The wife alleged that complete and 'normal' penetration of the passage had been affected and that the artificiality of the passage did not prevent her from consummating a marriage. Nonetheless, in judgement the court declared the wife to be incapable of consum-mating the marriage. What had taken place had been a 'mere con-nection ... between the parties. ... I do not consider that it [pene-tration] could be held to be consummation in the circumstances *having regard to the artificiality of her organ*' (p. 46–7; my emphasis).

In B v B, 'having regard to the artificiality of the organ', the constructed vagina transgressed nature: the genitals were not 'real'. It is interesting, therefore, that in the later case of SY v SY (Orse W.) [1963] P 37 – which is on the facts very similar to B v B – the court reached a rather different conclusion. As in B v B the husband petitioned for nullity whilst the wife contended that she was so capable and, in the alternative, if the marriage was not consummated then the husband had consented to and acquiesced in its non-consummation. Again, there was a defect on the part of the wife which prevented intercourse and counsel for the husband sought to invoke the reasoning of B v B:

> A connection in this way would no more constitute sexual intercourse than other forms of sexual gratification not within the vagina . . . there is nothing capable of being cured. . . . To amount to consummation there must be normal and natural intercourse, which can only occur within the natural vagina.
>
> (p. 48)

This time, however, the setting up of the ordinary/perverse dichotomy took place with a more explicit reference to male pleasure than had occurred in B v B. Male pleasure *per se* does not matter: 'he could have gratification through unnatural practices or in other orifices of the wife's body but that would not be sexual intercourse' (p. 48). What does matter is 'whether he substantially penetrates the vagina provided by nature for that purpose' – the pleasure is thus to be derived from intercourse. In the case of penetration of an artificial cavity, it was argued, 'in effect he would masturbate himself in an artificial passage. Were this form of connection to be held an act of intercourse the courts would be inviting perverted practice.' (p. 49). Male pleasure, as experienced in and through the penis, is thus made inseparable from the establishment of what 'true' genital connection may be. As for the 'artificial' vagina, 'a great many men would be repelled by a connection of this kind and would be incapable of penetrating the imitation vagina'. Moreover

> the artificiality of the imitation vagina is all important. . . . The best illustration is an artificial eye. It looks all right, but one cannot see with it, and the man with the artificial eye is still commonly regarded as a one-eyed man.
>
> (p. 49–50)

The normative case is made out to be the erectile capacity of an 'ordinary' man. The argument of counsel for the husband orders assessment of the 'natural' quality of a vagina around the issue of first-male pleasure and, second, male pleasure as experienced in and through the penis. Following the analogy with the eye, it is the natural *function* of the artificial vagina which would be thwarted. This function, presumably, is to engage in intercourse or what Ormrod J. was to later refer to as 'the essential role of the woman in marriage' (Corbett v Corbett). The woman with an artificial vagina, presumably, is therefore not a woman at all.

Karminski J. at first instance attempted to distinguish B v B on the facts from SY v SY, stating that 'it is possible to have marriage consummated in [a] case where a woman has created for her an artificial vagina' (p. 46). Throughout the judgement on appeal the court made clear that they were acutely aware of the implications of what they were deciding and, though the court eventually rejected the husband's argument, a familiar essentialism was to recur in the judgement. The importance of the 'natural' quality of the genitals is displaced but, crucially, the search for an essential definition retains a significance – only now 'the all important thing is the *initial* entry into the vagina' (p. 50; my emphasis). Alternatively, given that this clearly contradicts Lushington in D-e v A-g (*op. cit.*), it is said to be significant that the artificial vagina 'would be in the right place' (p. 51). In contrast to the later transsexual cases therefore, where the artifice is denied, here an artificial vagina *is* capable of being penetrated because, it would seem, 'it is in the right place':

> Vera copula . . . can exist even if it be created by a wholly artificial plastic vagina, provided that it occurs in the part of the body where a vagina is normally located.

> (p. 52)

Does this reduce consummation to a matter of geography? Are we then to reject Lushinton's formulae as 'an intolerable burden of dealing in inches' (p. 51)?

The above cases ostensibly concern the female anatomy and physiology. Yet it is a mapping of the sexed male body which signifies what is to be the 'natural' quality of the genitalia. Despite D-e v A-g's status as 'commanding authority', therefore, there is evidently no clear definition of what degree or 'quality' of penetration is required to constitute intercourse in law. In part, this is a

problem of the 'surfeit of truths' (Moran 1990: 158) which result
from the many techniques authorised by law to speak of the body.
Nonetheless, the search for some definitional essence to intercourse pervades the legal determinations of a consummated
marriage. At times it is to be derived from inches of penetration (as
in D-e v A-g), at other times this will be rejected as 'an intolerable
burden of dealing in inches' (SY v SY (Orse W.) [1963] P 37: 51).

Such contradictions abound in the cases on non-consummation.
In a case such as Corbett v Corbett the artificial quality of the genitals
rendered them incapable of 'true' intercourse. Yet, seven years
earlier, in SY v SY (*op. cit.*) we have seen that a surgically extended
vagina, though an 'artifice', was held to be capable of being penetrated because, it would seem, it was 'in the part of the body where the
vagina is normally located' (p. 52). It is difficult to account for the
difference between the two cases. The genital topography in SY v SY
is crude in the extreme but at least it recognises some of the implications of surgical transformation. If, as in in SYv SY, it was considered
difficult to see why the enlargement of a vestigial vagina should be
regarded 'as producing something different in kind from a vagina
artificially created from nothing' (p. 59), in Corbett v Corbett it was
precisely such a 'vagina . . . created from nothing' which faced the
court. On another level, however, there *is* a consistency to be found
here; for what marks out the naturalness, or otherwise, of the genitals
is not so much their relation to transformative surgery as something
much more subjective and difficult to quantify: male sexual pleasure.

Male sexual pleasure

The tension between pleasure and procreation had constituted a
recurring theme in ecclesiastical views of marital sex. By the end of
the sixteenth century at least some theologians had began to
consider that the married couple who have coitus, albeit without
any intention of conception, would not be deemed to be
committing a sin as long as nothing was done to impede
procreation (for example, Thomas Sanchez: D-e v A-g, *op. cit.*:
294). A shift in the Church's view of marital coitus thus entailed a
separation of pleasure and procreation as distinct concepts – at the
same time, paradoxically, as advocating their inseparability in
marital coitus. Tensions around the status of pleasure and procreation were, not surprisingly, replicated in non-consummation
cases.

Civil law has constructed the sexual pleasures to be derived from intercourse as qualitatively different for men and women. Women's sexual pleasure, though recognised, has frequently been constructed in relation to an awareness of the possibilities of conception taking place (for example, REL v REL (Otherwise R) [1948] P 211; 215). It is thus a 'woman's desire for motherhood' which is central to her desire for 'normal' marriage, not her desire for sexual satisfaction *per se*. The 'worthiest sentiments' of the unsatisfied wife are thus constructed as 'a burning desire for motherhood' (Darmon 1985: 103). Generally, female sexuality in law has been considered to be mysterious and has been shrouded by judges in metaphor and unknowability (Barker-Benfield 1976). There is a long tradition, in particular, of female orgasm and virginity as having inspired a poetic vein amongst physicians, churchmen and lawyers (Darmon 1985: 148; Flandrin 1985)

Yet it would be incorrect to claim that the possibility of conception is necessary for consummation to occur. Rather, what is implicit in a case such as Baxter v Baxter [1948] HL 278 is an assumption that without male erection there can be no sexual pleasure. In Cowen v Cowen [1946] P 36, the Court of Appeal had previously declared that

> sexual intercourse cannot be complete when a husband deliberately discontinues the act of intercourse before it has reached its natural termination . . . which is the passage of the male seed into the body of the woman.
>
> (p. 40)

To hold otherwise, it was stated, would be to 'intentionally frustrate' the principal end of matrimony (p. 40). Two years later, in Baxter v Baxter, the court had once again to consider the place of contraceptives when a husband sought an order that the marriage was null and void as a result of the wife's insistence that he wore a sheath (he consented to this, believing that if he did not do so there would be no intercourse at all). The conclusion is very different from Cowen, though the reasoning is similar. Once again we see counsel for the husband presenting male sexual pleasure as central in determining whether intercourse has taken place. Thus, although 'marriage is not consummated by an act designed merely to satisfy carnal lust' (p. 276) what is needed is 'penetration followed by emission of semen and deposit thereof within the vault of the vagina' (p. 276). The wearing of a sheath would thus thwart consummation – 'penetration is merely a preparation for consummation' (p. 277).

Pleasure is significant in this argument; the wearing of the sheath deprives the parties of 'actual contact . . . the woman does not enjoy the circulation of the seminal fluid' (p. 277). This attempt to valorise ejaculation over penetration was rejected by the court in Baxter and the court held that the husband was not entitled to a nullity decree. Frustration of the reproductive function of marriage, therefore, would not amount to non-consummation. However, the search for a verifiable essence to consummation remains:

> The essentials of consummation are erectio, intromissio and ejaculatio, viz, emission in the body of the women. Once these are present there is full intercourse and it does not matter what happens afterwards to the semen.
>
> (p. 279–80)

The test of consummation is 'whether the parties get full physical satisfaction from it, for example, whether an orgasm is produced in the woman' (p. 280). In judgement Viscount Jowllitt quoted the following words from Lord Stair's Institutions (1681: Book 1, para. 6). What is requisite 'is not the consent of marriage as it relateth to the procreation of children'. It is 'the conjunction of bodies as well as minds as the general end of the institution of marriage [it] is the solace and satisfaction of man.' Pleasure is thus given priority over procreation but it is a sexual pleasure which is to be derived from sexual intercourse.

Pleasure has a central place within marital sex, therefore, but it is a specifically *male* sexual pleasure which is central to the process of defining sexual intercourse in this context. Male sexual pleasure is to be derived primarily through the act of penetration (SY v SY (Orse W.) [1963] P 37: 49–50) and we have seen that assumptions have been made about the 'natural' function of an artificial vagina in terms of whether male pleasure will result from such intercourse. The question has been framed in terms of 'what the effect would have been on him'. Would a man 'obtain a large degree of satisfaction'? Would the wife 'get pleasurable sensations which would in turn communicate themselves to the husband'? After all 'a man is not very likely to get much enjoyment from a sexual act if the woman does not share at any rate in some degree with his feelings' (SY v SY: 42).

The anatomy of male pleasure has been located primarily in the penis itself. In some cases it has been as simple as a matter of inches of penetration. The greater the penetration, the greater the pleasure. In R v R (Otherwise F.) [1952] P 1194 a husband petitioned for nullity of marriage, only this time on the grounds of his own incapacity to consummate. He was able to effect an erection with his wife, and full penetration, but was unable to ejaculate. With another woman, however, with whom he had fallen in love, he was able to achieve 'penetration in the fullest sense'. Following the reasoning in Baxter v Baxter (*op. cit.*) the court concluded that it was penetration and not emission which results in consummation: 'only intercourse in the sense of vera copula is necessary to consummate a marriage' (p. 1198). Male pleasure, it appears, is to be derived from penetration but not necessarily emission (see also Willmer J. in White (Otherwise Berry) v White [1948] 2 All ER 151: 155). If a surgically treated vagina will 'admit the male organ and give its possessor sexual satisfaction . . . what ground is left for saying that the wife is incapable of consummating the marriage?' (SY v SY *op. cit.*: 62).

The very absence of male sexual pleasure has been considered problematic; after all, where 'there is not a natural indulgence of natural desire'

> almost of necessity disgust is generated and the probable consequences of other connexions with other men of ordinary self-control become almost certain . . . no man ought to be reduced to quasi-unnatural connexion and consequent temptation.
>
> (D-e v A-g *op. cit.*: 299)

A husband may have to 'submit to the misfortune of a barren wife' (p. 299), but as long as he can still experience pleasure he will not be tempted elsewhere. The dynamic which motivates male sexuality might clearly be expressed in natural or unnatural forms and the problem becomes one of male desire *not* being satisfied.

It is staggering to think that even if a man is admittedly the father of a child which is the result of a sexual relationship with his partner, a marriage may still be held to be unconsummated if 'full' intercourse did not take place. In Clarke (Otherwise Talbot) v Clarke [1943] 2 All ER 540 in the rare case of fecundatio ab extra, conception had taken place without penetration of the vagina. The child (12 years old at the date of the hearing) had been born after a protracted and difficult labour which ended after seventy-two hours with an instrumental delivery under general anaesthetic. Understandably, on such facts, 'the onus of satisfying the court lies heavily on the husband' (p. 541). Nonetheless, the court held the marriage to be unconsummated. There was to be no marriage notwithstanding the birth of a child of which the husband was admittedly the father. Even the difficulty of the birth was taken as evidence of the fact that the mother was a 'frigid woman whose sex life had been abnormal' (p. 543). Pleasure through penetration, it would seem, is more significant in determining consummation than the birth of a child. After sixteen years of marriage and the birth of a child there remains no legally recognised relationship.

This supreme indifference to the mother's perspective has been repeated in other cases. In Dredge v Dredge (Otherwise Harrison) [1947] 1 All ER p. 29 the wife was pregnant by the husband at the time of marriage, though intercourse did not take place following the ceremony. In the end, notwithstanding that a degree of nullity would bastardise the child, then aged 17 at the date of the hearing, the court held that in this case there was no legal marriage by reason of non-consummation. Even birth, it would seem, cannot supplant penetration as signifier of a legally committed relationship. More recently, in the Irish case of UF v JC [1991] 2 Irish Reports 330, a court granted a decree of nullity notwithstanding the birth of a child (aged 9 at the date of hearing) by reason of the 'homosexual nature' and 'incapacity to sustain a normal relationship' of one of the parties.

It is clear from the above cases that what it is that produces male pleasure is uncertain. In the context of legally consummating a marriage, male pleasure may be derived from penetration but not emission. There is implicitly something about the act of intercourse, but not ejaculation, which brings a marriage into being. As Moran (1986) has argued, the taxonomy is much more complicated than simply a matter of inches of penetration. It has involved no less than an assessment of pleasure, performance and person – and it is in this complexity that there lies the significance of the determination: what is potent masculinity?

To clarify: we have seen that simple penetration of somewhere between 3 and 4½ inches of the vagina (D-e v A-g, *op. cit.*) may not be sufficient. It certainly does not lead to a conclusive determination. Elsewhere it it is considered necessary for penetration to take place for an adequate, though unspecified, period of time. In W (Orse K) v W [1967] 1 WLR 1554, the husband was able to penetrate the wife on occassions but only for a short time. Soon after penetration his erection collapsed. The court held that such a penetration of the wife for such a short time and without ejaculation did not amount to ordinary and complete intercourse and was therefore insufficient to consummate the marriage. The judge declared that 'I do not think that there is any authority which binds me to hold that any penetration, however transient, amounts to consummation of marriage' (p. 1555). Indeed, the very frequency of attempts at intercourse on the part of the husband will be taken into account. In G v M [1885] AC 171 the court ascertained that, during the four month period after marriage, intercourse was attempted 'at intervals of two or three days, sometimes less'. The penis is to not just penetrate for a certain length of time; the frequency of attempts at penetration can be significant (see also Mason v Mason [1980] Family Law 144–8; O'Donovan 1993: 48).

Constructing the (im)potent male

What we have in the above cases is a complex assessment of the physical, temporal and performative aspects of sex. Crucially, this has involved establishing a normative sexual practice against which the sexual life of the married couple can be judged. It goes beyond determinations of simple bodily conjunction and to an assessment of the *marital life* itself; and it is at this point – in an assessment of the morphology of the sexually 'dysfunctional' – that a model of (im)potent masculinity emerges within and as an object of the judicial assessment of coitus. The focus on genital conjunction proving insufficient (out of kilter with discourses of normalisation concerned with the disciplining of the body, subjectivity, desire), the framing of the question shifts to a focusing on establishing sexual intercourse in terms of what it is not; or, more to the point, through constructing a model of the virile man in terms of what *he* is not: impotent.

It is in this way that we find in the cases judges moving away from a concern with establishing the physical essence of intercourse (defining an act) and instead moving towards an ostensibly more complicated but ultimately more productive and, for the judges, more liberating matter of ascertaining what actually might constitute an (im)potent male (establishing a person). What is he like? Well, he is not like us. What we are dealing with here is no less than the construction of a sexual being, a transgressive, deviant and

unacceptable masculinity, a masculinity which negates the hegemonic, potent ideal. It is not surprising that such a man, through
knowingly marrying, should be 'guilty of a most wicked and
abominable act' or a 'cruel wrong' (G v M [1885] AC 171 p. 207,
p. 202). It is a 'grave and wounding imputation' that a man is
impotent, the denial of a power 'which is commonly and rightly
considered to be the most characteristic quality of manhood' (per
Birkenhead L.C. C (Otherwise H) v C [1921] P 399, p. 400). He
offends religion and his wife's happiness; in other contexts judges
have ridden roughshod over women's feelings in the consummation cases. The impotent man, however, shifts this focus as a
rare sympathy for the married woman appears: 'few women can
endure indefinitely without serious injury to health' the strain and
humiliation of an impotent spouse (REL v REL (Otherwise R)
[1948] P 211).

A number of familiar elements of hegemonic masculinity
emerge here which retain a popular cultural and contemporary
resonance. Indeed, it has been suggested that

> the persistence and increased use of the stress inducing label
> impotence reflects a significant moment in the social construc-
> tion of male sexuality. The factors that create this moment
> include the increasing importance of life-long sexual activity in
> one's life, the insatiability of the mass media for appropriate
> sexual topics, the expansionist needs of speciality medicine and
> new medical technology, and the highly demanding male
> sexual script.
>
> (Tiefer 1987: 166)

Foremost amongst these is a presumption of male sexual activity/
initiation. Though he may be impotent a man is not to resort to what
Honoré (1978: 105) termed 'the passive role of the woman in intercourse'. Thus, to 'stimulate an impotent spouse' would be 'unnatural
to a sensitive woman' (REL (Otherwise R) v REL [1948] P 211, p.
214). An erection is to occur without such manual assistance therefore. Male sexual activity and initiation are thus presumed and,
indeed, advocated (S v S [1954] P 736, p. 739–40) as psychological
and physical techniques to promote male virility are judicially
endorsed (REL (Otherise R) v REL [1948] P 211, p. 212–3).

The male/active, female/passive dualism is enmeshed in the
familiar rhetoric of the 'reasonable man'. Implicitly, the normative
model of masculinity involves a rational calculation of sexual

propriety. Has the husband resorted to appropriate attempts to remedy the situation? What actions would he be justified in resorting to (G v M [1885] AC 171, p. 200)? He might have 'tried all means short of force' but

> it is permissible to wish that some gentle violence had been employed; if there had been it would either have resulted in success or would have precipitated a crisis so decided as to have made our task a comparitively easy one . . . [the husband] felt any attempt with even mild or gentle force would only hinder and not help the end he desired.
>
> (G v G [1924] AC 349, p. 357)

In this case simply 'loosening his pyjamas' was insufficient to manifest sexual intent (p. 362). What would a 'reasonable' husband do in such circumstances (G v M *op. cit.*, p. 193)? It is for the court to 'ask ourselves as reasonable men and apply . . . our experience of the ordinary circumstances of life to the case' (G v M [1885] AC 171). What is to be inferred when there is no intercourse after

> a man of fifty . . . married a young woman of twenty, described as handsome, desirable and one who is likely to create passionate sensation and lives with her for a period of at least two months?
>
> (p. 283)

He had 'one year and six months of lying beside this desirable young woman without even making an attempt to exercise his rights' (p. 208). What, then, did this say about him? What had been his sexual practices when younger (p. 176)? If he did masturbate when younger, why did he give it up (p. 200)? The 'reasonable man', it seems, might be found on the Clapham Omnibus, in the marriage bed or engaged in more solitary activities.

Indeed, the reasonableness of the man of law knows no bounds, particularly when it comes to ascribing sexualised meanings to the corporeality of women. The wife herself becomes an object of the representational process in constructing the reasonableness of male desire. Would the 'reasonable man' consider the wife in question to be attractive? In G v M she was considered to be a 'very handsome young woman of twenty . . . handsome, desirable, and one who is likely to create passionate sensation.' But what if she was not? Would male reluctance to penetrate then be considered understandable by the court?[2]

Implicitly, female attractiveness presumed the existence of a sexual relationship whilst proximity and male sexual hunger denote female frigidity. Thus, in Clarke (Otherwise Talbolt) v Clarke [1943] P 540, the 'frigid' Mrs Clarke was said to 'have no recollection of a number of matters which she cannot possibly have forgotten' (p. 543). Her 'aversion to the sexual act' was testified to by 'a desire for personal adornment and material possessions' (p. 543–4). The court, 'having found nothing which prevents me from concluding that Mr Clarke is telling the truth' (p. 545), constructed a difficult labour as signifier of frigidity both before and after the birth of a child.

A similar doubt is cast on the evidence of the 'frigid' (and hysterical?) wife in B v B [1955] P 42 (p. 47) and S v S [1954] P 736 (p. 738), illustrating the deep ambivalence to female sexuality evident throughout the consummation cases. Though the wife of the impotent male may be deserving of sympathy (being denied motherhood), one wonders what it might be about 'the shameful parts of women' which so disturbs the judges. The sexualisation of the corporeality of women serves to divert attention from the fragility of the potent/impotent dualism and renders problematic

> the violent force by which man feels himself drawn to the woman, and side by side with his longing, the dread that through her he might die and be undone.
>
> (Horney 1967a: 134; see also Horney 1967b; Hoch 1979: 68–71)

The denial of women's subjectivity has been perhaps most clear in relation to the fiction of the wife's permanent consent to sexual intercourse with her husband. This myth, in effect denying the wife legal autonomy over her body, had been accorded reverence by generations of judges until the recent R v R [1991].[3] She might have been able to withdraw consent for certain sexual acts (such as forced fellatio; R v Kowaliski [1987] 86 CAR, p. 339–4). In the case of intercourse, however, consent, once given, was irrevocable. The belief rested on a similar sexual reportoire to that which we can see in the non-consummation cases whereby it is a man's

> irrevocable privilege to have sexual intercourse with her during such time as the ordinary relations created by such contract subsist between them.
>
> (Hawkins J. in R v Clarence [1888] 22 QBD 22; O'Donovan
> 1993: 3)

What can be found in law is, in effect, a presumption of inter-course. This has been endorsed in a succession of cases which establish the legal fiction that given certain circumstances (proximity/attractiveness/opportunity) it will be presumed that intercourse will have occurred (for example, Dennis v Dennis [1955] 2 All ER 51, p. 53; Sapsford v Sapsford and Furtado [1954] P 394). Whether it did or did not is, of course, another matter. To make a case for the absence of intercourse it may become necessary to rebutt the presumption that intercourse would, given certain circumstances, 'naturally' take place. Implicitly it is the 'nature' of the male to have, and to seek, sexual intercourse (O'Donovan 1993: 67).

What we can see from these cases is no less than a picture of the psychology and physiology of the non-virile male. As Moran (1990: 165) has argued, this historical shift involved a transition from a concern with the performing of the *act* of intercourse to the constitution of the *identity* of a non-virile man.[4] In R v R (Otherwise F) [1952] P 1994 the court recounted at length the character and sexual history of the impotent male, noting his '. . . numerous illnesses . . . bronchitis, pneumonia, an operation on his ear, removal of glands in the neck and a complicated operation on the right groin' (p. 1195). He had been brought up in 'rather straight-laced circumstances'. Apart from 'the usual involuntary nocturnal emission', 'he showed very little interest in matters of sex'. In fact, penetration had been achieved in this case; the medical history related to his inability to ejaculate. Similarly, in G v G [1885] AC 171, although the court considered that 'it is not at all unusual for a man to fail within the first weeks of marriage' (p. 177), here was a

> nervous, bashful man, of delicate feeling, quiet and retiring, and it may be with want of passion and want of will, and therefore more easily repelled than a man of more violent temperament.
>
> (p. 178)

He was 'guilty of a most wicked and abominable act' (p. 281), a 'cruel wrong' (p. 202) and had subjected her to 'disgusting treat-ment' (p. 206). Had he any regard for her he would not have married (p. 203) and subjected her to such 'treatment degrading in the highest degree' (p. 206). Here, truly, was a husband that is emasculate, cold, languid, frozen to the marrow, and who can do nought of what he has promised his wife is the very quintessence of misfortune.

(D'Arreac, quoted by Darmon 1985: 62)

A concern with the act and identity converge in the cases on non-consummation. What we see is a man marked by a history of ill-health (R v R (Otherwise F) [1952] P 1194, p. 1195), a man whose sexual character and history exist to be assessed by the court; a man who is, thus disempowered, not really a man at all. The representations of potent masculinity which emerge from these cases are deeply phallocentric and if culturally sex is equated with intercourse then impotence can be seen to negate the sexual ideal itself. The double-edged nature of the (ever present) threat of impotence in these cases is proof that patriarchy can turn on those who betray its power and, most importantly, its secrets.

On the one hand the law is defining the norms by which implicitly every man might be able to confirm his potency. This is achieved through excluding from marriage the impotent man who is, in this sense, not a man at all (the man who is not potent). Kelley (1981: 126) captures well the signifying power of impotence in constructing masculinity:

The word impotent is used to describe the man who does not get an erection, not just his penis. When a man is told by his doctor that he is impotent or when the man turns to his partner and says he is impotent they are saying a lot more than that the penis cannot become erect.

(Quoted in Tiefer 1987: 165)

It has become almost a truism to say that men do not 'talk about their feelings' and are 'expected' to be 'strong and silent' (above p. 19). However, masculinity is much more complex than this rather simplistic language of emotional impoverishment implies. Men's social presence generally has been constructed through reference to the power they embody as men, their potential for activity. It is a combination of force, skill and the irresistable occupation of space as an expression of power which constitutes adult masculinity (Berger 1972; Connell 1983). The constructions of masculinity in the cases above do not stand apart, therefore, from this more general construction of the space and physicality of the male body. A nexus of body, space and power pervades the legal construction of male heterosexuality just as the 'sexual fix' of compulsory heterosexuality (Heath 1983: 2) itself constitutes the norm of commodified sexuality.

As 'victims' of the mythology of virility, the judges who pronounce on the bodies of women and men in these cases paradoxically testify to their own vulnerability and to the empowerment of a male subjectivity constituted through the 'natural' discourse of male sexuality. This masculinity does not just come about; it is ordered, regulated and sustained through discourses, such as law, which construct sexual pleasure through a normative mapping of the body in such a way as to valorise, and negate, certain sexual practices (note, for example, the ways in which the issue of consent is dispensed with in R v Brown [1993] 2 WLR 556). In the unconsummated marriage the abstracted legal concept and the experiential are integrated: failure to achieve sexual intercourse entails failure to enter the 'truly' married state. The unconsummated marriage thus transgresses the legal/institutional (conjugal) and social/subjective (experiential) norm, be the 'cause' of the maladaption on the part of the husband or the wife.

THE SOCIAL AND LEGAL CONSTRUCTION OF MALE SEXUALITY

The reading of heterosexuality presented above must be seen in the wider context of shifting strategies of normalisation which have been concerned with the constitution of the social body and the construction of 'the family' as a 'private' domain (Donzelot 1980; Minson 1985: 180–218: Chapter 2). From the mid-eighteenth century, Foucault has argued, it is possible to trace a class creating its own sexuality and forming a specific body based on it, a '"class" body with its health, hygiene, descent, and race; the autosexualisation of its body, the incarnation of sex in its body, the endogamy of sex and the body' (Foucault 1981: 124). What was also created was a knowledge of male sexuality 'as naturally active, penetrative, as forming the identity of the male . . . the key to a man's constitution, his character' (O'Donovan 1993: 67). This is a key stage of the construction of 'normal' masculinity in law.

The historical transformations of the nineteenth and twentieth centuries in relation to homosexuality and heterosexuality have involved a complex interdiscursive nexus of law, medicine, psychology and psychoanalysis; they have involved religion, science and sex, all (though in different ways) concerned with speaking of the body and revealing the 'truth' of our beings through our sexual status (Laqueur 1990). In the process of familialisation the body has been constituted as a surface upon which these multivarious discourses have provided a vocabulary, a way of talking, about sexuality (Gallagher and Laqueur 1987). But, crucially, this vocabulary has been open to those privileged to read through the empowered discourses of the 'psy' professions (Smart 1989a: 15) – of medicine, of the doctor, the surgeon, sexologist, the social worker, psychologist and psychoanalyst. That is, by those who have been privileged to reveal, to assess and construct what we have been, what we are and what we might become. The languages through which the body has been put into discourse have been derived from outside law, but they have been mediated through the power of law and the judicial gaze to determine what is, and what is not, of relevance for legal discourse.

This process has been both simultaneously subtle and crude. The criteria according to which the mapping of the body has taken place have not been sufficiently sophisticated as to begin to engage with the experiential/subjective nature of the structuring of emotional cathexis. They have been unable to integrate the complexities and contradictions within the psycho-sexual constitution of subjectivity in such a way that might accommodate the subjective gender of the transsexual, for example. The ordering is more precise, simple and clear-cut than that. It is genito-centric, heterosexual and familial. I have argued elsewhere (Collier 1992a) that there are five assumptions around sexual intercourse in law: sex is natural; what is natural is heterosexual; genital sex is primary and determining; 'true' sexual intercourse is phallocentric; and sex is something which takes place in marriage.

At the centre of this ordering is the privileged status of heterosexual intercourse in the institution of marriage. The transsexual, the homosexual and the impotent, all those who speak 'with the greatest precision [of] whatever is most difficult to tell' (Foucault 1981: 59), declare more than their ontological status and identity. They speak of the sexuality of the new social order itself. The exhortations to normative (hetero)sexuality so frequently propagated by judges, the dangers of deviancy stressed by sexologists and the general cultural advocation of the pleasures of heterosexuality together constitute a political economy of heterosexuality, a complex vocabulary which has been concerned to privilege one specific form of heterosexual marital relation. However, we must remember that the transformations of the late nineteenth century towards a more refined social regulation of extra-marital sexuality should not be understood in terms of a straightforward programme of 'social control' of a particular population, be they homosexual, unmarried or a sex-group in general (Foucault 1981: 103).

The social values and norms to which the body is used as a point of entry within this area of legal discourse are primarily phallocentric and heterosexual. This model of male sexuality, and the centrality of penetrative sex within this economy, continues today. It is not the archaic relic of a bygone age. In Britain, in what became known as the 'virgin mother' controversy in 1991, the objections to single women having children through artificial insemination (and, in particular, in those cases where the woman was a virgin) rested on the fact that the practice involved conception without penetration (for example, *The Guardian* 12 March 1991; *Daily Mail* 12 March 1991). It was motherhood *without men*, or more specifically without penetration, which was the real affront to the curious alliance of the 'pro-family' Right and the anti-abortionist lobby who objected to insemination in these cases. The heterosexual imperative was inscribed in the debates around legal change which followed.

What does this mean for the theorising of law and gender? The representations of male sexuality in law discussed in this and the preceding chapter, far from being preconstituted, unmediated artefacts, constitute a nexus of the physical and cognitive realms, of knowledge and experience of self and society and of those ideas in which individual subjectivity has been articulated and constituted (Rose 1987: 73). In the constitution of desire and sexuality it has been through the modalities of power, through languages of injunction/prohibition, pain/pleasure, natural/unnatural and order/disorder that legal discourse has been an important (but not the only) site within which intertextual constructions of sexuality have been produced and reproduced. Legal discourse remains a productive site for numerous exhortations of sexual difference and the appropriateness of certain forms of male and female sexual response. I have argued in this chapter that this history of male sexuality in law has been marked by a transformation in the technology of judicial surveillance of the sexed body (Moran 1990); a transformation of which the contours are now beginning to be mapped. The continuing significance of law in all this is perhaps best located in its continuing power within a complex unity which has been, and remains, involved in the opening up of the body to speech and to practice, to the constitution of the body and desire as objects of power and resistance. For this reason the analysis presented in this chapter constitutes a tentative beginning of the (re)writing of the relationship between male sexuality, masculinity and legal discourse.

CONCLUDING REMARKS

With regard to both the formation and the termination of marriage the meaning of sexual intercourse in law is far from clear. Generally, judges have constructed the male and female body in a crudely genito-centric manner focused around a phallocentric order and penis-use, resorting in the past to extensive medical examination in order to determine whether penetration had been possible. The context of nullity is very different today but the model of male sexuality implicit in these cases (we shall see in the following chapters) retains a contemporary purchase. The velvet glove of normalisation may have distanced itself from the crudity of the medical examinations which occurred in non-consummation cases well into the twentieth century but, enmeshed within the rhetoric of discipline, subjective commitment and control, the phallocentric imperative remains in place. Within this matrimonial 'penile economy' (Moran 1986) the law continues to reify the polymorphous possibilities of the body in a particular way, structuring emotional cathexis into a particular act (intercourse) and a particular part of the male body (the penis). Darmon (1985) is here writing regarding the impotency trials of pre-revolutionary France, but the conclusion applies equally in this context:

> Phallocentric indoctrination was so pervasive that it generated an irresistable need to reaffirm the figure of the virile male, and so the normal and the abnormal were systematically polarised.
>
> (Darmon 1985: 13)

Within this area of legal discourse the phallus has assumed the status of physical and psycho-sexual nexus of essential manhood, the quintessance of virility (Reynaud 1983). The penis is, on the above reading of the cases, the foundation upon which is built the marriage institution; without a 'functioning' penis there can be no marriage. Upon male pleasure, to be realised in a certain form, marriage depends. Or, as Helena Wright put it in 1937, 'nature has endowed every normal person with sex powers; the institution of marriage exists to satisfy all of them' (1937: 62). This is notwithstanding the fact that the institution of marriage is grounded in gender and society, not biology, and is historically variable. Indeed, the fact that the very legal definition, history and sociology of the family is unclear and contentious should alert us to the contingencies of (re)constructing familial histories in any particular ideological way (Poulter 1979). Within the process of the familialisation of society a piece of legislation such as Lord Hardwicke's Marriage Act of 1753 (Parker 1987) constitutes just one, albeit significant, moment. The shifts in the regulation of the point of entry to marriage and the institutionalising of the marital (hetero)sexual economy outlined in this chapter constitutes, I would argue, another such moment in the familialising of society. We have seen that the masculinist heterosexual economy is constructed through dichotomies and hierarchies more complex than a simple heterosexual/homosexual dualism. Within the parameters of matrimonial phallocentrism the legal treatment of sexual intercourse has involved not just the fissuring of the categories of the heterosexual/homosexual self but also the bifurcation of heterosexual masculinity itself into a virile/non-virile variant.

There are a number of more general implications to be derived from this reading of male heterosexuality in law. I have argued in this and the preceding chapter that deconstructing heterosexuality involves challenging the ideology of masculinism and questioning the interplay of law, gender and power within a division of labour and structure of emotion which has involved the institutionalised differentiation of male and female sexualities. On this division the reproduction of a sexual economy, an institutional order and a historically specific government of the self has been predicated. It is through seeking to explore further 'the emergence of male heterosexual sexuality within the institution of marriage' (Moran 1990: 171) that legal studies have now begun to fragment the model of unitary and monolithic heterosexuality which is to be found in law and in so doing have began to make visible that which was hitherto an absent presence; that is, the contingent, socially constructed and political nature of heterosexual familial relations in law (Hanscombe and Humphries 1987).

It has been a central argument of this chapter that the constitution of the family domain has been achieved in such a way as to historically entwine male authority with a construction of the male sexual imperative which rests on phallocentric presuppositions. The representations of heterosexuality in law discussed above are not necessarily consistent. They are mediated, infinite and bound up within the play of power relations. Above all they are political. Alternative social organisation is always possible and sexuality and social dis/order is reconstituted in every social interaction: gender itself

> is an identity tenuously constituted in time, instituted in an exterior space through a stylised repetition of acts . . . the mundane way in which bodily gestures, movements and styles of various kinds constitute the illusion of an abiding gendered self.
>
> (Butler 1990: 140).

At their best, recent studies of gender and power have begun to address the realities, the constraints and the possibilities of social *practice*. The legal structuring of heterosexual familial relations – what Helena Wright termed the *Art of Living the Married Life* back in 1937 – remains fundamental to an institutional order which continues to generate such inequalities. In questioning the politics of sexual identity, feminism, gay and lesbian studies and critical studies of masculinism have sought to resist this order and the oppressions of hegemonic masculinity and to rewrite the past, the present and the future of sexuality and the body. However, in constituting an overt anti-feminist 'backlash' (for example, see Ableman 1983; Amiel 1991; Andrew Stephen *The Observer* December 1991; Lyndon 1992)[5] the resurgence of naturalistic accounts of male sexuality have served only to obfuscate further one of the central dynamics of male power and prerogative – the continuing power and legitimacy of an ideology of male sexuality.

Through addressing historical change and continuity in the social and legal construction of masculinity it becomes possible to challenge those naturalistic and anti-feminist accounts of male sexuality which negate what Butler (1990) has called the 'performative character' of gender and the 'performative possibilities for proliferating gender configurations outside the restricting frames of masculinist domination and compulsory heterosexuality' (Butler 1990: 141; see also Rich 1980). Displacing discourses of gender premised on a masculinist, heterosexual imperative involves opening out to contest and resistance the body as politically regulated surface, a celebration of the contingencies and possibilities of challenge to the meanings of the phallocentric cultural context through which the subjective experiences of desire are articulated.

Critical studies of the construction of gendered subjectivity in law must begin, not from the pre-theoretical categories of male/female, masculinity/femininity, but by locating the body in its cultural context and seeking out the body as signifying practice in discourse, the body as a fluidity, a surface with a past, a present and a future; that is, a body which transcends the ontological status of 'being' and is grounded firmly, not in grand theories of oppression, but in the realities of social practice, yet mindful throughout of whose reality that may be.

Chapter 5

The 'good father' in law
Authority, work and the reconstruction of fatherhood

INTRODUCTION

The following two chapters are concerned with historical change in representations of familial masculinity. In this chapter I shall argue that fatherhood has, from the late nineteenth century to the present day, been 'modernised' in law and that, in this process, it has in important respects been rendered 'safe'. However, I wish to suggest that this reconstituted paternal masculinity remains bound up within discourses which both continue to construct fatherhood as involving specific claims to power and authority within the family (the focus of this chapter), and separate out this 'safe' paternal masculinity from other 'dangerous', extra-familial masculinities (the concern of Chapter 6). The ways in which the law has sought to incorporate hitherto extra-familial masculinities into the familial domain, at the same time as the institutional and ideological supports of the traditional patriarchal father have come under increasing attack, has led to a belief that modern paternal masculinity is itself in a state of 'crisis'. This belief, I shall argue, is mistaken.

Aspects of both 'dangerous' and 'familial' masculinities have been constructed in law as signifying (and celebrating) certain attributes which the judicial gaze has designated as appropriately 'masculine' in different contexts. However, for all the law's endeavours to bifurcate masculine subjectivities (through, I shall argue, resorting to the concept of a 'family man' in law who is, a priori, considered 'safe' and desirable), the dangerous and the familial share much more than is commonly acknowledged. At times that which is dangerous (for example men's violence, certain transgressive sexual behaviour) filters through (or 'leaks into') the familial domain. In different contexts certain values which are traditionally culturally considered to be 'masculine' (for example, competitiveness, a certain machismo, aggression) may be either celebrated or reviled depending on contingencies of class, timing and locale.[1] This chapter seeks to explore the nature of these connections through investigating the archaeology of this 'family man' in law.

Through addressing the emergence at a specific historical moment of the idea of modern fatherhood this chapter seeks to explore the legal rights and responsibilities of fathers, both married and unmarried. There is to be found in law a form of paternal masculinity which has been constructed through reference to historically and culturally specific ideas of masculine authority and masculinity as an economic resource within a sexual economy of hierarchic heterosexuality. The fatherhoods which exist in legal discourse have embodied this model of male subjectivity which has, in its effects, been central to the reproduction of the economic and familial order of gender hierarchy and compulsory heterosexuality.

What is interesting in the context of debates about family law in the early 1990s is that it is feminism which continues to be singled out as the 'cause' of a number of tensions around fatherhood. Yet the contradictions which exist in the construction of paternal masculinity in fact have a long history. They can be traced back to the contours of the construction of the modern father in law, and the re-drawing of the division between public and private in liberal legal discourse which took place in the late nineteenth and early twentieth centuries. It has been suggested that 'as our historical understanding of fatherhood increases, so will our ability to understand the present' (Richards 1987: 33–4). The historical modernising of fatherhood should not be seen as a liberalising, or de-gendering, of law. It is, rather, part of the more general *modernising of masculinity* which we have seen in Chapter 5. Before looking at the history of fatherhood in law, however, it is worthwhile examining some aspects of the contemporary context which has seen fatherhood, and the question of whether families do indeed 'need fathers', become increasingly problematic.

'MEN'S STUDIES' AND 'NEW FATHERS': CONSTRUCTING A CLIMATE OF CHANGE AND CRISIS

A concern with fatherhood has been central to many of the studies of men and masculinities which have emerged during the past decade. As we have seen in Chapter 1 there is no one politics or method to this burgeoning literature on masculinity. It should not surprise us therefore that such a political and methodological diversity is also replicated in accounts of fatherhood and masculinity. Nonetheless, a primary theme in the construction of the 'masculinity problematic' outlined above has been underlying assumptions that, first, masculinity is undergoing a profound change and, second, that this change is linked to a shift in the status of fatherhood. Crucially, this 'crisis' has been identified as having a specifically legal dimension in that it is a perceived breakdown of traditional masculine authority in relation to the family, and around men's relationships with women and children, which has become both the cause and the symptom of such a crisis. The relation between the two, however, is far from clear. Is it the cause of the crisis or does it indicate a deeper, underlying transformation in the family? Indeed, how can it be both the symptom and cause of this masculine crisis simultaneously?

On one level there is nothing new about this. Debates around fatherhood and legal change are well established in the politics of family law reform in England and Wales. From the reform of the divorce laws sought by the Campaign For Justice On Divorce in the late 1970s and early 1980s (Allan 1982; Alcock 1984), through to the joint custody campaigns of the 1980s and the continued (and, it appears, increasingly controversial) campaigns of Families Need Fathers in the 1990s,[2] it has been a perceived diminution of men's legal rights in relation to women, children and property which has been singled out for critique by those who have sought to argue that the law has now swung too far in favour of its 'spoilt darling'. This is, in essence, the heart of the argument of an international father's rights movement which has contended that fathers now get a 'raw deal' from the law. When allied to a 'pro-family', new right political perspective it is feminism itself which is seen as seeking to 'sack father' from the modern family (Morgan 1986; Anderson and Dawson 1986b).

In the early 1990s, prompted in part by the pervasive and powerful (if empirically questionable) ideology of the 'new fatherhood' (McKee and O'Brien 1982a; Lewis 1986; Lewis and O'Brien 1987; Smart 1989b; Brannen and Moss 1990), the politics of both family law and fatherhood have become enmeshed. Both the 'new fatherhood' ideology and the 'sociology of masculinity' genre have held out a belief that the modern father is indeed different from previous generations. It is in debates around family law reform, however, that these contested ideas of fatherhood have come to the fore.[3]

The example of child custody

In recent years analyses of the gendered juridification of child custody (Sevenhuijsen 1992) have prompted feminists to question both the masculinism of matrimonial law and the gendering of legal assessments of parenting capacity (Smart and Sevenhuijsen 1989). The legislation covering the future residence of children in England and Wales is formally gender-neutral (Matrimonial Causes Act 1973; Children Act 1989). Nonetheless, pre-1989 Children Act[4] research produced the generally consistent finding that it was mainly mothers who both claimed and obtained custody of children – whatever their status in the divorce petition. It was also clear that contested custody cases were very much the exception. With maintaining the continuity of care having 'overwhelming importance' (Bromley and Lowe 1987: 327), in the vast majority of cases what the courts were doing, therefore, was not so much determining whether the mother or father is the more 'appropriate' parent as simply making orders confirming the existing situation (Eekelaar *et al.* 1977). Around a mere six per cent of cases are eventually contested in court. Far from 'giving' care and control to the mother rather than the father, therefore, legal intervention has tended to simply confirm the existing division of labour in childcare. This is a division in which mothers have found themselves juggling with childcare responsibilities whilst participating in the workforce in ever greater numbers (Central Statistical Office 1991: Ch. 2).

In a minority of cases it became clear that some fathers were not obtaining custody even though they sought it (Maidment 1984). This, it was argued, was a result of judicial reliance on an out-dated view of gender roles which had no place in a society where women and men were, to all intents and purposes, equal in law. With this grievance articulated in the UK by groups such as Families Need Fathers, in the 1980s the issue took on a high public profile. Meanwhile, internationally, a range of other fathers' rights groups were similarly seeking to promote men's interests through engaging with law reform. One result has been to render it no longer possible for child custody to be constructed as an apolitical research topic, to be studied neutrally (for example through the gaze of the positivist and reformist 'socio-legal' scholar). Rather, it must be seen as an important part of the gender politics of family law itself (Brophy 1985; Brophy and Smart 1985; Sevenhuijsen 1986; Smart and Sevenhuijsen 1989).

All of this brings us to a paradox in the developing critique of masculinity – for child custody is also an area which exemplifies the tensions and contradictions within men's responses to feminism in a more general way. On one hand we have explicitly anti-feminist organisations, such as Families Need Fathers, which have drawn on the rhetoric of 'men's liberation' and, in the name of 'equal rights', have sought to extend the rights of all fathers in relation to children. At the same time, as we have seen in Chapter 1, a range of anti-sexist critiques of masculinism have also sought to challenge traditional notions of parenting and encourage men to take a greater role in child care (Hearn 1983). The cultural legitimation of the new father-hood ideology, which has had a significance and purchase which belies its foundation in any real changes in parenting practices, has further confused the picture through asserting that men are more involved in childcare than before – notwithstanding the fact that considerable disparities of power and status in marriage belie any notion that men and women are now truly 'equal'.

The last point is most important. The premise that men and women are now 'equal' in marriage is deeply problematic, as we shall see. In relation to financial provision on divorce and separa-tion, for example, the legal supplanting of 'need' with 'contri-bution' as the primary distributive concept has led some feminists to question how family law has functioned to ignore the material circumstances of divorcing women and children; what is a 'nice neat instance of conceptual progress to legal academics and law reformers does not necessarily help women's lives' (Fineman 1991a: 269). What *appears* to be a legal policy designed to advance 'equality' might, in reality, operate to the detriment of women through an insensitivity to the needs that motherhood and tradi-tional marriage create. As Fineman notes, 'need has no role to play in a true partnership of equals' (Fineman 1991a: 271). The rhetoric of equality, bolstered by a belief in the 'new fatherhood' and a reconstituted paternal masculinity, sits uneasily with the realities of the lives of many women and men.

Let us be clear what we are dealing with here. This apparent paradox around ostensibly 'progressive' fathering has been central to the double-edged nature, not just of the new fatherhood ideology, but also the recent growth of interest in masculinity itself. Yet it is also against this context that the generating idea of masculine 'crisis' (which may have both progressive and regressive resonances from a feminist perspective) has been constructed through reference to the formal *legal* rights of men and women. It has *not* been concerned with seeking to analyse and understand the historical background to these contemporary cultural in-securities around sexuality, gender and the family (notably under the sign of Aids). Instead, what has tended to happen has been an elision of the ideas of 'men's studies' and 'new fatherhood' which has in turn served to legitimate the reading of the historical development of fatherhood within the terms of a concern with the legal rights of individual men (thus men may be constructed as the 'victims' of feminism which has gone 'too far' in unbalancing hitherto 'equal' rights). Also this elision has deflected attention from the cultural climate in which the gender configurations of legal discourse and shifting representations of fatherhood have themselves been produced.

Against this background, the re-emphasis on fatherhood which has taken place in the late 1980s and early 1990s has tended to contrast a reconstituted paternal masculinity and the 'confusions' of the modern father with a pre-modern and 'authoritarian' (and 'sexist') father. The former becomes both product and signifier of 'post-feminist' equality; he is entrenched in legal reforms and popular culture as the 'new man' in the family. At times the 'new father' and 'new man' ideals have found it difficult to walk the tightrope of simultaneously celebrating masculinity and male (hetero)sexuality (Chapman 1988; Collier 1992b) whilst main-taining a fundamentally liberal anti-sexist position. The question is, how might we make sense of the tensions and contradictions which surround contemporary fatherhood, and which are testified to by the plethora of recent texts addressing the subject (Dorris 1990; Lee 1991; Corneau 1991; French 1992; Hoyland; 1992)?[5]

It is worthwhile looking at how the law has historically con-structed the relationship between fatherhood, paternal authority and male economic power. In particular, we need to explore how, through the processes of naturalising masculinity *per se*, hetero-sexual men generally have been constituted as subjects of a dis-course of paternal masculinity which constructs masculine subjectivity in such a way that the vast majority of men are not likely to want to be primary carer of their children.

To recap: at issue here are contested ideas of fatherhood and paternal masculinity which have become the currency in which a number of issues about law reform have been articulated. Yet fatherhood, as an interdiscursive construct, is at once both a public and a private concept. It is through trangressing this public/private division (see Chapter 2) and exploring its historical constitution in legal discourse that it is possible to open out to analysis an important, though curiously neglected, part of how the ideological division between men's public and private citizenship has been constructed in law. It is through charting the historical development of fatherhood in law and the shift from the 'premodern' to modern father that we might begin to make sense of some of the contradictions which pervade the legal construction of fatherhood in law. First we must ask ourselves – what do we mean by fatherhood?

ESTABLISHING PATERNITY

It is not so strange that I love you with my whole heart, for being a father is not a tie which can be ignored. Nature in her wisdom has attached the parent to the child and bound them together with a Herculean knot.

(Sir Thomas More 1517, quoted in Simpson *et al.* 1993: 1)

There are no more Knights of the open road, carrying or abandoning mate and offspring according to mere whim. Once a man has become a member of the wedding . . . once he has become a father, no matter how fleeting the connection, he is responsible in law to his partner and to his offspring. He is accountable. He has become part of the great chain of human relationships, with its ineluctable dependencies.

(Katz and Inker 1979: 13)

What is a father? Over the past twenty years the changes which have taken place in the familial and economic order of many western societies have, for some, marginalised fatherhood to such a degree that 'the social and indeed physical reproduction of the family are now possible without the continuity of role and person which fatherhood once implied' (Simpson *et al.* 1993: 1). In contrast to the bond between father and family evoked by the image of a 'Herculean knot', the father has instead been characterised as 'hanging on by his fingernails: socially, economically and emotionally obsolete' (ibid.: 1993). All of this is a far cry from the image of paternal responsibility depicted by Katz and Inker. Formally, at least, it is true that when a man becomes a father he becomes 'responsible in law to his partner and his offspring. He is accountable.' Whether he is 'responsible', for example by paying maintenance, is a different question. In seeking to render men accountable in the 'great chain of human relationships' it has been through reference to the legal concept of paternity that the nature of men's responsibility 'to his partner and to his offspring' has been established. At the outset, therefore, law has been fundamental in establishing paternity. Such a need to determine paternal status – to establish whether or not a man is for legal purposes the biological father of a child – has arisen in a number of different contexts. Whether he is to be subject to any maintenance obligations or what legal rights (if any) he may have in relation to the children will all depend on establishing his paternal status. From the child's perspective inheritance, nationality and succession rights might all depend on whether a link can be established with a particular man.

This might seem straightforward. The problem has been, however, that establishing biological paternity *per se* is not and has never been in itself sufficient to entitle a man to the legal rights and duties which come with parenthood (see further Smart 1987). Although recent developments in reproductive technologies have rendered the legal status of motherhood increasingly problematic (Stanworth 1987b), establishing an authoritative determination of paternity (proving the biological link) has historically posed considerable problems for legal systems. The importance of a man needing to be sure that a particular child is 'his' has, not surprisingly, been accorded a central place within a legal system in which property rights based on ownership and inheritance have traditionally passed through the male line. Within such a system of patrilineal, primogenital ordering, establishing with some degree of certainty a biological connection between a man and a child has assumed great importance.

In common law the 'illegitimate' child was the 'child of no one'. S/he was a stranger in law to the father, the mother and all other natural relatives; 'being nullius filius, he is therefore of kin to nobody, and has no ancestor from whom any inheritable blood can be derived' (Blackstone 1765). The concern with establishing the identity of a legitimate heir had led in the thirteenth century to the Statute of Merton (1234), an act which excluded the illegitimate child from inheriting the property of the father. By the mid-sixteenth century, and in order to avoid the unsupported child and mother becoming a charge on the parish, legislation imposed penalties on the parents; in particular, the unmarried woman would not be examined in order to establish who was the father of her child (O'Donovan 1985a: 40). As O'Donovan notes, bastardy was being created and constituted by legal provisions. The Poor Law Act of 1576 (18 Eliz. 1, c. 3) empowered justices to make an order on the putative father for the maintenance of an illegitimate child charged on the parish, though it was not to be until the Poor Law Amendment Act of 1844 that the mother was given the power to apply for an order for maintenance to be paid to herself. The 1576 Act meant that henceforward the illegitimate child should become the child of the community rather than the child of no one and, for the first time, a duty of support was placed on the parents of the illegitimate child. This Act may have continued to see bastardy in terms of transgression of 'God's law', but it was the economic imperative which had prompted the reform – the economics of who should support the 'bastard' child.

The law's subsequent response to the problem of establishing paternity has been to provide a range of mechanisms which might determine legitimate status in different contexts (e.g. Legitimation Act 1926; Legitimacy Act 1959; Legitimacy Act 1976; Family Law Reform Act 1987). Importantly, central to the organising of men's relationships with children has been the institution of marriage and the related concepts of legitimacy and illegitimacy. Where no marital link has existed between a man and the mother of 'his' child there has been no legal presumption as to his paternity. Though it might be possible to subsequently prove this biological relationship through blood testing (Bradney 1986) or, more recently, DNA fingerprinting, the entire process of establishing paternity has depended on recourse to law and the status of both child and father has depended on the existence of a marital link between the father and mother.

Crucially, it is through reference to the institution of marriage that the historical development of fatherhood must be located. At common law all children born in wedlock were a priori considered to be the legitimate children of the husband of the mother (Banbury Peerage Case [1811] 1 Sim & St 153). Indeed, such has been the importance of this bond between father and legitimate child that, in the past, neither husband nor wife could give evidence of non-access (lack of sexual intercourse) if the effect would be to bastardise a child born during the marriage.[6] Through reference to the legal fiction of the 'presumption of legitimacy' (in effect a presumption of paternity; Smart 1987) in certain circumstances the law has even been able to ignore the biological tie between man and child and create a legal relationship, notwithstanding evidence that the husband in question was not the biological father of the child. Law can, in other words, override biology (and law is, we have seen, a social construct).

To summarise: the legal status of a child has historically rested on the proof (or the absence of disproof) of a link with a particular *man*. The law has conferred a status on both men (as fathers) and children (as il/legitimate) through reference to the institution of marriage. The legal mechanisms which have established paternal rights in this way have been deceptively simple and have principally involved marital status (are the parents married?) and assigning to a child a particular legal status depending on whether s/he was born inside or outside marriage (is the child legitimate/ illegitimate?). It is the legal construct of marriage which has provided the principal means of uniting two people who are biologically unrelated, or distantly related, within the kinship networks of a hierarchic heterosexuality; and it is also the institution of marriage on which paternity has been dependent, rather than on proof of biological fatherhood.

This means that we can, at the outset, distinguish between paternity and fatherhood. 'Fatherhood' is the social construct through which the law has historically sought to attach men to children (Sevenhuijsen 1992). It is not a unitary concept and there is (as we shall see) no one fatherhood in law. A distinction may be made therefore between 'paternity', signifying a biological but not necessarily social connection with a child, 'biological fatherhood', which embraces the biological and social fathering relationship, and 'social fatherhood' in which the 'role' of fathering, and all the obligations it involves, occurs but without the presence of a biological relationship between man and child All of these are instances of men's relationships with children which have been established in law (Smart 1987). It is once paternity is proved that there may be a legal relationship between a man and child (his liability to pay maintenance is an obvious example), but the bundle of rights, obligations and duties which make up parenthood do not automatically follow from a finding of paternity. Thus, although the terms are often used synonomously, *paternity* is different from *fatherhood*. The former refers to the legal status of men who have biologically fathered a certain child or children. In a sense it is the law which 'gives' a man the status of fatherhood through recourse to the concept of paternity. Yet whether a man obtains the rights which go with fatherhood depends on other contingencies which are social in nature; of these the most important historically has been whether or not the father is married to the mother (in which case rights automatically vest in the husband).

It is misleading to read the legal history of fatherhood in terms of a distinction betwen the *rights* of *married* and *unmarried* fathers. Rather, I wish to approach the history of fatherhood in law through reference to how discourses of *paternal masculinity* have been constructed in law. Far from focusing on the content of juridical rights, this approach involves looking at how a masculine subject position in legal discourse has been constructed in such a way that it has become, at the present moment, increasingly available to both married and unmarried men. In effect, a paternal masculinity which has tended to be associated in the past with the married man has increasingly served to valorise *all* men's subjectivities whilst, by sleight of hand, rendering the overarching masculinity of the 'family man' invisible.

CONSTRUCTING FATHERHOOD IN LAW: FROM FATHER RIGHT TO FATHER ABSENCE

A historical snapshot: the 'golden age' of father's rights

The rights and obligations which married men have historically had over 'their' children must be socially, economically and politically located in the context of broader changes in family structure which resulted from the transformations of the agricultural and industrial revolutions of the eighteenth and nineteenth centuries. Sir William Blackstone, writing in the eighteenth century in his Commentaries on the Laws of England (1765), declared that at the time when the child reaches the age of twenty-one the 'empire of the father ... gives place to the empire of reason'. Until that time, however, the 'empire of the father continues even after his death' (Blackstone's

Commentaries on the Law of England, Vol. 1: 453, quoted in McKee and O'Brien 1982b: 27). The mother, in contrast, 'is entitled to no power, but only to reverence and respect'.

By the late nineteenth century the law had already began, albeit slowly, to move away from the common law 'empire of the father' position declared by Blackstone as a succession of legal reforms gradually brought increased legal rights to the mother (though rights were not formally equalised till the 1970s; Brophy 1985). Nonetheless contemporary family law textbooks continue to cite, as the apotheosis of 'absolute father right', the 1883 case of Agar-Ellis v Lascelles [1883] 24 Ch.D 317 and, perhaps of all the nineteenth century cases, this best illustrates the nature of the married fathers' rights at the time. Though almost a century later Lord Upjohn, in J v C [1970] AC 668 was to comment that he could 'only describe as dreadful' the decision in Agar-Ellis, the reasons given by Brett M.R. to endorse his view of the natural rights of the father retain a contemporary resonance.

In Agar-Ellis v Lascelles the father, a Protestant, had agreed at the time of his marriage that any children of that marriage would be brought up Roman Catholic. On the birth of the first child he changed his mind. The mother proceeded to teach the children Catholicism and, when the children later refused to go to a Protestant Church, the father made the children wards of court ([1878] 10 Ch. D 49). This prevented the mother from taking the children to confession and placed the father in control of the 'spiritual welfare' of the children. He then proceeded to remove the children from the mother, to censor the mother's letters and to restrict her visits to the children to once a month. Although the daughter had written to the judge begging to be allowed to live with her mother and to practise her religion, the father nonetheless continued to refuse fearing that the mother would alienate him from the affections of the child (although by this time the desire of the daughter to be with her mother was beyond doubt).

The mother's appeal against a first instance decision in favour of the father was dismissed on the ground that the court had no jurisdiction in a case such as this to interfere with the legal right of a father to control the custody and education of his children. It is the reasoning in the case which concerns us here. Father right was, first and foremost, natural and based on the reciprocity of obligation and paternal prerogative (per Brett M.R.: 327–8). Fathers' rights were 'sacred' rights with which, given their natural ordination, a court 'whatever be its authority or jurisdiction, has no right to interfere with' (per Vice-Chancellor Bacon in Re Plomley 47 LT 284). The Court must never forget, and will never forget . . . the rights of family life, which are sacred' (Brett M.R. in Agar-Ellis p. 337; see also In Re Curtis 28 LJ 458.) Above all, it was the sacred quality of these rights which Brett M.R. stated in Agar-Ellis that he 'endeavoured to express' (ibid.: 329) in his judgement. Why? This was 'on account of the general trust which the law reposes in the natural affection of the father this case is not brought within any of the rules which authorize the Court to interfere' (ibid.: 329).

It is interesting that the absence of paternal authority, like the absense of intercourse in the non-consummation cases, becomes bound up with a perceived threat to the familial and social order itself.[7]

> To neglect the natural jurisdiction of the father over the child until the age of twenty-one would be really to set aside the whole course and order of nature, and it seems to me it would disturb the very foundation of family life.
>
> (ibid.: 336)

Masculine authority in this case is, like the male sexualities of Chapter 4, *naturalised*; it needs no explanation, justification or further deliberation – it is impervious to questioning. To interfere with the rights of the father 'would be to ignore the one principle which is the most fundamental of all in this history of mankind, and owing to the full play of which man has become what he is' (ibid.: 337). Like sexuality, the authority of the father in the family is thus accorded a deep symbolic significance.

How might we read a case such as this? Or, rather, how might we present a 'critical genealogy of the naturalization of sex and of bodies' which occurs in this case (Butler 1990: 147)? Agar-Ellis provides us with a historically specific construction of masculinity in law. Yet we are dealing here, it must be remembered, with a judicial construct which is an *ideal* of paternal masculinity. The fatherhood Brett M.R. invokes (broadly, one of the Victorian paterfamilias) only ever related to the lives of some fathers. Specifically, it would register with those men socialised into the 'civilised self-control . . . rigidity of character structure' which marked the middle-class Victorian man (Cominos 1963, quoted in Richards 1987: 27). Class, geographic (for example rural/urban), religious and ethnic differences all divested the legal authority of fathers (as well as beliefs about sexuality) in different ways. This means that it would be misleading for us to simply assume that the sacramental bourgeois family depicted in the case (and to which this masculinity is seen as fundamental) was unproblematically diffused throughout the social order (Weeks 1981: 38). The 'separate spheres' ideology, which underlay the depiction of domestic arrangements in Agar-Ellis, did not apply universally. Furthermore, the cases which came to court at the time in this area only involved wealthy families. The legal 'disabilities' which befell married women at the time flowed from the fact that the wife's legal existence was incorporated into that of her husband; it was the equitable doctrines developed by the Court of Chancery which have lessened the harshness of the common law rules. Divorce was also heavily restricted and, importantly, permeated by the sexual double-standard which Brett M.R. reproduces in his judgement.

This means that the passionate homilies of judges to the symbolic good of 'the family' (be they from the 1880s or 1990s) must be seen as prescriptive rather than descriptive. They were addressing an *ideal* of familial masculinity. Historically, and bearing in mind occupational and regional differences in family structures, 'it is difficult to find any support for either a universal progressive democratization of family life or of the thesis of general cultural diffusion' (McKee and O'Brien 1982b: 18). However, this does not mean that to talk of representations of 'fatherhood' in law has no heuristic purpose in the light of the fragmentation of paternal masculinity through the contingencies of class, sexuality, age and ethnicity. Rather, what we are dealing with here is a particular *type* of masculinity which has been valorised in law. To understand why it took the form it did we must ask a rather different set of questions about the law. Far from constructing any unitary and universal model of masculinity from legal cases (which would continue to assign to law an epistemological significance of which, I have argued in Chapter 2, it is undeserving), it is more worthwhile to consider: how did this particular familial masculinity emerge at the time it did? How was it legitimated and promulgated and how, as one discourse of masculinity, does it continue to inform legal constructs of fatherhood? In the remainder of this chapter I wish to consider the *content* of contemporary paternal masculinity in law and how it differs from, and remains similar to, the masculinity evident in Agar-Ellis v Lascelles. Central to this discussion shall be the twin themes of masculine authority and publicly defined work.

Towards the 'best interests of the child'

Let us move forward a century to the 1980s. The 'sacred rights' of a father no longer exist as formal, legal, justiciable rights which he can assert in relation to 'his' children (or, indeed, 'his' wife). During the nineteenth century a change took place in social attitudes to children which was well under way by the time of Agar-Ellis in 1885 (Aries 1973). From a hitherto valuing of children by reference to their skilled labour capacities, the increasing power of a range of ideologies of childhood had began to stress the special and distinct quality of pre-adult years (Pinchbeck and Hewitt 1973). Alongside a succession of legal reforms (not least child protection legislation), childcare 'changed from a valuable family burden that men wished to control to a costly family asset that men wished to avoid' (Brown 1981: 242, quoted in Hearn 1992: 55).

In the subsequent reconstitution of the family as a distinctly modern and egalitarian household unit, however, the emergence in law of the 'welfare principle' made it necessary to ascertain just what the 'best interests of the child' as a 'paramount consideration' might actually be in any particular case (s. 1 Guardianship of Infants Act 1925; s. 1 Children Act 1989). By the 1920s (with the welfare principle entrenched in the 1925 Act), the father's role had already become increasingly problematic as, informed by a succession of childcare manuals, the role of the wife/mother was being emphasised in a celebration of the values of the family and marriage (Richards 1987: 32). Informed by 'scientific' paediatric discourses and shifting ideologies of childcare (as well as their own personal prejudices) (Bromley and Lowe 1987: 317) judges had already begun, from the late nineteenth century onwards, to detail a range of factors which together have been said to constitute the welfare principle in law and the best interests of the child in the companionate marriage. Thus, to this day, family law textbooks continue to list the 'factors' established in a succession of (frequently contradictory) Appeal Court cases (for example, employment and remarriage prospects) which determine the welfare principle at a particular historical moment (see Re L [1962] 1 WLR 886; Re K (Minors) (Wardship: Care and Control) [1979] 1

All ER 647). However, in practice, as feminist research has shown, this principle worked to assess women through the ideas of 'good' and 'bad' mothering (Smart 1984a).

One effect of the increasing influence of the welfare principle throughout the twentieth century has been to politicise fatherhood and to bring men's involvement in childcare into the public domain. On one level the *idea* of the companionate marriage presumed an increased joint activity on the part of both husband and wife. However, in reality tasks remained segregated along gender lines with the father a detached and often absent figure (see below). The emerging welfare principle thus fractured the basis of the father-right of Agar-Ellis through providing an alternative and child-centred moral imperative – in effect bringing fatherhood into the public and political domain. Do families need fathers? If so, why?

From the language of metaphysically ordained fathers' rights it is now the best interests of the child which moved onto centre stage. Yet, crucially, this did mean that discourses of paternal masculinity were no longer naturalised. Rather, as marriage has ceased to be the central vehicle of family law in the process of safeguarding (legal) fatherhood (Sevenhuijsen 1992: 80) a range of other legal concepts and techniques (for example the 'child of the family') have sought to walk the tightrope of doctrinal coherence whilst attaching men to children. However, the law has continued to reproduce a naturalist discourse of masculinity in seeking to protect fatherhood – no longer through granting to the father formal legal *rights* in relation to other family members but through constructing father-presence in the first place as desirable and natural for the well-being of *all* the members of the family.

We have seen above how, in the vast majority of custody cases the courts make decisions confirming the existing situation. As bearers of rights mothers and fathers formally appear equal before the law in England and Wales (Children Act 1989). Substantive inequalities of power, however, are evaded by

> taking mothers and fathers as degendered persons or simply 'parents', and then bring[ing] them under the jurisdiction of human rights reasoning and equality reasoning. Family law treats these persons *as if* they are equal. . . . Equality then comes down to equal treatment or consistency.
>
> (Sevenhuijsen 1992: 80)

This point is most important. The equal rights claim and equality norm (the language through which the fathers' rights movement and advocates of men's liberation have pitched their argument) is a claim the justice of which is hard to refute without denying the fundamental premise of liberal legal order (Smart 1989b). Indeed, the men and women involved in disputes over childcare articulate their claims through the language of equal rights (Smart 1991). Yet the equality model of marriage is based on a misunderstanding of how law has structured that relationship in the first place. It clashes with the material inequalities both within marriage and within society as a whole (O'Donovan 1982: 428), inequalities which mean that men benefit from market discrimination against women *and* the gendered division of labour and dependencies within the institution of marriage (Fineman 1991a, 1983). In short, 'dependency has not disappeared. . . . The care of children produces dependency, not only for the children, but for the primary caretaker' (Fineman 1991a: 270); and just because two parties may be legally equivalent for one purpose does not mean they are equivalent for all purposes (Westen 1982).

A further effect of this has been to depoliticise the gendering of male and female subjectivities in the first place, analysis of which would involve rejecting the conceptual baggage of liberal legalism. These are, crucially, subject positions which the law has gendered in quite specific ways. Parents do not come before the law as ungendered bearers of abstracted legal rights; they are beings subjectively committed to identities (father/mother, husband/wife) and institutions (marriage/the family) within which they might find themselves both powerful and powerless. Subjective interpretations of fatherhood, therefore, like heterosexuality and homosexuality (Chapter 3), are fluid. The possibility of agency remains ever present in opening out alternative discursive routes or 'ways of being' (Butler 1990: 143) through transcending the 'unnecessary binarism of free-will and determinism' (ibid.: 147). The law, however, has tended to fix fatherhood to a particular model of heterosexual masculinity which has systematically privileged certain categories of men and excluded others. Let us explore an aspect of such beliefs central to the father-absence idea in more detail – the relation between *men and work*.

Father absence and the 'masculine achiever'

The idea that the family sphere has been legally structured as the location for the exercise of power, authority and dominance by men has been central to feminist legal scholarship on the family (Fineman 1983, 1989; Atkins and Hoggett 1984; Smart 1984a, 1989a; O'Donovan 1985, 1993; Okin 1989). More generally the binding of paternal masculinity with ideas of male authority has been a recurrent theme in sociological research on the family, where a familiar image in accounts of family life (Willmott and Young 1962; Komarovsky 1964), as well as in pro-feminist critiques of masculinity (Tolson 1977: 8), has been that of an authoritarian father who somehow 'dominates' household arrangements.

A number of factors have recently come together to challenge this correlation between men and work. The increasing proportion of women in the workforce, alongside wider shifts in employment patterns resulting from economic restructuring, the impact of feminism, mass unemployment and shifts from industrial based to service economies have all thrown into question traditional ideas of paternal subjectivity and male familial commitment based on the centrality of work. Despite the cultural valorisation of leisure time and widespread unemployment, paid work nonetheless continues to assume a central place in accounts of masculine identity. Technical innovations consequent on capital reorganisation may have produced changes in the forms of male control and masculinity in the workplace (Cockburn 1983, 1991; Gray 1987); meanwhile crisis tendencies in the political sphere, which surfaced particularly vociferously during the 1980s in the UK, as labour movements sought to accommodate the demands of new social movements, have produced a trenchant critique of the 'masculinist' ethos of the traditional labour movement (Campbell 1985; Segal 1987; Cockburn 1988).

It is in this context that the rendering problematic of the men/work relation within the discourse of a 'crisis' of masculinity has taken place. Women's increased involvement in the workforce has rendered untenable the idea that the male/breadwinner, female/childrearer relation represents anything like the reality of family life for the majority. At the same time the development of new forms of commercialised masculinity, designed to meet the demands of sections of a male workforce with expendable income, has produced a commodification of men's working identities which, though it has in some respects undermined the traditional authoritarian father-figure, continues to reproduce the dominant man/work relation (Collier 1992b).

One of the problems for engaging with matrimonial law is that these changes in the man/work relation have come up against a familial ideology which in many respects continues to preserve the division between father/breadwinner and mother/childrearer. Married women have in the past been classified according to their husband's social class (Delphy 1984). In a sense, it remains is as if nothing has changed when such a familial ideology continues to inform matrimonial law and social policy (Carabine 1992) notwithstanding the realities of the labour market. In Britain women, for example, compose half the workforce and not simply 'secondary income earners'; women's participation in work also tends to take more varied forms, including the lowest paid and least-protected employment. The 'dual career', of wage-earner and mother, is not necessarily egalitarian; it may be potentially oppressive for many women 'who cannot do both, or cannot do both well' (Fineman 1991a: 271). Importantly, in the case of men it continues to be through a primary reference to his work and capacity for paid employment that masculine subjectivities (and more generally cultural understandings of masculinity) are understood as paternal masculinity continues to be defined in law through reference to men's capacities to provide economically for 'their' family (Land 1980; Barrett and McIntosh 1980). That is, with the few 'recognised' exceptions of sex discrimination law, equal pay and maternity provision, labour law

> is a world made up of full-time male breadwinners . . . the legal rules reflect this conception of the worker . . . the models labour lawyers employ to analyse and evaluate the rules are gender-blind in that they fail to recognise that for men and women experiences of work and the workplace may be very different.
>
> (Conaghan 1986: 380; see also O'Donovan and Szysczak 1988))

This has a number of implications for theorising paternal masculinity in law. We have here an ideological division of masculinity itself into 'public' and 'private' lives, premised on the dualisms of liberal legal discourse between public/private, work/home. Masculinity, as something which might be *mobilised as an economic resource*, has been systematically endorsed in law (Connell 1987:

106). The idea that paid employment has a central place in the maintenance of masculine identity and status recurs in a succession of legal cases (Tovey v Tovey [1978] 8 Fam Law 80; Billington v Billington [1974] 1 All ER 546; Williams v Williams [1974] 3 All ER 377.)[8] This is in marked contrast to legal constructions of the correspondence between maternity, childcare and women's familial role where ideas of the natural abilities of mothers have proved pervasive (for example, A v A [1988] 1 FLR 193–73: Re K (Minors) [1977] 1 All ER 651: Re C (Minors) [1978] 2 All ER 230). The corollary of these natural abilities of the mother is, of course, a belief that a man should be engaged in employment.

Even within the home a physical definition of masculinity has been sustained through a legally endorsed sexual division of domestic tasks (Atkins and Hoggett 1984: Ch. 6; O'Donovan 1985a, 1993: 71). In the cases of Wachtel v Wachtel [1973] 1 All ER 829, Cooke v Head [1972] 2 All ER 38 and Eves v Eves [1975] 3 All ER 768, a gendered division of domestic labour is constructed in such a way as to assess (and ultimately devalue) domestic tasks seen as 'female'. Some wives, it is clear, have done things a woman would not normally be expected to do:

> she stripped the wallpaper in the hall. She painted woodwork in the lounge and kitchen. She painted the kitchen cabinets. She painted the brickwork in the front of the house. She broke up concrete in the front garden. She carried the pieces to a skip. She, with him, demolished a shed and put up a new shed.
>
> (Eves v Eves [1975] 3 All ER 768)

'Male' jobs, in contrast to traditionally 'feminine' domestic tasks, require strength and certain traditionally masculine skills such as building, repairs, constructing the garden, digging, maintaining household machinery and maintaining cars (see also Burns v Burns [1984] 1 All ER 244; Langston v AUEW [1974] 1 All ER 980). In these cases the legal construction of 'housekeeping' takes place from a vantage point in which particular gendered roles for male and female are assumed (see further Bottomley 1993). Thus, when a marriage breaks up, the husband

> will have to go out to work all day and must get some woman to look after the house – either a wife, if he remarries, or a housekeeper, if he does not. . . . The wife will not usually have so much expense. She may go out to work herself, but she will

not usually employ a housekeeper. She will do most of the housework herself. . . . Or she may remarry, in which case her husband will provide for her.

(Wachtel v Wachtel [1973] 1 All ER 829)

The above cases bear the unmistakable imprint of Lord Denning (see also Thomas v Fuller Brown [1985] 1 FLR 237; Lloyds Bank Plc v Rosset [1988] 3 All ER 915; Hammond v Mitchell [1992] 2 All ER 109) and it might be argued that the division of labour evident in cases from the 1970s has no bearing in the 1990s. Yet this would be to misread how the law has reconstructed the man/work relation and underestimate how culturally powerful this idea of breadwinner masculinity remains. The idea of 'providing for the family' continues to bind men as financial providers to an economic system which structures household economies through allocating to a family member (usually the man) the role of primary wage earner (Wilson 1977; Land 1980). Yet it is misleading to try to understand this division through reference simply to a male 'role' of breadwinner. The idea of any unproblematic and given role, I have argued, fails to grasp the tensions which pervade the legal construction of breadwinner masculinity; and it is these tensions which are, at present, at the heart of many debates about family law reform.

In the 1990s it is this breadwinner masculinity, the general physical absence of fathers from the family domain (because they are or should be 'at work'), which sits uneasily with a new father-hood ideology which holds out that men's domestic lives *have* changed. Given these contradictions, it is interesting to consider legal responses to those men who, for differing reasons, find themselves caught up in those changes which have taken place around the men/work relation through, for a variety of reasons, rejecting its fundamental premise.

'DOING WHAT COMES NATURALLY': CONSTRUCTING BREADWINNER MASCULINITY

Given the primacy of the man/work relation, what of the man who chooses not to work in order to be involved in childcare? This issue brings together the themes of change in masculinity, men's libera-tion and the idea of the new fatherhood discussed above. In short, a central problem facing men who choose to take on primary childcare responsibilities has been 'the practical problem of fathers being able to cope' because of the demands of their full-time employment (Lowe 1982: 35). In two cases from 1985, both called B v B, just such a situation occurred.

In the first B v B (Custody of Child) [1985] FLR 462 (a case which has been subseqently cited with approval by Families Need Fathers in the UK), a central question for the court was how the father could maintain contact with his child. To keep up his contact he had to make arrangements to see that his son did not suffer in any way from the fact he had to go to work. He thus delegated day-to-day responsibility for childcare to his family, his mother and then sister (thus reproducing a traditional sexual division of labour). However, there was also a further division in the case between categories of fathers. This case, it was stressed, was not one of 'a father who has deliberately given up work in order to go on social security: circumstances have forced him to give up work . . . he is now unemployed and is likely to be for some time.' Unlike those fathers who 'choose' to go on social security *this* father's hand was forced through his employer's demands. A differentiation is thus made between different classes of un-employed fathers.

In the second B v B, however, it was just such a situation which occurred ([1985] FLR 166, [1985] Fam Law 29). Here the father decided that he *did* wish to live on social security so that he would be able to care for the child. At first instance the trial judge was unequivocal. He stated that the primary role of the father was to go to work and generate the resources whereby he would be able to provide support for himself and the child. It would be 'plainly wrong and silly if the father were to remain unemployed in order to look after one 4 year old boy' (p. 177). Indeed, he continued, 'I shall take a great deal of convincing that it is right that an adult male should be permanently unemployed in order to look after one small boy' (p. 174). Moreover

> a healthy young man like you must generate resources by your work to support your child and yourself . . . rather than have other people supporting you . . . through the tax payer.
>
> (p. 174)

The father's primary role must be by his work to generate resources which provide for the support and maintenance of his child and himself, rather than remain at home performing what traditionally is regarded as the mother's role.

(p. 177–8)[9]

The Court of Appeal subsequently allowed the father's appeal and awarded care and control to the father with reasonable access to the mother. However, they explicitly did not reject the construction of the relation between men and work that the trial judge had considered so important. Indeed, the Appeal Court went to great lengths to stress that they were not in disagreement with his reasoning:

> I do not for a moment wish to be thought unsympathetic to, or critical of, the judge's viewpoint that a young and able-bodied man ought to work; indeed, other things being equal, it is a view that I personally wholeheartedly subscribe to.

(p. 179)

It was stressed that 'the prospect of an able bodied man being permanently unemployed is . . . a relevant consideration' (p. 179), particularly where a father seemed 'fit and vigorous in appearance and manner' (p. 177).[10] The second B v B does not, therefore, involve a rejection of the idea that men should work to support their families or that a young child is best in the day to day care of the mother: 'it is not just the ties and incidence of nature. It is a hundred and one practical, common sense reasons' (p. 182). Indeed, it is interesting that it was the *special* circumstance of this case (highlighted throughout) which reveal this case as an exception which proves the rule – this father was quite unusual and not like other fathers. Indeed he 'lives in a kind of social cocoon . . . some day he is going to emerge from it.'

In both B v B cases, and in a succession of other custody cases, what is striking is the judicial concern with the arrangements which fathers may have to make in order to maintain contact with children (and thus not disturb the man/work bond; see also O'Donovan 1993: 70–1). In May v May [1986] 1 FLR 325 a father also made an arrangement with his employer to work restricted hours which would enable him to take the children to school and be available to collect them or be at home when they came home. In Re C (A), C v C [1970] 1 All ER 309 the father was 'usually at home at the time the infant gets back from school', whilst in Re W (A Minor) the judge noted that the father 'had the advantage of working in his own father's business which made it possible for him to arrange more flexible working hours than would be feasible for most men.'

In the second B v B case the father was 'trying to start a one-parent fathers club' (p. 181) (whilst presumably living in his 'kind of social cocoon'), but he was also assisted by a 'family circle living locally upon which he can call for assistance' (p. 182). He had available a wider network of support from his own relations 'and if necessary from other relations in the extended family' (see also May v May p. 329). In Re W the father also 'had the advantage of support from a number of members of his family who helped him with the onerous obligation . . .'. Fathers, it would seem, might need familial support and assistance with the parenting role that single mothers do not. Such assistance might then help them out with the 'onerous obligation' of childcare.

Perhaps it should not surprise us, given the centrality of the breadwinner masculinity constructed in these cases, that the benign influence of appropriate paternal masculinity can even be ascribed a temporal dimension. In May v May [1986] 1 FLR 325, Ackner L.J. stated that the crucial period when parents might have influence over their children is

> before they go to school and when they come home. Before they go to school there is the important training as to punctuality, tidiness, assistance in the household and the like, and when they come home there is the difficult conflict . . . between the time to be spent on homework, the time to be spent on television, and the time at which the child or children should go to bed. It seems to me that the father was given this crucial period during which he could exercise his influence.
>
> (per Ackner L.J. p. 330 in May v May)

This 'crucial period' interestingly corresponds with the times of the paternal presence afforded by the demands of work. Presumably more routine 'day-to-day' care (where the need for paternal discipline is not so acute?) may be left to the mother (or other family members).

It is not just the timing of the paternal presence which is at issue here. Even the quality of the paternal influence has been assessed by judges through reference to ideals of what are, and what are not, considered to be desirable masculine 'role models'. In May v May the central issue was a conflict of values between the two potential fathers who differed in their views on how to bring up the two boys, aged eight and six. The competence of both the mother and biological father in caring for the children was beyond question. Both parents 'by all standards have done a marvellous job together in bringing up these little boys' (p. 326). However, the mother and her new partner, a Mr Mitchell ('who had himself been divorced and since that divorce had lived with two other ladies': 326), were adjudged by the court to have

> a much freer and easier approach to life, and his approach to the discipline of the children (the time they should spend working, the time they should spend watching television and the like) and the emphasis on academic achievement would be significantly different from that of Mr May.
>
> (p. 328)

Mr May, by contrast, thought it appropriate 'to stimulate them from the educational point of view and to develop their character' (p. 329). The natural father, it was stressed, placed greater emphasis 'on fostering academic achievement. He would also inculcate different values – for example he chose to put some of Russell's birthday money in a building society account; Mrs May felt he should be allowed to spend it all.' It was noted (continuing a curious tradition of judicial interest in ideals of physical manliness) that both Mr May and Mr Mitchell were, according to the welfare report, 'keen sportsmen and can foster athletic development' in the boys (p. 328). However, 'Mrs May, because of her quiet nature, will need the support of her partner as the boys grow to test parental discipline' (p. 328) (implicitly she would need some man to help her). Extra-judicial input also, it seems, reproduces such ideas of masculinity (note also, on the father as disciplinarian, Re K (Minors) [1977] 1 All ER 651).

There is a clear class dimension to the assessment of paternal masculinities in May v May. What we are dealing with here are 'respectable' middle-class values, in which the appropriate paternal masculinity is assessed through reference to such concerns as 'academic achievement', an 'environment of discipline' and ability to 'foster athletic development' and so forth. The contrast with the lax, free and easy and 'different' atmosphere of the mother's house was thus seen to heighten the need for paternal discipline in a case concerning two boys; 'discipline was . . . very much in the mind of the father, the discipline meaning learning to discipline and organize one's own life' (p. 328–9). Mr

Mitchell could not be guaranteed to provide such discipline. The conclusion followed that it was in the best interests of the children to be brought up by the standards of the father as opposed to those of the mother.

What emerges from these cases is not just a class-based version of familial masculinity, however. There is also the familiar valorisation of the masculinity/work relation (albeit with some flexibility around working hours) which negates the value of men's involvement in childcare at the same time as promoting the ideal of breadwinner masculinity. The courts in England and Wales have, despite the arguments of the fathers' rights movement to the contrary, shown considerable sympathy with some (appropriate) fathers who wish to care for their children. With flexible working hours and, most importantly, a wider network of support (usually made up of female relatives), judges have constructed heterosexual paternal masculinity as a positive influence in the lives of children. Even better than practical support, a father's chances are increased if the female assistance takes the form of a mother-substitute figure within the household (thus reproducing the familial ideal; see Re C (Minors) [1978] 2 All ER 230).

It is important to remember that the paternal masculinity invoked in these cases remains premised on existing social and familial structural arrangements. It presumes heterosexuality and a clear division into 'appropriate' male/female relations with children. Whether a man works or not is not so much a moral choice; it is something which is presumed, that *as a father* his natural, primary duty is *to employment and not to childcare* (as is clear from the inadequacy of paternity leave provisions in the UK). This means that the man who actually gives up employment to care for children is not seen as acting on any 'natural' nurturing instinct but is, rather, acting against his natural bread-winner masculinity. It is simply not in the interests of children to have a father who is not working (Plant v Plant [1983] 4 FLR, p. 305). Ultimately the breadwinner ideology has at its heart the contradictory social values which run through familial masculinity; on the one hand a commitment to the economic and experiential significance of work and, on the other, a commitment to taking an increased part in childcare and domestic labour. The problem, as those men who have sought to take on primary carer responsibilities have found, can be very much one of trying to square the circle.

CONSTRUCTING THE FAMILY MAN: THE MODERNISING OF PATERNAL MASCULINITY:

How might we make sense of the above cases? We have seen constructions of paternal masculinity in law at two historical moments a century apart. We have moved, in a sense, from a concern with *father right* (Agar-Ellis) to the construction of a problematic of *father absence* (the breadwinner/custody cases). A range of familiar questions pervades texts on the latter issue. Do families need fathers? What are fathers for? Are feminists seeking to 'sack father' (Morgan 1986)? What are the acceptable parameters of paternal expressions of physical affection, given the evidence of sexual abuse by fathers? I believe that to make sense of what is going on here it is necessary to return to the historical and institutional emergence of discourses of masculinity concerned with constructing men *as* fathers. Such a historical approach has a particular utility, and not just for beginning to understand the transition which has taken place in the construction of paternal masculinity in legal discourse. It also helps clarify, at the present moment, why fatherhood has become such a contested issue.

Throughout the twentieth century the belief that families need fathers for the social, psychological and economic well-being of *all* the members of the family unit has underscored judicial hostility to autonomous motherhood. This belief has been couched primarily through reference to the welfare principle and the juridical assessment of maternal capability – the judging of the 'good' and the 'bad' mother. In the 1990s the centrality of fatherhood in the process of defining the 'familial' *per se*, as well as in negating the viability of extra-familial households (in particular those without men), remains evident in law. This has been particularly clear in recent developments around reproductive technology and in the law's continued (frequently convoluted and tortuous) attempts to attach unmarried men to children.[11] The presence of the father continues to be seen as a signifier of stability, 'normality' and, crucially, the 'healthy' adjustment of children. Ultimately, even riots and urban disorder have been laid at the door of the absent father (Dennis and Erdos 1992).

We are presented with a paradox when we consider the nature of the paternal presence, however. It is clearly not a *physical* presence (given the primary obligation to paid employment). Rather, the familial masculinity which pervades legal discourse –

the masculinity which has been attacked by the 'hostility of voci-
ferous minorities to the presence of men in families' (Anderson
and Dawson 1986b: 14) – is of a certain kind. After work, it involves
the second (and related) strand of the construction of fatherhood
in law – the presence of a *paternal heterosexual authority*. In short, not
any father will do. The family man of legal discourse is, we have
already seen in Chapter 3, heterosexual; but he is also a father who
is disciplined, economically responsible and who, perhaps above
all, embodies a particular kind of authority over women and
children in the family. In Agar-Ellis we witnessed a naturalising of
masculinity through reference to sacrament and social order.
Though rid of the metaphysical trappings of quasi-religious discourse, the law continues to reproduce functionalist ideas about
'stable' and 'healthy' families and men's authority. The law continues to ascribe the status of 'dysfunctional' to those families in
which an appropriate paternal masculinity is either absent (for
example in the case of lesbian motherhood; see Re P [1983] FLR
401; Eveson v Eveson [1980] unreported 27 November CA; C v C
[1991] FLR 223) or else is far removed from the hegemonic
heterosexual ideal considered to be desirable (as in the case of the
male homosexual parent; see Re D [1977] AC 617; Re G [1988]
unreported 23 March CA; Morris v Morris [1983] unreported 8
December CA; see further Bradley 1987).

Making fathers safe: the 'family man' in law

There have been two elements to this transformation of fatherhood from the times of the 'pre-modern' paterfamilias to the
'modern' father and family man of the purportedly 'symmetrical'
and egalitarian family. First it has been necessary to render fatherhood 'safe'; or, more accurately, to make a distinction between the
law's construction of familial paternal masculinities and other
'dangerous' masculinities. If this father is to be an equal partner in
the 'symmetrical family' it is important that he no longer embodies
the threat of the undomesticated male. It is an analysis of the
relation between these discourses of 'dangerous' and 'familial'
masculinities which constitutes the subject of the following
chapter. Second, and my immediate focus here, it has been necessary to construct father *presence* as *desirable* and father *absence* as
problematic. This has been achieved, we have seen above, through
reference to the father's presumed utility as an appropriate male

'role model' (utilising a crude and intellectually flawed variant of sex role theory).

Quite what this paternal 'role' involves is far from clear. For example, Maidment (1984: 187) comments in her discussion of child custody law that it 'is not known . . . whether low masculinity in boys is associated with adjustive difficulties in adult life.' The initial absence of paternal masculinity is presented by Maidment as the generating motor in a cycle of maladjusted males who have been denied the 'normal' paternal masculine presence. Yet just what the qualities of a normative and 'healthy' masculinity are (presumably pitched somewhere between 'low' and 'high' on an androgynous scale) remains unstated. Elsewhere, educational underachievement, delinquency, confused sexual identity, aggressiveness, promiscuity and poor verbal skills have all been laid at the door of the absent father (Anderson and Dawson 1986a). Positivistic accounts of the law/gender relation have tended to construct the 'scientific' discourse of child psychology as the signifier of what a 'just' and 'equitable' law should encompass. Yet the irony is that there remains no consensus amongst psychological theories as to the desirability and effects of father absence.[12] What judges have tended to do in child custody cases, therefore (with no objective proof of the universal effects of father-absence to turn to), is to resort to a simplistic and popularised version of sex role theory and sex-typing through which to legitimise their decisions about which parent a child should live with on divorce. What this means, of course, is that they then have considerable discretion to reproduce their own beliefs about 'appropriate' parental practices.

Of these beliefs, the idea of the functional family as source of social and individual stability has provided the most powerful (secular) basis of the argument that families 'need' fathers in law. Father presence is considered to be desirable because 'families' need fathers and, in particular, because the *children* of families do. It is thus through reference to their presumed utility as appropriate and 'natural' male role models that the law has sought to attach fathers to families; but fatherhood remains, as in Agar-Ellis, naturalised.

To recap; the construction of father absence as problematic in legal discourse has involved the mobilising of discourses which establish fatherhood as a desirable presence during marriage in the first place (for example, the economic provider discourse). The irony is that, given the economic rationality of advanced capitalism, the breadwinner masculinity of the 'good father' in fact entails a considerable physical absence from families for many men. The presence of paternal masculinity was always open-ended, however, and it is this which divorce reveals, making clear just what paternal masculinity, presumed by law to be desirable, actually entailed in the first place. Father absence really signifies something else – the desirability of the presence of masculinity within the family by embodying the three axes of authority, economic responsibility and heterosexuality. It is these which, together, constitute the idea of the 'good father' in law.

The familialisation of paternity

I referred above to the need to locate the historical emergence of fatherhood in relation to both the public and the private dimensions of men's citizenship. It is now necessary to broaden the scope of this discussion of fatherhood so as to embrace the position of the *unmarried* father – for it is at the interface of the married and unmarried man in law that paternal masculinity has itself been transformed.

The law has, we have seen above, sought to attach men to children through the concepts of paternity and fatherhood. Until the mid-nineteenth century, the only concern which the law had with the relation between fathers and illegitimate children was financial. Biological fatherhood was thus effectively separated from legal fatherhood (Smart 1987). Only the institution of marriage, dignified by the church with all its attributes of sanctity and endowed with the most valuable civil privileges, could then secure the claim for support from a proven biological father. In the case of the unmarried father, however, we face an apparent irony in the history of illegitimacy, for the mother of an illegtimate child has historically been in a stronger legal position regarding her children than the divorced mother. This does not mean that the law has looked in any sense with a degree of 'favour' on the unmarried mother. On the contrary, the history of illegitimacy has been marked by the view that it is an institutionalised relationship with a man which is the legally sanctioned locale for legitimate and 'lawful' sexual intercourse. The considerable social and legal 'misfortunes' which have historically befallen both the unmarried mother and her child (Macfarlane 1986; Gill 1977: 296) have stemmed from the centrality of marriage in constructing the 'legitimate' link between man and child.[13] Furthermore, the motives for granting unmarried mothers greater formal rights than their married counterparts have been primarily economic. The history of illegitimacy has thus been marked by a sexual double standard and by a concern for the public purse (see further Gill 1977; Laslett *et al.* 1980; O'Donovan 1985a; Smart 1987: 102). Throughout this history legal discourse has valorised and empowered a male subject position and the wishes of men in choosing whether or not to accept responsibility for a child.[14] Recently, however, and for a number of different reasons, the unmarried father's position in law has itself changed as the paternal masculinity of the 'family man' has come to embrace both the married and unmarried man.

Changes in marriage and birth status

Marriage, put simply, is now an inadequate securer of paternity. There has occurred a real and proportionate growth in the number of non-marital births (OPCS 1990). Over a half to two-thirds of illegitimate children are now born in stable partnerships. Some unmarried men, clearly, are not fleeing from parental responsibility. Meanwhile, the proportion of lone parents has doubled, rising from 8 per cent in 1971 to 19 per cent in 1991. More than one in six families are now headed by a lone mother (though of every three lone parents, only one is a woman who has never married). According to the 1991 General Household Survey (OPCS 1991: No. 22) only one in four households now consists of the 'traditional' family of a couple with dependent children. 'Illegitimacy' has not just become increasingly common but it is also being perceived by many as as a 'legitimate' parenting option – and thus, of course, as a threat to marriage and 'the family' (Wintour 1990; Utting and Laurence 1990).

In effect, for the past two decades (at least) the centrality of the institution of marriage in defining legal status has been super-ceded by other 'organising concepts' such as cohabitation and parenthood (Weitzman 1981; Pateman 1988). Cohabitation itself has increasingly corresponded to marriage, not just in its significance for determining of legal status of children, but also with regard to property entitlements on separation. In 1991, according to the General Household Survey, 8 per cent of men and 7 per cent of women aged between 16 and 59 were cohabiting and, as if in recognition of these legal changes, there has been a proliferation of legal texts on the subject of cohabitation law (Bottomley *et al.* 1981; Parker 1981; Parry 1981; Freeman and Lyon 1983) and, in some jurisdictions, specific legislation (New South Wales De Facto Relationships Act 1984). Far from security and status being derived from a marriage relationship, Glendon (1981) has argued, individuals now look to the state and employment as guarantors of the status which can be derived from the 'new property'.

All of this does not mean that marriage is not still central in attaching men to children. Rather, what has tended to happen is that hitherto 'extra-familial' domestic relationships have been embraced within a *reconstituted* familial domain. In other words, certain 'marriage type' relationships (specifically, heterosexual cohabitation with or without children) have become increasingly considered, assessed and regulated through reference to the best interests of the child doctrine and, importantly, through the juridical familial gaze of law. As such, the above changes in marriage and birth status can be seen as part of a more general reconstitution of ideas of the family which have occurred in the wake of the Divorce Reform Act 1969 and the Matrimonial Causes Act 1973. Familial ideology has been reconstructed as surviving and transcending the termination of individual relationships (O'Brien 1992) and this has a number of implications for how we understand paternal masculinity in law.

The idea that, whilst a marriage may be dead (or irretrievably broken down), 'the family' lives on, has been legitimated across a range of legal reforms (the Matrimonial and Family Proceedings Act 1984; Alcock 1984). However, this does not mean that the concept of fatherhood is no longer central to the constitution of a legal relationship between men and children. Law continues to define the 'familial' in the first place through reference to the presence of men. In the case of reproductive technologies, for example, practice takes place within parameters which prioritise the traditional family structure (Stanworth 1987a; Smart 1987; Dewar 1989b); and if the law has sought to detach the biological father from the child in the case of AID (Surrogacy Arrangements Act 1985), when it comes to the case of the rights of the unmarried father an opposite trend is identifiable (Smart 1987).[15] Embracing the hitherto extra-familial within the familial domain has brought about no less than a reconstitution of unmarried fatherhood.

We have seen how the emergence during the twentieth century of the concern with the welfare of the child redrew the boundaries of both the married and unmarried father's relationship with children. Welfarism, alongside the changing status of marriage, in effect brought the married and unmarried father closer together as significant and desirable presences in the lives of their children. One consequence of what is in effect a *familialising of paternity* has been to assign an increasing significance to the father/child bond. It is a bond which is 'in the interests of the child' and many men now desire their (extra-marital) relationship with children to be recognised in law. It has not been necessary to legitimate these changes through any 'reasonable man' referent; it can be achieved through reconstituting the welfare principle in such a way as to embrace this (naturalised) man/child bond. Extending the boundaries of 'the familial', therefore, has involved a widening of the net of paternal authority through facilitating the making of links between men and children just at the time when rising trends of divorce, cohabitation, step-parenthood and serial marriage might appear to have been breaking down the traditional family unit. Through the 'child of the family' concept, for example, all men can potentially be made responsible for the support of children who they had treated as a member of their family – there is no need to establish either marital or biological links (s. 52(1) Matrimonial Causes Act 1973)[16]. The related idea of 'social fatherhood' (a concept which may be found in legislation dealing with custody and maintenance on divorce, separation and nullity) has similarly transformed the legal significance of paternity and legitimacy through bringing into law a technique whereby all men may potentially have economic and social responsibilities towards children. Although such a legitimation of social parenting applies to women, it remains the case that women appear generally less likely to be in positions to provide maintainance/inheritance than men (given that progress towards equal opportunities for women in the labour market has been 'agonizingly slow'; Maclean 1991: 591).

Fatherhood can thus be seen to remain central to attaching men to children. It is simply a different conception of fatherhood. Though the child of the family/social fatherhood formulae is employed in specific statutes and has no general application, it has introduced into law a new relation between men and children and once again (as in the use of 'social parenthood' in cases of surrogacy) shows that it is through the concept of fatherhood that relationships between men and children, and thus the family, are established in law.

This has had a knock-on effect in bringing about a shift in attitudes to unmarried fatherhood. Most importantly, this has taken place just as the ideology of the new fatherhood has legitimated a belief that *all* men (married and unmarried) are more involved in shared parenting. As a result it was not surprising that, during the 1970s and 1980s, the legal disabilities which have historically attached to the unmarried father were reconsidered and strategies aimed at reforming the rights of the unmarried father took on all the hallmarks of a progressive liberal reform (Rights of Women, Family Law Subgroup 1985). This was, perhaps, most strikingly clear during the debates which preceded the reform of the legitimacy laws by the Family Law Reform Act 1987 (see further Law Commission 1979, 1982, 1986; National Council of One Parent Families 1980; Hayes 1980; Rights of Women, Family Law Subgroup 1985).

In the Family Law Reform Act 1987 'the status of illegitimacy was obscured but not obliterated' (Stevens and Legge 1987) and the entire debate which preceded it showed that perceptions of paternal masculinity were changing. Implicit had been the belief that 'a child could only have a proper status if it was linked to a man, and that it was not good enough to be the child of a woman' (Rights of Women, Family Law Subgroup 1985: 194–5). Or, as the 1979 Working Paper put it, 'the decision to exclude a father from all parental rights and duties is so important that it should not be the mother's alone' (Law Commission 1979: para. 4.25). The focus on disadvantages perceived to befall groups of *men* also tapped into the men's liberationist discourse (see Chapter 1) which was gaining ground in the context of a growing concern with men's rights in matrimonial law (for example the Campaign For Justice on Divorce; Allan 1982). As a result the ideas that men were somehow 'unequal' to women and that women were inadequate to parent alone were fused.

We can see several links in the law's seemingly disparate historical treatment of married and unmarried men, therefore. Though married and unmarried men may have historically had very different rights, legal discourse has constructed each through reference to a naturalised discourse of male sexuality whilst promoting female sexual fidelity and chastity within a marriage or, more recently, a marriage-type relationship. This has been the hallmark of a double standard which has been fundamental to the historical development of the provision of relief for unmarried mothers. It has pervaded the development of divorce law and continues, in the 1990s, to inform debates around welfare benefits, child support and single parenthood. The law, as debates in England and Wales around the Child Support Act 1991 make clear,[17] continues to be deeply ambivalent regarding fathers' abilities to be fathers in any other than the narrow economic sense (Simpson et al. 1993: 48).

In seeking to promote men's financial responsibility something of a twin-track approach has emerged in the law. On the one hand, seeking to *enforce* obligations through institutions and procedures designed to track down 'errant fathers' (such as the Child Support Act 1991); and, on the other, seeking to *encourage* financial responsibility through court orders regulating the post-divorce relationship. With regard to the latter, the popularity of the joint custody order during the 1980s was (as in North America and elsewhere) defended on the grounds that 'legal accountability may influence and shore up psychological and financial responsibility' (Wallerstein and Kelly 1980: 310). Without legal rights, put crudely, why should men be financially responsible? However, it is the very nature of this financial 'responsibility' which is at issue here, as has been shown all too clearly in the controversy surrounding the Child Support Act 1991 (Collier 1994). Legislative attempts to 'secure' paternity, enforce maintenance payments and, ultimately, to abolish the ill/legitimate distinction itself have all in the past floundered on the uncertain and problematic nature of 'fatherhood' as a social construct. What we can see in law is an acceptance of the potential irresponsibility of all men – and the implicit argument would appear to be that without *rights* there would be no *responsibility* on the part of men. It should not be surprising that British media coverage of the campaign against the Child Support Act has, almost without exception, presented the grievances of the father as legitimate and the maintenance payments set by the Child Support Agency as unjust. The campaign has tapped into some difficult truths about familial masculinity central to which has been the economic basis of fatherhood and the uncertain nature of masculine 'responsibility' in the family.

It is this very *individualising* which has served to negate analysis of the social production of the discourses of masculinity seen in this chapter and this, I have argued, has in turn served to empower men (married and unmarried) *as men*. The hierarchical structuring of marriage (far from a 'partnership of equals') and the rhetoric and limitations of reform strategies based on rule-equality (Fineman 1983, 1989) lead us to the structural and material realities of an unequal world. Far from ostensibly egalitarian family law reforms necessarily working in the interests of women (see Weitzman 1985; Minow 1986), laws have reconstituted the familial in such a way as to absolve men from any 'fault' by constructing the modern father as the personification of equality in the modern marriage. Side-stepping the structural inequalities which benefit all men, public policy continues to look to individual men as securers of financial security; that so many men seem not to want to take on such 'responsibility' does not indicate a 'change of heart' in the 'good father' when married to the 'irresponsible' divorcee. The problem transcends the question of personal problems and solutions and is part of the 'problem' of modern marriage. Rather, 'there is a continuity from marriage to divorce because the sexual division of labour that is celebrated as natural and desirable during marriage is precisely the basis of the main conflict upon divorce' (Smart 1984b: 21).

We have seen that specific societal perceptions of masculinity, as with perceptions of marriage and divorce, have shaped the ways in which judges, lawyers, spouses and legislators have considered the fairness (or otherwise) of provisions relating to children and property (Fineman 1991a: 265). Yet marriage no longer involves a life-long commitment to particular gender roles and the 'status' model of marriage has been supplanted by the companionate/ equality ideal. In this 'modern' family the husband/father is no longer predominantly responsible for the financial security of all family members. Yet it is this paternal masculinity which continues to be, in so many ways, bound up with naturalised ideas of masculinity as an economic resource and of women as financially dependent on men.

CONCLUDING REMARKS

I have argued in this chapter that the reconstitution of the public/ private during the late nineteenth and early twentieth centuries involved a division between 'public' and 'private' masculinities in legal discourse (see also Hearn 1992: 112–15). The diminution of father's legal rights did not necessarily mean a weakening the power of men generally. Rather, these changes can be seen as involving a reconstitution or modernisation of the power of men and masculinity in which, crucially, the discursive status of the 'family man' of law assumed a central significance. In bifurcating the public and the familial, a succession of legal provisions began to undermine the autonomy of families and to intensify the division between the man as breadwinner and woman as child-carer. This separation of home and work in liberal thought and legal discourse, in tune with the psychological characteristics valorised by the Protestant work ethic (Morgan 1992: 61), reconstituted the domestic sphere as signifier of comfort and renewal for men (Davidoff and Hall 1987); but it did so, crucially, at the same time as the institutionalisation of public masculinities in the public domain were also entrenching men's power.

The transformation of familial masculinity detailed above can be seen in a dialectical relation to the institutional incorporation of these distinctly 'modern' forms of public masculinities. In particular, the period 1870–1920 (remembering that Agar-Ellis dates from 1883) 'has appeared as the historical means by which men and masculinities came from the heroic "heights" of industrial capitalism in the mid-nineteenth century to become "modern men" of this century' (Hearn 1992: 96).

> That movement towards public patriarchies has provided the specific historical problem of 'public men', and in doing so made it contestable in both interpersonal and structural politics, struggles, and reflections. The movement to public patriarchies opened up both the incorporation of subjectivity into the public domains and the possibilities for radical challenges of subjectivity.
>
> (ibid.: 227)

This was a period during which a transition in ideas of masculinities *per se* was taking place (ibid.: 12) and the period of around 1870–1920, we have seen, saw not just the emergence of the welfare principle but also a succession of those legal reforms which brought about the diminution of men's formal legal rights in the family. Fatherhood in law was itself transformed as

> men in the private domains came to be defined less as fathers and more as husbands. . . . The state was sponsoring the means

to be uninvolved in active fathering or active parenting – and instead was assisting the creation of the detached father and the status of husband.

(ibid.: 114)

The incorporation of public masculinities was never a complete institutional closure. Rather, although masculinity was modernised in ways compatible with maintaining male dominance within the family of the new order, the masculinity of the man of law continued to embody ideals of class and respectability which did not relate to the lives, or masculinities, of all men. Domesticating masculinity, moving from the dangerous masculinities of dangerous classes (immoral, promiscuous, drunk, violent and so forth), involved also ridding masculinity of that which was the perceived essence of maleness at the time – the 'natural' force of male sexuality and its potentially destructive expression. It is no wonder that this process involved a de-sexualising of the father as he was transformed into the sex-less, safe and recognisable 'dad' of today. This point will be explored further in the following chapter.

What does all this mean for understanding fatherhood in the present? If it is true that the idea of extending autonomous motherhood to married parents would undermine the very basis of men's psychological investment in marriage, then the implicit argument would appear to be that without *rights* there would be no *responsibility* on the part of men. Writing in 1929, just four years after s. 1 of the Guardianship of Minors Act had enshrined the welfare principle in law, Bertrand Russell stated that he believed that any adapting of the law to the view that children 'belong' to the mother alone would result in women feeling that 'anything approximating to marriage as we know it now was an infraction of their independence and involved a needless loss of that complete ownership over their children which they would otherwise enjoy' (Russell 1929: 158). In Russell's words, such a position would 'diminish the seriousness of men's relations to women', turning them into 'mere pleasure, not an intimate union of heart and mind and body'. As a result men's 'serious emotions' would be diverted to 'his career, his country, or some quite impersonal subject'. His personal life would become 'trivial and thin, causing despair' (ibid.: 158–61). Over fifty years later, writing in the context of Australian joint-custody laws, Lehmann (1983) echoes such a concern:

If men can have their children confiscated from them irrespective of their own moral worth and effort, then they will be
obliged to avoid marriage, vasectomize themselves, become
narcissistic and use women as sexual objects.

(ibid.: 60)

It seems that the nature of men's commitment to the family,
though it is in many ways at the heart of matrimonial politics,
continues to be confused and ambiguous. The man/child connection must frequently be established in the face of men's resistance.
Russell's nightmare scenario of a man's family life without the
presence of legal obligation, responsibility and commitment raises
some fundamental questions about men and families. Why is
motherhood without men perceived as so threatening? And does
our society really know what fathers are 'for'? (Moore 1993)?

I have argued in this chapter that there is to be found in law a
familial paternal masculinity. This has emerged within a historical,
social and economic context which also saw a more general transformation in discourses of masculinity. On one level I recognise
that it is difficult to talk of paternal discipline and authority at all
without becoming caught up within broader ideas of parental
responsibility and social order. Clearly, paternal authority no
longer resembles that of 'the absolute monarch . . . characterised
by hierarchical social relations and by the governance of the
father, the husband, the master and the lord' (McKee and O'Brien
1982b: 17). Yet the law continues to construct masculinity in terms
of authority and many fathers today, as we shall see in the following
chapter, retain adequate opportunity to exercise control over
objects, situations and other people in the family. We have seen in
this chapter how 'legal discourse cannot conceive of a person in
whom gender is not a fundamentally determining attribute'
(O'Donovan 1993: 60).

The language of welfarism and the rhetoric of the best interests
of the child both point to degendered legal agents coming before
a neutral law seeking equality. Yet the subjectivities of women and
men remain gendered through reference to quite traditional
notions of male authority and discipline. In this chapter I have
sought to explore some of the contours of the subjectivity of this
'detached' modern father and the ideal of a familial masculinity
which continues to be bound up with class-based notions of
economic and sexual propriety and authority (both in terms of the

family and society generally). Authority and (legitimate/at work) absence, bonded by the breadwinner ideology, remain central to the construction of the husband in legal discourse.

In the following chapter we shall see how the 'family man' or 'detached father' which emerged in legal discourse during the late nineteenth and early twentieth centuries took on all the trappings of a benign and safe/domesticated masculinity – a masculinity marked by the dualism of a public/private divide which legitimated his absence from childcare whilst maintaining the structural supports whence he derived his economic power. We have seen in this chapter how men did not cease to be powerful in families simply because they had less formal rights than before. In constructing the modern family the gendered subjectivities of women and men were transformed through the shifting power relations of the reconstituted family (Donzelot 1980). Paternal authority was transformed by the disciplinary mechanisms of the new governmental order in such a way that mobilising paternal power no longer depended on resorting to such a juridical right. However, the cost of the transformation was assigning to the extra-familial values which did not accord with this image of the modern and safe father, a censure which in turn rendered the married father safe. It is to these masculinities that we must now turn.

Chapter 6

'Family men' and 'dangerous' masculinities

INTRODUCTION

I have argued in Chapter 5 that the construction of modern fatherhood involved rendering paternal masculinity 'safe' through the making of a distinction between the law's construction of the familial masculinity of the 'good father' and other 'dangerous' masculinities. In this chapter I wish to explore the ways in which this dichotomy continues to function so as to divert attention from the problematic nature of masculinity *per se* and, in particular, how it involves an obfuscation of the socially destructive nature of masculinities *inside* the family. In so doing I wish to challenge those dualisms through which we continue to think of men and masculinity (public/private, work/home, safe/dangerous, family/non-family). It is inadequate to frame questions about men's violences, I shall argue, in terms of asking the question 'how could a family man' act in a particular way. This presumes that 'being a family man' discounts any propensity for violence. Instead, it becomes necessary to understand how the *very idea* of the 'family man' has itself been constructed historically in law through reference to these extra-familial masculinities. To do this we need to clarify just how this family man has achieved such a powerful status within legal discourse. The idea of the 'family man' is, I want to suggest, in many respects a contradiction in terms.

THE 'FAMILY' MAN AND 'RESPECTABLE' MASCULINITY

The masculinity of the man of law

Who is the 'man' of law? The subject of liberal legal discourse, and more generally of social and political theory, is a gendered subject

(O'Donovan 1985a, 1993; Pateman 1988; Okin 1989), but the legal subject is not just a man, he is also a particular *type* of man. He is 'a competitive entrepreneur, a successful market individual who fosters his own interests and has an eye to the main chance' (Naffine 1990: 100). This man has been depicted within classical social theory as acting in the public domain on behalf of his family (that is, on behalf of women and children whose legal identities have been, in certain respects, subsumed under his; see O'Donovan 1985a: Ch. 2; Pateman 1988). It has been through highlighting the inconsistencies which bedevil social contract theory, premised on this gendered separation of work/home, that feminists have questioned the many inequalities within the marriage relationship which had come to be seen as part of a 'natural' social condition (the belief, for example, that 'both before and after the social contract it was presumed that men would exercise sexual rights over an obedient woman'; Naffine 1990: 104; also Okin 1989).

As a Weberian ideal-typical legal subject, Ngaire Naffine has argued in her book *Law and the Sexes: Explorations in Feminist Jurisprudence* (1990) that the masculinity of this man of law mirrors the interests of a particular grouping of men; specifically, that his characteristics are closely related to the worldview of the socially powerful:

> Included within the membership of this elite – indeed exemplifying its very character – are the judiciary and the top echelons of the legal profession: they may be viewed as prototypical members of the dominant group. Simply, this group is white, educated, affluent and male. Law's institutions and principles, its general orientation, may all be seen to reflect and reinforce the priorities of those who interpret and administer the law. Law's sense of the social order and the nature of people is, in many ways, their sense of the natural order.
>
> (Naffine 1990: 100)

This construction of a legal person who reflects the moral and social priorities of these persons is also to be found in family law, a subject which has itself tended to focus on the problems of economically privileged groups in constructing the '"typical" problems and "proper" solutions' to be addressed by the law (Fineman 1991a: 267). The 'family man' of law, to adapt Naffine's term, is 'a middle class man; and he evinces the style of masculinity of the middle-classes'. We have seen in Chapter 5, in relation to the breadwinner ethic and man/work relation, how this has involved a masculinity which projects the subjectivity and motivations of economic man as a rational, acquisitive and calculating activist in the development of commercial capitalism. It is this rationality, and the fact that men and women appear to do things differently, which has led feminist legal scholars to question the nature of this 'rationality' of law (Boyle 1985a; Frug 1985; Smart 1989a; see also Gilligan 1977). This is a masculinity infused with the values of participation, investment and commitment to the ethics of the capitalist order:

> The man of the social contract, the man of the marketplace, is nobody's fool. He is aware that the public sphere is a battle-ground and that only the best man will win. The man of law competes, pushes his own suit and succeeds. He flourishes in a legal system which is essentially adversarial, in which there are winners and losers, which is based on conflict. In this mould, our man of law might be seen as the archetypal tough-minded businessman – the entrepreneur.
>
> (Naffine 1990: 116)

Yet, in the domain of family law, this cannot be *all* he is. The family domain appears not quite as compatible as the commercial sphere with a legal subject and a model of masculinity which embodies the qualities of effort, endurance and virtue, an ideal of manliness which 'encourage[s] accomplishment, autonomy and aggression – all in the service of an intense competition for success in the market-place' (Rotundo 1987b: 37). He may be, primarily, a worker, a provider and an economic agent; but he is also a father, a lover, a partner in the 'companionate marriage'. He is not, given all his other commitments to the world of work, left with much time for childcare. To be a 'man', we have seen, is to be affixed in so many ways within the 'public' domain (Hearn 1992).

Reproducing the man of law

There is a history to all this. The man of law was established in legal discourse at around the same time as urbanisation, industrial-isation and capital accumulation were transforming pre-industrial conceptions of civil society and, crucially, of ideas of parenthood itself. Together these changes brought about no less than a reconstitution of familial, household and gender relations at the same time as male power within the 'public' domain of work, the market and industrial capital was being entrenched through the incorporation of distinctly 'public' masculinities (Hearn 1992):

> To become adult men . . . they must provide a livelihood which made possible domestic establishment where they and their dependents could live a rational and morally sanctioned life. The masculine persona which emerged was organised around a man's determination and skill in manipulating the economic environment
>
> (Davidoff and Hall 1987: 229)

In 'mirroring' these middle-class concerns, the masculinity of the man of law can be historically located in the context of the emergence of the 'public' masculinities of the rising middle class in the nineteenth century. In terms used by both Naffine (1990) and O'Donovan (1993) we are dealing here with the masculinity of the men of the *Gesellschaft*, of those with lives suited to the impersonal and market forces of free market capitalist society. At its heart is the ideology of separate spheres, the rational imperatives of industrialisation, industrial production and the standardisation of labour and products (Allen and Crowe 1989; Naffine 1990: 105). The historical binding of manhood with employment which we have seen in Chapter 5 is perhaps best exemplified by the concept of the 'family wage' which developed at this time (and which was articulated most clearly by the 'respectable' craft unions; see Land 1980).

Such a masculinity closely corresponds with Rotundo's (1987a) notion of the 'Masculine Achiever' as a historically specific standard of male behaviour. This ideal was, Rotundo argues, held up to middle-class men and generally held sway throughout the nineteenth century. It was an ideal which related not just to the man of law, however, but also to other associated ideas of manliness which were considered to be desirable qualities for middle-class men during the mid- to late nineteenth century (Hammerton 1992: 149). Vance (1985), for example, notes that the influential ideal of 'Christian manliness' of the time celebrated the qualities of 'physical courage, chivalric ideals, virtuous fortitude with additional connotations of military and patriotic virtue' (see also Davidoff and Hall 1987: 110; Springhall 1987). As with the masculine achiever, such an ideal can be taken as referring to 'a cluster of traits, behaviour and values that the members of a society believe a person should have as a woman or a man' (Rotundo 1987b: 35). Writing in 1838 the American lawyer Charles Theodore Russell[1] captured the essence of this masculine achiever as denoting a man who was 'made for action, and the bustling scenes of moving life, and not the poetry or romance of existence.'

To recap; on one level the breadwinner masculinity seen in Chapter 5 constitutes a contemporary variant of the masculine achiever ideal. What we have here is, above all, a model of the man as father and as provider. Yet the characteristics of the 'man of law', as an archetypal legal subject, clash in several respects with the idea of the man as a 'partner' in an egalitarian modern marriage. It is not just that the primacy of masculinity as an economic resource cuts across any notion of the father as equal participant in childcare. This 'man of law is also, and importantly, an ideal grounded in a particular *class* position. With this class-specificity in mind, therefore, it is interesting to consider how the masculinities of the 'masculine achiever' and the 'man of law' have come together in a class-based version of a respectable manliness in law. For it is just such an ideal of a *respectable masculinity* which, Mangan and Walvin (1987) suggest, emerged around the same time as the masculine achiever ideal was beginning to gain dominance across a range of discourses of masculinity.

A range of socio-economic and cultural changes brought about the emergence of this idea of respectable masculinity. In part, the sedentary and literate masculinity of the middle-class male was consciously set against the aristocratic masculine values of 'gambling, duelling, sporting and sexual prowess' (Davidoff and Hall 1987: 205). For the middle-class man, in contrast, reward lay in 'wealth, power and cerebral control of the world'. Though it was initially confined to the specific social milieu which the 'respectable' middle classes formed, as a gender ideal it nonetheless overlapped with the values of the wider culture in which the cultural choices of those addressed by this discourse became inscribed. It involved an ideal of masculinity which, importantly, did not just come about. Considerable efforts were made legitimating and promulgating a discourse of respectable familial masculinity 'through the printed word and via prestigious and proliferating educational institutions' (Mangan and Walvin 1987: 1). The scale of this reconstruction should not be underestimated therefore (Vance 1985; Rotundo 1987a). Traversing such diverse fields as the emergence of the boy scouts movement in disciplining youth

(Warren 1987), through to the pervasive masculinism of the public schools system (Mangan 1987) and the institutionalisation of sport (Park 1987; Walvin 1987), the late nineteenth and early twentieth centuries witnessed a profusion of discourses of masculinities in a more general sense. But these masculinities tended to be based, crucially, on notions of *respectability* and *sexual propriety* (frequently constructing the male body as a metaphor for the spiritual and economic health of the nation). Whilst such developments can be seen in the wider context of changes taking place in and across other discourses on adolescence, education, literature and art, all were concerned with organising the moral rectitude of the middle and, increasingly, the working classes. This was also, importantly, the period which witnessed the construction of homosexuality (Chapter 3) and the proliferation of discourses concerned with constructing the normative sexual potency of the married family man (Chapter 4), as well as the 'deviance' of those sexualities which transgressed this ideal.

As an interdiscursive nexus, the respectable family man can, in short, be seen as a historically specific construct. The formal legal changes detailed in the previous chapter tell us only one part of this history, however. We must also not lose the wider context and, in particular, the fact that this masculinity was set against and constructed in relation to what were perceived to be the extra-familial and 'dangerous' masculinities of the undomesticated male. The rest of this chapter is, accordingly, concerned with how these 'dangerous' masculinities have been and continue to be reproduced in law.

DANGEROUS MEN, DANGEROUS MASCULINITIES: THE LIMITS TO RESPECTABILITY

I have argued that this respectable familial masculinity must be located in relation to the emergence of the public masculinities of the rising middle class in the nineteenth century. The bifurcation between the dangerous and the familial took place just as the entrenchment of the public/private division had itself brought about an institutional incorporation of public masculinities (Hearn 1992). This meant that, alongside those concerted attempts to discipline men to the familial order, men's power was also being established in the domain of paid employment (Hearn 1992). The 'private' sphere of the companionate marriage stood in contrast to the (harsh, impersonal) public domain where men's power and prerogatives were being established (for example through denying women entry into professions or 'masculinising' careers hitherto dominated by women).

As an ideal of manliness, however, it never succeeded in permeating the social order. During the late nineteenth and early twentieth centuries, notwithstanding the efforts to set the ideals of respectable masculinity 'before the proletariat by pedagogues and publishers . . . pressed on them by charitable organisations and philanthropic activists' (Mangan and Walvin 1987: 4), they only ever permeated in part the working class. This point is most important, for although the ideal of respectable familial masculinity

> made important inroads . . . in middle-class schools, churches and homes . . . it is open to serious doubt whether [it] managed to take root and grow at the lower end of the social scale, where it encountered the antipathy of the poor, ill-educated and aggressive urban youths who remained the perennial but hostile target of proponents of this middle-class ideal.
>
> (Mangan and Walvin 1987: 5)

The masculinity of the man of law and the concomitant ideas of respectability and familialism may, in other words, have been ascribed to by considerable numbers of men, notably the middle-class agents of moral reform who had primarily influenced legal change and in whose image, in Naffine's terms, the man of law can be seen to be 'mirrored'; but its values did not permeate the social order.

To understand why this was so we need to identify the archaeology of its deployment. The historical entrenching of the idea of a 'respectable' familial masculinity took place in contrast to the masculinities of the extra-familial domain and, more generally, of what were perceived to be the dangerous and undomesticated classes of the late nineteenth century (the relationship between the two is, we shall see, symbiotic). The respectable masculinity of the man of law was set against the gender order of the irresponsible and sexually licentious 'dangerous classes' who haunted the Victorian imagination. The impact of industrialisation and urbanisation had brought with it an undermining of the traditional social controls which had regulated sexuality in the pre-industrial world. The 'sexual waywardness' perceived to be endemic amongst the dangerous classes at the time was, in fact, a consequence of the more general proliferation of pre-, extra- and intra-marital sexual styles which had accompanied industrial-isation. The sexual 'transgression' of the lower orders were, how-ever, rapidly seen from the view-point of a sex and class-based notion of sexual propriety (Finer and McGregor 1974: para 59). Meanwhile, laws on inheritance and illegitimacy continued to reflect the economic interests of middle-class men concerned with entrenching their entitlements to estates and (accumulating) industrial wealth through ensuring that property and titles would be inherited throughout the male line with order and certainty. From 'darkest Africa to darkest England' (Showalter 1992: 5), and trading on eugenic fears of race degeneration (Stedman-Jones 1976), chroniclers of the nineteenth century had, as the century progressed, depicted a netherworld of a chronically poor class who were yet to be civilised into the gender norms of the new familial order (Booth 1976; Keating 1976).

The transgression of the familial ideal took a number of forms. The continued existence of the pre-industrial pursuits and 'sinful recreations' (Walvin 1978: 33) of a significant section of the urban population, for example, had already informed the policing and demarcation of urban areas into those 'safe' for both capital development and 'respectable' domestic space (Cohen 1981; Storch 1981). The potential sources of obstruction which faced both capital reorganisation and familial reconstruction in the urban context included not only dealing with an archaic urban infrastructure but also the persistent threat of

> strikes, political mobilizations and organized crime . . . the development of street cultures and their irregular economies, upon which whole working-class communities came to depend as a means of local livelihood and identity against the anarchy of impersonal market forces.
>
> (Cohen 1981: 116)[2]

The perceived threat constituted by the dangerous classes during the nineteenth century should not be underestimated, therefore. By the late nineteenth century the patterns of street and neigh-bourhood usage of this 'undomesticated' working class had created an urban environment unsympathetic to the trans-formations of capitalist planning. The masculine subjects of the dangerous classes were clearly a far cry from the Victorian pater-familias (accompanied by his 'Angel in the House'; see Weeks 1981: 57–72) and the paternal masculinity evident in Agar-Ellis

(p. 186). They were also, importantly, far removed from the familial ideal and the models of marriage and fatherhood of the late nineteenth and early twentieth centuries which were emerging in legal discourse. These legal transformations were, I have argued above, fundamental to empowering the masculinity of the 'detached' father.

'SACRIFICIAL MEN' AND 'ERRANT FATHERS'

The 'sacrificial' man of law

We have seen how, in constructing the 'man of law', Naffine (1990) stresses the *class*-based nature of this ideal of male subjectivity. Indeed, she notes that it is ironic that feminists 'who object to the treatment of women as a homogeneous group' (ibid.: 115) should repeat such an essentialist 'grand theorising' in relation to law and masculinity. Naffine thus endorses Connell's (1987: 63) depiction of 'multiple masculinities' and the disaggregation of the concept of 'the male'. What this means is that, while there may be a masculine style which retains a discursive dominance in the public domain, we cannot say that all males are afforded equal access to this discourse or that all masculinities are equally privileged.

This has a number of implications for law and the family. The masculinity of the 'man of law' (as an ideal-typical legal subject) is, we have seen, that which is 'considered desirable by a dominant, middle-class type of male who is able to earn a living through his intellect rather than with his hands'. His is 'a distinctive masculinity shaped by the circumstances, expectations and priorities of the men of his class . . . a masculinity of the boardroom or the legal chambers, not of the football club' (Naffine 1990: 118). It is this masculinity which continues to be reproduced through the institutions of law and which retains a powerful cultural purchase in British public life.

One effect of this has been to render 'marginal in the eyes of the law' (ibid.: 102) those 'poor, ill-educated and aggressive urban youths' (Mangan and Walvin 1987: 5) who ill-fit this masculine ideal. Traditionally it has been in the context of criminal law and the criminal justice system that what Naffine calls the 'sacrificial man' has primarily encountered the law. It is when we stray from the concerns of the propertied classes, in other words, that such 'subordinated' masculinities enter the judicial gaze. It is, for example, those 'young, poor and uneducated' males (Naffine 1990: 124) who remain the principal object of criminological discourse and the criminal justice system (Box 1983: 54). The subjectivity of the man of law as a middle-class economic agent does not easily correspond with 'the role accorded the real men who are brought before the criminal courts'.

This has in turn generated problems for accused persons seeking to extract 'justice' from the law (Carlen 1976; Naffine 1990: 130–1) who, though they are guaranteed a right to a hearing, have their ability to speak and be understood limited by a socially subordinate position and the dominant mode of courtroom discourse (White 1991). In the field of criminal justice there exists an enormous social distance between those who are passing sentence and those who are, in the vast majority, on the receiving end of that 'justice' (Bankowski and Mungham 1976; Carlen 1976; Box 1983). This can be seen in terms of a hierarchy of masculinities within the criminal court; indeed, magistrates courts are a showground for competing masculinities. The assessments by judges of the propriety of the actions of 'lower' class males involve, crucially, judgements about masculinity. Indeed, the overwhelming maleness not just of crime but of the criminal justice system itself is the single most obvious fact which, ironically, criminology has largely failed to address (Jefferson 1992).[3]

This also has a number of implications for how we understand the masculinities of family law, for such men are also fathers, partners, husbands and sons. The gendered assumptions which pervade empirical and theoretical accounts of crime illustrate the nature of the overlap between familial ideology (male/breadwinner, female/childrearer) and the constitution of criminality. For example, assumptions are made about men's familial responsibilities; in the constitution of the family as a source of social control it is assumed that men engage in primary breadwinner responsibilities as providers for their family (Eaton 1986). The problem is, of course, that not all men are afforded equal access to employment opportunities and cannot equally so 'provide'. Men are assessed within terms of the familial ideology but, signified by economic rather than sexual/gendered considerations, it appears to be assumptions about social class and race which inform their status (for example ideas of 'dangerous', 'disrespectful' masculinity) rather than more obviously or overtly gendered considerations (for example the 'good mother', 'good housekeeper' idea). The familiar assumption would seem to be that when a man meets a woman, then his life becomes 'anchored' because of his new found responsibilities.

The pervasiveness of the construction of masculinity as an economic resource is illustrated by those theories of male offending which have generally tended to take as axiomatic the idea that the central activity of the men under scrutiny is paid employment (Farrington and Morris 1983). Yet we also know that prevailing notions about the effect of unemployment on crime cannot be sustained when it is female, and not male, crime which is the object of study (Naffine and Gale 1989). Moreover, the gender culture which unites the masculinities of perpetrators of 'white-collar'/ corporate crime (Box 1983: 39) and the more 'routine' crimes of the criminal justice system involves value systems, motivational imperatives and access to public space which are common to men of all classes. Nonetheless the attentions of the criminal justice system remain directed towards the property crimes of the 'lower' classes.

How does all this relate to the man of law? The relationship between the values of the dominant group (as 'mirrored' in the man of law) and the jurisprudential tradition of doctrinal exegesis is symbiotic. The legal subject remains, to this day, a gendered subject which embodies the masculinity of a particular group of males whose character is exemplified by 'the judiciary and the top echelons of the legal profession . . . [a] dominant group' which is 'white, educated, affluent and male' (Naffine 1990: 100). This does not necessarily accord with the subject positions of all men. Given the power of elite males to construct a moral discourse of their own gender, the marginalisation of working-class cultures and these 'sacrificial' masculinities in legal discourse is perhaps unsurprising. However, the problem with the above analysis – or of simply seeing masculinity in terms of class – is that it side-steps the power which law accords to *all* men *as men.*

On the one hand it is important to recognise the diversity of masculinities and the fact that all men are not constituted the same way in law. The example of the 'sacrificial men' of the law shows how familial assumptions can inform the construction of masculinities in criminal law discourse. Nonetheless there are limits to this notion of competing masculinities. The politics of gender cut across traditional party politics. It would be misleading at this point, therefore, simply to 'enlist sympathy for the working-class family as subject to surveillance by experts' (O'Donovan 1993: 22). What we need to do here, in the light of the above discussion of the historical constitution of the man of law and the idea of 'respectable' familial masculinity, is to relate this idea of class-mediated masculinities to the gender politics of the matrimonial domain. In other words, it is necessary to bring together these concerns with class and masculinity in an analysis of how the idea of the 'family man' works to benefit all heterosexual men but also to effectively marginalise those men who 'fail' to live up to the dominant constitutive element of this masculinity.

To recap: the legal subject is gendered, he is masculine, but his is a certain kind of masculinity. The 'man of law' emerged just as masculinity was itself being bifurcated into public/private spheres of men's lives. All men might be potential 'good fathers' – but all men were not, and could not, be economically 'successful' as providers for 'their' family. The ideological power of the idea of the 'family man', as a kind of rhetorical glue, has served to detract attention from the basic contradictions which run through the 'family man' ideal and the very deep ambiguity which continues to mark the legal construction of fatherhood in law. I want to illustrate this through a detailed discussion of an issue which has assumed considerable political significance in the early 1990s in the UK. It is an issue which clarifies and exemplifies themes already discussed in Chapter 5 in relation to the social construction of father-absence. It also, importantly, illustrates how class-based notions of dangerous masculinities can be reproduced in debates about family law reform. In relation to the construction of single motherhood as a social problem the above themes of father-absence, class and 'subordinated' and 'hegemonic' masculinities coalesce.

'A normal father's love': constructing the 'errant father' discourse

Men? Who needs them? Far from single mothers being the objects of shame or pity they once were, more and more women are opting to have babies independent of traditional reproduction and family structure. And age seems no barrier. But is this a revolution out of control?

(*The Guardian* 18 February 1993)

During July 1993 a high-profile and apparently orchestrated[4] political row took place in Britain following comments made by the Conservative Cabinet Minister John Redwood. He had suggested that some single women were deliberately becoming pregnant, with no intention of marrying, in the knowledge that they would then be supported by the state. Moreover, he declared, lone mothers should not receive state benefit until the 'errant father' had been found and forced to return to the family. Redwood was not simply suggesting that fathers should make a financial contribution to the upkeep of their child. This was already accepted in law in England and Wales and its implementation was the task of the Child Support Agency, set up by the government under the Child Support Act 1991. What Redwood was stating was that fathers should return to the household so that they might offer what he called 'the normal love and support that fathers have offered down the ages' (*Guardian* 3 July 1993).

Redwood's comments were populist and crude but they were also the catalyst for an extensive public debate about what he termed 'one of the greatest social problems of our day'. A succession of government ministerial statements followed his lead in blaming the numbers of single mothers on such diverse influences as the church, 'politically correct' ideas and a feminist movement which 'has given encouragement to the concept that it is all right to have a child and bring the child up on your own' (*Guardian* 6 July 1993).[5] Whilst some sought to distance themselves from such comments',[6] what the ensuing controversy did was to scapegoat single mothers as an 'undeserving' poor whilst, conveniently, placing on the political agenda the possibility of further cuts in welfare benefits (cuts which were soon to follow).

What was marked about this and other debates about single motherhood, both in Britain and elsewhere, was the absence of critical discussion of paternal masculinity. This absence then made it easier for rhetorical appeals to 'the normal love that fathers have offered' to side-step a number of difficult questions about contemporary fathering and men's relationships to women and children. Fathers were, therefore, largely absent from the debates even though 'father absence' was itself the central problem. Out of sight and out of mind, there was a systematic failure to address the fact that generations of men have been considered effectively redundant by the women with whom they have children because they either cannot or will not pay maintenance (Smart 1985a; Edwards and Halpern 1990b, 1990c). Rather, when paternal masculinity was considered it was through reference to the familiar myths and images of fathering which combine ideas of class and culture in constructing paternal masculinity. In particular, what the single mother debates in Britain did was to construct an 'irresponsible', feckless (lower-class) father and, in contrast, the 'normal love' offered by responsible and respectable married men (such as Redwood and his Cabinet colleagues).

In this process the ideal of the responsible and respectable family man discussed above was consciously invoked, notwithstanding the fact that the majority of women who petition and are eventually divorced 'find themselves on their own with their children, virtually abandoned by their husbands, struggling to make ends meet on half their original income, 75 per cent of the husbands and fathers making no contribution to the household' (Robinson 1991: 270). Divorce research shows that the majority of cases are marked by a pattern of proactivity on the part of women and reactivity on the part of men (Burgoyne et al. 1987: 33). That is, women are not only likely to be the initiators of divorce but they are also less likely to regret the decision (Davis and Murch 1988). In 1990, for example, 72 per cent of divorces were granted to women and in 55 per cent of these cases the grounds cited were the husband's unreasonable behaviour (OPCS 1992; see further Simpson et al. 1993: 2)

The scale of father-absence is staggering. In Britain, it has been suggested, as many as 47 per cent of fathers lost contact with their children following divorce (Bradshaw and Millar 1991) and, at a current estimate, around 750,000 children have lost contact with their fathers. Yet during a subsisting marriage, as we have seen in Chapter 5, fathers are also often absent from the family due to the demands of work. So whatever we mean by a father's presence in the family cannot be taken as necessarily referring to a substantial physical presence; rather, as we have seen, the law has constructed this paternal presence through reference to men's employment capacity.

This issue brings together the ideas of class and the respect-able family man. The problem at issue here, as in debates around the Child Support Act 1991, is not simply one of 'forcing' fathers to pay (Edwards and Halpern 1990a; Wilton 1990; Collier 1994). It is, rather, about 'cultures of masculinity that mean men will not co-operate with women and take care of their children' (Campbell 1993: 310). There is a growing consensus that fathers should be financially responsible for their children. What there does not appear to be, however, is any understanding of how *cultures of masculinity* which are inimical to men's involvement with childcare have themselves been reproduced through law and how they continue to inform understandings of the morality, economics and the politics of single parenthood. It is this failure to engage with cultures of masculinity which has been particularly evident in the historical construction of the errant father discourse.

The idea of the 'errant' and irresponsible father, which has surfaced so clearly in recent debates, taps into and reproduces deep-seated ideas about respectable familial masculinity. I have argued above that the separating out of a 'safe' paternal masculinity from other 'dangerous' masculinities involved making an association between the extra-familial and ideas of economic irresponsibility and sexual licentiousness. Sex, class and morality have been bound together in projecting the idea of the 'responsible' father. The history of the illegitimacy laws illustrates clearly how the sexualities and subjectivities of all men, married and unmarried, have been valorised in law (Smart 1987; above p. 204). What we are dealing with in the case of the errant father discourse, however, is an ideological division between discourses of 'respectable' and 'irresponsible/dangerous' masculinities which are, in fact, two sides of the same coin. It is a *male* culture, not simply a *class* culture, which is at issue here (Campbell 1993). It is misleading, Campbell has argued, to interpret the 'flight of fathers' either as a purge orchestrated by mothers or through reference to a 'heyday of respectability as the proper regime of family life' where that 'respectability' was expressed through the economic power of the father (Campbell 1993; c.f. Dennis and Erdos 1992). That respectability was premised in the first place, as we have seen in Chapter 5, on a legally structured male authority derived from the man/work relation. What is shared, in other words, between classes of males through the cultures of masculinity, irrespective of marital status, is far more than is usually allowed. In the present context what these classes of males can be seen to share is a *lack* of any involvement in childcare.

Yet a class-based construct of masculinity continues to inform the idea of the 'family man' in law. In Britain this has been particularly clear in recent debates about the existence of an urban *underclass*, which curiously echoes nineteenth century concerns about the 'dangerous classes'. Just as in the late nineteenth century the emerging familial masculinity of the modern father was contrasted with the urban proletarian 'mob', in the early 1990s a similar idea of a sexually, economically and socially irresponsible dangerous class has resurfaced in the debates (in Britain and elsewhere) around single motherhood and child maintenance. This has happened through assigning to this 'underclass' a range of values and behaviour which are seen as underpinning the 'problem' of lone parenthood (for example greed, 'loose' morals, inability to work, absent fathers who are more commited to crime than to providing for their family). Indeed, this idea of an underclass (which has been promoted in both Europe and North America by politicians and academics from different political persuasions) has come to signify a working class residuum unwilling or unable to adapt to economic, sexual and familial norms (Galbraith 1992; Robinson and Gregson 1992; Campbell 1993: 306).

The deceit, hypocrisy and gender-blindness with which the debate about single mothers has been constructed is indicative of the contemporary purchase not just of the underclass thesis but also of the discursive power of the ideology of the family man. It is within this section of society, specifically, that the problem of the 'flight of fathers' has been primarily constructed. Yet such an image is deliberately misleading; the continued political concern with single mothers who have never married obscures the fact that around two-thirds of lone mothers are divorced, separated or widowed.[7] That is, made up of women who have tried the nuclear ideal but have found, for whatever reason, that it does not always work. This is a context in which it is already the case that lone mothers are less likely to work outside the home than married mothers and pregnant women continue to be discriminated against in employment. Meanwhile the lack of childcare facilities continues to confine many women to marginal, low-paid and low-status employment. In reducing child welfare to a matter of financial arrangements (Bryant 1992), one effect of legislation such as the Child Support Act 1991 appears to have been to thrust lone parents even deeper into hardship.

There is a further deceit to the dominant construction of single mothers and absent fathers, however, and to address this we need to understand the ways in which the family man discourse is reproduced. It promotes a belief that the problem is a question of the irresponsibility of a single group of men and women (read underclass) and not one of cultures of masculinity generally (cultures which pervade socio-economic groupings and which are, we have seen, reproduced in law). That generations of judges have reproduced these beliefs in family law – and that they should be so grossly insensitive to the needs of single mothers – should not surprise us when it is remembered that they 'belong to a generation whose mothers and wives are likely to live out the myth of the idealised family' (O'Donovan 1993: 31). It is the invisibility of fatherhood therefore, secured through reference to a catch-all, benign but illusive, family man, which has functioned to make the scapegoating of single mothers possible; a family man which has embedded in its definition a breadwinner masculinity which negates men's involvement in childcare in any case. Women, as mothers, are associated with nurturing and compassion. Men, constructed as potentially feckless and irresponsible, are excluded from such a caring ethic (the vast majority of fathers living away from their children are, we know, unwilling to support them).

What are these errant fathers like? Well, they are not like us. From the class-mediated perspective of the judicial gaze this objectification of the 'errant father' has served to divert attention from the masculinities of the elite males who are setting the parameters of the debate, those who are cutting benefits and who are, at the end of the day, returning home to their (usually second) wives and children to provide their 'normal love and support'. Yet however politicians and the media might construct this issue the failure to engage emotionally and economically with women and children cannot be confined to a particular class of men. Historically masculinity has been constituted as emotionally distant (Seidler 1987). It is not just the 'irresponsible' behaviour of a 'bunch of jobless teenagers', therefore, but is one end of a continuum of what is considered to be 'acceptable' masculine behaviour, and therein, lies the problem:

> It is not only unemployed men from inner city dumps who feel that it is perfectly OK to procreate and move on. All kinds of men think children basically belong to women, that their part in the process ends as soon as they put their trousers back on . . . we can't even have a debate if no one is going to ask the most obvious and fundamental question: how do you get men to change?
>
> (Suzanne Moore, *Guardian* 16 July 1993)

Disturbing the perceptual grid which renders male heterosexuality invisible makes it possible to 'recognize the extent of the complex, mutually reinforcing nature of men's power, as a class, and the diversity of men and men's power' (Hearn 1992: 96). The historical emergence of discourses of 'underclass' masculinity, from the late nineteenth century to the present day, can be seen in relation to ideals of a 'respectable' masculinity. In fact the 'errant' fathers, aggressive youths and dangerous masculinities (the very stuff of traditional criminological discourse)

> have more in common with the men who represent the nation, the rowdy louts in the Palace of Westminster, whose manners are modelled on an upper-class cult of conflict. The lads on the terraces behave more like MPs on the benches than school dinner ladies and secretaries, and the women who have to put up with them.
>
> (Campbell 1993: 313)

At the heart of the errant father discourse is something with which we are now familiar – a naturalised discourse of male sexuality. It is this which has been the ever-present 'other side' of the responsible, committed family man. The very *fragility* of men's familial commitment, the almost disbelief that men might want to take on responsibility, has never been far below the surface of family rhetoric. Implicitly, it is accepted than men desert women and leave them to care for children. In the debates which preceded the Divorce Reform Act 1969, O'Donovan (1993: 78) notes, the divorcing husband was constructed as a 'middle-aged Casanova . . . "a butterfly flitting from flower to flower". Men desert women. Women are ditched'. What the recent controversies around single mothers have shown is how these stereotypes retain their power. Yet to really appreciate the paradox of the simultaneous power and fragility of the family man discourse, it is worthwhile to look elsewhere – to those areas where familial masculinity transgresses both the familial ideal and the law.

In the next section of this chapter I wish to illustrate how the idea of the family man can work to divert attention from what I shall term the 'dangerous' qualities of familial masculinity. In particular, I want to explore the reproduction of the family man discourse in areas where the prevalence of men's violence and power has raised fundamental questions about what we understand 'normal' male heterosexualty to be in the first place. Specifically, I shall look at legal responses in two areas where male heterosexuality transgresses the idea of a 'safe' family man. These are prostitution and child sexual abuse.

THE FAMILY MAN AS 'OTHER': CASE STUDIES

The example of prostitution: the Sexual Offences act 1985

The history of the legal regulation of prostitution has been marked by a sexual double standard, oppressive legislation and the powerful ideology of male sexual 'needs' (McIntosh 1978b). If it is true that the 'power of a discourse resides in the way it passes as truth and in the way its premises and logic are taken for granted' (Holloway 1981: 33), then the discourse of male sexuality continues to exert considerable power in framing understandings of prostitutes and their clients. In England and Wales the post-Wolfenden (1957) strategy of the law has been to manage prostitution in an 'acceptable' form (the parameters of which have varied historically). But even within its own liberal terms, existing legislation has had a limited effect on stopping prostitution (Matthews 1985: 1986).

There is now a wealth of feminist literature which has explored prostitution's legal and social history (Millet 1975; Jaget 1980; Walkowitz 1980a, 1980b, 1984; McLeod 1982: Ch. 4; Wilson 1983; Smart 1985). Prostitution is also one area where the politics of male sexuality has, for a century at least, been of central importance in framing understandings of legal intervention. Traditional accounts of law and prostitution (Sion 1977; Honoré 1978) are full of essentialist constructions of sexuality. What is interesting in such accounts is how the

> cravings of men constitute the overt, socially recognised problem. Men consciously experience and express 'needs' that go beyond monogomy . . . the idea that male sexual needs are themselves socially produced would be considered unscientific because they depend on things that cannot be directly observed.
>
> (McIntosh 1978b)

We have seen in Chapters 3 and 4 how a judicial acceptance of this 'hydraulic' model of male sexuality has proved pervasive in both criminal and matrimonial law. It is perhaps not surprising, therefore, that it was not until the 1980s that the behaviour of the male clients of prostitutes was criminalised for the first time. Until the enactment of the Sexual Offences Act 1985, the kerb-crawling client of the prostitute effectively escaped prosecution. For the prostitute, however, non-payment of fines continued to mean that prison remained a possible punishment (Matthews 1985).

The Sexual Offences Act 1985 is, in effect, a piece of legislation concerned with setting limits as to what constitutes 'legitimate' male sexual adventuring. Masculinity and male sexuality are central to the Act. It was prompted, however, not by any expectation of finally erradicating street prostitution (though the legislators considered that that would be desirable), but by the evidence of tenant associations, community groups and local councils which had made clear that a range of public order and nuisance problems in 'red-light' areas were resulting more from the customers, rather than the sellers, of sex. The pressure to 'do something' about this nuisance led to a perceived need to try and circumscribe the opportunities in which the male kerb-crawling client can seek sex. It was a concern with nuisance with which the Act was primarily concerned, therefore, and not prostitution *per se*. As was stressed during the parliamentary debates, MPs did not feel they were being asked 'to take a moral view. They are asking us to prevent abuse and nuisance' (T. Marlow, 82 Hansard; Col. 660, 5 July 1985).

How does this relate to the family man discourse? It has been difficult to escape questions of morality in legislating around prostitution and nowhere has this moralising been more evident than in relation to assigning a deviant sexual status to the 'common' prostitute herself (Smart 1985). The kerb-crawling client, in contrast, may have evoked an image of particular masculinity; an image of a sad, joyless, sexually frustrated outsider (though in fact research suggests that the vast majority are 'just like other men – ordinary' (see McLeod 1981, 1982)). Until the 1985 Act, however, he had not been subject to criminal sanction. This idea that the client was different from the respectable family man recurred during the parliamentary debates which preceded the passing of the Sexual Offences Act 1985 (just as it had been an assumption which had blighted the investigation into the murders by Peter Sutcliffe; see further Holloway 1981; Smith 1989: 117). The 1985 Act, ostensibly breaking ground by criminalising the male kerb-crawling client, in fact drew heavily on and reinforced existing sexual ideologies. In particular, and although the public nuisance dimension was clearly foremost in the mind of legislators, we can see other issues running through the parliamentary debates which preceded the Act. First, there was a concern expressed that local women, characterised as 'innocent', were being inadvertently singled out by the kerb-crawling clients of the prostitute, and that these women should be afforded adequate protection from certain men. Second, there was a concern running through the debates that whatever legislation did result should adequately protect 'innocent' men who might be charged with soliciting a prostitute. Each issue derives from a particular understanding of the family man in law.

The 'ordinary woman' and the 'men who fall from the kerb'

The Sexual Offences Act 1985, which followed a private members bill and the recommendations of the Criminal Law Revision Committee in their Report *Prostitution in the Street*, made kerb-crawling an offence for the first time in England and Wales. However, the parliamentary debates which preceded the Act traded in a succession of stereotypes which drew on a belief in the inevitability of prostitution whilst continuing to censure the female prostitute as an outcast. A consensus appeared that prostitution (though for unspecified reasons) was inevitable; it has 'always existed and always will exist' (M. Parris, 79 Hansard: Col. 678, 17 May 1985). For some MPs a preferable solution would have been to ensure that it take place in 'a less offensive . . . more civilised way because it simply won't go away' (J. Fraser, ibid.: Col. 680). At the turn of the century the Home Secretary of the time had similarly commented that 'To get rid of prostitution . . . is out of the question so long as human nature is what it is' (quoted by Weeks 1981: 85). Legislation in Britain continues, it seems, to construct prostitution as an eternal mystery, shrouded in the language of fatalism and biological imperative.

What was interesting in the debates around the Act was how women's sexuality was itself assessed within masculinist parameters (drawing on a long tradition of the law's construction of the prostitute as sexual object: see further Smart 1985). The problem arose when the object of the solicitation was not a prostitute but a particular kind of woman:

an ordinary woman – one's sister, wife or someone else's daughter – going home to visit a friend and not dressed in any way that could be described as extravagent or sexually provocative.

(D. Mellor, 82 Hansard: Col. 670, 5 July 1985)

The 'ordinary' woman is here defined through reference to her (familial) relationship to a man. This would seem to be the reason she needs protection. Heaven forbid that one's wife or sister or other member of the family might dress in a sexually provocative manner:

> How would a member of the Committee feel if he [sic] went home tonight and was greeted by his wife who broke down and cried because she was accosted by a kerb-crawler who wanted to know how much money she wanted to have sex with him. A man who has any respect for his wife would find that absolutely repugnant . . . [what] am I supposed to say to constitutents who come to my surgery, sometimes with their husbands or boy-friends to complain about being victims of kerb-crawlers?
>
> (T. Cox, Hansard Standing Committee C: Col. 63–4, 27
February 1985)

Crucially, the problem is here set up from the perspective of the family man. How would a man feel? He would find it repugnant. He becomes part of the trauma. The discourse which emerges sets up the 'respectability' of the family man (the innocent man to be protected from false accusation) through reference to the 'innocent' non-prostitute women that need to be protected from men's advances. Thus, what would on the surface appear to be a concern with nuisance and public order is then constructed through reference to a masculinist perspective on prostitution 'so that even when we are not looking at male sexuality as such we are looking at the world within its frame of reference' (Weeks 1986: 38). This reflects the more general way in which legal institutions have tended to 'protect' only those women who conform to male expectations and interpretations of 'woman' (see Bumiller 1991; Grbich 1991). It also reveals the ways in which women's status is imbued with matters arising from their gender. As Smart notes, when women go to law they do so as

> mothers, wives, sexual objects, pregnant women, deserted mothers, single mothers and so on. They are not simply women (in distinction to men) and they are most definately not un-gendered persons.
>
> (Smart 1990b: 7)

The contrast with men is stark. MPs stressed their concern that the 'true punishment' of arrest under the Act would be 'the wrecking of a person's reputation and career . . . comments made from car windows to women on the street are so liable to misinterpretation there is always the possibility of a mistake' (M. Parris, 79 Hansard Col. 672, 17 May 1985). Any charge might have a catastrophic effect 'on his reputation . . . on a man's marriage. It would have a catastrophic effect on a man's family life' (T. Marlow, 82 Hansard: Col. 661, 5 July 1985). This concern with 'reputation' and 'career' has, clearly, a distinct class dimension.

It is interesting that the attitude to the 'natural' quality of the male sexual urge which underpins prostitution was much more ambiguous. Thus 'great concern' was expressed about the police tactic of using policewomen as decoys; after all 'the WPCs in Leicestershire are attractive ladies and . . . some innocent people might be tempted down the wrong road', though if they were so 'tempted' what then happens to their 'innocent' status (P. Brunivels, 79 H.C. Debates: Col. 670, 17 May 1985)? The general strategy is part of an acceptance of an individualising of the prostitute's client through reference to psychological and psychiatric explanations of why men might seek the services of a prostitute. There is no integration of feminist discourses, for example, which might stress the structural context in which prostitution takes place. Instead, psychiatric explanations served to cast the client as somehow 'sick' and thus render any solution individual rather than societal (whilst, importantly, simultaneously diminishing his responsibility). They also, of course, distance the client from the 'normal' family man.

This individualising can be seen in relation to the construction of the 'red light' area of many British cities (frequently inner city areas with low-grade housing) as the locus of male sexual threat. Yet, as McLeod (1982) has pointed out, the problem of male physical and sexual harassment cannot be confined to 'innocent' (non-prostitute) women living in or passing through 'red light' areas. Women generally are brought up not to go out alone after dark, be it in the country or an inner city area when the 'threat of male assault and harassment of women on the streets is geographically universal in this country' (see further Chadwick 1986).

The subsequenct reluctance to enforce the Act[8] is, however, perhaps understandable when it is remembered that both police and Crown Prosecution Service (who are responsible for bringing criminal prosecutions in England and Wales) had, shortly after the enactment of the Sexual Offences Act, got their fingers burnt over the arrest and prosecution of 'leading' public figures (and, in particular, members of the judiciary). In 1986 Colin Hart-Leverton QC, a leading and well-respected barrister, was prosecuted by the Metropolitan Police. His initial conviction was quashed on appeal at the Crown Court, and this case appeared to have prompted caution on the part of the police in bringing further prosecutions. However, the 1985 Sexual Offences Act and the efficacy of the law relating to prostitution achieved its highest public profile in recent years in Britain in 1991, following the case of another public figure arrested for kerb-crawling – only this time it was the Director of Public Prosecutions, the head of the Crown Prosecution Service and the man who was in charge of bringing prosecutions under the Act in the first place.

We have seen above how the idea of a division between innocent/guilty women was reproduced around the Sexual Offences Act. In the case of the arrest of Allan Green, the former Director of Public Prosecutions for England and Wales, we can see how the family man discourse can function to protect the 'innocent' but to chastise those men who 'fall from the kerb' (*The Times*, 4 October 1991). On the morning of 4 October 1991 the national press in Britain made much play of a photograph of Sir Allan Green and his wife, Eva, just after he received his knighthood. The disjuncture of this image with the facts of his arrest (in the streets around King's Cross, one of London's areas most notorious for prostitution) prompted deliberations in the British media on the 'Fatal Attraction of Prostitutes' and the seeming perennial problem of those 'men who fall from the kerb'. The legal profession quickly rallied to Green's defence. As the senior legal official in the country, in charge of criminal prosecutions in England and Wales, his resignation produced shock and sadness among the legal profession. The Attorney-General 'bitterly regretted what has happened', whilst the Home Secretary described the case as a 'personal tragedy'. However, there remained a recognition that resignation was inevitable and that he had, in the words of the Home Secretary, 'done the right thing' in resigning.

The responses of both the media and the legal profession to Allan Green's resignation tapped into and reproduced the discourse of the family man. Green's actions were, it was stressed, an abberation, a flaw in an otherwise honourable personality.

Frequenting prostitutes was, within this discourse, an *individual* failing on the part of men (though Green was, in fact, the latest of a succession of public figures disgraced by charges of kerb-crawling including peers, politicians and media celebrities). He was, in the words of a High Court Judge, 'the very last person I would have expected this of' (*The Times*, 4 October 1991). For the *Daily Telegraph* (4 October 1991) the resignation was 'another body blow to justice . . . already hit by a catalogue of cases involving mis-carriage of justice'. For others the punishment was 'out of all proportion to the offence' and it was 'odd in what is claimed to be a libertarian society that willing partners cannot enter into a contract, however temporary or meaningless, for their own satis-faction' (Nicholas Fairbairn in *The Independent*, 4 October 1991)

Ideas of class and masculinity come together here. Married with two children (and a knighthood), Sir Allan Green represented an archetypal 'family man'; much was made in the media of his social status. But, crucially, the familialism this involved needed to be contrasted with the Other and, in the case of prostitution, this has tended to involve a narrative structure which invokes images of the 'world he left behind'. So, much is made of the idea of the 'dangerous area' – the litter-strewn, decaying streets around King's Cross, the locale for 'shifty men . . . fast-food shops' (the locale of *other* males, not the respectable man). This is contrasted with the elegant offices of the Director of Public Prosecutions at Queen Anne's Gate in London (implicitly the narrative reads 'how could this man fall so far?'). This is, we should remember, not just a media construction of one man's tragedy but also a perspective which pervades sociological and cultural texts on prostitution.

This contrast between the image of the middle-class family man and a 'working class prostitute' (very much part of the history of prostitution) was strikingly clear in Britain in what has become a now notorious summing up in the libel trial brought by Jeffrey (now Lord) Archer. Jeffrey Archer is a former Conservative MP, but he is perhaps best known as the author of a number of financially successful novels. He was also, for a brief period, Chairman of the Conservative Party and is thus a high profile public figure in Britain. When a national newspaper alleged that he had made payments to a pro-stitute in order to secure her silence (implying there had been a sexual relation), he took action for libel. His case in the High Court is culturally, if not legally, significant in this context for it revealed the judicial construction of familial masculinity with which we are now becoming increasingly familiar. Though it did not concern the Sexual Offences Act 1985, its parameters were squarely within the sexual ideology which informed the Act and thus reveal further aspects of the family man ideal.

We have seen how the judicial gaze has sexualised the corporeality of women in the non-consummation cases in Chapter 4. Importantly, in the Archer case, the sexualising of Mary Archer, Jeffrey Archer's wife, became inseparable from the construction of Archer's middle-class familial masculinity as respectable and therefore not in need of sexual 'servicing'. Both the media and the judge made much of her attractiveness; her image, the judge commented, was one of 'elegance' and 'fragrance' and without the strain of the trial she would have a 'radiance'. The jury were explicitly asked to consider her sexual status: 'What is she like in physical features? In presentation?' Her 'happy married life' was linked to the presence of intercourse – she thus comments 'with delicacy' that 'Jeffrey and I lead a full life' (they were 'blessed . . . with two sons who are possibly at their most attractive ages'). Thus, there was clearly no 'abstinence from marital joys for Archer – for Jeffrey', (*The Times*, 24 July 1987). As in the non-consummation cases, intercourse is presumed and it is intercourse which signifies normality.

The way in which this masculinity is depicted is simple. Archer is first constructed as a man engaged in a healthy marital sexual relationship. Then, the foundation laid, we are informed that he embodies the respectable values and manliness of the middle-class male. 'His history . . . is worthy and healthy and sporting . . . he's fit looking . . . he's still interested in an athletic life.' Then comes the pay-off: given all these respectable hetero- sexual qualities, the subtext becomes *'how could he?'*.

> Is he in need of cold, unloving, rubber-insulated sex in a seedy hotel, round about a quarter to one on a Tuesday morning after an evening at the Caprice with his editor?
>
> (*The Times*, 24 July 1987)

This paean to the familial does not negate an essentialist discourse of male sexuality. He is not in need of 'cold, unloving rubber-insulated sex' because he is sexually satisfied in marriage (even though it appears that the majority of prostitutes' clients are married; McLeod 1982). If his wife is 'fragrant' and 'elegant', the other woman at the centre of the case, a Monica Coghlan, is described as a 'working-class prostitute' who would work her 'beat' for a 'miserable three or four hours a night'; she would 'shrink into alleyways to avoid being arrested'. She would use 'guile and cunning' to get her way (*The Times*, 24 July 1987). She was not, as the newspapers reported each day of the trial as they contrasted the fashions of the leading ladies, quite so 'elegant and fragrant' in appearance. She was beyond the familial as constructed through the masculinist aesthetic.

> Under the present meaning of 'woman' it is always *she* who will be scrutinized and unveiled before a court simply because it is still women who are constituted around male aesthetics and male sexuality.
>
> (Grbich 1991: 74)

Prostitution serves as an example of how the discourse of familial masculinity can be reproduced in a particular legal context – and how 'like much of our public culture, prostitution contributes to the casting of women as object and man as subject and thus to the prevailing ideology' (McIntosh 1978b: 63–4). It reveals a dialectical relation between the family man discourse and the sexualising of women's bodies. There are, of course, different views of prostitution available. The English Collective of Prostitutes, based in King's Cross and concerned with prostitutes' rights and working conditions, brought a very different view to bear on the case of Allan Green. In their input into the media, in the days after his arrest, they stressed that male violence was an everyday threat for prostitutes and that it remained primarily economic factors which drove women to prostitution. Recent cutbacks in child and housing benefits, alongside male unemployment, had simply exacerbated the problems which prostitutes face. Moreover, it was stressed, around 70 per cent of working prostitutes in Britain were single parents (one of the very groups being scapegoated as 'undeserving' poor by the Conservative government).

Such facts, of course, do not square with the ideology of male sexual needs and the ideal of the family man. Instead, we find that it is the image of 'innocent' women and 'deviant' masculinity which continues to inform the legal regulation of prostitution. Prostitution raises many difficult questions about masculinity and the nature of 'sexual connection'; it is part of contemporary masculinity that men pursue, initiate, harass or force women (Coward 1982). Yet it would be misleading to read the law regarding prostitution as simply revealing the power of the ideology of male sexual needs, however powerful these ideologies are for both men and women (the idea that men, 'being men', means nothing can be done).

The failure of the Sexual Offences Act 1985 to 'do something' about the problems of kerb-crawling is palpable. Despite its progressive resonances, it has perpetuated and reinforced a normative sexual discourse which has, ironically, legitimated in many respects the behaviour it sought to eradicate. The criminalisation of the male heterosexual client by the Sexual Offences Act 1985 does not represent any significant departure in the legal conception of 'legitimate' male sexual behaviour. An ideolology of male sexual needs continues to be reproduced in debates around prostitution. If we wish to understand how this ideology is reproduced then we also need to challenge the ways in which the discourse of familial masculinity separates out 'safe' and 'dangerous' men. Ultimately, the 1985 Act simply continues a long legal history of ambiguity and uncertainty about the morality of prostitution and the 'acceptable' parameters of male heterosexual expression.

Child sexual abuse and masculinity: constructing the abuser.

The example of prostitution reveals a bifurcation of heterosexual masculinity into the 'safe'/respectable and dangerous/deviant. This division has also informed the ways in which the law has responded to child sexual abuse. The questions raised by child sexual abuse about 'normal' masculinity are manifest; the nature of men's involvement with children, the sexual division of labour (and the public/private dichotomy on which it is based), the differential forms of men's interaction with girls and boys, the relationship between men in private (for example, fathers) and men in public (for example, police, lawyers, social workers), as well as the historical binding of fatherhood with ideas of authority (see Chapter 5) are all implicated in attempts to tackle the relationship between masculinity and familial sexual violence (Hearn 1990: 66).

I have argued above that constructing the masculinity of the 'detached father' in law involved assigning to extra-familial masculinities (both heterosexual and homosexual) values which did not accord with the ideal of the modern and 'safe' father. In the case of child sexual abuse what we can see is how it has been through a sexualising of masculinities *external* to the family that the threat of men's violence *inside* the family has been evaded

(Macleod and Saraga 1988a, 1988b). This is not to say that male sexualities both inside and outside the familial are not premised on a naturalised discourse of male sexuality – the idea traverses both sides of the dichotomy between the safe and the dangerous. However, what this means is that the behaviour of a sexually abusive father may, in one instance, be seen as a result of a 'natural' sexual urge which is blocked (for example due to non-access to wife or partner). Thus, evidence of either non-access or sexual activity on the part of a daughter has counted as a mitigating factor (Mitra 1987).

At the same time, it has also been necessary to construct this behaviour as unnatural because of the threat it clearly poses to the family. In a sense, therefore, it is both natural and unnatural, and it is partly for this reason that in the context of child sexual abuse the discourse of the family man has facilitated the (re)integration of men into the family unit. So natural is the normal paternal masculinity of the modern father that imagining him as dangerous, violent and so forth becomes impossible unless one challenges the gender order of the family itself. The 'external' threat (the paedophile, the pervert) is depicted as a powerful but dangerous sexuality; but this male sexuality is banished to the extra-familial. It is no wonder that, given these confusions, 'the problem of child sexual abuse is, for feminism, the problem of masculine sexuality. This is not a problem that admits of easy solutions' (Smart 1989a: 50).

It has been in feminist writings on child sexual abuse that male sexuality and men's power have become the central problem (Macleod and Saraga 1988a). This is in marked contrast to the traditional, though still influential, focus on individual pathology (the 'sick man') or family dysfunction/family therapy (the 'sick family'). It is such feminist work on child sexual abuse which has attempted to bring together the structural (that is the differential power of men and women in society) and the interpersonal (the fact that although all men might potentially abuse, it is necessary to account for the psychic reasons why some men do – and some men do not). All men, clearly, are not abusers. One result of feminist excavations of the histories of child sexual abuse has been to make public the voices of those who have been hitherto silenced; that is, women and children who have survived men's violence. However, through charting historical shifts in perceptions of the male abuser, feminists have also challenged the dominant conception that men as fathers are, a priori, safe. Yet the law in England and Wales appears to continue to find it immensely difficult to respond to any suggestion that a 'family man' might himself constitute a danger to the family. This reluctance is perhaps more understandable when we consider how child sexual abuse, male sexuality and the family man ideal have been constructed in civil and criminal law in this context.

In 1885 the Criminal Law Amendment Act entrenched in law a fundamental tension (which continues today) between, on the one hand, a recognition that children need to be protected from men's violences and, on the other, a deep-seated ambivalence towards the victims of abuse (see further Smart 1989a: 51). This tension, however, makes more sense from the vantage point of the late twentieth century when we consider just *who* is being constructed here as the potential abuser. We have seen in Chapter 5 how the period 1880–1920 saw a shift from 'father-right' to the emergence of the 'modern' father in which the child became the legal object of the 'welfare principle'. The 1885 legislation had been the result of a moral panic around the sale of children into prostitution (Bristow 1977; Gorham 1978); amongst its other provisions the Act therefore raised the age of consent for girls from 13 to 16 years in an effort to protect those perceived to be 'at risk'. Its aim had been, bearing in mind the context of widespread prostitution in the towns and cities of Britain at the time, to deter men, and in particular upper-class, propertied men, from abusing (mainly) working-class girls. The threat to children and the family here takes the form of a 'degenerate aristrocrat who thought nothing of "ruining" working-class girls' (Smart 1989a: 52); the object of the law's protection was, from the outset, class-based.

However, this concern with protection (part of the more general concern with working-class welfare; above p. 221) sits ill at ease with the concomitant sexual double standard of the time which in many respects *legitimated* men's extra-familial sexual adventuring, notably in the form of prostitution and differential divorce laws. On one estimate prostitution was, by the mid-nineteenth century, the fourth largest female occupation (Weeks 1981: 85). Thus, whilst on the one hand the law was beginning to curtail once-acceptable masculine prerogatives (the 1885 Act), it also continued to embody a double standard which sought to control working-class women (notably under the Contagious Diseases Acts of the 1860s) while simultaneously legitimating male sexual adventuring in the form of prostitution (Walkowitz

1980a; Weeks 1981: Ch. 5). From its beginning, in other words, legislation concerned with child sexual abuse had emerged in a moral, legal and cultural climate in which, in many other respects, the inevitability of a naturalised discourse of male sexuality was accepted.

In relation to the respectable/dangerous division it is clear that the parameters of the abuser-discourse were being set from the class-perspective of those who were concerned with the ill-disciplined and undomesticated 'lower orders'. It is interesting, for example, that the subsequent 1908 Punishment of Incest Act followed a succession of reports which had located the widespread prelevance of incest amongst the cramped living conditions and the slum housing of the urban poor (Bailey and Blackburn 1979). Indeed, to the present day the belief that sexual abuse occurs primarily, if not exclusively, in working-class families has continued to feed into constructions of the abuser as someone who transgresses, rather than embodies, an ideal of a respectable familial masculinity (Campbell 1988: 108). Implicit in such a belief, Smart notes, is a

> Victorian stereotype of the cramped, poor (and hence working-class) living conditions, coupled with the contemporary view of the dire consequences of women shirking their marital, sexual obligations to their husbands.
>
> (Smart 1989a: 56)

The 1908 Act made sexual abuse of children within the family a criminal offence for the first time in England (see further Bailey and Blackburn 1979: 709). Yet it is clear that this and subsequent criminal laws (in particular the consolidating Sexual Offences Act 1956) have patently failed to 'do something' about child sexual abuse – either in the short-term sense of prosecuting men who abuse and protecting women and children or in that of a longer-term aim of reducing the incidence of abuse. In part we might put this down to the adversarial nature of proceedings and the evidential minefield which child abuse raises (Bazell 1989). For some this has led to calls to abandon the criminal law and adopt civil law mechanisms. Nonetheless the failure of the criminal law to protect and prosecute must also be seen in the light of the masculinisation of the procedures of interrogation, assessment and policing of abuse which have themselves continued to embody a deep antipathy to the idea that men in families sexually abuse children; and, at the heart of this belief, is the continued power of the family man ideal. The (dis)belief in the existence of child sexual abuse in the family (of which there are many judicial illustrations; see Mitra 1987) has been reproduced through reference to a two-fold process.

First, the bifurcation of the naturalised discourse of male sexuality has involved assigning to the familial domain a natural (pre-theoretical) heterosexual masculinity. It is this which is embodied by the family man. This is the model of the father as provider, as respectable and preferably propertied; that is, he not working class and/or already subject to state surveillance. This has in turn facilitated the construction of non-heterosexual masculinity and other stigmatised masculinities which have come to signify the extra-familial in this context (perhaps the most obvious example is the homosexual 'pervert' or the homosexual as threat to children). The abuser is thus someone who is, from the perspective of the family man, 'outside' of the abused family looking 'in'. He is not, importantly, *of* the family.[9] It is, therefore, not so surprising that believing the evidence of sexual abuse can prove so difficult when we come up against the ideology of the family man:

> For the police . . . sexual abuse faces them with an accusation against their own gender. Police and judicial mastery over evidence has for over a century enabled them to banish the sexual experiences of women and children . . . did the evidence say the unsayable? Did it detonate a taboo which failed to forbid sexual abuse but only succeeded in keeping it secret, keeping it outsde *social* knowledge? Evidence is not neutral, nor does it fall from the sky: it has to be discovered.
>
> (Campbell 1988: 78).

The 'accusation against' masculinity which child sexual abuse constitutes fractures the concept of the family man as natural, pre-theoretical and safe.

Second, the continuing purchase of the discourse of male sexuality inside the family has resulted in an objectification of women's and children's corporeality in such a way as to justify and 'explain' sexual violence (Dominelli 1987; Mitra 1987). Usually this has been in terms of a 'blocked' legitimate channel of male sexuality (as in the discourses around non-consummation and prostitution). This then facilitates a reading of child sexual abuse from the perspective of family dynamics and family therapy.

Through sexualising the wife/mother, the abusing man is effectively absolved of responsibility for the abuse. In the crudest form of such mother-blaming it is the mother who is responsible for securing the children's well being (Mrazek and Bentovim 1981; Bentovim *et al.* 1988). As Smart puts it, 'each trial therefore confirms this truth of child sexual abuse, namely that proximity causes abuse, women's frigidity causes abuse, abnormal stress causes abuse, and that this form of abuse is rare – men are rendered invisible in this catalogue' (Smart 1989a: 56).

This model of masculinity repeats the idea, already seen in the context of 'legitimate' sexual intercourse in marriage, that men somehow cannot control their own sexuality and that women and children must then be responsible for ensuring that *they* do not arouse men. An effect of this is to both accept the inevitability of child sexual abuse whilst, ultimately, holding women responsible for controlling male sexuality.

We have here conflicting images of paternal masculinity in which contradictory ideas of 'natural' male sexuality abound. The dominant image of the child sexual abuser in the late-twentieth century remains that of the paedophile and the child pornographer (McIntosh 1988); that is, a man who is *external* to the family and who threatens both child and family life itself. This image ill-fits the scale of the evidence which implicates male sexuality inside the *family*; 'the more child sexual abuse was depicted as a horrible pathology, the less could "ordinary" fathers be seen as enacting such deeds' (Smart 1989a: 52). One effect of the Cleveland controversy in England (Butler-Sloss 1988; Campbell 1988) has been to mobilise the discourse of parental rights (Sharron 1987: though this is, in effect, a concern with paternal rights) against an 'over-zealous' and oppressive state (Campbell 1989; note also the letter from consultant paediatricians, *The Guardian* 18 February 1989). Again, what is being defended here is a notion of respectable family privacy which derives from the ideal of a respectable paternal masculinity. The 'good father' could not act in such a way.

Ultimately child sexual abuse questions both masculinity and the family. Sexual abuse appears in the past to have been something which can be understood, if not accepted, so long as it happens in other people's families, in strange families and strange places. The problem of male sexuality in our society cannot be confined to a specific locale, however. As Campbell argues:

Sexual abuse of children presents society with the ultimate crisis of patriarchy, when children refuse to protect their fathers by keeping their secrets. We know the alternative – that children put their father's pain before their own and protect them, as they always have, with their silence. Until now all the institutions of the state and civil society have conspired to protect the men in general and fathers in particular.

(Campbell 1988: 71)

Child sexual abuse presents a crisis for law and the state; not just in relation to the use of criminal and civil law in responding to the problem, of evidential requirements and the relation between law and other discourses, but in how we think about crime and punishment, how the law treats children as objects (O'Donovan 1993: 91) and, I have argued, how we think about 'normal' male hetero-sexuality.

CONCLUDING REMARKS

In this chapter we have seen two consequences of the repro-duction in legal discourse of the idea of the respectable mascu-linity of the 'family man'. First it has served to separate out mascu-linities in law through reference to the normative masculinity of the 'man of law'. Though I have focused on class differences in this chapter, masculinities are also differentiated in other ways (notably differences of race and ethnicity). I have argued that it would be misleading to read from this a view that such 'sacrificial' or 'subordinated' masculinities are not *also* empowered in a legal discourse which valorises such a construct of masculinity.

This leads us to the second point – the way in which this masculine idea serves to negate political engagement with the destructive or dangerous behaviour of men *inside* the family. The examples of prostitution and child sexual abuse have sought to illustrate some of the ways in which the discourse of the family man continues to be reproduced in law. This has involved drawing on the construction of masculinity in Chapter 5, around work/ authority, to show how this understanding of familial masculinity has placed men in a position of power in families. Legal responses to dangerous masculinities, be they in the areas of criminal or matrimonial law, have tended to support those 'features of family life' and have been marked by a commitment to the preservation of the family unit and a failure to engage with reasons as to why women may be ambivalent about resorting to law in the first place.

Where does this leave our understanding of the power of law? Mainstream theorists of social justice have failed to pay much attention to the internal inequalities of the family, whilst functionalist sociology, we have seen in Chapter 2, has idealised the family as a social institution par excellence for providing 'stable' gender identities and facilitating the development of a sense of justice in its individual members (Okin 1989: 134–5). Feminist studies, in contrast, have fundamentally questioned not just the role of law in being able to 'do something' about dangerous masculinities, but have also sought to explore how law can be seen to reproduce such masculinities in the first place (Freeman 1980, 1984a; Hanmer and Stanko 1985). As Freeman comments:

> Violence by husbands against wives should not be seen as a breakdown in the social order, as orthodox interpretations perceive it, but as an affirmation of a particular sort of social order. Looked at in this way domestic violence is not dysfunctional: quite the reverse, it appears functional . . . it must be considered in a particular cultural context.
>
> (Freeman 1984a: 51)

Although the legal system may no longer force men and women to adopt rigidly opposed roles, it does still support and define an ideology which promotes separate spheres of activity for men and women. One effect of this has been that laws which set out to deal with the socially destructive consequences of masculinity have themselves been seen to contribute to expectations of male dominance. Moreover, the mere existence of a specific law or legal remedy, as in the case of prostitution or domestic violence,[10] does not mean that that remedy is going to be effective. Indeed, the appearence of law as providing a 'solution' can ultimately prove counterproductive through promoting the belief that at least something has been done about a seemingly intractable social problem.

The case of domestic violences, for example, raises clear problems about the law's response to the socially destructive characteristics of modern masculinities. The scale of men's violence in the home testifies against the idea that the family is necessarily a safe place for women and children. In 1990 there were 226 female homicide victims. Of these 43 per cent were killed by their partners (present or former spouse, cohabitant or lover), 19 per cent by another member of the family and 11 per cent by strangers. Of the 381 male homicide victims that year, in contrast, 9 per cent were killed by partners, 17 per cent by another member of their family, 36 per cent by friends or other associates and 24 per cent by strangers (Home Office 1992a, Section 95: 22). These figures echo the central finding of research into the scale of violence in the family; not just in that the home can be a dangerous place, but also in that the 'most significant problem damaging the health and safety of women [is] husbands, boyfriends, former spouses and intimate companions' (Stanko 1993; see further Stanko 1987, 1988). According to a recent survey one in ten women have been beaten by their partners in the past year (*The Guardian*, 22 February 1993).

Yet notwithstanding the clear evidence of the scale of men's violence in the family, the law has historically shown a marked resistance to recognising and responding to the extent of the social problems associated with the socially destructive aspects of modern masculinities (Martin 1976; Walker 1979; Dobash and Dobash 1980; Borkowski *et al.* 1983; Wilson 1983; Pahl 1985a; Adler 1987; Edwards 1987, 1989). Judges have resorted to various excusatory and explanatory ideologies of male violence in order to construct men's familial violence through reference to protectionist and paternalist notions of women as men's property (O'Donovan 1985a). Yet, as Joan Smith states, three or four times a year we go through a ritual known as 'Outcry Over Judge's Remarks In Rape Case'. Then 'the whole business dies down – until it happens again' (Smith 1989: 1; see also Patullo 1983).

I have argued in this chapter that challenging dominant ideas of masculinity must be a central issue in seeking to understand and combat the prevalence of male violences in the family (Stanko 1987, 1990). Beyond the family, however, the very scale of men's violence questions what we understand by 'normal' masculinity. Men's violences in the public domain, accounted for within the language of public masculinities, may be comprehended. The masculinity of the mob, of the pub fight, of urban disorder, the masculinism of public spaces generally – of cities, towns and villages – all might be accommodated within an account of public masculinities as claims to power and prerogative. These violences exist in the street, round the corner; they permeate the public domain. It is through challenging the division of public and private masculinities (and the concomitant belief that only these public violences are deserving of legal recognition as crimes) that feminist studies have thrown into question the universally benign and natural qualities of familial masculinity. The prevalence of male violences *within* the family, in short, jars with any image of masculinity as a priori 'safe' and desirable.

Ultimately, challenging the 'dangerous' aspects of the 'familial' masculinity, and the relation between the two, must involve addressing the legal structuring of women's dependent position in the household and the ways in which male authority within that family continues to be constituted through a naturalised discourse of masculinity. Deconstructing the ideas of the 'family man' and the 'good father', I have argued in this and the preceding chapter, must be part of this challenge.

Chapter 7

Changing masculinities, changing law

Concluding remarks

In this book I have sought to explore how heterosexual masculinity has been constructed in family law. I have argued that masculinity, as a discursive position, is constantly constructed within a process which has involved both resistances and challenges to the constitution of the hegemonic norm of heterosexual familialism. Legal determinations of relationships between men, women and children have involved a complex interdiscursive process through which legal discourse has brought together a range of ideas about men and masculinity. The exclusions of legal discourse – what is not said as much as what is about being a man in law – must be seen, I have argued, as an important part of the history of masculinity. At times the ideas of masculinity to be found in law can be seen to be contradictory. There is no general consistency to the representations of masculinity in law and the law does not uniformly reflect or embody an omnipotent and omnipresent male power. However, what does tend to unite the constructions of masculinity discussed above is their combined function in establishing the power of a more overarching idea – that of a *familial masculinity* in law.

In this final chapter I wish to draw together the themes explored in this book and, by way of conclusion to this study of masculinity, law and the family, to assess how some of the implications of this analysis might bear on the politics of changing our understandings of both masculinities and of law.

BEYOND THE FAMILY: MASCULINE AUTHORITY AND LEGAL DISCOURSE

I have argued in Chapter 6 that the male subject in family law does not stand apart from manifestations of masculinity in other areas of law (for example criminal, commercial or contract law). It is also misleading, I have argued in Chapter 2, to see the substantive content of the doctrinal subject 'family law' as somehow separate from the broad range of laws and regulatory strategies which have been concerned with gendering men and women in the family. In Chapter 6 we have seen how the diverse legal and quasi-legal responses to prostitution, domestic violence and child sexual abuse have operated 'to signify the dominance of a specific notion of sexuality, [to] reaffirm a particular form of heterosexuality and disqualify women's experiences' (Smart 1989a: 50).

In relation to the family there has been a clear correlation, entrenched in legal discourse, between such a 'form of hetero-sexuality' privileged in law and the fusing of claims to familial authority and men's paid employment. The economic structuring of the gendered subject (for example through regulation of personal fiscal management) has, in particular, constituted mascu-linity as an economic resource. One consequence of this has been to economically disadvantage (and stigmatise) households in which there is no father. The reproduction of familial structures premised on such economic presuppositions continues to limit choice in forming households outside the familial model. How-ever, the increased incidence of divorce, single parenthood and cohabitation, the increasing number of women and men living on their own, of elderly and lesbian and gay households all testify to the diversity of sexualities and gender identities within house-holds. The traditional model of the family is, I have argued, increasingly challenged by those whose voices it excludes.

The analysis of masculinity presented in this book has involved, in particular, a deconstruction of the division between 'public' and 'private' masculinities (Hearn 1992) and it is the mystifying nature of this division which is, I have argued, central to obfuscating the ways in which men's authority is reproduced in law. In rejecting sociology's traditional sexual divisions of public/work and private/home (and the concomitant gendered definition of 'work' as, a priori, a public-related activity), an apparently seamless web of masculine authority has been revealed. This authority has encompassed both the familial and the institutional terrains of interpersonal relationships, employment, the state and the public spaces of leisure and the street. This has meant that any ideas we may have of masculine authority can no longer be confined to the familial domain. They can no longer be conceived through reference to the public/private division (Chapter 2). They should, instead, be seen as embracing aspects of both private (men at home) and public (men at work) masculinities, as well as the dialectical relation between the two.

One result of this is that the legal structuring of paternal authority depicted in Chapter 5 cannot be calibrated in zero-sum terms. It would be erroneous to assume, for example, that a range of working-class 'subordinated' or 'sacrificial' masculinities (Chapter 6) necessarily take an authoritarian or 'hypermasculine' form as a mechanistic response to threat in another area of life (the 'I am weak at work therefore I will be strong at home' argument). This does not mean, however, that class-based judgements of masculinity do not stem from this belief and do not continue to inform intra-male relations (for example through the complex codes through which working-class masculinities are denigrated and patronised). There is, I have argued, no *one* masculine authority to be found in law. Masculine authority transcends social class. This does not mean that men in general are not powerful in relation to women and children or that some men do not exert authority in relation to other men (Pleck 1980). What this does mean is that in constructing men as masculine subjects we cannot find any single, universal, unitary model of masculine authority in legal discourse. Rather than search for any omnipotent and omnipresent masculine authority (the problem with the 'grand theorising' seen in Chapter 2), it is more useful to engage with the ways in which masculine authority has been constructed in different legal contexts. This I have tried to do in Chapters 4 to 6.

My focus in this book has been the family. A similar engagement with masculinity might equally consider other areas of law. Criminal law, for example, is also a rich source of representations of heterosexual masculinity; the masculinity of criminology is, in many ways, only beginning to be considered. The *family man* in law, I have argued in Chapter 5, has historically embodied claims to authority and power which have been sanctioned across diverse areas of law. In particular, this empowering of male subjectivity has involved claims to economic authority and sexual prerogative in the familial domain. One result of the pervasive breadwinner ideology has been, as O'Donovan (1993: 69) suggests, to promote a certain 'instrumentality' with regard to a man's sense of self. This has involved, as experiential accounts within the men against sexism writings illustrate, a construction of masculinity through reference to a denial of emotion (the discourse of men as 'failures' in the family and in relationships, of men as errant fathers and wayward sons) and the defining of men's 'success' through social and economic status and, importantly, familial responsibility.

The associations between masculinity and control cannot be confined to the family sphere and the above division of masculinities has tended to divert attention from how masculine authority has been constructed in a more general sense. To understand how the configurations of masculinity seen in this book have been (and continue to be) reproduced we must look *beyond the family*. The study of masculinity, law and the family needs, in other words, to transcend the family – in the sense of looking outside the parameters of the legal subdiscipline 'family law' in order to analyse the contours of familial masculinity and, in particular, the 'dangerous' dimensions of masculinity discussed in Chapter 6. The obstacle to such a study, however, remains the powerful perceptual grid of doctrinal legal method which continues, in so many ways, to negate a critical engagement with the social constitution of gendered subjectivity. The social order of hierarchic heterosexuality embodied in family law continues to achieve its hegemony by naturalising those discourses (for example in relation to care of children) which legitimate and support existing social arrangements.

Recognising the *diversity* of masculinities is a key to fracturing the unity of the idea of public and private male subjects. It is essential in engaging with the fluid nature of masculine authority. This public/private divide has, in a more general way, functioned so as to dichotomise the world (Thornton 1991). As embedded in liberal legal discourse, it has represented a systematic form of what Connell (1987) has termed the 'purification' attempted by a dichotomised sexual ideology. It is just such a naturalising of the sociality of gender which has run throughout the construction of sexual divisions in law (O'Donovan 1985a). It has also, we have seen, informed the law's drive for dichotomous purification in relation to gendering the legal subject in the family. Thus, for example, we have seen how the law has been involved in the mapping of a rigid (hetero)sexual dichotomy on the human body through constituting a division between hetero- and homosexualities (Chapter 3). Similarly, in Chapter 5, we have seen how in childcare cases a bifurcation of masculinity has taken place in the construction of the worlds of work and home. In relation to custody and divorce, perhaps ironically, it is that very legal intervention, and the calling upon of the juridical gaze, which fractures the hitherto (uneasy) relation between the private and public faces of masculinity. The example of custody illustrates how, on divorce, the trajectories of public demands on men (notably as primary breadwinner) might clash with the commitment to a private affective and emotional family life (for example the father who may desire fuller involvement in childcare).

The historical account of fatherhood in Chapters 5 and 6 helps us make sense of these tensions and has sought to show how this bifurcation into public and private masculinities has also, importantly, facilitated the institutionalisation and incorporation of men's power. The law has constructed elements of public patriarchies (employment, sexual status, ideas of masculinity as an economic resource and so forth) in terms of and through ostensibly 'private' relationships which transgress the public/private boundary. However, procreation, sexuality, violence and the heterogeneity of ideas we have of 'family life' all are open to a re-reading from a perspective which integrates the sociality of masculinity. We cannot, therefore, confine emotion, affective relations, sexuality and so on to the domestic, the familial and the 'private' sphere. Indeed, it has long been a deceit of liberal legalism that 'it is to women that law assigns the job of holding the two halves [public and private] together. The invisibility of women's work, the efforts of emotional succour, enable the legal man to appear in the public world of Gesellschaft free of encumbrances' (O'Donovan 1993: 33).

Looking beyond the family in this way brings into focus the range of material practices which reproduce sexual divisions of labour. In Britain the attacks by the Conservative government on the public sector, for example, the negation of social collective responsibility for childcare and the 'feminisation' of both poverty and community care (Lewis 1989) have all served to undermine and fragment families. Yet a 'pro-family', 'pro-fathers' political agenda continues to restrict the choices of those who wish to live their lives outside the traditional family and marriage. Most importantly, a law-centred focus on *individually* perceived injustices (the hallmarks of the father's rights approach) diverts attention from the more general social construction of masculinity through reference to hierarchy and authority (a construction which unites the safe/dangerous masculinities of Chapters 5 and 6). The juridical model of power, we have seen in Chapter 2, sees law as the provider of rights; but, in so doing, it individualises the power of both law and of masculinity. Through focusing on the discursive construction of masculinity, however, it becomes possible to see how masculinity has been in a much more general way permeated with ideas of hierarchy and claims to authority.

The fragmentation of paternal authority facilitates the making of a contrast between what has been termed a 'core' (the terrain of public masculinities) and a 'periphery' (for example men's localised power within families; Connell 1987: 109) in the power structure of gender. I have argued in Chapter 5 that, although the law no longer embodies anything as crudely patriarchal as 'absolute father right', this does not mean that family law can no longer be said to reproduce patriarchal relations or that masculinity does not remain constructed through reference to the iconography of paternal authority. The diminution of men's formal legal rights by egalitarian legal reforms has not necessarily eroded paternal authority. This authority has, I have argued, been modernised.

(RE)CONSTRUCTING THE FAMILY MAN

This modernisation of masculinity has taken place by constructing the 'family man' as an ideal of (hetero) familial masculinity. It is an ideal which remains a dominant motif in law. It has been constituted across a multiplicity of discourses and practices, not towards any one overarching purpose, but as an effect of power. In this process fatherhood has been reconstructed in such a way as to maintain economic and social arrangements that benefit all men as men. The shift from absolute father-right to the emergence of the 'modern' family (Chapter 5) took place alongside the growth of a range of regulatory strategies and techniques of surveillance and normalisation which were more attuned to the disciplinary mechanisms of the modern order. However, these regulatory agencies were themselves concerned with reproducing masculinity in ways compatible with maintaining male dominance within the family of the new order. It should not surprise us, therefore, that both legal and extra-legal agents tap into an ideology of masculinity.

The analysis presented in this book has sought to avoid falling back on any notion of a mythical past of a 'functional' pre-modern family in depicting this process of familialisation. Paternal authority was *transformed* by the disciplinary mechanisms of the new governmental order in such a way that mobilising paternal power no longer depended on resorting to a juridical 'right'. As a result of the increased availability of divorce and the rise in the proportion of births outside the institution, marriage was in any case no longer the central vehicle of family law in the process of safeguarding legal fatherhood. What we have seen in Chapter 5 is how other legal concepts and techniques have subsequently sought to attach men to children; and how, in many respects, the legal status of the unmarried man has become more like that of the married.

I have argued that there have been two elements to this transformation of fatherhood from that of the pre-modern paterfamilias to the 'modern father' of the purportedly symmetrical and egalitarian family. First, father absence has been constructed as problematic (the focus of Chapter 5). Second, fatherhood has been reconstituted as 'safe' (the concern of Chapter 6). One result has been that masculinities outside the familial heterosexual matrix have tended to be sexualised; the iconography of the extra-familial is thus replete with such images as the 'promiscuous' homosexual, the 'irresponsible' unmarried father who evades his responsibilities, the sexually suspect male who fails to marry after 'sowing his wild oats' and so forth. Such representations draw on diverse notions of sexual propriety, bodily hygiene and, in particular, ideas of male sexuality as a potential threat to children (most clear in relation to homosexuality, but a threat which attaches to all men beyond the frame of heterosexual familialism).

At the same time women have been sexualised through reference, in particular, to the discourse of the naturalised male sexual drive. This, in effect, has denied them any legitimate subject position in law. Within present gender-based power relations the 'safe' subject position remains that of hierarchic heterosexuality, a lasting relationship and, ultimately, marriage. Thus, as we have seen in Chapter 6, it has been at the cost of rendering unmarried paternal masculinity invisible – or rather collapsing this male subjectivity into the clichés of 'absence' and 'economics' – that what I have called the 'errant father' discourse has constituted the single unmarried mother as a social 'problem'. Maintaining the centrality of fatherhood in the construction of the familial has involved a systematic negation of the legitimacy of autonomous motherhood. Thus, for example, in the case of reproductive technologies and in the historical development of laws on legitimacy, the law has tended to valorise paternity and fatherhood whilst devaluing motherhood and maternity outside the heterosexual familial matrix. It is hoped that through deconstructing the nature of the claims of a naturalised fatherhood it may be possible to ensure that

> legal and social policy does not relegate caring and nurturing by women to the lowest priority by redefining women's objections [to the assertion of father's rights] as individual pathologies or selfish vested interest.
>
> (Smart 1989b: 25–6)

I have argued in Chapter 6 that, in contrast to the 'sexually wayward' unmarried mother, there is no alternative, readily accessible discourse of unmarried paternal masculinity to resort to in this instance (beyond the idea of men as 'irresponsible', 'promiscuous' begetters of children, of men as socially and economically immature). It is not surprising that the 'errant father' in legal discourse should be reduced solely to his economic capacity to provide for those for which he is responsible. This is, after all, what underlies the construction of fatherhood itself (Chapter 5). Legislation continues to construct fatherhood in terms of economics and not quality of interaction. The enactment of the Child Support Act 1991 in England and Wales, for example (Family Policy Studies Centre 1991; Montgomery 1991), will do little to 'improve' parental responsibility so long as there remains a deep confusion around just what such responsibility entails. Such legislation diverts attention from the responsibilities of the state (in the name of protecting the public purse) and, in enforcing the private maintenance obligation, re-establishes a protective, paternalistic masculinity compatible with the hegemonic ideal depicted in this book. This is part of a more general lack of any coherent policy in relation to families on the part of the liberal state (Leach and Hewitt 1993).

In effect there exist in law two, seemingly contradictory, images of masculinity in this context; one very much according with the reconstruction of a safe heterosexual fatherhood (and thus deserving of legal rights); the other (the errant, irresponsible father) a throwback to some pre-familial order of undomesticated men. Both, however, tap into discourse of individual rights; and both masculinities are, I have argued in Chapter 6, really just two sides of the same coin. Or, rather, they are co-existing discourses whose subject-positions must be seen as fundamental to the construction of heterosexual masculinity in law *per se*.

What appears to have been ignored in many debates around law reform is how, for heterosexual men, it is possible to shift *between* these subject positions. The 'good father' may not always be so good and today's 'family man' might be tomorrow's 'errant father'. Heterosexual familial masculinity has been historically fragmented into notions of marital and extra-marital paternity which have been, and continue to be, mediated by discourses of class and ethnicity. The subjective commitments of both married and unmarried men must be seen against the valorising of economic, sexual and procreative capacity and status in discourses of masculinity. It is important not to underestimate the strength of these commitments and, I believe, any praxis of 'rejecting' fatherhood, which can be found in some men against sexism writings, is arguably unhelpful here. In the current political climate any idea that the 'notion of fatherhood must be smashed or more precisely dropped bit by bit into the ocean' (Hearn 1983) seems a long way off. This does not so much redescribe the possibilities which already exist as reproduce a model of paternal masculinity as inherently oppressive. Chapters 5 and 6 point, instead, to the performative possibilities of embracing new ways of fathering and to how ways of establishing as political 'the very terms through which identity is articulated' might question the foundationalist frame of gender as an identity politics (a frame which itself 'presumes, fixes and constrains the very "subjects" that it hopes to represent and liberate' (Butler 1990: 148)).

The ideological split between familial/safe and dangerous/ extra-familial masculinities remains with us today, just as important aspects of what might be termed pre-modern paternal masculinities continue to appear in legal discourse. Violence, for example, has itself been central to the history of fatherhood in law: 'the social and historical meaning of fatherhood includes the treatment of children as possessions, appropriated from the mother . . . even a man who is a "nice" father carries with him the possibility of becoming a "nasty" or violent one' (Hearn 1990: 76). Paternal authority, in an age of widespread divorce, continues to be exerted through men seeking to enforce relationships with children, sometimes by using demands for custody to coerce their former partners (Neely 1984). In relation to children it is perhaps

also cautionary to recall that 'one of the most extreme consequences of paternal authority for young people, especially girls, is
incest' (Hearn 1990: 76).

To conclude these comments on the reconstruction of fatherhood, I believe that the importance of the institutionalisation of
the idea of a respectable familial masculinity detailed in Chapters
5 and 6 lies in its two-fold influence in: first constituting the
masculinities of public institutions as the 'other' domain of public
masculinities (Hearn 1992) and; second as a form of respectable
class masculinity which continues to stand in contrast to the unacceptable, dangerous masculinities of the extra-familial and,
more generally, of those masculinities which transgress the economic and cultural norms of class-based notion of 'manliness'. Those
who fail to attain the economic power or sexual orientation to
enter the comforting world of familial heterosexuality (with all its
complex codes of courtship, coupledom and irretrievable breakdown) continue to speak in tongues alien to the notions of economic and sexual propriety of the class of elite males (white, upper/
middle class) whose interests the law continues, in so many
respects, to represent. Davidoff and Hall capture well the tautologous logic through which 'normal' masculinity is produced:

> The images of middle-class men . . . vary in kaleidoscopic
> patterns, helping to define the boundaries of that entity called
> the middle-class and guiding both the beliefs and actions of
> men. What all have in common, however, is the masculine
> penumbra of these activities. What men did was defined as
> man's work; because they did it, they were men.
>
> (Davidoff and Hall 1987: 271)

In the development of family law, legal fatherhood has been maintained not so much by the institution of marriage as via a nexus of
de-gendered humanism, rights discourse and liberal legal claims
to equality. The shifts in securing paternity detailed in Chapter 5
are themselves symptomatic of and attest to the fragmented nature
of gender identity and the subversion of hitherto dominant,
naturalised discourses of masculinity. Paternal authority is no
longer legitimated by appeals to God's will. Men 'do' things differently now. However, it would be a mistake to locate the historical
reconstruction of fatherhood in a process of liberalisation. This
process, like the politics of men's liberation in the present, has
been ultimately concerned with modernising masculinity.

Carrigan *et. al.* (1985) have captured well the contradiction which lies at the heart of the fathers' rights argument in this respect:

> It is not, fundamentally, about uprooting sexism or transforming patriarchy, or even understanding masculinity in its various forms . . . what it is about is the modernizing of hegemonic masculinity. It is concerned with finding ways in which the dominant group – the white, educated, heterosexual, affluent males . . . can adapt to new circumstances without breaking down the social-structural arrangements that actually give them their power.
>
> (Carrigan *et al.* 1985: 577)

What recent developments signify is not the emergence of a 'new man' in family law but a modernising of – and not a fundamental challenge to – a form of hegemonic masculinity. Meanwhile proponents of fathers' rights do not work against the social order of advanced capitalism. The arguments of the fathers' rights movement 'continue to make an impact both in terms of conventional wisdom about the treatment of fathers in custody disputes . . . and in discussion on law and contemporary legal practice in this field' (Brophy 1985: 115; also 1982). Allied to a men's liberationist perspective, men are the 'victims' of work, of long hours, limited interpersonal skills and emotionally impoverished personal lives. But where does this leave the so-called 'new man'? One day the 'new man' is to blame for a rise in the number of suicides amongst young men (*The Independent*, 3 November 1993). The next the 'new man image takes a battering' as research reveals that women continue to undertake the bulk of domestic labour (*The Independent*, 21 December 1993; see also Game and Pringle 1984).

The 'new man' idea is simply part of the liberationist rhetoric, a superficially attractive but deeply misleading image of changing masculinities. I have argued above that enforcing a construction of masculinity as an a priori economic resource, whilst at the same time seeking to increase men's involvement in childcare, is a bit like trying to square the circle. But fathers' rights advocates do not necessarily seek greater involvement *in* childcare so much as an increased power *over* the day to day care of children (Brophy 1989). The argument that men are now unequal before the law has thus served their ends and, welded to the men's liberation discourse, inequalities have been seen as individual issues and not as issues around the collective practices and powers of men and women. As Ehrenreich has stated:

male culture seems to have abandoned the breadwinner role without overcoming the sexist attitudes that role has perpetuated: on the one hand, the expectation of female nurturance and submissive service as a matter of right; on the other hand, a misogynist contempt for women as 'parasites' and entrappers of men.

(Ehrenreich 1983: 182)

Advocates of fathers' rights seek to promote a male authority through resorting to legal right whilst retaining the benefits which accrue to men (Sevenhuijsen 1986; Graycar 1989). In the present moment it is simply too easy for the fathers' rights movement to advocate 'equality' without reference to the historical, social and economic context in which the discourses of masculinity, through which the rights claim is articulated, have been produced (and with reference to which the heterosexual familialism defended by fathers' rights groups continues to derive its social power). The paucity of this vision is its political and theoretical downfall.

The success of hegemonic masculinity at reconstituting itself should not be underestimated. In recent years the reformulation of sexual politics into a 'sex war' rhetoric has shown that the 'backlash' to the perceived gains of feminism has expressed itself both in a vituperative misogyny and, interestingly, in the rediscovery of a 'natural' masculinity which is to be celebrated. In this context men's anti-sexist critiques aimed at going 'through or going beyond man made constructions or images' in order to take 'the surface seriously, examining how it is constructed and how it functions' (Morgan 1992: 1) have accorded well with the fragmentations of postmodernity. Yet there remains an underlying political pessimism to both the sex-war rhetoric and those abstracted deconstructions of gender which sometimes appear to float free of any material base in the real lives of women and men (Segal 1990: 36).

How do we see the 'family man'? If God the Father remains one of the most powerful mythologies, 'the father as man, man the father, is a still more mysterious creature' (Segal 1990: 28). Whilst feminism has scrutinised motherhood as a concept, distinguishing between the *biological* capacity of women to have children and the *social* institution and experience of motherhood, it remains the case that '"fatherhood" is usually still used as a single unitary concept' (Sevenhuijsen 1986: 338). But what does fatherhood involve? Fatherhood has become, Suzanne Moore has argued, a cipher for various ideologies which define father absence in the negative. Far from any 'contemporary crisis' of masculinity, the dilemmas of men and masculinity continue to take priority over wider questions of social/structural change. The representations of fatherhood discussed in this book hold out historically specific beliefs about familial and sexual relations which relate to, and must be seen as constitutive elements of, the cultural nexus within which subjective commitments and aspirations to family life and material power are activated (in other words, the lives of those women and men who 'come before' the gaze of the law). However, it is this culture which is, I have argued, fracturing under the weight of the demands of those it excludes. There are 'real and unresolvable differences' which emerge when discussing family law at the present moment (Fineman 1991a: 266). What 'family', what image of the world, what 'responsibilities' are we talking about? The home may be permeated with the codes of heterosexual familialism but the multivarious subjectivities which have proliferated outside this gender order testify to a diversity which undermines any claims to 'normality' for the globalising, heterosexual subject.

Ultimately, legal representations of masculinity, male sexuality and fatherhood articulate a male subjectivity which remains premised on the coherent, unified, univocal and rational essence of liberal humanism. It is a masculinity which confines emotion and vulnerability to (heterosexual) familial relations, which valorises calculative rationality and a competitive economic individualism which is in the end – as celebrated in longer working hours, material gain and the striving for economic 'success' – destructive of men's relationships with women, other men and the children they so rarely see.

MARRIAGE, LAW AND MALE SEXUALITY

I have argued in Chapter 3 that the law has fissured the categories of man/woman and sought to bifurcate male sexuality into hetero- and homosexualities. Similarities in the social expression of homosexuality and heterosexuality have been negated in the legal promulgation of an ideology of natural sexual difference between male/female and hetero/homosexual. It is on the basis of these differences, importantly, that the institution of marriage is founded. The structuring of power relations *between* masculinities which this process has involved thus exists in a dialectical relationship to the male/female axis. The social construction of heterosexual masculinity must be located not just within a network of power relations whereby a 'normal' adult heterosexuality is a path through which a gender identity might be negotiated; it must also be seen through reference to those other masculinities which may deviate from this hegemonic norm. Thus, something like male impotence, for example (as a deviant/non-virile masculinity), can be seen as a crucial organising moment within the construction of the hegemonic male sexuality and hetero-virility (Chapter 4).

These dichotomies (man/woman, hetero/homosexual, virile/non-virile) are not simply constructed at the level of discourse. They are supported within relations of power and they interplay with the division of labour and the structuring of familial relations in law. On one level it is possible to see the institutionalised differentiation of these masculinities in law as having been inscribed and taking effect at the level of state policy (for example, through decisions that homosexuals may not marry or adopt children). The historical construction of masculinities outlined in this book can thus be seen as part of a struggle for resources and power – as inescapably political questions.

Shaped at the juncture of subjectivity and objectivity, I have argued that a particular form of male heterosexuality has been fundamental in constituting the potentialities of men's bodies in law. In locating sexuality as a construct of the social realm, the physiology and morphology of the body provide the preconditions of human sexuality. These potentialities are transformed and given meaning in social relationships (Chapter 3). The emergence of the phallocentric heterosexual masculinity of Chapter 4 must, therefore, be seen in the context of the more general 'sexualisation' of society. We are, Foucault states

> in a society of 'sex', or rather a society 'with a sexuality'. . . . Through the themes of health, progeny, race, the future of the species, the vitality of the social body, power spoke of sexuality and to sexuality: the latter was not a mark or a symbol, it was an object and a target.
>
> (Foucault 1981: 147)

The diversity and heterogeneity of discourses 'speaking of sex' has run throughout this account of masculinity, law and the family.

Yet, amongst the plethora of texts addressing the perfection of sex technique (for example the legal cases of Chapter 4), just what it is that is so very 'natural' about heterosexuality is open to question. The natural male sexuality, it would appear, is much of the time in need of education and assisted 'technique'. The male sexuality at issue here is, in short, deeply phallocentric. It is the penis which is, on the reading of legal cases in relation to homosexuality, trans-sexualism and impotence (Chapters 3 and 4), the foundation upon which is built the marriage institution – and it is through reference to the institution that law has then proceeded to historically construct fatherhood.

Locating matrimonial law within the wider historical context in which heterosexuality has emerged as a distinct construction within legal discourse has involved disturbing the polarities of the purportedly natural categories of 'man', 'woman', 'masculinity' and 'femininity' upon which the institution of marriage has been based. In law, as we have seen in relation to transsexualism and homosexuality, the categories of 'man' and 'woman' are far from unproblematic. Although positivist law continues to treat them as prediscursive entities, what has marked the construction of hetero-sexuality in these contexts has been the need to affirm and institu-tionalise a form of (hetero) sexuality within the institution of marriage. When the binary oppositions which traverse matri-monial law are disturbed, however (as they are by the case of transsexualism), the resulting fracture runs through to the very basis of marriage, the family and those sexual divisions on which the institution has been predicated and legally structured.

One result of this has been to fragment the coherence of ideas of 'sexual identity' in law and, instead, to valorise the dissonant and often contradictory nature of human experience, the idea of a multiple, shifting identity 'asserting difference in a non-hierarchical manner, refusing to disembody and therefore to de-sexualize the vision of the subject' (de Lauretis, quoted in Bottomley 1993: 68). This development has undermined con-structions of male and female as antithetical, exclusive categories (Butler 1990). It has also challenged essentialist conceptions of male sexuality as natural, genital and a priori heterosexual. The multivarious discourses which speak of sex and the body all (though in different ways) provide a vocabulary for, a way of talking about, heterosexuality. Law is, on this view, one discourse among many which sets the limits of the possible. However, through denying the sociality of (hetero)sex, positivist legal discourse has sought to 'control' the undifferentiated lusts of men through establishing the locale for 'natural' sexual expression as the institution of marriage. The trouble has been, of course, that the resulting network of familial power has never been stable and finally settled. When (within these liberal legal terms) male sexuality 'breaks out' of the confines of its legitimate locale (as in the cases of prostitution or, in a different way, in the sexual abuse of children), it becomes then necessary to reconstruct the familial as the site of the dangerous, asocial masculinity. This is, we have seen in Chapter 6, notoriously difficult to do so long as imagining the family man as dangerous is anathema to familial ideology and the essentialist discourse of male sexuality.

MASCULINITY, FEMINISM AND 'CRITICAL' FAMILY LAW: SOME CONCLUDING REMARKS

To conclude this book, I wish to present some (tentative) thoughts on a number of issues raised by this study of masculinity and law. 'Change' has been envisaged by proponents of 'men's studies' (as a separate discipline) and advocates of a 'critical study of masculinity' as something which might take place at the general level of developing non-patriarchal forms of masculinity and also in terms of the more specific and local aim of seeking to develop 'pro-feminist' research on men and masculinity.[1] This book, in a sense, bridges the critique of masculinity and the critical study of law. I now, by way of conclusion, wish to consider what the critical engagement with masculinity might mean for the relationship between men and feminism in the institutions of legal education, academia and practice. In Chapter 1 I referred, in passing (p. 12), to problems which might follow developing the study of masculinity and law. Before ending a book which has sought to do just that, it is perhaps appropriate to return to this issue in some more depth. The following comments are speculative but they do, I hope, raise some important questions about the future direction of research in masculinity and law.

Men, feminism and legal education

Perhaps it is difficult to talk of men in academia 'supporting' feminism (in writings if not in deed) when the definition of, and interests represented by, feminism can seem so fragmented and elusive. Nonetheless within both explicitly 'critical' and more traditionally doctrinal textbook legal scholarship it is possible to find many examples of male academics who have sought to take on the implications of feminist scholarship for their own area of law (though there also remain, of course, many examples of texts which remain impervious to feminist work).

For some, sympathies may amount to no more than altering their terminology in speech and writing from the universal 'he' to 's/he'. For others, self-policing and self-interest in setting the parameters of 'politically correct' liberal discourse within the law school may determine the times and the places of what, and what not, to say. Nonetheless all this may be seen as a sign of feminism's presence within the academy. Yet the relation of men to feminism in law remains, I wish to suggest, far from clear. Indeed it has become increasingly problematic at a time when more and more male legal academics (such as myself) have been seeking to integrate feminist scholarship into their own legal research. When it comes to directing resources into researching men and masculinity (the 'men's studies' position) the problem is compounded by allegations of opportunism and appropriation of feminist knowledges;

> Where were these men five years ago, when feminists searched in vain for more than minimal support from male social scientists. . . . Why do they all appear now, when further education and higher education are increasingly threatened? . . . Is it a coincidence that [the new men' studies] is being constructed in the present context as a source of potential research, publishing deals, and (even more) jobs for the already-well-paid boys holding prestigious posititons?
>
> (Canaan and Griffin 1990: 208)

As a discourse which claims to speak some 'truth' about men, the discourse of 'men's studies' exercises, and is justified by, forms of power which value its own particular notions of truth. Those discourses which would render to men's studies a claim to 'scientificity' within the academic discursive hierarchy are arguably patriarchal in that they would at the same time rank feminist 'knowledges' as inferior. It would not be desirable, I believe, to see 'men's studies' emerge as a distinct approach to law within the legal academy. How can we talk of 'men and the law' when the law is already, in so many ways, male?

It might be claimed that men who wish to support feminism in their academic research face a paradox in that, in a sense, they can't win. But, Canaan and Griffin argue, as men we are winners already and that is the whole point. Should we really care about the poor men who so desire to be seen as politically correct, but as (predominantly) white, heterosexual men are already, and inescapably, the beneficiaries of patriarchy? That is, the very system they/I seek to challenge through writing on 'patriarchalism and law'? What is the aim of such writings? Why do we write on gender, sex and subjectivity (why have I?)? Feminist legal methodology has stressed the importance of valorising women's experience; what has happened to the 'personal' in this book? The men against sexism tradition also highlights the importance of the experiential, of 'being a man'; yet why do I remain wary of here bringing in 'my own' experience? (In part, I think, because this mirroring of the methodological developments of feminism does seem to so easily lead to a self-indulgent introspection.) I do not know; but the story of law in this book does come from experience in that it comes from one social perspective. It is 'biased' in that there can be no 'unbiased' view.

It is clear that the men/feminism problematic works on different levels. On the level of equitable academic practice is the vexed question of appropriate citation, with possibly undue deference given to the traditional legal academic canon resulting in a failure to cite those feminists whose work has influenced one's own research. This is a particular problem in a discipline whose method has itself being premised on reference to the sacred texts of the law (and a problem which traverses both doctrinal and ostensibly 'critical' legal studies).

There is also the problem of the abstraction of patriarchy referred to in Chapter 1, whereby the power of masculinity becomes for the legal scholar something 'out there' – something which might speak of the law and lawyers but not the reproduction of academic practice itself. It is clear that it is now inadequate for the analysis of law and gender to be limited to the question of 'women in law' (Jardine 1987: 56) and the recent interest in the study of masculinity in law can be seen in the wider context of feminism's impact on the liberal humanities (Jardine and Smith 1987). I have argued in Chapter 1 that if methodological reflexivity may be commonplace in sociology (which is questionable), in law it remains more akin to heresy. This demand for reflexivity cannot be confined to doctrinal black-letter law, however. It has been forcefully argued that feminism and critical legal studies, for example, are not the same political project (Bottomley *et al.* 1987). One of the main differences between feminism and critical legal studies could be seen to be how they look at the world. Feminism starts from the experiential point of view of the oppressed, dominated and devalued, while 'the critical legal studies critique begins – and some would say remains – in a male constructed, privileged place in which domination and oppression can be described and imagined but not fully experienced' (Menkel-Meadow 1988: 61).

It is essential, therefore, that critiques of the doctrinal ortho-doxy (whatever rubric they take place under, 'critical' or other-wise) recognise the methodological and epistemological impli-cations of the body of feminist legal scholarship which has rendered problematic the relationship between legal studies, men and feminism (for example Graycar 1986; Bottomley 1987; Menkel-Meadow 1988; Hantzis 1988). It is one thing to locate the masculinism of law and legal practice, to point out sexist bias, the assumptions and prejudices of the law and the masculinism of legal method. What this means for those men who seek to be supportive of feminism in their own legal practice is a very different, and complex, question. How have men in legal studies responded to feminist critiques of their work, their law and their practices – in their teaching, in their research and, in a more general sense, as legal agents?

The politics of masculinity involves recognising that historically specific institutional practices – for example, how lawyers and legal academics behave, how they interact with colleagues, clients and students and how the 'working' lives of such professionals relate to the 'home' lives – contribute to, draw upon and transform a gender order in which at present hegemonic masculinism constitutes a powerful ideology. The components of masculinism Brittan describes (1989: 4) are also features of law schools, law teaching and the legal profession. Professionalism, Connell has argued

> has been constructed historically as a form of masculinity: emo-tionally flat, centred on a specialist skill, insistent on pro-fessional esteem and technically based dominance over other workers, and requiring for its highest (specialist) development the complete freedom from childcare and domestic work.
>
> (Connell 1987: 181)

This stands as a fair description of a 'successful' legal or academic career for many men (can we think of the professional men of law whose masculinities accord with such a description?). Masculinism, in short, is not just bound up with the power of law (Smart 1989a) but also with the occupational closures of professions (Witz 1990). The concept of homosociality perhaps serves to illustrate the point that ideologies of masculinism must be understood within terms of the gender order of specific institutions.

Institutionalising masculinity: the example of male homosociality in law

The *homosocial* dynamics of male/male interactions have been identified both by feminists and within the sociology of masculinity as an important factor in the reproduction of patriarchal relations. Homosociality is also a useful concept in understanding the social dynamics of a range of institutions of the law and a range of male cultural practices. (For example, see the notion of 'male horse-play' adopted in R v Aitken [1992] WLR 1006. In this case horse-play was taken to cover the setting on fire of a man by fellow RAF officers 'in the context of a celebratory evening in the mess' (p. 1019). The contrast with R v Brown [1991], p. 105 is informative).

How does this relate to men as legal academics? Take, for example, the following comments. Hamerton's *The Intellectual Life* (1929) consists of a series of essays 'To a Young Man' who is thinking of embarking on a 'life of the mind'. Commenting on happiness, personal and mental hygiene (and the search for a correct, intellectually compatible partner) for the aspiring male intellectual, he also considers:

> The professor may love his wife, and fully appreciate her qualities as a housekeeper, but he passes a more interesting evening with some male friend whose reading is equal to his own. Sometimes the lady perceives this, and it is an element of sadness in her life . . . although he would open his mind with the utmost frankness to a male aquaintance over the evening whiskey-toddy, there was not whiskey enough in all Scotland to make him frank in the presence of his wife.
>
> (Hamerton 1929: 234–5)

The homosocial dynamics of many male working practices have been identified by feminists as crucial to maintaining the exclusion of women from loci of decision-making. Hamerton's reflections in *The Intellectual Life* reveal one significant dynamic of male-male heterosexual relations. Lipman-Blumen (1976) has argued for the analytic usefulness of a 'homosocial theory of sex roles' to explain a limited range of social phenomena, such as the psychodynamics of institutionalised segregation in the structured domains of work and leisure. Homosocial behaviour has also been identified as constituting an important dynamic within the maintenance of a male heterosexual identity predicated on genital performance (Hoch 1979; Person 1980; Lyman 1987; Sherrod 1987). Central to this idea of homosociality is the notion that while men are in competition with each other, men are simultaneously attracted to, stimulated by and profoundly interested in other men (Pleck 1980).

It is of course by no means original to identify the heterosexual as the denial/negation of homosexual desire (Easthope 1987). However, at the descriptive level this concept of homosociality serves as an accurate reflection of any number of social institutions of the legal and political world; from university senior common rooms, criminology and law conferences to the House of Lords and Commons, barristers chambers and the upper echelons of the Law Society and firms of solicitors (Spencer and Podmore 1987b; Rogers 1988). When Hearn asks what might the study of masculinity tell us about 'parliament, industry, the city, the professions?' (Hearn 1987: 22), then the pervasive homosociality of these institutions may be one answer. In a profession where patronage, contacts and secrecy continue to inform recruitment and progression, such homosociability appears to have worked against women's advancement. The psychodynamics of male homosociality as institutionalised in the patriarchal structures of legal institutions are evident in the systems of deference, patronage and resource allocation which are hallmarks of progression in the profession (Thornton 1989a: 122; on stereotypes of gender in the recruitment process generally see Equal Opportunities Commission 1986; the role of patronage in academia should also not be underestimated).

In the work of writers such as Thornton (1989a), Rogers (1988), Lipman-Blumen (1976) and Ramazanogolu (1987) therefore a picture emerges of working environments which are suffused with the 'male club ethos' and a masculinism which emphasises exclusivity, the accumulation of resourses and, crucially, the exclusion of women, whose presence 'would dilute the atmosphere and function of these bastions of male homosociability' (Lipman-Blumen 1976: 30). It is not simply that male homosociality can here serve to make women feel 'awkward' or produce an unpleasant working environment. One of its effects is to promote the exclusion of women and those men whose masculinities might deviate from the normative hegemonic ideal.

This exclusion in turn has material consequences in the denial of access to information, input to decision-making, access to resources, etc. In relation to law such an exclusion of women has historically served as an institutional imperative of the legal world. If, at the contemporary moment, the corporate-commercial City law firms might initiate minimal crèche facilities, and show degrees of sympathy to childcare, it remains the case that more women than men leave the law, differential earnings continue and, notwithstanding the evolution of women-only firms, the legal profession remains predominantly male (Chambers' 1990: 20–5). As Apter (1985) notes, drawing attention to the sexual division of labour which underpins this gendering of professional career 'success', 'women don't have wives'. Men do.

'Who's that man?' Feminist masculinities and hidden agendas

> Like other men, sociologists also have sex lives and 'even this' may be intellectually consequential. In loyalty tinged with bitterness, most stick it out to the end with wives who saw them through graduate school, while others practise serial polygamy . . . it is my strong but undocumented impression that when some sociologists change their work interests, problems, or styles, they also change mistresses or wives.
>
> (Gouldner 1970: 56–7; quoted by Scraton 1990: 10)

If the above comment is true then, judging by the numbers of men whose work interests have turned to the subject of men and masculinity in recent years, there would appear to have been many broken relationships. Perhaps men's turning to masculinity has been prompted in part by a disillusionment with traditional critical legal theory (and in particular marxism) whereby for post-modern nihilist and post-marxist alike:

> The experience of being left out, on the sidelines, was the new and threatening reality for many a young male radical, no

longer feeling as certain as he had in the 1960s of his own
participation in the making of history.

(Segal 1990: 280)

If we look upon the legal academy as dependent on a 'market' for
the research produced (publication determining career progress,
or obtaining employment in the first place) then the advocacy of a
study of masculinity may amount to no more than another method
of reproducing the individual and collective power of men.
Academics seek new markets, new forms of expression and new
things to express in the tortuous path of the academic career
(Bankowski and Mungham 1976). Research on masculinity may
therefore amount to no more than the seeking out of another
'market', a subfield within gender studies to be exploited by male
academics, excluded from feminism, but who find themselves ill at
ease within malestream scholarship such as a traditional marxism
or, more recently, postmodernism. Masculinity has, interestingly,
moved increasingly centre-stage in the discipline of criminology.
Yet as Moore (1993) has put it, 'Every other subject is already
unofficially men's studies – isn't the demand for a separate discipline to study masculinity just another classic case of the way men
want to have their cake and eat it?'

There is an important issue here which relates to both how we
understand the construction of the masculine subject in feminist
discourse and the ways in which the masculinity problematic is
being reproduced at this moment in legal studies. It is revealing to
look at how feminist concepts and methods have been appropriated in texts which have sought to develop the critique of
masculinity in the context of law.

In legal studies perhaps one of the most obvious manifestations
of the introspective self-pity which has bedevilled so much of the
writing on men and masculinity is Fraser's (1988) article 'What's
Love Got To Do With It? Critical Legal Studies, Feminist Discourse
and the Ethic of Solidarity'. This article is interesting in several
respects. Fraser's principal aim appears to be to state (but not to
analyse) the tensions, confusions and contradictions involved in
being a male legal academic who has sought to engage with
feminism in his research and teaching. Like much of the literature
purporting to be sympathetic to feminism, it is (frequently)
extremely self-conscious in declaring the academic/personal
aspirations and good faith of the author. Above all, Fraser means

well and is at pains to stress his good intentions. Commenting on the feminist challenge to his academic life he comments:

> Sex. I am a white, male, heterosexual law professor, and when I talk about sex, people listen. . . . The feminist project hits us where we live. It threatens to, at the grossest level, cut off our cocks.
>
> (Fraser 1988: 53)

Leaving aside an interesting conception of castration/depowerment, Fraser would seem to be saying that he does indeed live in his, and perhaps all, 'cocks' (an interesting literal and metaphorical personification of phallocentrism). Men do seem to feel tensions between their academic and their personal aspirations, between keeping 'good faith' with feminism and simultaneously 'exploring' the politics of masculinity in their own academic careers. Men writing about feminism often seem to desire to be 'correct' in what they do (and Fraser provides just one example of this self-consciousness; see also Rowen (1987)).

> Questions plague me. Does she desire me or her 'law professor and his power'? Can the two be separated? . . . If I, as professor, approach a student, I engage in sexual harassment, for I cannot escape 'professor' status. . . . This is my experience in law school. I want connection. . . . As a white, male, heterosexual, CLS law professor I . . . struggle *for the politically correct position* on love in the law school.
>
> (Fraser 1988: 80; my emphasis)

It is not clear what the 'politically correct' position on love in the law school is. What is it? One which does not subordinate women or one where Fraser will be able to know if she desires him or his professorial power? How is he to know? Does she know when he makes his 'approach' to her? He wants 'connection', and turns to feminism for assistance.

If this is the face of legal studies 'taking feminism seriously' then we may be better off without it. Traditional legal method may be passionless but to turn to some generic feminism for 'authentic connection' (assuming there is such a thing) is a misguided appropriation of feminism and is more akin to the politics of 'men's liberation'. As Bottomley *et. al.* (1987) have argued,

> In so far as feminism is held together by an acceptance that women are subordinated and their position must be changed

this, of itself, says little. It is like saying that we all like demo-
cracy. Feminists divide over many major issues. To conflate is
not simply to confuse but to patronise and to attempt to control
through simplification and caricature. We cannot merely be
added to the agenda. We may actually be tearing the agenda up.
We don't yet know.

(Bottomley *et al.* 1987: 49)

It is to Fraser's credit that he at least questions his own practice, and
it is this academic practice which feminists – not just in law, but
throughout the academy generally – have identified as in so many
respects oppressive, as inimical to women's autonomy and as an
obstacle to programmes of equality (Perreault 1983; Thornton
1989a). However, he also identifies some of the dangers in developing work on masculinity and law. 'What's Love Got to Do With It?'
provides a good example of the qualities of appropriation, egocentric
self-interest and the power of the hegemonic masculinity which is
ostensibly the object of critique. Given these problems, what does the
future hold for developing the study of law and masculinity?

'Taking masculinity seriously'?

Just as the growth in the 'sociology of masculinity' or 'men's
studies' has been considered problematic from a feminist perspective, so too might the engagement with masculinity in legal
studies. Yet it appears, with an almost predictable regularity, that
whenever 'new directions' for research are referred to then this
will be taken to include the study of men and masculinity. Usually
this is phrased in terms of a need to 'take masculinity seriously'
(see Stanko and Hobdell 1993). However, just what 'taking masculinity seriously' might involve is far from clear.

This book, alongside many others, has sought to investigate
aspects of the masculinism of law and legal practice. Notwithstanding
concerns which have been raised in this section about the relation of
men to feminism, it appears that the time is now propitious for the
study of masculinity and law. In a sense, legal studies have slowly
begun, albeit tentatively, to consider debates which have become well
established in the discipline of sociology. In the latter field there has
been no end to the prescriptive 'do's and don'ts' of desirable methodological and epistemological practice in engaging with feminist
scholarship (for example Hearn 1987: 1992).

It is important to recognise at the end of this study of masculinity and law that there is nothing inherently progressive or pro-feminist about men addressing masculinity. As Thornton has pointed out, simply pre-fixing 'women and' and 'men and' to the subject of research may itself legitimate the gender regime of the liberal state and the legal order (Thornton 1989a: 126), the regime which had ostensibly been the object of critique. It would be naive in engaging in research on men and masculinity to be blind to the politics of the production and reproduction of 'knowledge' and to write with no more than a:

> boyish enthusiasm for anything new combined with an age old thrust to colonise, particularly if it looks like a field where no angel has yet trodden or at least registered a thesis topic.
>
> (Bottomley *et al.* 1987: 48)

Notwithstanding these concerns I believe that it remains important that legal studies address the masculinism at the heart of its own practices, method and institutions. I hope that this book, and what it has had to say about masculinity, law and the family, is some small contribution towards doing just that.

Notes

PREFACE

1 For example Carol Smart's (1989a) *Feminism and the Power of Law* and Katherine O'Donovan's (1993) *Family Law Matters.*
2 For example Jeff Hearn's *Men in the Public Eye* (1992).
3 For example Ngaire Naffine's (1990) *Law and the Sexes: Explorations in Feminist Jurisprudence.* See further Chapter 6, p. 216.

1 INTRODUCTION: ON LAW AND MASCULINITY

1 See further on this literature, and these distinctions, Morgan (1992).The 'men's studies' discipline appears more developed in the US than in the UK. On the 'critical study' of masculinity in the UK, Hearn and Morgan (1990) is a good introduction to the issues; also Hearn (1992). I am here using the term 'sociology of masculinity' in a broader sense to cover work which may not necessarily be pro-feminist. The 'critical' study of masculinity denotes explicitly anti-sexist scholarship in this context.
2 It is arguable that liberal legalism has reconstituted itself in such a way as to (largely) avoid the overt discriminatory statements of judges. Discrimination, however, continues in other forms (O'Donovan 1993). It has been the perceived inadequacy of 'progressive' liberal legal reforms which has led some feminists to question the utility of engaging with law. Others (see below) have conceived of the law itself as inherently 'male' and oppressive.
3 See note 1, above. The discussion which follows owes much to the (pioneering) work of Carrigan *et al.* (1985) and Connell (1987) on the sociology of masculinity literature.
4 I will return to this issue in more detail in Chapter 7. See further on this point the work of Middleton (1992) and Morgan (1992).
5 Canaan and Griffin (1990) provide a useful overview of some of these problems.
6 For example Schwerger (1984); Woodcock (1984): Riedman (1987).

7 Vance (1985).

8 Wernick (1987); Mort (1988); Collier (1992b).

9 Connell (1983); Dunning (1986); Walvin (1987); Jefferson (1989).

10 Mercer and Julien (1988); Sinha (1987); Gary (1987); Cazenave and Leon (1987); Franklin (1984, 1987); Hoch (1979); Jefferson (1993).

11 Jackson (1990); Cohen (1992). Experiential accounts of men's lives are common in much of the men's anti-sexist writings.

12 For example Easthope (1987).

13 I do not mean this list to be exclusive. The above constitute just a small selection of the diverse writings in these areas.

14 Wood (1982); Lees (1983); Abraham (1989).

15 Willis' account in *Learning to Labour* (1977), though not from within the anti-sexist tradition, has perhaps been one of the most influential studies of male working-class adolescents. Much of the writings in this area comes from a social work focus, with the emphasis on practice and intervention.

16 Fennell *et al.* (1988: Ch. 5). This is, I believe, a relatively unexplored area and deserving of more attention.

17 I am aware of the cultural specificity of many of these (and my own) accounts of the social construction of masculinity. Just as masculinity and heterosexuality are often 'taken for granted', sometimes implicit assumptions are also made about race and ethnicity in accounting for masculinity. The subject of this book is heterosexual masculinity in legal discourse and I am aware that what follows is just one story, from one perspective, and is necessarily limited.

18 For example Metcalf and Humphries (1985); Kaufman (1987a); Kimmell (1987a); Brod (1987b); Hearn (1987); Brittan (1989); Hearn and Morgan (1990); Middleton (1992); Rutherford (1992); Hearn (1992); Morgan (1992). See further Ford and Hearn (1988). Again, this list is selective.

19 I am using these 'themes' for heuristic purposes. I am aware that one might equally point out other distinctive traits of the genre. Nonetheless I believe that these do tend to be issues which recur in the writings on masculinity. The idea of 'crisis' will be explored in more detail below.

20 See note 10, above.

2 THEORISING MASCULINITY AND THE FAMILY

1 See also Hawes v Evenden [1953] 2 All ER 737. In this case 'family' was held to include a cohabiting couple who have children.

2 See Ghandi and MacNamee (1991) on the need to take into account cultural differences and the non-essential nature of family structures. The distinctions made between people in family law should be based, Ghandi and MacNamee (1991: 127) argue, on actual relationships between individuals, for example financial dependence, what has been shared, length of time living together and so forth.

3 For example, on autopoetic theory see O'Donovan (1993: 27).

4 See also Harding (1986); Fraser and Nicholson (1988); Smart (1989a).

5 Not least of which are a latent anti-feminism and tendency to appeal to a notion of a 'golden age' of the mythical family. See further Bennett *et al.* (1981); Barrett and McIntosh (1982).

3 LAW, SEX AND MASCULINITY

1 See also on the heterosexual/homosexual dichotomy Wilkinson and Kitzinger (1993).

2 Just as men may feel threatened by women's critiques of masculinity, so heterosexual women may appear to have ambivalent feelings about articulating heterosexuality. It has been claimed that 'there is not as strong a conceptual bond between femininity and heterosexuality for females as there is between masculinity and heterosexuality for males' (Hunter 1993: 157).

3 See S. LeVay (1992) 'Are Homosexuals Born and Not Made?', *The Guardian*, 9 October 1992. My focus here is on social/cultural responses to homosexuality – how homosexuality has been constituted as 'other' in legal discourse.

4 Article Eight is concerned to guarantee a person's 'right to respect for his private and family life, his home and correspondence'. Article Twelve concerns the right to marry.

5 For example, the Christian Institute (Campaigns) Paper 'Adoption and Fostering by Homosexual Couples' (1991) exemplifies this attempt to mobilise against relationships of homosexuals with children. The report seeks to emphasise that 'the law does not regard a homosexual way of life as neutral, rather it considers a homosexual household to be a negative factor in weighing up the welfare of a child'.

6 'Registered partnerships' in Denmark are still defined through reference to heterosexual marriage, however; O'Donovan (1993: 51).

7 The Irish case UF v JC The Irish Reports [1991] 2 IR 330 is particularly interesting on assessing degrees of homosexuality in a heterosexual institution. The idea is that one might reach such a degree of homosexuality beyond which one should not be able to marry. Quite what this degree is, however, is far from clear.

8 Weeks (1985: Ch. 4) contains an excellent discussion of the background, development and influence of the sexological tradition.

9 At the time of writing the most recent case is that of Miss B. (B v France [1992] 2 FLR 249).

10 Including Belgium, Denmark, Finland, France, Germany, Italy, Luxembourg, Portugal, Spain, Sweden, the Netherlands and Turkey.

11 See also Morris (1984); April Ashley (*The Times*, 7 June 1980); Mark Rees (*The Guardian*, 18 November 1986); Caroline Cossey (*The Guardian*, 24 October 1990).

4 'LOVE WITHOUT FEAR': REPRESENTATIONS OF MALE HETEROSEXUALITY IN LAW

1 Canon law recognised three types of impotence: accidental impotence, resulting from injury, illness or surgical operation; and respective impotence and relative impotence, as intermittent and selective forms of impotence affecting, in the latter case, only one of the partners (Darmon 1985: 22–3). Both structural and psychological causes of non-consummation have come within the judicial gaze for the purposes of determining whether intercourse has taken place.
2 See further p. 159.
3 R v R [1991] 4 All ER 481; [1991] 3 WLR 766. See further on this case Giles (1992); Laird (1992).
4 A transition evident in the cases of Welde v Welde [1731], G v M [1885] and N v M [1853]. See further on this change Moran (1990).
5 On anti-feminism in newspapers see Zoe Heller, 'Don't Look Back' (*The Independent on Sunday*, 22 March 1992). Ableman's polemical *The Doomed Rebellion* (1983) is a particularly venemous attack on feminism. What is perhaps most interesting about Neil Lyndon's (1992) shoddy *No More Sex War* is the extraordinary amount of publicity its publication attracted.

5 THE 'GOOD FATHER' IN LAW: AUTHORITY, WORK AND THE RECONSTRUCTION OF FATHERHOOD

1 This will be explored further below. I have in mind here the idea of 'subterreanean values'; see Matza and Sykes (1961); Matza (1964).
2 See Sally Weale 'Parental Rights and Wrongs' (*The Guardian*, 7 April 1993).
3 The controversies during 1993 in England and Wales surrounding the workings of the Child Support Act 1991 illustrate how ideas of fatherhood can be bound up in debates around family law reform. This legislation, which came into force in April 1993, set up a Child Support Agency, the stated aim of which was to prevent maintenance becoming a source of conflict between parents. In practice, however, it soon appeared that the Agency was focusing on hitherto 'responsible' fathers who were already making maintenance payments (any monies the Agency obtains do not benefit the mother; they are deducted from her benefit). Following widespread, and highly publicised, protests from absent fathers and second families about the inflexible way the Agency worked, the government announced changes to the way that maintenance contributions were to be calculated. In the debates around the Act a clear distinction was made between the 'respectable/responsible' father and the 'errant/ runaway' father. See further on this distinction Collier 1994.
4 The implementation of the Children Act 1989 has radically transformed the legal relationships between men and women, parents and children (see White, Carr and Lowe 1990). It has, for the first time,

brought the hitherto separate areas of 'private' and 'public' laws relating to the family together in one Act (Bainham 1990, 1991). Strictly speaking the very language of 'child custody' is now obsolete and, under section 8 of the Act, a new range of orders in relation to children have been enacted. However, and notwithstanding the major changes in terminology introduced by the Act, the essence of the legal determination of the arrangements regarding children remains the same. Decisions are to be made with the welfare principle as 'paramount consideration' (section 1(1)). I will, for reasons of clarity and because the research discussed concerns pre-Children Act cases, continue to use the term child custody in this book.

5 Though its empirical foundations may be dubious, one effect of the ideology of the 'new fatherhood' has been to feed in to an explicit anti-feminist backlash (Faludi 1992: Roberts 1992; cf. Lyndon 1992). On representations of fatherhood in popular culture see Collier (1992b).

6 Such was a rule 'founded in decency, morality, and polity' (Stevens v Modd *et al.* [1777] 2 Cowp 591, p. 594 per Lord Mansfield).

7 This argument is particularly clear in the writings edited by Anderson and Dawson (1986a). On homosexuality as threat to social order and national security see Moran (1991).

8 Also Campbell v Campbell [1976] 3 WLR 572; Clarke v Clarke [1980] 9 Fam Law 15.

9 A view also evident in Tovey v Tovey [1978] 8 Fam Law 80

10 It is curious the extent to which in custody (and other) cases judges comment on the 'fit and vigorous' (or otherwise) nature of a man's physicality, perhaps betraying their own beliefs about appropriately 'masculine' comments.

11 This was particulary clear in the recent controversies in North America and Europe surrounding the practice of 'virgin births'. See further p. 170.

12 For example Pilling and Kellmer-Pringle (1978). This, and other, research is discussed by Maidment (1984).

13 It would be misleading to claim that the law has 'improved' the situation of the illegitimate when we recall that the law has been the source of the 'misfortunes' in the first place.

14 For example, having established in 1841 that only the unmarried mother would have sole rights to her child, the 1844 Poor Law Amendment Act proceeded to take bastardy proceedings out of the hands of the Poor Law authorities and turn them into a civil matter between the parents. The mother was thus given a civil action for maintenance against the putative father of her child and affiliation proceedings became a civil matter between the parents of the child. This meant was that henceforward any responsibilities the father might have would only be realised if the mother took civil action for maintenance against him. Making affiliation proceedings a civil matter between the parents of the child effectively put the ball in the mother's court (Smart 1987: 103). Not until 1844 (and following the

abolition of all the laws on bastardy in 1841) did the mother obtain the legal right to maintenance from the father. The Poor Law Guardians, in contrast, had the power to make a charge on the putative father as far back as 1576. The subsequent history of illegitimacy laws has revealed just how difficult the enforcing of this right has been. See further Smart 1987.

15 Particularly evident in the Family Law Reform Act (1987) and the Chidren Act (1989 s. 4).

16 The child of the family concept is also to be found in legislation of support after death: Inheritance (Provision for Family and Dependants) Act (1975); Fatal Accidents Act (1976) (as amended by the Administration of Justice Act 1982).

17 See note 3 above.

6 'FAMILY MEN' AND 'DANGEROUS' MASCULINITIES

1 Quoted in Rotundo (1987b: 36).

2 Such irregular economies and street cultures, we must remember, continue to exist today in areas which are economically and culturally marginalised See further Campbell (1993).

3 Women commit fewer crimes of all types and proportionally fewer serious and violent crimes than men. There were, for example, about 1,600 female offenders in prison on 30 June 1990 compared with around 43,000 men, and of the 509,000 offenders found guilty or cautioned for indictable offences in 1990 only 17 per cent were women. Only 7 per cent of the female population will have had a conviction for a serious offence by the age of 31 compared with 33 per cent of males (Home Office 1992b: 3.4, p. 7). It is not just that crime appears an overwhelmingly male activity. Women, although the number in each agency is increasing, remain the minority in senior positions across all criminal justice agencies: (19 per cent of practising barristers in private practice are women, 5 per cent of QC's are women and less than 20 per cent of solicitors in private practice in England and Wales are women, 10 per cent of partners in solicitors firms are women (Chambers 1990). In 1992 12 per cent of police officers were women. Although on 1 January 1992 45 per cent of lay magistrates were female, only 5 per cent of circuit judges, 5 per cent of recorders and 10 per cent of assistant recorders were women (*Gender and the Criminal Justice System* 1992).

4 At the 1992 Conservative Party conference the Secretary of State for Social Security had, in a parody of the Mikado, spoken of 'young ladies who get pregnant just to jump the housing list and dads who won't support the ladies they have . . . kissed (*Observer*, 14 November 1993). Following Redwood's comments in July 1993 it emerged that Peter Lilley, the Social Security Secretary, had known in advance what Redwood was going to say. Further statements from ministers appear to suggest that both Lilley and the Prime Minister were happy for a

high-profile debate about single parents at a time of public spending
cuts. According to John Perry, Institute of Housing Policy Director,
there is no evidence that single parents on waiting lists are allocated
better housing more quickly.

5 Tom Sackville, *Guardian*, 6 July 1993.

6 Peter Lilley told MPs 'We are certainly not against lone parents. . . .
The state has to step in with monetary help if parents are unable to
support those children but we can never substitute for that love or
commitment' (*The Independent*, 5 July 1993).

7 Of such single mothers who have never married half are older than
25. Figures suggest that the typical lone mother has been married, is
probably divorced, is aged 35 to 39 and has two children. Whilst it is
true that the number of never married lone mothers has risen sharply
(representing in 1993 6.4 per cent of all families compared with 1.2
per cent in 1971), changes in family structures have meant that
around 20 per cent of all households are made up of single parents,
of which 1.4 per cent are headed by men.

8 See Edwards (1987). In part the problems which have faced the police
and the Crown Prosecution Service in enforcing the Act have
stemmed from the wording of the Act itself and, in particular, the
meaning of 'persistent' soliciting; see Darroch v Director of Public
Prosecutions [1990] 91 Cr App R 378; Hughes v Holley [1988] 86 Cr
App R 130; Paul v Director of Public Prosecutions [1990] 90 Cr App R
173); Susan Edwards (*Guardian*, 4 October 1991).

9 See Campbell (1988: 69–82) on police practices in Cleveland in
relation to this disbelief that abuse could take place inside the family.

10 The legal difficulties which women faced in gaining protection, alongside the growing awareness of the scale of the problem, led to the
passing of the Domestic Violence and Matrimonial Proceedings Act
1976. Yet the nature and inadequacies of this and subsequent legal
responses to the problem (McCann 1985) have led some to question
the role of law in 'solving' the problem of domestic violence. Cases
since 1976 have tended to focus on the housing of the parties, the
circumstances in which men may be excluded from the home and the
need to reconcile a woman's need for protection with the laws res-
pecting a man's rights of property (for example see Davis v Johnson
[1979] AC 264; Spindlow v Spindlow [1979] 1 All ER 169; Richards v
Richards [1984] AC 174; Myers v Myers [1982] 1 WLR 247). What
emerges from much research is a commonly held belief that domestic
violence is a 'crime' only in the most serious of cases and a judicial
antipathy to the view that the interests of husband and wife may not,
in all instances, be the same (see Hoskyn v Metropolitan Police Commissioner [1979] AC 474 per Lord Wilberforce p. 488, also Lord
Salmon p. 495; Boyle 1980). Furthermore domestic cases would
appear to often receive lower sentences than in other cases of violence
(Binney *et al.* 1981; note R v Cutts [1987] Fam Law 311).

7 CHANGING MASCULINITIES, CHANGING LAW: CONCLUDING REMARKS

1 For Brod (1987b), for example, violent men can be seen as 'victims' of masculinity in the sense that they are the impersonal locus of forces that move them. In relation to rape and violence against women, therefore, Brod advocates treatment programmes or forms of 'masculinity therapy' which might tackle the socially destructive effects of masculinity at root. From this perspective 'men's studies' actually is a feminist project, feminist scholarship applied to the case of men. Resources should, on this argument, be diverted to such masculinity therapy because 'prevention' is better than 'cure'. This view has a number of implications for social work as preventative of men's violence (Hearn 1990: 79) and raises difficult questions about what to do with men who do not take responsibility for their violence. Hearn (1990: 83) suggests that a distinction can be made between short-term strategies (aimed at avoiding men's violence in specific situations), medium-term strategies which work against violence in men and long-term ones which challenge the social institutions and laws and attitudes which produce and reproduce violence.

Bibliography

Abbott, F. (1990) (ed.) *Men and Intimacy: Personal Accounts. Exploring the Dilemmas of Modern Male Sexuality*, London: Crossing Press.

Abel, R. (1973) 'Law Books and Books About Law', *Stanford Law Review* 26: 175.

Ableman, P. (1983) *The Doomed Rebellion*, London: Bee in Bonnett/Zomba Books.

Abraham, J. (1989) 'Gender Differences and Anti-School Boys', *The Sociological Review* February, 37: 65.

Adler, Z. (1987) *Rape On Trial*, London: Routledge and Kegan Paul.

Alcock, P. (1984) 'Remuneration or Remarriage? The Matrimonial and Family Proceedings Act 1984', *Journal of Law and Society* 11, 3: 357.

Allan, D. (1982) *One Step From The Quagmire*, Aylesbury: Campaign For Justice On Divorce.

Allen, H. (1987) *Justice Unbalanced*, Milton Keynes: Open University Press.

Allen, G. and Crowe, G. (1989) *Home and Family: Creating the Domestic Space*, London: Macmillan.

Allen, J. (1988) 'The Masculinity of Criminality and Criminology: Interrogating Some Impasses' in M. Findlay and R. Hogg (eds) *Understanding Crime and Criminal Justice*, Sydney: Law Book Company.

—— (1987) '"Mundane Men": Historians, Masculinity and Masculinism', *Historical Studies* 22: 617.

Allen, S. and Harne, L. (1988) 'Lesbian Mothers: The Fight For Child Custody' in B. Cant and S. Hemmings (eds) *Radical Records*, London: Routledge.

Altman, D. (1983) *The Homosexualisation of America*, Boston: Beacon Press.

—— (1971) *Homosexual Oppression and Liberation*, New York: Outerbridge and Dienstfrey.

Altman, M. (1984) 'Everthing They Always Wanted You to Know: The Ideology of Popular Sex Literature' in C. Vance. (ed.) *Pleasure and Danger: Exploring Female Sexuality*, London: Routledge..

Amiel, B. (1991) 'Men and their natural sexuality on trial', *The Sunday Times*, 15 December.

Anderson, D. and Dawson, G. (eds) (1986a) *Family Portraits*, London: Social Affairs Unit.

—— and —— (1986b) 'Popular but Unrepresented: The Curious Case of the Normal Family' in D. Anderson and P. Dawson (eds) *Family Portraits*, London: Social Affairs Unit.

Anderson, M. (1980) *Approaches to the History of the Western Family 1500–1914*, London: Macmillan.

—— (1971) *Family Structure in Nineteenth Century Lancashire*, Cambridge: Cambridge University Press.

Apse, S.M., Gregory, J.G. and Purcell, M.H. (1984) 'The Inflatable Penile Prosthesis, Recuperation and Patient Satisfaction: A comparison of statistics obtained from patient record review with statistics obtained from intensive follow-up research', *Journal of Urology* 131: 894.

Apter, T. (1985) *Why Men Don't Have Wives*, Basingstoke: Macmillan.

Archer, J. and Lloyd, B. (1982) *Sex and Gender*, Harmondsworth: Penguin.

Aries, P. (1985) 'Thoughts on the History of Homosexuality' in P. Aries. and A. Bejin (eds).*Western Sexuality: Practice and Precept in Past and Present Times*, Oxford: Basil Blackwell.

—— (1973) *Centuries of Childhood*, Harmondsworth: Penguin.

—— and Bejin, A. (eds) (1985) *Western Sexuality: Practice and Precept in Past and Present Times*, Oxford: Basil Blackwell.

Astrachan, A. (1986) *How Men Feel: Their Response to Women's Demands for Equality and Power*, Anchor City, NJ: Doubleday.

Atkins, S. and Hoggett, B. (1984) *Women and the Law*, Oxford: Blackwell.

August, E.R. (1985) *Men's Studies: A Selected and Annotated Bibliography*, London: Libraries Unlimited, Littleton College.

Bailey, R. (1979) 'A Note on C v D', *Australian Law Journal* 53: 659.

Bailey, V. and Blackburn, S. (1979) 'The Punishment of Incest Act 1908: A Case Study of Law Creation', *Criminal Law Review.* 708.

Bainham, A. (1991) *Children The New Law: The Children Act 1989*, Bristol: Jordans.

—— (1990) 'The Children Act 1990: The State and the Family', *Family Law* 20: 231.

Bancroft, J. (1982) 'Erectile Impotence: Psyche or Soma?', *International Journal of Andrology*, 5: 353.

Bankowski, Z. and Mungham, G. (1976) *Images of Law*, London: Routledge and Kegan Paul.

Banks, T.L. (1988) 'Gender Bias in the Classroom', *Journal of Legal Education* 38: 137.

Banner, L. (1989) 'Review', *Signs* 14: 3.

Barker-Benfield, B. (1976) *The Horrors of the Half-Known Life: Male Attitudes Towards Women and Sexuality in Nineteenth Century America*, New York: Harper and Row.

—— (1972) 'The Spermatic Economy: A Nineteenth Century View of Sexuality', *Feminist Studies* 6: 45

Barrett, M. (1980) *Women's Oppression Today*, London: Verso.

—— and McIntosh, M. (1982) *The Anti-Social Family*, London: Verso/New Left Books.

—— and —— (1980) 'The Family Wage: Some Problems for Socialists and Feminists', *Capital and Class* 11: x.

Bartholomew, G.W. (1960) 'Hermaphrodites and the Law', *University of Malaya LJ* 2: 83.

Barton, C. (1987) 'Incest and Prohibited Degrees', *New Law Journal* May: 29.

Barz, H. (1991) *For Men Too; A Grateful Critique of Feminism*, Illinois: Chricon.

Bazell, C. (1989) 'Evidential and Procedural Problems in Child Abuse Cases', *Family Law* 19: 35.

Beach, F.A. (1976) 'Cross-Species Comparisons and the Human Heritage' in F.A. Beach (ed.) *Human Sexuality in Four Perspectives*, Baltimore: Johns Hopkins University Press.

Beaumont, P. (1990) 'Church Gay Controversy', *The Observer* 11 February.

Beauvoir, S. de (1972) *The Second Sex*, trans by H.M. Parshley, Alfred A. Knopf, Harmondsworth: Penguin.

Becker, M.E. (1989) 'Obscuring the Struggle: Sex Discrimination, Social Security and Stone, Seidman, Sunstein and Tushnet's "Constitutional Law"', *Columbia Law Review* 89: 264.

Bedell, G. (1993) 'Absent Fathers', *The Independent on Sunday*, 11 July.

Bell, C. and Newby, H. (1976) 'Husbands and Wives: The Dynamics of the Differential Dialectic' in S. Allen and D. Barker (eds) *Dependence and Exploitation in Work and Marriage*, London: Longman.

Bell, C., Mckee, L. and Priestly, K. (1983) *Fathers, Childbirth and Work*, Manchester: Equal Opportunities Commission.

hooks, b. (1984) *Feminist Theory: From Margin to Centre*, Boston: South End Press.

—— (1981) *Ain't I a Woman: Black Women and Feminism*, Boston: South End Press.

Bem, S. (1976) 'Probing the Promise of Androgyny' in A.G. Kaplan and J.P Bean (eds) *Beyond Sex Role Stereotypes: Readings Towards a Psychology of Androgyny*, Boston: Little Brown and Co.

—— (1974) 'The Measurement of Psychological Androgyny', *Journal of Consulting and Clinical Psychology* 42: 155.

Bender, L. (1988) 'Lawyer's Primer on Feminist Theory and Tort', *Journal of Legal Education* 38: 3.

Benhabib, S. (1986) *Critique, Norm and Utopia: A Study of the Foundations of Critical Theory*, New York: Columbia University Press.

Benjamin, H. (1953) 'Transvestism and Transsexualism', *International Journal of Sexology* 7: 12.

Benn, S. and Gaus, G. (1983) *Public and Private in Social Life*, London: Croom Helm.

Bennett, F., Coward, R. and Campbell, B. (1981) 'Feminists: Degenerates of the Social?', *Politics and Power* 3, London: Routledge and Kegan Paul.

Benton, S. (1986) 'But why do they call themselves feminists? ' *New Statesman*, 19 September: 13.

Bentovim, A. *et al.* (eds) (1988) *Child Sexual Abuse Within the Family*, London: Wright.

Berger, B. and Berger, P. (1983) *The War Over the Family*, London: Hutchinson.

Berger, J. (1972) *Ways of Seeing*, Harmondsworth: Penguin.

Berkovits, B. (1981) 'The Family and the Rent Acts: Reflections on Law and Policy', *Journal of Social Welfare Law.* 83.

Bernardes, J. (1988a) 'Founding the New Family Studies', *The Sociological Review* 36, 1: 57.

—— (1988b) 'Whose Family? A Note on the Changing Sociological Construct of the Family', *The Sociological Review* 36: 2.

Binney, V., Harknell, G. and Nixon, J. (1981) *Leaving Violent Men*, Shaftsbury, Dorset: Women's Aid Federation.

Blackstone, W. (1765) Commentaries on the Laws of England, 1978 edn, New York: Garland.

Bliss, S. (1986) 'Changing Men's Publications', *Men's Studies Newsletter* 3: 2.

Bly, R. (1991) *Iron John*, Shaftesbury, Dorset: Element Books.

Booth, W. (1976) 'In Darkest England and the Way Out', in P. Keating (ed.) *Into Unknown England 1866–1913*, London: Fontana.

Borkowski, M., Murch, M. and Walker, V. (1983) *Marital Violence: The Community Response*, London: Tavistock.

Boswell, J. (1980) *Christianity, Social Tolerance and Homosexuality*, Chicago: University of Chicago Press.

Bottomley, A. (1993) 'Self and Subjectivities: Languages of Claim in Property' in A. Bottomley and J. Conaghan (eds) *Feminist Theory and Legal Strategy: Journal of Law and Society: Special Issue*, Oxford: Blackwell.

—— (1992) 'Feminism: Paradoxes of the Double Bind' in I. Gregg-Spall and P. Ireland (eds) *The Critical Lawyers Handbook*, London: Pluto.

—— (1987) 'Feminism in Law Schools' in S. McLaughlin (ed.) *Women and the Law*, London: University College London, Faculty of Law, Working Paper No. 5.

—— (1985) 'What is Happening to Family Law? A Feminist Critique of Conciliation', in J. Brophy and C. Smart (eds) *Women in Law: Explorations in Family, Law and Sexuality*, London: Routledge and Kegan Paul.

—— (1984) 'Resolving Family Disputes: A Critical View', in M. Freeman (ed.) *State, Law and the Family*, London: Tavistock.

—— and Conaghan, J. (eds) (1993) *Feminist Theory and Legal Strategy: Journal of Law and Society: Special Issue*, Oxford: Blackwell.

—— (1993b) 'Feminist Theory and Legal Strategy' in A. Bottomley and J. Conaghan (eds) *Feminist Theory and Legal Strategy: Journal of Law and Society: Special Issue*, Oxford: Blackwell.

——, Gibson, S. and Metyard, B. (1987) 'Dworkin – Which Dworkin? Taking Feminism Seriously', *Journal of Law and Society* 14, 2: 47.

——, Gieve, K., Moon, G. and Weir, A. (1981) *The Cohabitation Handbook*, London: Pluto.

Bouchier, D. (1983) *The Feminist Challenge: The Movement For Women's Liberation in Britain and the USA*, London: Macmillan.

Bowles, G. and Klein, R. (1983) *Theories of Women's Studies*, London: Routledge.

Bowman, K. and Engle, B. (1960) 'Sex Offences: The Medical and Legal Implications of Sex Variations', *Law and Contemporary Problems* 25: 292.

—— and —— (1957) 'Medico-Legal Aspects of Transvestism', *American Journal of Psychiatry* 113: 583.

Box, S. (1983) *Power, Crime and Mystification*, London: Tavistock.

Boyd, S. (1989) 'From Gender Specificity to Gender Neutrality? Ideologies in Canadian Child Custody Law' in C. Smart and S. Sevenhuijsen (eds) *Child Custody and the Politics of Gender*, London: Routledge.

Boyle, C. (1985a) 'Book Review', *Canadian Bar Review* 63: 427.

—— (1985b) 'Sexual Assault and the Feminist Judge', *Canadian Journal of Women and the Law* 1: 93.

—— (1980) 'Violence Against Wives', *Northern Ireland Law Quarterly* 35: 50.

Bozett, F.W. (1987) *Gay and Lesbian Parents*, New York: Praeger.

Bradley, D. (1987) 'Homosexuality and Child Custody in English Law', *International Journal of Law and the Family* 1: 155.

Bradney, A. (1987) 'Transsexuals and the Law', *Family Law* 17: 350.

—— (1986) 'Blood Tests, Paternity and the Double Helix', *Family Law* 16: 353.

—— (1979) 'The Family in Family Law', *Family Law* 9: 244.

Bradshaw, J. and Millar, J. (1991) *Lone Parent Families in the UK*, London: HMSO.

Braidotti, R. (1991) *Patterns of Dissonance: A Study of Women in Contemporary Philoshopy*, London: Polity.

—— (1987) 'Fathers in Dual Earner Households Through Mothers' Eyes' in C. Lewis and M. O'Brien (eds) *Reassessing Fatherhood*, London: Sage.

Brannen, J. and Moss, P. (1990) *Managing Mothers: Dual Earner Households After Maternity Leave*, London: Unwin Hyman.

Brannon, R. (1976) 'The Male Sex Role: Our Cultures Blueprint of Manhood and What It's Done For Us Lately' in D. David and R. Brannon (eds) *The Forty-Nine Per Cent Majority: The Male Sex Role*, Reading, MA: Addison-Wesley.

Bray, A. (1982) *Homosexuality in Renaissance England*, London: Gay Men's Press.

Brindle, D. (1990) 'Errant Fathers Plan Will Cut Benefits', *The Guardian*, 30 October.

—— and Wintour, P. (1990) 'Tough Levy For Errant Fathers', *The Guardian*, 19 July.

Bristow, E.J. (1977) *Vice and Vigilance: Purity Movements in Britain Since 1700*, Dublin: Gill and Macmillan.

Brittan, A. (1989) *Masculinity and Power*, Oxford: Blackwell.

—— and Maynard, M. (1984) *Sexism, Racism and Oppression*, Oxford: Blackwell.

Britton, A. (1983) *Cary Grant: Comedy and Male Desire*, Newcastle: Tyneside Cinema.

Brod, H. (1987a) 'Towards a New Men's Studies' in H. Brod (ed.) *The Making of Masculinities: The New Men's Studies*, London: Allen and Unwin.

—— (1987b) (ed.) *The Making of Masculinities: The New Men's Studies*, London: Allen and Unwin.

—— (1987c) 'A Case For Men's Studies' in M. Kimmell *Changing Men: New Directions in Research on Men and Masculinity*, London: Sage.

Broker, M. (1976) 'I May be Queer, but at least I'm a Man: Male Hegemony and Ascribed Versus Achieved Gender' in D. Leonard, J. Barker and S. Allen (eds) *Sexual Divisions in Society*, London: Tavistock.

Bromley, P. and Lowe, N. (1987) *Family Law*, 7th edn., London: Butterworth.

Brophy, J. (1989) 'Custody Law, Childcare and Inequality in Britain' in C. Smart and S. Sevenhuijsen (eds) *Child Custody and the Politics of Gender*, London: Routledge.

—— (1987) *Family Law: Review of Child Care Law: Custody – Rights Of Women Response*, London: Rights of Women.

—— (1985) 'Child Care and the Growth of Power' in J. Brophy and C. Smart (eds) *Women in Law; Explorations in Family, Law and Sexuality*, London: Routledge.

—— (1982) 'Parental Rights and Children's Welfare: Some Problems of Feminist Strategy in the 1920's', *International Journal of the Sociology of Law* 10, 2: 149.

—— and Smart, C. (1985) *Women in Law: Explorations in Family, Law and Sexuality*, London: Routledge.

—— (1981) 'From Disregard To Disrepute: The Position of Women in Family Law', *Feminist Review* 9: 3–15.

Brown, A. (1990) 'A Christian Ceremony That Has Became a Mixed Blessing', *The Independent*, 21 February.

Brown, B. (1986a) 'Women and Crime: The Dark Figures of Criminology', *Economy and Society* 15: 355.

—— (1986b) 'Review of "Sexual Divisions in Law"', *Journal of Law and Society* 13: 436.

Brown, C. (1981) 'Mothers, Fathers and Children: from private to public patriarchy', in L. Sargent (ed.) *Women and Revolution: The Unhappy Marriage of Marxism and Feminism*, London: Pluto.

Brownmiller, S. (1975) *Against Our Will*, London: Penguin.

Brunt, R. (1982) '"An Immense Verbosity": Permissive Sexual Advice in the 1970s' in R. Brunt and C. Rowen (eds) *Feminism, Culture and Politics*, London: Lawrence and Wishart.

Bryant, M. (1992) 'Hard Cash, Soft Targets', *The Guardian*, 16 October.

Buffalo Symposium (1985) 'Feminist Discourse, Moral Values and the Law: A Conversation', *Buffalo Law Review* 34: 11.

Bullough, V.L. (1977) 'Challenges to Societal Attitudes Toward Homosexuality in Late Nineteenth Century and Early Twentieth Century', *Social Sciences Quarterly* 1: 58.

—— (1972) 'Sex in History: A Virgin Field', *The Journal of Sex Research* 8, 2: 101.

Bumiller, K. (1991) 'Fallen Angels: The Representation of Violence Against Women in Legal Culture' in M. Fineman and N. Thomadsen (eds) *At The Boundaries of Law: Feminism and Legal Theory*, London: Routledge.

Burgoyne, J., Ormrod, R., and Richards, R. (1987) *Divorce Matters*, Harmondsworth: Penguin.

Burniston, S., Mort, F. and Weedon, C. (1978) 'Psychoanalysis and the Cultural Aquisition of Subjectivity' in *Women Take Issue*, CCCS, London: Hutchinson.

Busby, K. (1989) 'The Maleness of Legal Language', *Manitoba Law Journal* 18: 191.

Butler, J. (1990) *Gender Trouble: Feminism and the Subversion of Identity*, London: Routledge.

Butler-Sloss, L.H. (1988) *Report of the Inquiry into Child Abuse in Cleveland*, London: HMSO Cmnd. 412.

Byers, K. (1990) *Man In Transition*, California: Journeys Together.

Cain, A. (1988) 'Teaching Feminist Legal Theory at Texas: Listening to Difference and Exploring Connections', *Journal of Legal Education* 38: 165.

Cain, M. (1990) 'Realist Philosophies and Standpoint Epistemologies or Feminist Criminology as a Successor Science' in L. Gelsthorpe and A. Morris (eds) *Feminist Perspectives in Criminology*, Milton Keynes: Open University Press.

—— (1986) 'Realism, Feminism, Methodology and Law', *International Journal of Law and Society* 14, 34: 255.

Calverton, V.F. and Schmalhausen, S.D. (eds) (1929) *Sex in Civilization*, London: Allen and Unwin.

Cameron, D. and Frazer, E. (1987) *The Lust to Kill: A Feminist Investigation of Sexual Murder*, Cambridge: Polity.

Campbell, B. (1993) *Goliath: Britain's Dangerous Places*, London: Methuen.

—— (1989) 'Cleveland's Dilemma', *New Statesman*, 24 February.

—— (1988) *Unofficial Secrets*, London: Virago.

—— (1985) 'Politics Old and New', *New Statesman* 8 March.

——(1980) 'A Feminist Sexual Politics: Now You See It Now You Don't', *Feminist Review* 5: 1.

Canaan, J.E. and Griffin, C. (1990) 'The New Men's Studies: Part of the Problem or Part of the Solution?' in J. Hearn and D. Morgan (eds) *Men, Masculinities and Social Theory*, London: Unwin Hyman.

Caplan, J. (1981) 'Sexuality and Homosexuality' in Cambridge Women's Studies Group (eds) *Women in Society*, London: Virago.

Caplan, P. (ed.) (1987) *The Cultural Construction of Sexuality*, London: Tavistock.

Carabine, J. (1992) '"Constructing Women": Women's Sexuality and Social Policy' in *Critical Social Policy* 12, 31: 23.

Card, C. (1991) 'Intimacy and Responsibility: What Lesbians Do' in M. Fineman and N. Thomadsen (eds) *At The Boundaries of Law: Feminsim and Legal Theory*, London: Routledge.

Carlen, P. (1976) *Magistrates Justice*, London: Martin Robertson.

Carlton, E. (1980) *Sexual Anxiety: A Study of Male Impotence*, Oxford: Martin Robertson.

Carrigan, T., Connell, R. and Lee, J. (1985) 'Towards a New Sociology of Masculinity', *Theory and Society* 14: 551.

Cavadino, M. and Dignan, J. (1992) *The Penal System: An Introduction*, London: Sage.

Cazenave, N.A. and Leon, G.H. (1987) 'Men's Work and Family Roles and Characteristics: Race, Gender and Class Perceptions of College Students' in M. Kimmell (ed.) *Changing Men: New Directions in Research on Men and Masculinity*, London: Sage.

Central Statistical Office (1991) *Social Trends 21*, London: HMSO.

Chadwick, K. (1986) 'The Company of Wolves', *New Socialist*, June 6.

Chambers, G. and Millar, A. (1983) *Investigating Sexual Assault*, Edinburgh: Scottish Office.

Chambers, M. (ed.) (1990) *Chambers and Partners Directory of the Legal Profession 1990*, London: Chambers and Partners Publishing.

Chapman, R. (1988) 'The Great Pretender: Variations on the New Man Theme' in R. Chapman and J. Rutherford (eds) *Unwrapping Masculinity*, London: Lawrence and Wishart.

Charver, J. (1983) *Feminism*, London: Dent.

Chesser, E. (1941) *Love Without Fear: A Plain Guide To Sex Techniques For Every Married Adult*, London: Rich and Cowan.

Christian Institute (1991) *Adoption and Fostering by Homosexual Couples*, Newcastle upon Tyne: Christian Institute Campaign.

Clark, A. (1987) *Men's Violence, Women's Silence: Sexual Assault in England 1770–1844*, London: Pandora.

Cloward, R.A. and Ohlin, L.E. (1960) *Delinquency and Opportunity: A Theory of Delinquent Gangs*, London: Macmillan.

Coates, D. (1991) *Running the Country*, Milton Keynes: Open University Press.

Cockburn, C. (1991) *In The Way of Women: Men's Resistance to Sex Equality in Organizations*, Basingstoke: Macmillan.

—— (1988) 'Masculinity, the Left and Feminism' in R. Chapman and J. Rutherford (eds) *Unwrapping Masculinity*, London: Lawrence and Wishart.

——(1983) *Brothers: Male Dominance and Technological Change*, London: Pluto.

Cohen, A. (1955) *Delinquent Boys: The Culture of the Gang*, London: The Free Press.

Cohen, D. (1992) 'Oh The Torture of Being a Man!', *The Independent*, 16 September.

Cohen, P. (1981) 'Policing the Working Class City' in M. Fitzgerald, G. McLennan and J. Pawson (eds) *Crime and Society: Readings in History and Theory*, Milton Keynes: Open University Press.

Cole, W.S. (1978) 'The Constitutionality of Chromosome Testing', *San Diego Law Review* 15: 331.

Colker, R. (1991) 'Feminism, Sexuality and Authenticity' in M. Fineman and N. Thomadsen (eds) *At The Boundaries of Law: Feminism and Legal Theory*, London: Routledge..

—— (1988) 'Feminism, Sexuality and Self: A Preliminary Enquiry into the Politics of Authenticity', *Boston University Law Review* 68: 217.

Collier, R. (1994) 'The Campaign Against the Child Support Act: "Errant Fathers" and "Family Men"', *Family Law*, July: 384–7.

—— (1993) '"The Good Father": Reconstructing Masculinity in Family Law', paper given at the Law and Society Association Annual Conference, Chicago, May.

—— (1992a) '"The Art of Living the Married Life": Representations of Male Heterosexuality in Law', *Social and Legal Studies*, 1: 543.

—— (1992b) 'The New Man: Fact or Fad?', *Achilles Heel* 13: 34.

—— (1991) 'Masculinism, Law and Law Teaching', *International Journal of the Sociology of Law* 19: 427.

Collins, H. (1982) *Marxism and Law*, Oxford: Clarendon Press.

Collins, R. (1977) 'Language, History and Legal Process: A Profile of the "Reasonable Man"', *Rutgers Law Review* 8: 311.

Comfort, A. (1977) *More Joy of Sex*, London: Quartet Books.

—— (1968) *Sex in Society*, Harmondsworth: Penguin.

Cominos, P. (1963) 'Late-Victorian Sexual Respectability and the Social System', *International Review of Social History* 8: 18.

Conaghan, J. (1986) 'The Invisibility of Women in Labour Law: Gender Neutrality in Model Building', *International Journal of the Sociology of Law* 14: 377.

Connell, R. (1987) *Gender and Power*, Cambridge: Polity Press.

—— (1985) 'Theorising Gender', *Sociology* 19, 2: 265.

—— (1983) *Which Way is Up?*, Sydney: George Allen and Unwin.

Coombs, M.I. (1988) 'Crime in the Stacks, or a Tale of a Text: A Feminist Response to a Criminal Law Textbook', *Journal of Legal Education* 38: 117.

Cooper, D. (1971) *The Death of the Family*, Harmondsworth: Penguin.

Corneau, G. (1991) *Absent Fathers, Lost Sons: The Search For Masculine Identity*, London: Shambhta.

Cossey, C. (1992) *My Story*, London: Faber.

Coveney, L., Jackson, M., Jeffrey, S., Kaye, L. and Mahibey, P. (1984) *The Sexuality Papers: Male Sexuality and the Social Control of Women*, London: Hutchinson.

Coward, R. (1982) 'Sexual Violence and Sexuality', *Feminist Review* 11: 15.

Crane, P. (1982) *Gays and the Law*, London: Pluto.

Crawford, M. (1993) 'Identity, "Passing" and Subversion' in S. Wilkinson and C. Kitzinger (eds) *Heterosexuality: A Feminism and Psychology Reader*, London: Sage.

Cretney, S. (1992) *Elements of Family Law*, London: Sweet and Maxwell.

—— and Masson, J. (1990) *Principles of Family Law*, 5th edn, London: Sweet and Maxwell.

Dalton, C. (1987–8) 'Where We Stand: Observations on the Situation of Feminist Legal Thought', *Berkeley Women's Law Journal* 3: 1.

—— (1988) 'The Political is Personal in Tenure Decisions', *Harvard Law Record*, 22 April.

Daly, M. (1985) *Beyond God the Father: Towards A Philosophy of Women's Liberation*, London: The Women's Press.

—— (1984) *Pure Lust: Elemental Feminist Philosophy*, London: The Women's Press.

—— (1979) *Gyn/Ecology*, London: The Women's Press.

Darmon, P. (1985) *Trial By Impotence: Virility and Marriage in Pre-Revolutionary France*, London: Chatto and Windus/Hogarth Press.

Davenport-Hines, R. (1990) *Sex, Death and Punishment*, London: Collins.

David, D.S. and Brannon, R. (1976) *The 49 per cent Majority*, Reading, MA: Addison Wesley.

David, E.S. (1975) 'The Law and Transsexualism: A Faltering Response to a Conceptual Dilemma', *Conn. Law Review* 7: 288.

Davidoff, L. and Hall, C. (1987) *Family Fortunes*, London: Hutchinson.

Davis, G. and Murch, M. (1988) *Grounds for Divorce*, Oxford: Oxford University Press.

Davis, K. (1939) 'Illegitimacy and the Social Structure', *American Journal of Sociology* 45: 215.

Davis, L.A. (1988) 'A Feminist Justification for the Adoption of an Individual Filing System', *Southern California Law Review* 62: 197.

Deakin, N. and Wicks, M. (1988) *Families and the State*, London: Family Policy Studies Centre.

Debray, R. (1984) *Critique of Political Reason*, trans. by D. Maccey, London: Verso/New Left Books.

Deech, R. (1980) 'The Case Against Legal Recognition of Cohabitation' in J. Eekelaar and S.M. Katz (eds) *Marriage and Cohabitation in Contemporary Society*, London: Butterworth.

Delmar, R. (1986) 'What is Feminism' in J. Mitchell and A. Oakley (eds) *What is Feminism?*, Oxford: Blackwell.

Delphy, C. (1984) *Close to Home: A Materialist Analysis of Women's Oppression*, London: Hutchinson.

—— (1976a) 'Continuities and Discontinuities in Marriage and Divorce' in D.L. Barker and S. Allen (eds) *Sexual Divisions and Society: Process and Change*, London: Tavistock.

—— (1976b) 'The Main Enemy' in *The Main Enemy: A Materialist Analysis of Women's Oppression*, London: Women's Research and Resources Centre.

Dempster, T. (1990) 'Consent and Marital Rape', *New Law Journal* 10 August: 1149.

Dennis, N. and Erdos, G. (1992) *Families Without Fatherhood*, London: Institute of Economic Affairs.

Derrida, J. (1978) *Writing and Difference*, trans. A. Bass, Chicago: University of Chicago Press.

—— (1976) *Of Grammatology*, trans. G.C. Spivak, Baltimore: Johns Hopkins University Press.

—— (1975) 'The Purveyor of Truth', *Yale French Studies* 52: 31.

Devlin, P. (1959) *The Enforcement of Morals: Maccabean Lecture on Jurisprudence*, London: Oxford University Press.

Dewar, J. (1989a) *Law and the Family*, London: Butterworth.

—— (1989b) 'Fathers in Law: The Case of AID' in R. Lee and D. Morgan (eds) *Birth Rights*, London: Routledge.

—— (1985) 'Transsexualism and Marriage', *Kingston Law Review* 15: 58.

Dickey, A. (1982) 'The Notion of family in Law', *University of W A Law Review* 14: 417.

Dingwall, R., Eeekelar, J. and Murray, T. (1984) 'Childhood as a Social Problem: A Survey of the History of Legal Regulation', *Journal of Law and Society* 11, 2: 207.

—— (1983) *The Protection of Children: State Intervention and Family Life*, Oxford: Basil Blackwell.

Dobash, R. and Dobash, R. (1987) 'The Responses of British and American Women's Movements to Violence Against Women' in J. Hanmer and M. Maynard (eds.) *Women, Violence and Social Control*, Atlantic, Highlands: N.J. Humanities Press International.

—— and —— (1980) *Violence Against Wives: The Case Against Patriarchy*, London Open Books.

Dominelli, L. (1987) 'Judicial Discourse in Father Daughter Incest: Patriarchy's Shameful Secret', *Critical Social Policy* 16, 6: 8.

Donzelot, J. (1980) *The Policing of Families*, London: Hutchinson.

Dorris, M. (1990) *The Broken Cord: A Father's Story*, London: Warner/Futura.

Douzinas, C. and Warrington, R. (1987) 'On the Deconstruction of Jurisprudence: Fin(n)is Philosophiae', *Journal of Law and Society* 14, 1: 33.

——, —— and McVeigh, S. (1990) *Postmodern Jurisprudence*, London; Routledge.

Dover, K.G. (1978) *Greek Homosexuality*, London: Duckworth.

Dunning, E. (1986) 'Sport as a Male Preserve: Notes on the Social Sources of Masculine identity', *Theory, Culture and Society* 3, 1: 79.

Durham, M. (1991) *Sex and Politics: The Family and Morality in the Thatcher Years*, Basingstoke: Macmillan.

Dworkin, A. (1987) *Intercourse*, London: Arrow Books.

—— (1981) *Pornography: Men Possessing Women*, London: The Women's Press.

Dyer, R. (1985) 'Male Sexuality in the Media' in A. Metcalf and M. Humphries (eds) *The Sexuality of Men*, London: Pluto.

Easlea, B. (1987) 'Patriarchy, Scientists and Nuclear Warriors' in M. Kaufman (ed.) *Beyond Patriarchy: Essays by Men on Pleasure, Power and Change*, Oxford: Oxford University Press.

—— (1983) *Fathering the Unthinkable: Masculinity, Scientists and the Nuclear Arms Race*, London: Pluto.

—— (1981) *Science and Sexual Oppression: Patriarchy's Confrontation with Woman and Nature*, London: Weidenfeld and Nicholson

Easthope, A. (1987) *What A Man's Gotta Do: The Masculine Myth in Popular Culture*, London: Paladin.

Eaton, M. (1986) *Justice for Women? Family Court and Social Control*, Milton Keynes: Open University Press.

Edelsky, C. (1981) 'Who's Got the Floor?', *Language in Society* 10: 383.

Edleson, J.L., Eisikovits, Z. and Guttman, E. (1985) 'Men Who Batter Women: A Critical Review of the Evidence', *Journal of Family Issues* 6, 2: 229.

Edwards, S. (1992) 'Battered Women Syndrome', *New Law Journal*: 1350.

—— (1990) 'Battered Women Who Kill', *New Law Journal*: 1380.

—— (1989) *Policing Domestic Violence*, London: Sage.

—— (1988) 'Made, Bad or Pre-Menstrual?', *New Law Journal*: 456.

—— (1987) 'The Kerb-Crawling Fiasco', *New Law Journal*, 137: 1209.

—— (1985) 'Male Violence Against Women: Excusatory and Explanatory Ideologies in Law and Society' in S. Edwards (ed.) *Gender, Sex and the Law*, London: Croom Helm.

—— and Halpern, A. (1990a) 'Maintenance in 1987: Fact or Fantasy?', *Family Law* 18: 113.

—— and —— (1990b) 'Making Fathers Pay' *New Law Journal*: 1687.

—— and —— (1990c) 'The Continuing Saga of Maintaining the Family After Divorce', *Family Law* 18: 31.

Eekalaar, J. (1989) 'What is Critical about Critical Family Law?', *Law Quarterly Review* 105: 144.

—— (1984) *Family Law and Social Policy*, London: Weidenfeld and Nicholson.

—— and Maclean, M. (1986) Maintenance after Divorce, Oxford: Clarendon Press.

——, Clive, E. and Raikes, S. (1977) *Custody After Divorce*, Oxford, Centre For Socio-Legal Studies, Wolfson College.

Ehrenreich, B. (1983) *The Hearts of Men and the Flight from Commitment*, London: Pluto.

Eichler, M. (1980) *The Double Standard*, London: Croom Helm.

Eisenstein, H. (1984) *Contemporary Feminist Thought*, London: Unwin.

Elisonfon, H. (1983) 'A Historical and Comparative Study of Bastardy', *Anglo-American Law Review* 2: 306.

Elliot, M.L. (1985) 'The Use of "impotence", and "frigidity": Why Has Impotence Survived?', *Journal of Sex and Marital Therapy* 11: 51–6.

Ellis, H. (1946) *The Psychology of Sex* London: Heinemann.

Elshtain, J.B. (1982) 'Aristotle, the Public/Private Split and the Case of the Suffragists' in J.B. Elshtain (ed.) *The Family in Political Thought*, Sussex: Harvester Press.

Engels, F. (1972) *The Origins of the Family, Private Property and the State*, London: Lawrence and Wishart.

Equal Opportunities Commission (1990) *Women in Britain*, Manchester: EOC.

Fallon, B., Rosenberg, S. and Culup, D. (1984) 'Long Term Follow-Up in Patients with an Inflatable Penile Prosthesis', *Journal of Urology* 132: 270.

Faludi, S. (1992) *Backlash: The Undeclared War Against Women*, London: Chatto and Windus.

Family Policy Studies Centre (1992a) *The Family Today: Fact Sheet No. 1*, London: FPSC.

—— (1992b) *Family Finances: Fact Sheet 4*, London: FPSC.

—— (1992c) *One Parent Families: Fact Sheet 3*, London: FPSC.

—— (1991) *Supporting Our Children: The Family Impact of Child Maintenance*, London: FPSC.

Faragher, T. (1985) 'The Police Response to Violence Against Women in the Home' in J. Pahl (ed.) *Private Violence and Public Policy: The Needs of Battered Women and the Responses of the Public Services*, London: Routledge.

Farrell, W. (1974) *The Liberated Man*, New York: Bantam.

Farrington, D.P. and Morris, A. (1983) 'Sex, Sentencing and Reconviction', *British Journal of Criminology* 23: 229.

Featherstone, M. (ed.) (1988a) *Special Issue on Postmodernism, Theory, Culture and Society* 5, 2/3, London: Sage.

——(1988b) 'In Pursuit of the Postmodern: An Introduction' in M. Featherstone (ed.) *Special Issue on Postmodernism, Theory, Culture and Society* 5, 2/3, London: Sage.

Fennell, G., Phillopson, C. and Evers, H. (1988) *The Sociology of Old Age*, Milton Keynes: Open University Press.

Ferriman, A. (1991) 'Lesbian Mothers Warn of Aids Risk', *The Observer*, 17 March.

Fineman, M. (1991a) 'Societal Factors Affecting the Creation of Legal Rules for Distribution of Property at Divorce' in M. Fineman and N. Thomadsen (eds) *At The Boundaries of Law: Feminism and Legal Theory*, London: Routledge.

—— (1991b) 'Introduction' in M. Fineman and N. Thomadsen (eds) *At The Boundaries of Law: Feminism and Legal Theory*, London: Routledge.

—— (1989) 'Societal Factors Affecting the Creation of Legal Rules for Distribution of Property on Divorce', *Family Law Quarterly* 23, 2: 279–99.

—— (1986) 'Illusive Equality', *American Bar Foundation Journal* 781.

—— (1983) 'Implementing Equality: Ideology, Contradiction and Social Change: A Study of Rhetoric and Results in the Regulation of the Consequences of Divorce', *Wisconsin Law Review* 789.

—— and Thomadsen, N.S. (1991) *At The Boundaries of Law: Feminsim and Legal Theory*, London: Routledge.

Finer, M. (1974) *The Finer Report on One Parent Families*, London: Cmnd 5629.

—— and McGregor, O.R. (1974) 'The History of the Obligation to Maintain', Appendix 5 to the *Report of the Committee on One-Parent Families*, London: Cmnd. 5629.

Finley, L.M. (1989a) 'A Break in the Silence: Including Women's Lives in a Torts Course', *Yale Journal of Law and Feminism* 1: 41.

—— (1989b) 'Breaking Women's Silence in Law: The dilemma of the gendered nature of legal reasoning', *Notre Dame Law Review* 64: 886.

Fitzpatrick, P. and Hunt, A. (ed.) (1987) *Journal of Law and Society Special Issue on Critical Legal Studies*, Oxford: Blackwell.

Flandrin, J.L. (1985) 'Sex in Married Life in Early Middle Ages: The Church's Teaching and Behavioural Reality' in P. Aries and A. Begin (eds) *Western Sexuality: Practice and Precept in Past and Present Times*, Oxford: Blackwell.

Fletcher, R. (1977) *The Family and Marriage in Britain*, 3rd edn, Harmondsworth: Penguin.

Folsom, R. and Roberts, N. (1979) 'The Warwick Story: Being Led Down the Contextual Path of Law', *Journal of Legal Education*, 30: 166.

Ford, D. and Hearn, H. (1988) *Studying Men and Masculinity*, Bradford: University of Bradford Applied Social Studies.

Foucault, M. (1986) *The History Of Sexuality: Vol. 2, The Uses of Pleasure*, Harmondsworth: Penguin.

—— (1981) *The History of Sexuality Vol. 1: An Introduction*, Harmondsworth. Penguin.

—— (1980) *Power/Knowledge*, (ed. Colin Gordon), Brighton: Harvester Press.

—— (1979) 'On Governmentality', *Ideology and Consciousness* 6: 5.

—— (1970) *The Order of Things*, London: Tavistock.

—— (1967) *Madness and Civilisation*, trans. R. Howard, London: Tavistock.

Fox, R. (1967) *Kinship and Marriage*, Harmondsworth: Penguin.

Franklin, C.W. (1987) 'Surviving the Institutional Decimation of Black Males: Causes, Consequences and Intervention' in H. Brod (ed.) *The Making of Masculinities: The New Men's Studies*, London: Allen and Unwin.

—— (1984) *The Changing Definition of Masculinity*, New York: Plenum Press.

Fraser, D. (1988) 'What's Love Got to Do With It? Critical Legal Studies, Feminist Discourse and the Ethic of Solidarity', *Harvard Women's Law Journal* 11: 53.

Fraser, N. and Nicholson, L. (1988) 'Social Criticism without Philosophy: an encounter between feminism and postmodernism', *Theory Culture and Society* 5, 2/3: 373.

Freeman, A. and Mensch, E. (1987) 'The Public Private Distinction in American Law and Public life', *Buffalo Law Review* 36: 237.

Freeman, M.D.A (1985) 'Towards a Critical Theory of Family Law', *Current Legal Problems* 38: 153.

—— (1984a) 'Legal Ideologies, Patriarchal Precedents and Domestic Violence' in M.D.A. Freeman (ed.) *State, Law and the Family: Critical Perspectives*, London: Tavistock.

—— (ed.) (1984b) *State, Law and the Family: Critical Perspectives*, London: Tavistock.

—— (1980) 'Violence Against Women: Does the Legal System Provide Solutions or Itself Constitute the Problem?', *Journal of Law and Society* 17: 215.

—— and Lyon, C.M. (1983) *Cohabitation Without Marriage*, Aldershot: Gower.

French, S. (1992) *Fathers and Sons*, London: Faber.

Frug, M.J. (1985) 'Re-reading contracts: A feminist analysis of a contracts casebook', *American University Law Review* 34: 1065.

Fudge, J. (1987) 'The Public/Private Distinction: The Possibilities of and Limits to the Use of Charter Legislation to Further Feminist Struggles', *Osgoode Hall Law Journal* 25: 485.

Fuss, D. (ed.) (1987) *Inside/Out: Lesbian Theories, Gay Theories*, London: Routledge.

Galbraith, J.K. (1992) 'Culture of Contentment', *New Statesman and Society* 8 May: 14.

Gallagher, C. and Laqueur, T. (eds) (1987) *The Making of the Modern Body: Sexuality and Society in the Nineteenth Century*, Berkeley: University of California Press.

Gamarinkow, E., Morgan, D., Purvis, J. and Taylorson, D. (eds) (1983) *The Public and the Private*, Aldershot: Gower.

Game, A. and Pringle, R. (1984) 'Production and Consumption' in D. Broom (ed.) *Unfinished Business*, Sydney: Allen and Unwin.

Gardiner, J. (1983) 'Power, Desire and Difference: Comment on Essays from Signs Special Issue on Feminist Theory', *Signs* 8: 733.

Garland, D. and Young, P. (eds) (1983) *The Power to Punish: Contemporary Penality and Social Analysis*, London: Heinemann.

Gary, L.E. (1987) 'Predicting Interpersonal Conflict Between Men and Women: The Case of Black Men' in M. Kimmell (ed.) *Changing Men: New Directions in Research on Men and Masculinity*, London: Sage.

Gelles, R. (1972) *The Violent Home*, Beverley Hills: Sage.

Gelsthorpe, L. and Morris, A. (1990) *Feminist Perspectives in Criminology*, Milton Keynes: Open University Press.

Getes, R. (1979) *Family Violence*, Beverley Hills, California: Sage.

Ghandi, P.R. and MacNamee, E. (1991) 'The Family in UK Law and the International Covenant on Civil and Political Rights 1966', *International Journal of Law and the Family* 5: 104.

Gilder, G. (1986) *Men and Marriage*, Gretna, Louisiana: Pelican.

Giles, M. (1992) 'Judicial Law-making in the Criminal Courts: The Case of R v R', *Criminal Law Review.* 407.

Gill, D. (1977) *Illegitimacy, Sexuality and the Status of Women*, Oxford: Basil Blackwell.

Gilligan, C. (1982) *In A Different Voice: Psychological Theory and Women's Development*, London: Harvard University Press.

—— (1977) 'In A Different Voice: Women's Conceptions of Self and Morality', *Harvard Law Educational Review* 47: 481.

Glendon, M.A. (1981) *The New Family and the New Property*, London: Butterworth.

—— (1978) 'Statization and De-juridification of Family Relationships' in M.Freeman (ed.) *State, Law and the Family: Critical Perspectives*, London: Tavistock.

—— (1977) *Family Law in Transition in the United States and Western Europe*, Amsterdam: North-Holland.

Goldberg, H. (1976) *The Hazards of Being Male: Surviving the Myth of Masculine Privilege*, New York: Signet.

Goldberg, S. (1973) *The Inevitability of Patriarchy*, New York: William Morrow.

Goldstein, J., Freud, A. and Solnit, A.J. (1973) *Beyond the Best Interests of the Child*, London: Collier Macmillan.

Goodrich, P. (1990) *Languages of Law*, London: Weidenfeld and Nicolson.

—— (1987) *Legal Discourse*, London: Macmillan.

—— (1986a) *Reading the Law: A Critical Introduction to Legal Methods and Techniques*, Oxford: Blackwell.

—— (1984) 'Law and Language', *Journal of Law and Society* 11: 173.

Gorham, D. (1978) 'The "Maiden Tribute of Modern Babylon" Re-examined', *Victorian Studies* 21, 3: 353.

Gorz, A. (1982) *Farewell to the Working Class*, London: Pluto.

Gough, E.K. (1971) 'The Origins of the Family', *Journal of Marriage and the Family* 30: 760.

—— (1959) 'The Naguars and the Definition of Marriage', *Journal of the Royal Anthropological Institute*, 89: 23.

Gould, R.E. (1974) 'Measuring Masculinity by the Size of a Paycheck' in J. Pleck and J. Sawyer (eds) *Men and Masculinity*, New Jersey: Prentice Hall.

Gouldner, A. (1970) *The Coming Crisis of Western Sociology*, London: Heinemann.

Grady, K.E., Brannon, R. and Pleck, J. (1979a) *The Male Sex Role: A Selected and Annotated Bibliography*, Rockville MD: US Department of Health, Education and Welfare.

——, —— and —— (1979b) *Men's Studies Bibliography*, Massachusetts Institute of Technology Humanities Library, 4th edn, MIT, Mass.

Graham, H. (1983) 'Do Her Arguments Fit His Questions? Women and the Survey Method' in E. Garminkow (ed.) *The Public and the Private*, London: Heinemann.

Gray, S. (1987) 'Sharing the Shopfloor' in M. Kaufman (ed.) *Beyond Patriarchy: Essays By Men on Pleasure, Power and Change*, Oxford: Oxford University Press.

Graycar, R. (1989) 'Equal Rights Versus Fathers' Rights: The Child Custody Debate in Australia' in C. Smart and S. Sevenhuijsen (eds) *Child Custody and the Politics of Gender*, London: Routledge.

—— (1987–8) 'Review of Katherine O'Donovan's "Sexual Divisions in Law"', *Journal of Family Law* 26: 265.

—— (1986) 'Yes Virginia, There is a Feminist Legal Literature', *Australian Journal of Law and Society* 3:

—— and Morgan, J. (1990) *The Hidden Gender of Law*, Sydney: Federation Press.

Grbich, J. (1991) 'The Body in Legal Theory', in M. Fineman and N. Thomadsen (eds) *At the Boundaries of Law*, London: Routledge.

—— (1987) 'The Position of Women in Family Dealing: The Australian Case', *International Journal of the Sociology of Law* 15: 309.

Green, K. (1992) 'Review of P. Goodrich's *Languages of Law: From Logics of Memory to Nomadic Masks*', *Social and Legal Studies*, 2, 3: 361.

Greer, G. (1992) 'Two Fingers To The Bully', *The Guardian*, 23 September.

Griffin, S. (1981) *Pornography and Silence*, London: The Women's Press.

Griffith, J. (1985) *The Politics of the Judiciary*, 3rd edn, London: Fontana.

Griffith, M.E. (1989) 'Sexism, Language and the Law', *West Virginia Law Review* 91: 125.

Griffiths, S. (1992) 'A Knock at the Men's Room Door' *The Times Higher Education Supplement*, 4 September: 36.

Grigg-Spall, I. and Ireland, P. (1992) *Critical Lawyers Handbook*, London: Pluto.

Grosz, E. (1987) 'Feminism and Social Theory', unpublished paper presented at the Department of Anthropology and Sociology, University of Queensland, 30 October.

Hacker, H. (1957) 'The New Burdens of Masculinity' *Marriage and Family Living* 19 August: 229.

Hall, A. (1991) *Hidden Anxieties: Male Sexuality 1900–1950*, Cambridge: Polity Press.

Hall, C. (1992) *White, Male and Middle-Class*, London: Polity.

Hall, S. and Jefferson, T. (eds) (1976) *Resistance Through Rituals*, London: Hutchinson.

Hamerton, P.G. (1929) *The Intellectual Life*, London: Macmillan.

Hammerton, A.J. (1992) *Cruelty and Companionship: Conflict in Nineteenth Century Married life*, London: Routledge.

Hammond, D. and Jablow, A. (1987) 'Gilyamesh and the Sundance Kid: The Myth of Male Friendship' in H. Brod (ed.) *The Making of Masculinities: The New Men's Studies*, London: Allen and Unwin.

Hanmer, J. and Maynard, M. (eds) (1987) *Women, Violence and Social Control*, Atlantic, Highlands NJ: Humanities Press International.

—— and Stanko, E. (1985) 'Stripping Away the Rhetoric of Protection: Violence to Women, Law and State in Britain and the USA', *International Journal of the Sociology of Law* 13: 357.

Hanscombe, G. and Humphries, M. (eds) (1987) *Heterosexuality*, London: Gay Men's Press.

—— and Forster, J. (1982) *Rocking the Cradle: Lesbian Mothers*, London: Sheba.

Hantzis, C.W. (1988) 'Kingsfield and Kennedy: Reappraising the Male Models of Teaching', *Journal of Legal Education*, 38: 155.

Harding, S. (1986) *The Science Question in Feminism*, Milton Keynes: Open University Press.

Harland, R. (1987) *Superstructuralism: The Philosophy of Structuralism and Poststructuralism*, London: Methuen.

Harris, C.C. (1979) *The Family: An Introduction*, London: Allen and Unwin.

Hart, H.L.A. (1963) *Law, Liberty and Morality*, London: Oxford University Press.

Hartley, R.E. (1974) 'Sex Role Pressures and the Socialisation of the Male Child' in J. Pleck and J. Sawyer (eds) *Men and Masculinity*, New Jersey: Prentice Hall.

Havil, A. (1939) *The Technique of Sex: Towards a Better Understanding of Sexual Relationships*, London: Wales Publishing.

Hayes, M. (1980) 'Law Commission Working Paper No. 74: Illegitimacy', *Modern Law Review* 43: 299.

Hearn, J. (1992) *Men in the Public Eye*, London: Routledge.

—— (1990) '"Child Abuse", and Men's Violence' in Violence Against Children Study Group (ed.) *Taking Child Abuse Seriously*, London: Unwin Hyman.

—— (1987) *The Gender of Oppression: Men, Masculinity and the Critique of Marxism*, Brighton: Harvester Wheatsheaf.

—— (1983) *Birth and Afterbirth: A Materialist Account*, London: Achilles Heel.

—— and Morgan, D. (eds) (1990) *Men, Masculinities and Social Theory*, London: Unwin Hyman.

—— and Parkin, W. (1987) *'Sex', and 'Work': The Power and Paradox of Organisation Sexuality*, Brighton: Wheatsheaf.

Heath, S. (1987) 'Male Feminism' in A. Jardine and P. Smith (eds) *Men in Feminism*, London: Methuen.

—— (1983) *The Sexual Fix*, London: Macmillan.

Hetherington, E.M. (1981) 'Children and Divorce' in R.W. Henderson (ed.) *Parent-Child Interaction: Theory, Research and Prospects*, New York: Academic Press.

Hey, V. (1984) *Patriarchy and Pub Culture*, London: Tavistock.

Hill, C.L. (1988) 'Sexual Bias in the Law School Classroom: One Student's Perspective', *Journal of Legal Education*, 38, 1/2: 603.

Hirschfeld, M. (1952) *Sexual Anomalies and Perversions*, London: Encylopaedic Press.

Hite, S. (1981) *The Hite Report on Male Sexuality*, New York: Ballatine.

—— (1978) *The Hite Report on Female Sexuality*, London: Talmy Franklin.

Hoch, P. (1979) *White Hero, Black Beast*, London: Pluto.

Hocquenham, G. (1978) *Homosexual Desire*, London: Allison and Busby.

Hoggett, B. (1987) *Parents and Children: The Law of Parental Responsibility*, 3rd edn, London: Sweet and Maxwell.

—— and Pearl, D. (1987) *The Family, Law and Society: Cases and Materials*, London: Butterworth.

Holloway, W. (1989) *Subjectivity and Method in Psychology: Gender, Meaning and Science*, London: Sage.

—— (1981) '"I Just Wanted to Kill a Woman: Why?" The Ripper and Male Sexuality', *Feminist Review* 9: 33.

Home Office (1992a) *Criminal Justice Act 1991, Section 95: Gender and the Criminal Justice System*, London: HMSO.

Home Office (1992b) *Criminal Statistics for England and Wales*, London: HMSO.

Honoré, T. (1978) *Sex Law*, London: Duckworth.

Horder, J. (1992) *Provocation and Responsibility*, Oxford: Clarendon Press.

Horney, K. (1967a) 'The Dread of Women' in K. Horney *Feminine Psychology*, New York: WW Norton.

—— (1967b) 'On the Genesis of the Castration Complex in Women' in K. Horney, *Feminine Psychology*, New York: WW Norton.

Horowitz, M. (1982) 'The History of the Public Private Distinction', *University of Pennsylvania Law Review*, 130: 1427.

Hoyland, D. (ed.) (1992) *Fathers and Sons*, London:. Serpents Tree.

Hunter, A. (1993) 'Same Door: Different Closet: A Heterosexual Sissy's Coming Out Party' in S. Wilkinson and C. Kitzinger (eds) *Heterosexuality: A Feminism and Psychology Reader*, London: Sage.

Hutter, B. and Williams, G. (eds) (1981) *Controlling Women: The Normal and the Deviant*, London: Croom Helm.

Interrante, J. (1981) 'Dancing Along the Precipice: The Men's Movement in the 1980's', *Radical America* Sept–Oct, 15: 53.

Jackson, B. (1985) *Semiotics and Legal Theory*, London: Routledge.

Jackson, B. (1984) *Fatherhood*, London: George Allen and Unwin.

Jackson, D. (1990) *Unmasking Masculinity A Critical Autobiography*, London: Unwin Hyman.

Jackson, E. (1993) 'Catherine Mackinnon and Feminist Jurisprudence: A Critical Reappraisal', *Journal of Law and Society* 19: 195.

Jacob, H. (1989) 'Another Look at No-fault Divorce and the Post-divorce Finances of Women', *Law and Society Review* 23: 95.

Jaget, C. (ed.) (1980) *Prostitutes – Our Life*, Bristol: Falling Wall Press.

Jardine, A. (1987) 'Men in Feminism' in A. Jardine and P. Smith (eds) *Men in Feminism*, London: Methuen.

—— and Smith, P. (eds) (1987) *Men in Feminism*, London: Methuen.

Jefferson, T. (1994) 'Theorising Masculine Subjectivity' in E. Stanko and T. Newburn (eds) *Just Boys Doing Business?: Men, Masculinity and Crime*, London: Routledge.

—— (1993) '"Tougher Than the Rest": Mike Tyson and the Destructive Desires of Masculinity', paper presented to the British Criminology Conference, University of Cardiff, July.

—— (1992) 'Men and Crime', *Achilles Heel*, Summer: 10.

—— (1989) 'On Men and Masculinity', *Changes* 7, 4: 124.

Jeffrey-Poulter, S. (1991) *Peers, Queers and Commons*, London: Routledge.

Jump, T.L. and Haas, L. (1987) 'Fathers in Transition: Dual Career Fathers Participating in Child Care' in M. Kimmell (ed.) *Changing Men; New Direction in Research on Men and Masculinity*, London: Sage.

Kagan, J. and Moss, H.A. (1962) *Birth To Maturity*, New York: Wiley.

Kairys, D. (ed.) (1982) *The Politics of Law: A Progressive Critique*, New York: Pantheon Books.

Kamenka, E. and Tay, A. Erh-Soon (1975) 'Beyond Bourgeois Individualism: The Contemporary Crisis in Law and Legal Ideology' in E. Kamenka and Erh-Soon Tay (eds) *Feudalism, Capitalism and Beyond*, London: Edward Arnold.

Karpf, A. (1992) 'The Unbearable Rightness of Being PC', *The Guardian*, 24 September.

Katz, A. (1978) 'Studies in Boundary Theory: Three Essays in Adjudication and Politics', *Buffalo Law Review* 28: 383.

Katz, S.N. and Inker, M. (eds) (1979) *Fathers, Husbands and Lovers: Legal Rights and Responsibilities*, New York: American Bar Association Library.

Kaufman, M. (ed.) (1987a) *Beyond Patriarchy: Essays by Men on Pleasure Power and Change*, Toronto: Oxford University Press.

—— (1987b) 'The Construction of Masculinity and the Triad of Men's Violence' in M. Kaufman (ed.) *Beyond Patriarchy: Essays by Men on Pleasure Power and Change*, Toronto: Oxford University Press.

Keating, P. (ed.) (1976) *Into Unknown England 1866–1913*, London: Fontana.

Keen, S. (1992) *Fire in the Belly: On Being a Man*, London: Priaktus.

Kelley, S. (1981) 'Some Social and Psychological Aspects of Organic Sexual Dysfunction in men', *Sexuality and Disability* 4: 123.

Kellner, D. (1988) 'Postmodernism as Social Theory: some challenges and problems', *Theory, Culture and Society* 5, 2/3: 239.

Kelman, M (1984) 'Trashing', *Stanford L Rev* 36: 292.

Kennedy, D. (1982) 'Legal Education as Training for Hierarchy' in D. Kairys (ed.) *The Politics of Law: A Progressive Critique*, New York: Pantheon Books.

Kennedy, H. (1992) *Eve Was Framed: Women and British Justice*, London: Vintage.

Kenny, M. (1986) 'The Ideological Battle Over the Family' in D. Anderson and G. Dawson (eds)*Family Portraits*, London: Social Affairs Unit.

Kimmell, M. (ed.) (1987a) *Changing Men: New Directions in Research on Men and Masculinity*, London: Sage.

—— (1987b) 'Teaching a Course on Men: Masculinist Reaction or "Gentlemen's Auxiliary?"' in M. Kimmell (ed.) *Changing Men: New Directions in Research on Men and Masculinity*, London: Sage.

—— (1987c) 'The Contemporary Crisis of Masculinity' in H. Brod (ed.) *The Making of Masculinities*, London: Allen and Unwin.

Kingdom, E. (1985) 'Legal Recognition of a Woman's Right to Choose' in J. Brophy and C. Smart (eds) *Women in Law: Explorations in Family, Law and Sexuality*, London: Routledge.

Kinsey, A.C., Pomeroy, W.B. and Martin, C.E. (1948) *Sexual Behaviour in the Human Male*, London: Saunders.

Kinsman, G. (1987) 'Men Loving Men: The Challenge of Gay Liberation' in H. Brod (ed.) *The Making of Masculinities*, London: Allen and Unwin.

Kitzinger, C. (1987) *The Social Construction of Lesbianism*, London: Sage.

Komarovsky, M. (1964) *Blue Collar Marriage*, New York: Vintage Books.

Krafft-Ebing, R.V. (1931) *Psychopathia Sexualis: A Medical Forensic Study, with Especial reference to the Antipathic sexual instinct*, New York: New York Physicians and Surgeons Book Company.

Krane, R.J., Siroky, M.B., Goldstein, I. (1983) *Male Sexual Dysfunction*, Boston: Little Brown.

Kristeva, J. (1981) 'Oscillation between power and denial', in E. Marks and I. de Courtivron (eds) *New French Feminisms*, Brighton: Harvester.

Lacey, N., Wells, C. and Meure, D. (1990) *Reconstructing Criminal Law: Texts and Materials*, London: Weidenfeld and Nicolson.

Lahey, K. (1991) 'Reasonable Women and the Law' in M. Fineman and N. Thomadsen *At The Boundaries of Law: Feminsim and Legal Theory*, London: Routledge.

—— (1985) 'Until Women Themselves Have Told All They Have To Tell', *Osgoode Hall Law Journal* 23, 3: 519.

—— and Salter, S.W. (1985) 'Corporate Law in Legal Theory and Legal Scholarship: From Classroom to Feminism', *Osgoode Hall Law Journal* 23, 3: 543.

Laing, R.D. and Esterson, A. (1964) *Sanity, Madness and the Family*, London: Tavistock.

Laird, V. (1992) 'Reflections on R v R', *Modern Law Review* 55: 386.

Land, H. (1984) 'Changing Women's Claims to Maintenance' in M. Freeman (ed.) *State, Law and Family: Critical Perspectives*, London: Tavistock.

—— (1983) 'Poverty and Gender: The Distribution of Resources Within the Family' in M. Brown (ed.) *The Structure of Disadvantage*, London: Heinemann.

—— (1980) 'The Family Wage', *Feminist Review* 6: 55.

—— (1976) 'Women: Supporters or Supported?' in D.L. Baker and S. Allen (eds) *Sexual Divisions and Society: Process and Change*, London: Tavistock.

Laqueur, T. (1990) *Making Sex: Body and Gender From the Greeks to Freud*, Cambridge, MA: Harvard University Press.

Larrabee, M.J. (1993) *An Ethic of Care; Feminist and Interdisciplinary Perspectives*. London: Routledge.

Lasch, C. (1977) *Haven in A Heartless World: The Family Besieged*, New York: Basic Books.

Laslett, P. (1977) *Family Life and Illicit Love in Earlier Generations*, Cambridge: Cambridge University Press.

—— and Oosterven, K and Smith, R.M. (eds) (1980) *Bastardy and Its Comparative History*, London: Edward Arnold.

Law Commission (1986) *Illegitimacy: Second Report No 157*, London: Law Commission.

—— (1982) *Report on Illegitimacy, No. 118*, London: Law Commission.

—— (1981) *Family Law: The Financial Consequences of Divorce. No, 112*, London: Law Commission.

—— (1979) *Illegitimacy: Working Paper No. 74*, London: Law Commission.

Lehmann, G. (1983) 'The Case for Joint Custody', *Quadrant* 27: 60.

Le Vay, S. (1992) 'Are Homosexuals Born and Not Made?', *The Guardian*, 9 October.

Leach, E.R. (1955) 'Polyandry, Inheritance and the Definition of Marriage', *Man* 199.

Leach, P. and Hewitt, P. (1993) *Social Justice, Children and Families*, London Institute for Public Policy Research.

Lee, J. (1991) *At My Father's Wedding*, London: Piatkus.

Lees, S. (1983) 'How Boys Slag Off Girls', *New Society* 66: 51.

Leigh, W. (1979) *What Makes a Woman Good in Bed?*, London: Mayflower/Granada Books.

Lewis, C. (1986) *Becoming a Father*, Milton Keynes: Open University Press.

—— and O'Brien, M. (1987) *Reassessing Fatherhood: New Observations on Fathers and the Modern Family*, London: Sage.

Lewis, J. (1989) 'It all really starts in the family: Community Care in the 1980s', *Journal of law and Society* 16, 1: 83.

Lewis, R.A. and Salt, R. (1986) *Men In Families*, London: Sage.

Lindsey, B. and Evans, W. (1928) *The Companionate Marriage*, London: Bretanos.

Lipman-Blumen, J. (1976) 'Toward a Homosocial Theory of Sex Roles: An Explanation of the Sex Segregation of Social Institutions', *Signs* 1, 3: 15.

Lloyd, G. (1984) *The Man of Reason: 'Male', and 'Female' in Western Philosophy*, London: Methuen.

Locke, J. (1967) *Two Treatises of Government*, ed. P. Laslett, 2nd edn, Cambridge: Cambridge University Press.

Lockyer, D. (1987) 'The Woman with the Shampoo and Set Turned Out to be a Builder from Clapham called Greg', *Today* June 22.

Lorenz, K. (1967) *On Aggression*, London: Methuen.

Lowe, N. (1982) 'Fathers and the Law' in L. McKee and M. O'Brien (eds) *The Father Figure*, London: Tavistock.

Lummis, T. (1982) 'The Historical Dimension to Fatherhood: A Case Study 1890–1914' in L. McKee and M. O'Brien (eds) *The Father Figure*, London: Tavistock.

Lyman, P. (1987) 'The Fraternal Bond as Joking Relationship: A Case Study of the Role of Sexist Jokes in Male Group Bonding' in M. Kimmell *Changing Men: New Directions in Research on Men and Masculinity*, London: Sage.

Lyotard, J.F. (1984) *The Postmodern Condition*, Manchester: Manchester University Press.

Lyndon, N. (1992) *No More Sex War*, London: Sinclair Stevenson.

MacAndrew, R. (1946) *Friendship, Love Affairs and Marriage: An explanation of men to women and women to men*, London: Wales Publishing.

Macauley, J. (1987) 'Women Academics: A Case Study in Inequality' in A. Spencer and D. Podmore (eds) *In A Man's World*, London: Tavistock.

McCann, K. (1985) 'Battered Women and the Law' in C. Smart and J. Brophy (eds) *Women in Law*, London: Routledge.

Macfarlane, A. (1986) *Marriage and Love in England: Modes of Reproduction 1300–1840*, Oxford: Basil Blackwell.

McGregor, D.R. (1957) *Divorce In England*, London: Heinemann.

McIntosh, M. (1988) 'Family Secrets: Child Sexual Abuse', *The Chartist*, January.

—— (1978a) 'The State and The Oppression of Women' in A. Kuhn and A. Wolpe (eds) *Feminism and Materialism*, London: Routledge.

——(1978b) 'Who Needs Prostitutes? The Ideology of Male Sexual Needs' in B. Smart and C. Smart (eds) *Women, Sexuality and Social Control*, London: Routledge.

—— (1968) 'The Homosexual Role', *Social Problems* 16, 2: 82.

McKee, L. and Bell, C. (1986) 'His Unemployment, Her Problem' in S. Allen (ed.) *The Experience of Unemployment*, London: Macmillan.

—— and O'Brien, M. (eds) (1983) 'Interviewing Men: Taking Gender Seriously' in E. Garmarinkow (ed.) *The Public and the Private*, London: Heinemann.

—— and —— (eds) (1982a) *The Father Figure*, London: Tavistock.

—— and —— (1982b) 'The Father Figure: Some Current Orientations and Historical Perspectives' in L. McKee and M. O'Brien (eds) *The Father Figure*, London: Tavistock.

Mackinnon, C. (1989) 'Feminism in Legal Education', *Legal Education Review* 1: 85.

—— (1987) *Feminism Unmodified: Discourses on Life and Law*, London: Harvard University Press.

—— (1983) 'Feminism, Marxism, Method and the State: Towards a Feminist Jurisprudence', *Signs* 8, 2: 635.

—— (1982) 'Feminism, Marxism, Method and the State: An Agenda For Theory', *Signs* 7, 3: 515

—— (1979) *Sexual Harassment of Working Women*, New Haven: Yale University Press.

Maclean, M. (1991) *Surviving Divorce: Women's Resources After Separation*, London: Macmillan.

McLellan, D. (1979) *Marxism After Marx*, London: Macmillan.

—— (1971) *The Thought of Karl Marx*, London: Macmillan.

McLeod, E. (1982) *Women Working: Prostitution Now*, London: Croom Helm.

—— (1981) 'Man Made Laws For Men: The Street Prostitutes Campaign Against Control' in B. Hutter and G. Williams (eds) *Controlling Women: The Normal and the Deviant*, London: Croom Helm.

Macleod, M. and Saraga, E. (1988a) 'Challenging the Orthodoxy: Towards a Feminist Theory and Practice', *Feminist Review*, 28: 16.

—— (1988b) 'Against Orthodoxy', *New Statesman*, 1 July: 16.

—— (1987) 'Abuse of Trust', *Marxism Today* August: 10.

McMullen, R. (1990) *Male Rape: Breaking the Silence on the Last Taboo*, London: Gay Men's Press.

Maidment, S. (1984) *Child Custody and Divorce*, London: Croom Helm.

Mair, L. (1971) *Marriage*, Harmondsworth: Penguin.

Malos, E. (ed.) (1980) *The Politics of Housework*, London: Allison and Busby.

Mangan, J. (1987) 'Social Darwinism and Upper Class Education in late

Victorian and Edwardian England' in J. Mangan and J. Walvin (eds) *Manliness and Morality: Middle-Class Masculinity in Britain and America 1800–1940*, Manchester: Manchester University Press.

—— and Walvin, J. (eds) (1987) *Manliness and Morality: Middle-Class Masculinity in Britain and America 1800-1940*, Manchester: Manchester University Press.

Martin, D. (1976) *Battered Wives*, New York: Simon and Schuster.

Matteson, D. (1987) 'The Heterosexually Married Gay and Lesbian Couple' in F. Bozett (ed.) *Gay and Lesbian Parents*, New York: Prager.

Matthews, R. (1993) *Kerb-Crawling, Prostitution and Multi-Agency Policing Police Research Group*, paper 43, London: HMSO.

—— (1986) 'Beyond Wolfenden? Prostitution, Politics and the Law' in R. Matthews and J. Young (eds) *Confronting Crime*, London: Sage.

—— (1985) 'Streetwise? A Critical Review of the CLRC Report on Prostitution in the Street', *Critical Social Policy* 12: 102.

Matza, D. (1964) *Delinquency and Drift*, London: Wiley.

Matza, D.M. and Sykes G. (1961) 'Juvenile Delinquency and Subterreanean Values', *American Sociological Review* 26: 712.

May, G. (1930) *Social Control and Sex Expression*, London: Allen and Unwin.

Mead, M. (1950) *Male and Female: A Study of the Sexes in a Changing World*, London: Gollancz.

—— (1943) *Coming of Age in Samoa*, Penguin, London:

—— (1935) *Sex and Temperament in Three Primitive Societies*, New York: William Morrow.

Menkel-Meadow, C.M. (1988) 'Feminist Legal Theory, Critical Legal Studies and Legal Education or "The Fem-Crits Go to Law School"', *Journal Of Legal Education* 38, 1/2: 61.

—— (1985) 'Portia in a Different Voice: Speculations on a Woman's Lawyering Process', *Berkeley Women's Law Journal* 1: 39.

Mercer, K. and Julien, I. (1988) 'Race, Sexual Politics and Black Masculinity' in R. Chapman and J. Rutherford (eds) *Unwrapping Masculinity*, London: Lawrence and Wishart.

Messner, M. (1987) 'The Meanings of Success: The Athletic Experience and the Development of Male Identity' in H. Brod (ed.) *The Making of Masculinities: The New Men's Studies*, London: Allen and Unwin.

Metcalf, A. and Humphries M. (eds) (1985) *The Sexuality of Men*, London: Pluto.

Michael, J. (1988) 'Homosexuality and Privacy', *New Law Journal* November, 11: 831.

Middleton, P. (1992) *The Inward Gaze: Masculinity and Subjectivity in Modern Culture*, London: Routledge.

Miedzian, M. (1991) *Boys Will Be Boys: Breaking the Link Between Masculinity and Violence*, Garden City NY: Doubleday.

Mill, J.S. (1929) *On the Subjection of Women*, London: Dent.

—— (1910) *On Liberty*, London: Dent.

Miller, S. (1983) *Men and Friendship*, London: Gateway Books.

Miller, W. (1958) 'Lower Class Culture as a Generating Milieu of Gang Delinquency', *Journal of Social Issues* 14: 5.

Millet, K. (1975) *The Prostitution Papers*, London: Paladin.

Minow, M. (1988) 'Feminist Reason: Getting it and Losing it', *Journal of Legal Education* 38, 1/2.

—— (1986) 'Consider the Consequences', *Michigan Law Review* 84: 900.

—— (1985a) '"Forming Underneath everything that grows": Towards a History of Family Law', *Wisconsin Law Review.* 819.

—— (1985b) 'Beyond State Intervention in the Family: For Baby Jane Doe', *University of Michigan Journal of Law Reform* 19: 933.

Minson, J. (1985) *Genealogies of Morals: Neitzsche, Foucault, Donzelot and the Eccentricity of Ethics*, New York: St Martins Press.

Mitra, C. (1987) 'Judicial Discourse in Father-Daughter Incest Appeals Cases', *International Journal of the Sociology of Law* 15, 2: 121.

Moi, T. (1985) *Sexual/Textual Politics*, London: Methuen.

Montgomery, J. (1991) *The Child Support Act 1991: Text and Commentary*, London: Sweet and Maxwell.

Moore, R. and Gillette, D. (1992) *King Warrier, Magician Lover*, San Francisco: HarperCollins.

Moore, S.(1993) *Guardian* 16 July.

—— (1991) 'Trivial Pursuits of Stags at Bay', *Observer*, 9 January.

—— (1988) 'Getting A Bit of the Other: The Pimps of Postmodernism' in R. Chapman and J. Rutherford (eds) *Unwrapping Masculinity*, London: Lawrence and Wishart.

Moran, L. (1991) 'The Uses of Homosexuality: Homosexuality For National Security', *International Journal of the Sociology of Law* 19: 149–70.

—— (1990) 'A Study of the History of Male Sexuality in Law: Non Consummation', *Law and Critique* 1, 2: 155.

—— (1987) 'Masculinity and Legal Education', paper delivered to Critical Legal Conference, University of Newcastle-upon-Tyne, September.

—— (1986) 'Dr. Lushington's Sexual Fix', paper delivered to Critical Legal Conference, University of Kent, September.

Morgan, D. (1992) *Discovering Men*, London: Routledge.

—— (1987) 'It Will Make a Man of You: Note on National Service, Masculinity and Autobiography', *Studies in Sexual Politics*, L. Stanley and S. Scott (series eds), Manchester University Sociology Department, Manchester.

—— (1981) 'Men, Masculinity and the Process of Sociological Enquiry' in H. Roberts (ed.) *Doing Feminist Research*, London: Routledge.

—— (1975) *Social Theory and the Family*, London: Routledge and Kegan Paul.

Morgan, P. (1986) 'Feminist Attempts to Sack Father: A Case of Unfair Dismissal? in D. Anderson and G. Dawson (eds) *Family Portraits*, London: Social Affairs Unit.

Morris, J. (1974) *Conundrum*, London: Faber.

Mort, F. (1988) 'Boys Own? Masculinity, Style and Popular Culture' in R. Chapman and J. Rutherford (eds) *Unwrapping Masculinity*, London: Lawrence and Wishart.

—— (1987) *Dangerous Sexualities: Medico Moral Politics in England Since 1830*, London: Routledge.

Moss, P. and Branner, J. (1987) 'Fathers and Employment' in C. Lewis and M. O'Brien *Reassessing Fatherhood: New Observations on Fathers and the Modern Family*, London: Sage.

Mossman, M.J. (1988) 'Portia's Progress: Women as Lawyers – Reflections on Past and Future', *Windsor Yearbook Access to Justice* 8: 252.

—— (1986) 'Feminism and Legal Method: The Difference It Makes', *Australian Journal of Law and Society* 3: 30; also in M. Fineman and N. Thomadsen (1991) *At The Boundaries of Law: Feminsim and Legal Theory*, London: Routledge.

—— (1985) 'Otherness and the Law School: A Comment on Teaching Gender Inequality', *Canadian Journal of Women and the Law* 1: 213.

Mount, F. (1983) *The Subversive Family*, London: Counterpoint.

Mrazek, P.B. and Bentovim, A. (1981) 'Incest and the Dysfunctional Family System' in P.B. Mrazek and C.H. Kempe (ed.) *Sexually Abused Children and their Families*, Oxford: Pergamon Press.

Murphy, W.T. and Rawlings, R. (1982) 'After the Acien Regime: The writings of Judgements in the House of Lords 1979/80', *Modern Law Review*, 34.

Myers, M.F. (1989) *Men and Divorce*, New York. Guildford Press.

Naffine, N. (1990) *Law and the Sexes: Explorations in Feminist Jurisprudence*, Sydney: Unwin Hyman.

—— and Gale, F. (1989) 'Testing the Nexus: Crime, Gender and Unemployment', *British Journal of Criminology* 29, 2: 144.

National Council of One Parent Families (1980) *An Accident of Birth – A Response to the Law Commission Working Paper on Illegitimacy*, London: National Council of One Parent Families.

Nava, M. (1988) 'Cleveland and the Press: Outrage and anxiety in the Reporting of Child Sexual Abuse', *Feminist Review* 28: 103.

Neely, R. (1984) 'The Primary Caretaker Parent Rule: Child Custody and the Dynamics of Greed', *Yale Law and Policy Review* 3: 168.

Nelson, C. (ed.) (1986) *Theory in the Classroom*, Chicago: University of Illinois Press.

Nelson, D. (1991) 'Isle of Man Set to Defy Whitehall on Gays Ban', *Independent on Sunday*, 3 February.

—— (1987) 'A Gay Marriage', *New Society*, 2 January: 7.

Neustatter, A. (1992) 'A Very Delicate Matter', *Independent on Sunday*, 11 October.

Nichols, J. (1975) *Men's Liberation*, New York: Penguin.

Nicholson, J. and Linda, A. (1986) *Gender and History: The Limits of Social Theory in the Age of the Family*, New York: Columbia University Press.

Nielson, L. (1990) 'Family Rights and the "Registered Partnership" in Denmark', *International Journal of Law and the Family* 4: 297.

Norris, C. (1982) *Deconstruction: Theory and Practice*, London: Methuen.

O'Brien, R. (1992) 'Branch Lines and Family Trees', *The Guardian*, 15 September.

Ochberg, R.L. (1987) 'The Male Career Mode and the Ideology of Role' in H. Brod (ed.) *The Making of Masculinities: The New Men's Studies*, London: Allen and Unwin.

O'Donovan, K. (1993) *Family Law Matters*, London: Pluto.

—— (1989) 'Engendering Justice: Women's Perspectives on the Rule of Law', *University of Toronto Law Journal* 39: 127.

—— (1985a) *Sexual Divisions in Law*, London: Weidenfeld and Nicholson.

—— (1985b) 'Protection and Paternalism' in M.D.A. Freeman (ed.) *State, Law and the Family*, London: Tavistock.

—— (1985c) 'Transsexual Troubles: The Discrepancy Between Legal and Social Categories' in S. Edwards (ed.) *Gender, Sex and the Law*, London: Croom Helm.

—— (1984) 'Legal Marriage – Who Needs It?', *Modern Law Review* 47: 112.

—— (1982) 'Should All Maintenance of Spouses be abolished?', *Modern Law Review* 45: 424.

—— (1981) 'Before and After: The Impact of Feminism on the Academic Discipline of Law' in D. Spender (ed.) *Men's Studies Modified*, Elmsford: Pergamon Press.

——(1979) 'The Male Appendage: Legal Definitions of Women' in S. Burman (ed.) *Fit Work For Women*, London: Croom Helm.

—— and Szyszczak, E. (1988) *Equality and Sex Discrimination Law*, Oxford: Basil Blackwell.

Office of Population Censuses and Surveys (OPCS) (1992) *Marriage and Divorce Statistics*, London: HMSO.

—— (1991) *General Household Surveys, 22*, London: HMSO.

—— (1990) *Population Trends, 59*, London: HMSO.

Okin, S.M. (1989) *Justice, Gender and the Family*, London: Basic, HarperCollins.

—— (1979) *Women in Western Political Thought*, Princeton: Princeton University Press.

Olsen, F. (1989) 'Feminist Theory in Grand Style', *Columbia Law Review* 89: 1147.

—— (1985) 'The Myth of State Intervention in the Family', *University of Michigan Journal of Law Reform*, 18, 4: 835.

—— (1984) 'The Politics of Family Law', *Law and Inequality* 2: 1.

—— (1983) 'The Family and the Market: A Study of Ideology and Legal Reform', *Harvard Law Review* 96: 1497.

Omolade, B. (1991) 'The Unbroken Circle: A Historical Study of Black Single Mothers and their Families' in M. Fineman and N. Thomadsen (eds) *At The Boundaries of Law: Feminism and Legal Theory*, London: Routledge.

Ormrod, R. (1976) 'The Medico-Legal Aspects of Sex Determination', *Medico-Legal Journal* 40: 78.

Pace, P.J. (1983) 'Sexual Identity and the Criminal Law', *Criminal Law Review* 317.

Pahl, J. (ed.) (1985a) *Private Violence and Public Policy: The Needs of Battered Women and the Responses of Public Services*, London: Routledge.

—— (1985b) 'Refuges for Battered Women: Ideology and Action', *Feminist Review* 19: 25.

Pannick, D. (1983) 'Homosexuals, Transsexuals and the Sex Discrimination Act', *Public Law*: 279.

Park, R.J. (1987) 'Biological Thought, Athletics and the Formation of a

"Man of Character": 1830–1900' in J. Mangan and J. Walvin (eds) *Manliness and Morality: Middle-Class Masculinity in Britain and America 1800–1940*, Manchester: Manchester University Press.

Parker, S. (1987) 'The Marriage Act 1753: A Case Study of Family Law Making', *International Journal of Law and the Family* 1: 133.

—— (1981) *Cohabitees*, Chichester: Barrory Rose.

Parkinson, L. (1987) 'Independent Divorce Mediation Services in Britain' in *The Role of Mediation In Divorce Proceedings: A Comparative Perspective*, Vermont: Vermont Law School Dispute Resolution Project, Vermont Law school Vermont.

—— (1983) 'Conciliation: A New Approach to Family Conflict Resolution', *British Journal of Social Work* 13: 19.

Parry, M. (1981) *Cohabitation*, London: Sweet and Maxwell.

Parsons, T. (1964) *Essays in Social Theory*, New York: Free Press.

—— and Bales, R.F. (1956) *Family, Socialisation and Interaction Processes*, London: Routledge and Kegan Paul.

Pateman, C. (1988) *The Sexual Contract*, Cambridge: Polity Press.

—— (1983) 'Feminist Critiques of the Public Private Dichotomy' in S.I. Benn and G.F. Gaus (eds) *Public and Private in Social Life*, Canberra: Croom Helm.

Patullo, P. (1983) *Judging Women: A Study of Attitudes that Rule our Legal System*, London: NCCL.

Perelman, M. (1984) 'Rehabilatitive Sex Therapy for Organic Impotence' in R.T. Segraves and E.J. Haeberce (eds) *Emerging Dimensions in Sexology*, New York: Praeger.

Perreault, G. (1983) 'Contemporary Feminist Perspectives on Women and Higher Education' in C.C. Gould (ed.) *Beyond Domination: New Perspectives on Women and Philosophy*, London: Rowman and Allanhead.

Person, E.S. (1980) 'Sexuality as the Mainstay of Identity', *Signs*, 5, 4: 605.

Phillips, A. (1991) 'Pregnant Pause', *The Guardian*, 9 April.

Pilling, D. and Kellmer-Pringle, M. (1978) *Controversial Issues in Child Development*. London: Elek.

Pincheck, I. and Hewitt, M. (1969) *Children in English Society: Vol. 1 From Tudor Times Till the Eighteenth Century*, London: Routledge and Kegan Paul.

—— and —— (1973) *Children in English Society Vol. II*, London: Routledge and Kegan Paul.

Pleck, J.H. (1987a) 'American Fathering in Historical Perspective' in M. Kimmell (ed.) *Changing Men: New Directions in Research on Men and Masculinity*, London: Sage.

—— (1987b) 'The Theory of Male Sex-Role Identity: Its Rise and Fall 1936 to the Present' in H. Brod (ed.) *The Making of Masculinities: The New Men's Studies*, London: Allen and Unwin.

—— (1981) *The Myth of Masculinity*, Cambridge, MA: MIT.

—— (1980) 'Men's Power with Women, Other Men, and Society: A Men's Movement Analysis' in J.H. Pleck and E.H. Pleck (eds) *The American Man*, Englewood Cliffs, NJ: Prentice Hall.

—— and Pleck, E.H. (1980) *The American Man*, Englewood Cliffs, NJ: Prentice Hall.

—— and Sawyer J. (eds) (1974) *Men and Masculinity*, Englewood Cliffs, NJ: Prentice Hall.

Ploscow, M. (1951) *Sex and the Law*, New York: Prentice-Hall.

Plummer, K. (ed.) (1981) *The Making of the Modern Homosexual*, London: Hutchinson.

—— (1975) *Sexual Stigma: An Interactionist Account*, London: Routledge and Kegan Paul.

Polan, D. (1982) 'Towards a Theory of Law and Patriarchy' in D. Kairys (ed.) *The Politics of Law: A Progressive Critique*, New York: Pantheon Books.

Porter, K. and Weeks, J. (1991) *Between the Acts: Lives of Homosexual Men 1885–1967*, London: Routledge.

Poster, M. (1978) *Critical Theory of the Family*, London: Pluto.

Poulter, S. (1979) 'The Definition of Marriage', *Modern Law Review* 42: 409.

Power, H. (1993) 'Entrapment and Gay Rights', *New Law Journal*, 15 January: 47.

Pringle, K. (1992) 'Child Sexual Abuse Perpetrated by Welfare Personnel and the Problem of Men', *Critical Social Policy* 12, 3: 4.

Radford, J. (1987) 'Legalising Woman Abuse' in J. Hanmer and M. Maynard (eds) *Women, Violence and Social Control*, Atlantic, Highlands NJ: Humanities Press International.

Ramazanogulu, C. (1987) 'Sex and Violence in Academic Life, or You Can Keep a Good Woman Down' in J. Hanmer and M. Maynard (eds) *Women, Violence and Social Control*, Atlantic, Highlands NJ: Humanities Press International.

Raymond, J. (1979) *The Transsexual Empire*, London: The Women's Press.

Reich, W. (1972) *The Functions of the Orgasm: Sex Economic Problems of Biological Energy*, London: Panther Books.

Reinharz, S. (1993) 'How My Heterosexuality Contributes to My Feminsim and Vice Versa' in S. Wilkinson and C. Kitzinger (eds) *Heterosexuality: A Feminism and Psychology Reader*, London: Sage.

Reuben, D. (1972) *Any Woman Can!*, London: WH Allen.

—— (1970) *Everything You Always Wanted To Know About Sex . . .*, London: WH Allen.

Reynaud, E. (1983) *Holy Virility: The Social Construction of Masculinity*, London: Pluto.

Rhode, D.L. (1986) 'Feminist Perspectives in Legal Ideology' in J. Mitchell and A. Oakley (eds) *What is Feminism?*, Oxford: Blackwell.

Rich, A. (1980) 'Compulsory Heterosexuality and Lesbian Existence', *Signs*, 5, 4: 631.

—— (1977) *Of Woman Born*, London: Virago.

Richards, M. (1987) 'Fatherhood, Marriage and Sexuality: Some speculations on the English middle-class family' in C.Lewis and M. O'Brien (eds) *Reassessing Fatherhood: New Observations on Fathers and the Modern Family*, London: Sage.

—— (1982) 'How Should We Approach the Study of Fathers?' in L. McKee and M. O'Brien (eds) *The Father Figure*, London: Tavistock.

Riedman, J.D. (1987) 'Re-reading American Literature from a Men's

Studies Perspective: Some Implications' in H. Brod (ed.) *The Making of Masculinities: The New Men's Studies*, London: Allen and Unwin.

Rifkin, J. (1980) 'Toward a Theory of Law and Patriarchy', *Harvard Women's Law Journal* 3: 53.

Rights of Women, Family Law Subgroup (1985) 'Campaigning Around Family Law: Politics and Practice', in J. Brophy and C. Smart (eds) *Women in Law: Explorations in Family, Law and Sexuality*, London: Routledge.

—— (1984) *Lesbian Mothers on Trial: A Report on Lesbian Mothers and Child Custody*, London: Rights of Women.

Roberts, H. (1981) *Doing Feminist Research*, London: Routledge and Kegan Paul.

Roberts, Y. (1992) *Mad About Women*, London: Virago.

Robinson, M. (1991) *Family Transformation Through Divorce and Remarriage: A Systemic Approach*, London: Routledge/Tavistick.

Robinson, F. and Gregson, G. (1992) 'The Underclass: A Class Apart?', *Critical Social Policy* 12, 1: 38.

Rogers, B. (1988) *Men Only*, London: Pandora.

Rosaldo, M.Z. (1974) 'Women, Culture and Society: An Overview' in M.Z. Rosaldo and L. Lamphere (eds) *Women, Culture and Society*, Stanford: Stanford University Press.

Rose, N. (1987) 'Transcending the Public/Private', *Journal of Law and Society* 14, 1: 61.

Ross, M. (1983) *The Married Homosexual Man*, London: Routledge.

Rotundo, E.A. (1987a) 'Patriarchs and Participants: A Historical Perspective on Fatherhood' in M. Kaufman (ed.) *Beyond Patriarchy: Essays by Men on Pleasure Power and Change*, Toronto: Oxford University Press.

—— (1987b) 'Learning about Manhood: Gender Ideals and the Middle-class Family in Nineteenth Century America' in J. Mangan and J. Walvin (eds) *Manliness and Morality: Middle-Class Masculinity in Britain and America 1800–1940*, Manchester: Manchester University Press.

Rowen, J. (1987) *The Horned God: Feminism and Men as Wounding and Healing*, London: Routledge and Kegan Paul.

Rowland, J. (1986) *Rape: The Ultimate Violation*, London: Pluto.

Russell, B. (1929) *Marriage and Morals*, London: George Allen and Unwin.

Russell, G. (1983) *The Changing Role of Fathers*, St Lucia: University of Queensland Press.

Rutherford, J. (1992) *Men's Silences: Predicaments in Masculinity*, London: Routledge.

—— (1988) 'Who's That Man?' in R. Chapman and J. Rutherford (eds) *Unwrapping Masculinity*, London: Lawrence and Wishart.

Sachs, A. and Wilson, J.H. (1978) *Sexism and the Law: A Study of Male Beliefs and Judicial Bias*, Oxford: Martin Robertson.

Scales, A.C. (1980) 'Towards a Feminist Jurisprudence', *Indiana Law Journal* 56: 375.

Schneider, E.M. (1991) 'The Dialectics of Rights and Politics: Perspectives from the Women's Movement' in M. Fineman and N. Thomadsen (eds) *At The Boundaries of Law: Feminism and Legal Theory*, London: Routledge.

Schwarz, W. and Sharratt, T. (1990) 'Gay Priest Study to Liberal to be Aired', *The Guardian*, 10 February.

Schwerger, P. (1984) *Phallic Critiques*, London: Routledge and Kegan Paul.

Scraton, P. (1990) 'Scientific Knowledge or Masculine Discourses? Challenging Patriarchy in Criminology' in L. Gelsthorpe and A. Morris (eds) *Feminist Perspectives in Criminology*, Milton Keynes. Open University Press.

Scruton, R. (1986) *Sexual Desire: A Philosophical Investigation*, London: Weidenfeld and Nicholson.

Scutt, J.A. (1985) 'Sexism in Legal Language', *Australian Law Journal* 59: 163.

Segal, L. (1990) *Slow Motion: Changing Masculinities, Changing Men*, London: Virago.

—— (1987) *Is the Future Female? Troubled Thoughts on Contemporary Feminism*, London: Virago.

—— (ed.) (1983) *'What is to be Done about the Family?'*, Harmondsworth: Penguin.

Seidler, V. (1992) *Men, Sex and Relationships: Readings From Achilles Heel*, London: Routledge.

—— (1991) *The Achilles Heel Reader: Men, Sexual Poilitics and Socialism*, London: Routledge.

—— (1989) *Rediscovering Masculinity*, London: Routledge.

—— (1987) 'Reason, Desire and Male Sexuality' in P. Caplan (ed.) *The Cultural Construction of Sexuality*, London: Tavistock.

—— (1985) 'Fear and Intimacy' in A. Metcalf and M. Humphries *The Sexuality of Men*, London: Pluto.

Sevenhuijsen, S. (1992) 'The Gendered Juridification of Parenthood', *Social and Legal Studies* 1: 71.

—— (1986) 'Fatherhood and the Political Theory Of Rights: Theoretical Perspectives of Feminism', *International Journal of the Sociology of Law* 14, 3/4: 329.

Sharron, H. (1987) 'Parent Abuse', *New Society*, 13 March.

Sherrod, D. (1987) 'The Bonds of Men: Problems and Possibilities in Close Male Relationships' in H. Brod (ed.) *The Making of Masculinities: The New Men's Studies*, London: Allen and Unwin.

Shiffman, M. (1987) 'The Men's Movement: An Exploratory Empirical Investigation' in M. Kimmell (ed.) *Changing Men: New Directions in Research on Men and Masculinity*, London: Sage.

Shorter, E. (1975) *The Making of the Modern Family*, London: Collins.

Showalter, E. (1992) *Sexual Anarchy*, London: Bloomsbury.

—— (1987) ' Critical Cross Dressing: Male Feminists and the Woman of the Year' in A. Jardine and P. Smith (eds) *Men in Feminism*, London: Methuen.

Simpson, B., Corlyon, J., McCarthy, P. and Walker, J. (1993) *Post-Divorce Fatherhood: Discussion Document*, Family and Community Dispute Research Centre, Newcastle, University of Newcastle-upon-Tyne.

Sinha, M. (1987) 'Gender and Imperialism: Colonial Policy and the Ideology of Moral Imperialism in Law in Nineteenth Century Bengal' in M. Kimmell (ed.) *Changing Men: New Directions in Research on Men and Masculinity*, London: Sage.

Sion, A. (1977) *Prostitution and the Law*, London: Faber and Faber.

Slovenko, R. (1965) *Sexual Behavior and the Law*, Illinois: Charles C Thoman.

Smart, C. (ed.) (1992a) *Regulating Womanhood: Historical Essays on Marriage, Motherhood and Sexuality*, London: Routledge.

—— (1992b) 'The Woman of Legal Discourse', *Social and Legal Studies* 1: 29.

—— (1991) 'The Legal and Moral Ordering of Child Custody', *Journal of Law and Society* 18, 4: 485.

—— (1990a) 'Feminist Approaches to Criminology: Or, Postmodern Woman Meets Atavistic Man' in L. Gelsthorpe and A. Morris (eds) *Feminist Perspectives in Criminology*, Milton Keynes: Open University Press.

—— (1990b) 'Law's Truth: Women's Experience' in R. Graycar (ed.) *Dissenting Opinions: Feminist Explorations in Law and Society*, Sydney: Allen and Unwin.

—— (1989a) *Feminism and the Power of Law*, London: Routledge.

—— (1989b) 'Power and the Politics of Child Custody' in C. Smart and S. Sevenhuijsen (eds) *Child Custody and the Politics of Gender*, London: Routledge.

—— (1987) 'There is Of Course a Distinction Dictated by Nature: Law and the Problem of Paternity' in M. Stanworth (ed.) *Reproductive Technologies*, Cambridge: Polity Press.

—— (1986) 'Feminism and Law: Some Problems of Analysis and Strategy', *International Journal of the Sociology of Law* 14: 109.

—— (1985) 'Legal Subjects and Sexual Objects: Ideology, Law and Female Sexuality' in J. Brophy and C. Smart (eds) *Women in Law: Explorations in Family, Law Sexuality*, London: Routledge.

—— (1984a) *The Ties That Bind*, London: Routledge and Kegan Paul.

—— (1984b) 'Marriage, Divorce and Women's Economic Dependency: A Discussion of the Politics of Private Maintenance' in M. Freeman (ed.) *The State, The Law and the Family: Critical Perspectives*, London: Tavistock.

—— (1976) *Women, Crime and Criminology*, London: Routledge and Kegan Paul.

—— and Sevenhuijsen (1989) *Child Custody and the Politics of Gender*, London: Routledge.

Smith, D.K. (1971) 'Transsexualism, Sex Reassignment Surgery and the Law', *Cornell Law Review* 56: 969.

Smith, J. (1989) *Misogynies*, London: Faber.

Snodgrass, J. (ed.) (1977) *For Men Against Sexism*, Albion, California: Times Change Press.

Solanas, V. (1967) *SCUM Manifesto*, New York: Olympia.

Somerville, J. (1989) 'The Sexuality of Men and the Sociology of Gender', *The Sociological Review* 37, 2: 308.

Speight, N. (1989) 'Child Abuse: A Paediatricians View', *Family Law* 19: 29.

Spelman, E.V. (1989) *Inessential Woman: Problems of Exclusion in Feminist Thought*, Boston: Beacon Press.

Spencer, A. and Podmore, D. (eds) (1987a) *In A Man's World*, London: Tavistock.

—— (1987b) 'Women Lawyers: Marginal Members of a Male Dominated Profession' in A. Spencer and D. Podmore (eds) *In A Man's World*, London: Tavistock.

Spender, D. (ed.) (1981) *Men's Studies Modified*, Oxford: Pergamon.

Spiegelman, P.J. (1988) 'Integrating Doctrine, Theory and Practice in the Law School Curriculum: The Logic of Jake's Ladder in the Context of Amy's Web', *Journal of Legal Education* 38: 243.

Springhall, J. (1987) 'Building Character in the British Boy: The Attempt to Extend Christian Manliness to Working Class Adolescents 1880–1914' in J. Mangan and J. Walvin (eds) *Manliness and Morality: Middle-Class Masculinity in Britain and America 1800–1940*, Manchester, Manchester University Press.

Stang Dahl, T. (1987) *Women's Law*, Oxford: Oxford University Press.

—— (1986) 'Taking Women as the Starting point: Building Women's Law', *International Journal of the Sociology of Law* 14: 239.

Stanko, E. (1993) Book Review, *British Journal of Criminology* 33, 3: 449.

—— (1992) *Intimate Intrusions*, London: Routledge.

—— (1990) *Everyday Violence*, London: Pandora.

—— (1988) ' Hidden Violence To Women' in M. Maguire and J. Pointing (eds) *Victims of Crime: A New Deal?*, Milton Keynes: Open University Press.

—— (1987) 'Typical Violence, Normal Precaution: Men, Women and Interpersonal Violence in England, Wales, Scotland and the U.S.A.' in J. Hanmer and M. Maynard (eds) *Women, Violence and Social Control*, Atlantic, Highlands NJ: Humanities Press International.

—— and Hobdell, K. (1993) 'Assault on Men; Masculinity and Male Victimization', *British Journal of Criminology* 33, 3: 400.

Stanley, C. (1988) 'Training For Hierarchy? Reflections on the British Experience of Legal Education', *The Law Teacher* 22, 2/3.

Stanley, L. and Wise, S. (1983) *Breaking Out: Feminist Consciousness and Feminist Research*, London: Routledge and Kegan Paul.

Stanworth, M. (1987a) 'The Deconstruction of Motherhood' in M. Stanworth (ed.) *Reproductive Technologies*, Cambridge: Polity Press.

—— (ed.) (1987b) *Reproductive Technologies*, Cambridge: Polity Press.

Stearns, P. (1979) '*Be a Man! Males in Modern Society*', New York: Holmes and Meir.

Stedman-Jones, G. (1976) *Outcast London: A Study in the Relationship between Classes in Victorian Society*, Harmondsworth: Penguin.

Stekel, W. (1971) *Impotence in the Male*, New York: Liversight.

Stevens, R. and Legge, A. (1987) 'Illegitimacy Obscured but not Obliterated: An Analysis of the Family Law Reform Act 1987', *Family Law* 17: 409.

Stewart, R.J. (1991) *Celebrating the Male Mysteries*, Bath: Arcara.

Stoltenberg, J. (1977) 'Refusing to Be a Man' in J. Snodgrass (ed.) *For Men Against Sexism*, Albion, California: Times Change Press.

Stone, L. (1990) *The Road to Divorce: England 1530–1987*, Oxford: Oxford University Press.

—— (1977) *The Family, Sex and Marriage in England: 1500–1800*, London: Weidenfeld and Nicholson.

Storch, R. (1981) 'The plague of the Blue Locusts: Police Reform and Popular Resistance in Northern England 1840–57' in M. Fitzgerald, G. McLennan and J. Paulson *Crime and Society: Readings in History and Theory*, Milton Keynes: Open University Press.

Strauss, S.A. (1967) 'The Sex Change Operation: Two Interesting Decisions', *South African Law Journal* 84: 214.

Taitz, J. (1988) 'A Transsexual's Nightmare: The Determination of Sexual Identity in English Law', *International Journal of Law and the Family* 2: 139.

Tannahill, R. (1980) *Sex in History*, London: Hamish Hamilton.

Tatham, P. (1992) *The Making of Maleness: Men, Women and the Flight of Dedalus*, London: Karna Books.

Taub, N. and Schneider, E. (1982) 'Perspectives on Women's Subordination Under the Rule of Law' in D. Kairys (ed.) *The Politics of Law: A Progressive Critique*, New York: Pantheon Books.

Temkin, J. (1987) *Rape and the Legal Process*, London: Sweet and Maxwell.

Thomas, A. (1993) 'The Heterosexual Feminist: A Paradoxical Identity' in S. Wilkinson and C. Kitzinger (eds) *Heterosexuality: A Feminism and Psychology Reader*, London: Sage.

Thomas, D. (1993) *Not Guilty*, London: Weidenfeld and Nicholson.

Thompson, K. (ed.) (1992) *Views from the Male World*, London: Aquarian.

Thorne, B. and Yalom, M. (eds) (1982) *Rethinking the Family: Some Feminist Questions*, New York: Longman.

Thornton, M. (1991) 'The Public Private Dichotomy: Gendered and Discriminatory', *Journal of Law and Society* 18, 4: 448.

—— (1989a) 'Hegemonic Masculinity and the Academy', *International Journal of the Sociology of Law* 17: 115.

—— (1989b) 'Women and Legal Hierarchy', *Legal Education Review* 1: 97.

—— (1986) 'Feminist Jurisprudence; Illusion or Reality?', *Australian Journal of Law and Society* 3: 5.

Thornton, W.E. and James, J. (1979) 'Masculinity and Delinquency Revisited', *British Journal of Criminology* 19: 225.

Thrasher, F.M. (1927) *The Gang*, Chicago: University of Chicago Press.

Tiefer, L. (1987) 'In Pursuit of the Perfect Penis: The Medicalisation of Male Sexuality' in M. Kimmell (ed.) *Changing Men: New Directions in Research on Men and Masculinity*, London: Sage.

Tolson, A. (1977) *The Limits of Masculinity*, London: Tavistock.

Torry, M., Casey, J. and Olsen, K. (1990) 'Teaching Law in a Feminist Manner: A Commentary from Experience', *Harvard Women's Law Journal* 13: 87.

Turner, B. (1984) *The Body and Society*, Oxford: Blackwell.

Turnstall, J. (1962) *The Fisherman*, London: MacGibbon and Kee.

Tushnet, M. (1986) 'Critical Legal Studies: An Introduction to its Origins and Jurisprudence', *Journal of Legal Education* 36, 4: 506.

Unger, R.M. (1983) *The Critical Legal Studies Movement*, Harvard: Harvard University Press.

Utting, D. and Laurence, J. (1990) 'Family Fallout', *Sunday Correspondent*, 15 July.

Van der Velde, T. (1928) *Ideal Marriage: Its Physiology and Technique*, London: Heinemann.

Vance, C.S. (ed.) (1984) *Pleasure and Danger: Exploring Female Sexuality*, London: Routledge and Kegan Paul.

Vance, N. (1985) *The Sinews of the Spirit: The Ideal of Christian Manliness in Victorian Literature and Religious Thought*, Cambridge: Cambridge University Press.

Veyne, P. (1985) 'Homosexuality in Ancient Rome' in P. Aries and A. Bejin (eds) *Western Sexuality: Practice and Precept*, Oxford: Blackwell.

Walker, L.E. (1979) *The Battered Woman*, New York: Harper and Row.

Walkowitz, J.R. (1984) 'Male Vice and Feminist Virtue: Feminism and the Politics of Prostitution in Nineteenth Century Britain', *History Workshop Journal* 13: 77.

—— (1980a) *Prostitution and Victorian Society: Women, Class and the State*, Cambridge: Cambridge University Press.

—— (1980b) 'The Politics of Prostitution' in C.R. Stimpson and E. Spector-Person (ed.) *Women, Sex and Sexuality*, Chicago: University of Chicago Press.

Wallerstein, J.S. and Kelly, J. (1980) *Surviving the Breakup: How Children and Parents Cope With Divorce*, London: Grant McIntyre.

Walsh, B. (1989) 'Whiting v Whiting: Whither the Clean Break Principle?', *Family Law* 19: 157.

Walvin, J. (1987) 'Symbols of Moral Superiority: Slavery, Sport and Changing World Order, 1800–1940' in J. Mangan and J. Walvin (eds) *Manliness and Morality: Middle-Class Masculinity in Britain and America 1800–1940*, Manchester: Manchester University Press.

—— (1978) *Leisure and Society*, London: Longman Educational.

Warner, M. (1990) 'Homo-Narcissism: or Heterosexuality' in J. Boone and M. Cadden (eds) *Engendering Men*, London: Routledge.

Warren, A. (1987) 'Popular Manliness: Baden Powell, Scouting and the Development of Manly Character' in J. Mangan and J. Walvin (eds) *Manliness and Morality: Middle-Class Masculinity in Britain and America 1800–1940*, Manchester: Manchester University Press.

Weedon, C. (1987) *Feminist Practice and Poststructuralist Theory*, Oxford: Blackwell.

Weeks, J. (1991) 'Pretended Family Relationships' in D. Clark (ed.) *Marriage, Domestic Life and Social Change: Writings for Jacqueline Burgoyne*, London: Routledge.

—— (1987) 'Questions of Identity' in P. Caplan (ed.) *The Cultural Construction of Sexuality*, London: Tavistock.

—— (1986) *Sexuality*, London: Tavistock.

—— (1985) *Sexuality and Its Discontents*, London: Routledge and Kegan Paul.

—— (1982) 'The Development of Sexual Theory on Sexual Politics' in M. Brake (ed.) *Human Sexual Relations*, Harmondsworth: Penguin.

—— (1981) *Sex, Politics and Society: The Regulation of Sexuality Since 1800*, London: Longman.

—— (1977) *Coming Out: Homosexual Politics in Britain From the Nineteenth Century to the Present*, London: Quartet.

Weintraub, J. (1990) 'The Theory and Politics of the Public/Private

Distinction', paper presented to the annual meeting of the American Political Science Association, San Francisco.

Weir, S. (1993) 'No Orgasms Please, We're Labour', *New Statesman and Society* 12 February: 34.

Weitzman, L. (1985) *The Divorce Revolution: The Unexpected Social and Economic Consequences for Women and Children in America*, New York: Free Press.

—— (1981) *The Marriage Contract: Spouses, Lovers and the Law*, New York: Free Press.

Wells, C. (1985) 'Law Reform, Rape and Ideology', *Journal of Law and Society*', 12, 1: 63.

Wernick, A. (1987) 'From Voyeur to Narcissist: Imaging Men in Contemporary Advertising' in M. Kaufman (ed.) *Beyond Patriarchy: Essays by Men on Pleasure, Power and Change*, Toronto: Oxford University Press.

West, D.J. (1977) *Homosexuality Revisited*, London: Duckworth.

West, R. (1991) 'The Difference in Women's Hedonic Lives: A Phenomenological Critique of Feminist Legal Theory' in M. Fineman and N.S. Thomadsen (eds) *At The Boundaries of Law: Feminsim and Legal Theory*, London: Routledge.

—— (1988) 'Jurisprudence and Gender', *University of Chicago Law Review* 55: 1.

West, R., Nichols, F. and Roy, C. (1978) *Understanding Sexual Attacks*, London: Heinemann.

Westcott, C., Mills, V. and Reader, A. (1988) 'Joint Custody Orders', *Family Law* 18: 95.

Westen, P. (1982) 'The Empty Use of Equality', *Harvard Law Review* 95: 537.

White, A. (1985) 'Laying Down Machoism and Taking Up Knitting', *The Guardian*, 16 July.

White, L. (1991) 'Subordination, Rhetorical Survival Skills and Sunday Shoes: Notes on the Hearing of Mrs. G.' in M. Fineman and N. Thomadsen (eds) *At The Boundaries of Law: Feminsim and Legal Theory*, London: Routledge.

White, R., Carr, P. and Lowe, N. (1990) *A Guide to the Children Act 1990*, London: Butterworth.

Whyte, W.F. (1943) *Street Corner Society*, Chicago, Chicago University Press.

Wicks, M. (1989) 'A Contradiction Where There Should be a Strategy', *The Independent*, 28 September.

Wikeley, N. (1991) 'The Maintenance Enforcement Act 1991', *Family Law* 21: 353.

Wilkinson, S. and Kitzinger, C. (1993) *Heterosexuality: A Feminism and Psychology Reader*, London: Sage.

Williams, B. (1979) *Committee on Obscenity and Film Censorship*, London: Cmnd. 7772.

Williams, J.C. (1989) 'Deconstructing Gender', *Michigan Law Review* 87: 797.

Willis, P. (1977) *Learning to Labour*, London: Saxon.

Willmott, P. and Young, M. (1973) *The Symmetrical Family*, London: Routledge and Kegan Paul.

—— (1962)*Family and Kinship in East London*, Harmondsworth: Penguin.
Wilson, E. (1983) *What is to be Done about Violence Against Women?* Harmondsworth: Penguin.
—— (1977) *Women and the Welfare State*, London: Tavistock.
Wilton, S. (1990) 'I Can't Pay, He Won't Pay', *New Law Journal* 6 July: 976.
Wintour, P. (1990) 'Changing Attitudes Shake Family Values', *Guardian*, 9 October.
Witz, A. (1990) 'Patriarchy and the Professions: The Gendered Politics of Occupational Closure', *Sociology* 24, 4: 675.
Wolfenden, J. (1957) *Report of the Committee on Homosexual Offences and Prostitution*, London: Cmnd 247.
Wood, J. (1982) 'Boys Will be Boys', *New Socialist* May–June: 5.
Woodcock, B. (1984) *Male Mythologies: John Fowles and Masculinity*, Brighton: Harvester Press.
Woodcraft, E. (1988) 'Child Sexual Abuse and the Law', *Feminist Review* 28: 122.
Wright, H. (1937) *The Sex Factor in Marriage: A Book For Those Who Are or Are About To Be Married*, London: Wales Pub.
Young, A. (1993) 'The Authority of the Name' in S. Wilkinson and C. Kitzinger (eds) *Heterosexuality: A Feminism and Psychology Reader*, London: Sage.
—— (1990) *Femininity in Dissent*, London: Routledge.
Young, I. (1987) 'Child Abuse – Key Considerations For Lawyers', *Family Law* November: 369.
Yural-Davis, N. (1993) 'The (Dis) Comfort of Being Hetero' in S. Wilkinson and C. Kitzinger (eds) *Heterosexuality: A Feminism and Psychology Reader*, London: Sage.
Zedner, L. (1991) *Women, Crime and Custody in Victorian England*, Oxford: Clarendon Press.
Zilbergeld, B. (1980) *Men and Sex*, London: Fontana.

TABLE OF CASES

Carega Properties v Sharratt [1979] 2 All ER 1084
Clarke v Clarke [1980] 9 Fam Law 15
Clarke (Othewise Talbolt) v Clarke [1943] 2 All ER 540
Corbett v Corbett (Orse Ashley) [1971] P 83, [1970] 2 All ER 33
Cooke v Head [1972] 2 All ER 38
Cossey v UK [1991] 2 FLR 492
Cowen v Cowen [1946] P 36; [1945] 2 All ER 197

Darroch v Director of Public Prosecutions [1990] 91 Cr App R 378
Davis v Johnson [1979] AC 264; [1978] 1 All ER 1132
D-e v A-g (falsely calling herself D-e) [1845] 1 Rob Ecc 280
De Reneville (Otherwise Sheridan) v De Reneville [1948] 1 All ER 56 P
    100
Dennis v Dennis [1955] 2 All ER 51
Dredge v Dredge (Otherwise Harrison) [1947] 1 All ER 29
Dyson Holdings v Fox [1976] QB 503; [1975] 3 All ER 1030

E.A. White v British Sugar Corporation [1977] 1 IRLR 121
Eves v Eves [1975] 3 All ER 768
Eveson v Eveson [1980] unreported 27th November (CA)

G v G [1924] AC 349
G v M [1885] AC 171
Gammans v Ekins [1950] 2 All ER 140

Harrogate Borough Council v Simpson [1985] 17 HLR 205; [1986] 2 FLR
    91
Hammond v Mitchell [1992] 2 All ER 109
Hawes v Evenden [1953] 2 All ER 737
Helby v Rafferty [1979] 1 WLR 13; [1978] 3 All ER 1016
Hoskyn v Metropolitan Police Commissioner [1979] AC 474; [1978] 2 All
    ER 136
Huges v Holley [1988] 86 Cr App R 130
Hyde v Hyde and Woodmansee [1866] LR 1 P & D 130

J v C [1970] AC 668; [1969] 1 All ER 788

Knuller v DPP [1973] AC 435

Langston v AUEW [1974] 1 All ER 980
Lloyds Bank Plc v Rosset [1988] 3 All ER 915

M v M [1979] Fam Law 92
M v M (Orse B) [1957] P 139; [1956] 3 All ER 769
Mason v Mason [1980] Family Law 144
May v May [1986] 1 FLR 325
Morris v Morris [1983] Unreported 8th December (CA)
Myers v Myers [1982] 1 WLR 247

N v M [1853] 163 ER 1435

Paul v Director of Public Prosecutions [1990] 90 Cr App R 173
Plant v Plant [1983] 4 FLR 305

R v Aitken [1992] WLR 1006
R v Boyea [1992] Crim LR 574
R v Brown [1993] 2 WLR 556
R v Clarence [1888] 22 QBD 22
R v Cozins [1834] 6 C & P 351
R v Cutts [1987] Fam Law 311
R v Donovan [1934] 2 KB 498
R v Gray [1981] 74 Crim App Rep 324
R v Ford, Redgrave [1981] 74 Crim App Rep 10
R v Hall [1964] 1 QB 273
R v Hornby & People [1946] 2 All ER 487
R v Hunt [1950] 2 All ER 291
R v Immigration Appeal Tribunal, ex parte Windestedt [1984] *The Times*
    12 December 1984
R v Kirkup [1981] *The Guardian* 10 November
R v Kowaliski [1987] 86 Crim App Rep 339
R v Lines [1844] 1 Car & Kir 393
R v Miskell [1954] 1 All ER 137
R v Plimmer [1975] 61 Crim App Rep 264
R v Preece [1977] 1 QB 770
R v R (otherwise F) [1952] P 1994
R v R [1991] 3 WLR 766
R v R [1991] 4 All ER 481; [1991] 3 WLR 766
R v Tan [1983] 2 All ER 12
Re C and D (falsely calling herself C) [1979] 28 ALR 524; 35 FLR 340
Re C (Minors) [1978] 2 All ER 230
Re D [1977] AC 617
Re K (Minors) [1977] 1 All ER 647
Re L [1962] 1 WLR 886; [1962] 3 All ER 1
Re North *et al.* and Matheson [1975] 52 DLRP 280
Re P [1983] FLR 401
Re X [1957] *Scots Law Times* 61
The Rees Case: Rees v UK [1987] 2 FLR 111
REL v REL (Otherwise R) [1948] P 211

Richards v Richards [1984] AC 174
Sapsford v Sapsford and Furtado [1954] P 394
Sefton Holdings v Cairns [1988] 2 FLR 108
Shaw v DPP [1962] AC 220
S v S (otherwise C) [1954] P 1; [1954] 3 All ER 736
SY v SY [1963] P 37
SY v SY (Orse W) [1963] P 37
Spindlow v Spindlow [1979] 1 All ER 169

Talbolt (Otherwise Poyntz) v Talbolt [1967] 111 Sol Jou 213
Thomas v Fuller Brown [1985] 1 FLR 237
Tovey v Tovey [1978] 8 Fam Law 80

UF v JC [1991] 2 Irish Reports 330

W (Orse K) v W [1967] 1 WLR 1554

Wachtel v Wachtel [1973] 1 All ER 829
Welde v Welde [1731] 161 ER 447
White (Otherwise Berry) v White [1948] 2 All ER 151
Williams v Williams [1974] 3 All ER 377

Index